KU-845-024

THE SOKAGAKKAI AND
MASS SOCIETY

Stanford Studies in Comparative Politics, 4

JAMES W. WHITE

THE SOKAGAKKAI AND MASS SOCIETY

STANFORD UNIVERSITY PRESS
STANFORD, CALIFORNIA
1970

Stanford University Press
Stanford, California
© 1970 by the Board of Trustees of the
Leland Stanford Junior University
Printed in the United States of America
ISBN 0-8047-0728-6
LC 75-93498

For Stephen Galatti and
Marius B. Jansen

Preface

THE SŌKAGAKKAI is by no means an exclusively Japanese organization. According to the chief of the Sōkagakkai Overseas Bureau, there are over 150,000 members living abroad in more than thirty-five different countries. In an organization of several million persons, however, these overseas believers constitute a slim minority; and in visiting their meetings one sees immediately that cultural differences render the overseas Sōkagakkai significantly different from the Gakkai in Japan. This study is concerned in part with the political significance of the Sōkagakkai; but the Society has explicitly rejected political activity outside Japan. For all of these reasons, the descriptive data presented in this study and the generalizations offered deal with the Sōkagakkai only as a Japanese phenomenon.

In the course of preparing this book I became indebted to a great number of persons in the United States and Japan. Nobutaka Ike, Kurt Steiner, Sidney Verba, Gabriel Almond, and Thomas C. Smith of Stanford University read various preparatory papers and offered cogent criticism at many points in the study. Miyake Ichirō of Kyoto University was of great assistance in analyzing and evaluating the survey data so generously made available by the research team, headed by Sidney Verba, conducting the Cross-National Project for Political and Social Change.

In Tokyo, the officials and members of the Sōkagakkai were at all times cooperative, thoughtful, and of incalculable aid in developing a balanced picture of the organization. President Ikeda Daisaku gave his valuable time, as did Hōjō Hiroshi, Akiya Einosuke, and Tada Shōgo, and Kōmeitō Diet member Kuroyanagi Akira. Akiyama Tomiya and Sasaki Toshiyuki of the Sōkagakkai Public Relations Bureau answered innumerable questions and assisted in locating materials of all types. Toda Takahisa granted a long and very pleasant interview in which he spoke at length concerning his father, Toda Jōsei.

Nagai Michio and Hara Yoshio of the Tokyo Institute of Technology gave me numerous suggestions about the place of the Sōkagakkai in the Japanese political system, as did several members of the faculty of Tokyo University, including Ikeuchi Hajime and Kyōgoku Jun'ichi, and especially Watanuki Jōji, whose own works on Japanese politics were of great value.

Other observers of the Japanese political and religious scenes who contributed time and data to this study were Ikado Fujio of the Japanese Ministry of Education; Hugh Burleson and Nishiyama Sen of the United States Information Service, Tokyo; the Reverend Joseph Spae, Director of the Oriens Institute, Tokyo; and Jerrold Schecter, Tokyo Bureau Chief for Time Magazine. Supplementing the information given by these gentlemen, several research agencies made available a large quantity of survey data. Nishihira Shigeki of the Institute for Statistical Mathematics, Tajima Tadashi of the Prime Minister's Office, Asano Tadanobu of the Central Research Service, Adachi Keigo and Miss Koshitani Kazuko of the *Mainichi Shimbun*, and Hiraoka Sachirō of the *Yomiuri Shimbun* were all most cooperative in unearthing previously unpublished data on the Sōkagakkai and Kōmeitō contained in earlier surveys by their respective organizations.

This book would not have been possible without financial assistance from the Office of Education of the U.S. Department of Health, Education, and Welfare, which made a grant available to me under Title IV of the National Defense Education Act, and from the Foreign Area Fellowship Program, which provided a grant enabling me to remain in Japan for a sufficient period and supported me during the writing of this study.

J.W.W.

Contents

Tables

THE SOKAGAKKAI AND
MASS SOCIETY

Introduction

IN THE YEARS since 1945, when the American Occupation began its breathtaking experiment in constitutional engineering, scholars and statesmen have followed closely the fortunes of democratic politics in Japan. That the new political framework could be assimilated without strain or that its existence would be unimperiled no one expected; except for an unsuccessful experiment with parliamentary institutions before the war, Japan had no tradition of democratic politics, however defined. Today, though, Japan stands as an example of relatively stable parliamentary democracy in a context of rapid economic growth, a rarity among Asian nations. But neither democratization nor development has been without strain; social, psychological, and political discontinuities have meant insecurity, bewilderment, and frustration for large numbers of people. And though today stabilization is the trend in Japanese politics, economy, and society, elements of social and economic instability remain, and opponents of the democratic political process are active on both left and right.

In the 1950's a movement emerged that many observers took to be a new manifestation of the undemocratic threat—the Sōkagakkai,* a militant religious movement of lay believers in a traditionally nationalistic Buddhist sect, Nichiren Shōshū.† As a religion the Gakkai was described as fanatical, millenarian, and intolerant; when its political interest became publicized it was called fascist, chauvinist, and totalitarian.

* Translatable as "Value-Creation Academic Society."
† Translatable as "Orthodox Nichiren Sect," and named for its founder, Nichiren, a bellicose thirteenth-century Japanese monk.

In many ways the Sōkagakkai is a new phenomenon in Japanese history. Its size, its theology, its peculiar combination of religion and politics, and the particular social element constituting its membership render it an intrinsically interesting subject for study. But perhaps more important are its political implications for Japan: an organization claiming over ten million members, the third strongest party in the nation in total legislative assembly seats held, commands attention as a potentially critical actor in politics.

In the literature on democracy's sources and problems, two works are of particular relevance in studying the Gakkai. One is William Kornhauser's *The Politics of Mass Society*; the other, Seymour Martin Lipset's *Political Man*. Kornhauser is concerned with the phenomenon of mass movement and describes its major political implications—notably marked dysfunction for stable democratic political systems.[1] Lipset, approaching the subject sociologically, predicates that the lower classes—those social strata most often identified as the primary constituents of the Gakkai's membership—tend toward undemocratic beliefs and behavior.[2] Of the various types of threats to democratic systems the Gakkai seems most amenable to analysis through Kornhauser's mass movement concept. Lipset is one of many who treat sociological aspects of political systems; his study, however, is especially relevant as a conceptual treatment of the political implications of lower-class life.

CONCEPTS

The concept of a "mass society" has been defined by Daniel Bell as follows:

The revolutions in transport and communication have brought men into closer contact with each other and bound them in new ways; the division of labor has made them more interdependent.... Despite this greater interdependence, however, individuals have grown more estranged from one another. The old primary group ties of family and local community have been shattered; ancient parochial faiths are questioned; few unifying values have taken their place. Most important, the critical standards of an educated elite no longer shape opinion or taste. As a result, morals and mores are in constant flux.... At the same time greater mobility, spatial and social, intensifies concern over status. Instead of a fixed or known status symbolized by dress or title, each person assumes a multiplicity of roles and constantly has to prove himself in a succession of new situations. Because of all this, the individual loses a coherent sense of self. His anxieties increase. There ensues

---

[1] Numbers refer to Notes (pp. 323–50), primarily citations of sources and relevant collateral material. Footnotes are designated by asterisks (*) and daggers (†).

a search for new faiths. The stage is thus set for the charismatic leader, the secular messiah, who, by bestowing on each person the semblance of necessary grace, and of fullness of personality, supplies a substitute for the older unifying belief that the mass society has destroyed.[3]

Many writers have dealt with this so-called mass society, differing greatly in their opinions of its causes, its particular characteristics, and its consequences.[4] Most of these theorists have approached the problem in a total fashion: is a given society a mass society, or is it not? While agreeing with Bell on the unlikelihood that any fully mass—in the sense of atomized and alienated—society has ever existed,[5] I believe that at any point in time, in any social system, some elements may be characterized as "masses."

The definitions of mass and related concepts used here are those offered in *The Politics of Mass Society*. There Kornhauser defines "mass man" as man *unattached* to any broad social groupings (such as class, society, or nation), either objectively (i.e., he *has* few interpersonal relationships) or subjectively (i.e., he *feels* no sense of belonging to or identification with such groupings).[6] Moreover, mass man is *alienated*—from himself; from his fellow men as human beings; and from the social, economic, and political systems of which he is objectively a member.[7] Aggregating those members of any society who may be characterized as mass men, Kornhauser visualizes the masses as "large numbers of people who are not integrated into any broad social groupings, including classes."[8] Where the masses constitute the predominant social element in a society, one may speak of a mass society. Kornhauser does not suggest any threshold beyond which a society becomes "mass," but he states that any "social system in which elites are readily accessible to influence by non-elites and non-elites are readily available for mobilization by elites" may be termed a mass society.[9] The non-elite mass man is available because he has few attachments to secondary groups that would serve as a screen between himself and the elites; similarly, elites in mass society are accessible to non-elites because there are no strong intermediate groups to mediate and structure the influence that non-elites exert over the selection and behavior of the elites.

The modal behavioral pattern of mass men, according to Kornhauser, is "mass behavior." Characteristically, the focus of attention is remote from personal experience and everyday life and tends rather toward direct, activist response (i.e. behavior unmediated by social relations). Such activity is unstable, periods of intense activity alternating with long periods of apathy.[10] Where mass behavior is politically relevant one may speak of "mass politics": "large numbers of people engaging in political activity outside of the procedures and rules instituted by a society to govern political action."[11] If such mass behavior, political or otherwise, maintains continuity as a pattern of purposes and effort organized around a program, then one may speak of a "mass movement"; or, if the leaders of the movement have totalitarian inclinations, of a "totalitarian movement."[12]

The manner in which Kornhauser expands his model from mass man to mass society, from individual mass behavior to mass movement, indicates that he considers mass man a microcosm of mass movement and mass society. His mass society is best considered an ideal type, as Bell advises.[13] But for the present we shall assume that individuals fitting the model of mass man do exist and that movements closely approximating Kornhauser's mass movements also exist, and that both have the behavioral characteristics he imputes to them.

The social, psychological, and behavioral syndrome by which Kornhauser typifies mass men and movements is, by his definition, subversive of democratic political systems.[14] The behavioral tendencies of such people and movements directly contravene the constitutional order; and because of their alienation and isolation mass men are readily mobilized to act on these tendencies. In Japan, the totalitarian trend of the early twentieth century may have reflected a response of this sort to the disintegrative effects of the Meiji Restoration. Or perhaps it did not; other factors may have been active in that period. But there are factors in Japan today—and their parallel to the Meiji aftermath is striking—that could well herald the rise of mass movements: devastating military defeat followed by extremely rapid economic development; concomitant widespread disintegration of older, more stable social structures as urbanization increases; a normative vacuum following the discrediting of the prewar ethical system; and wholesale implantation of novel political structures and processes, the roots of which are still of questionable strength and legitimacy.[15]

MASS MAN AND DEMOCRACY

There are many reasons why men may find themselves without attachments to social groups. The dissolution of social entities, the fruitlessness of membership in groups that have lost all ability to satisfy the needs brought to them, and the emergence of new needs or the intensification of old ones owing to environmental change all contribute.[16] Whatever the causes, this nonattachment or isolation brccds normlessness, anxiety, and a susceptibility to mobilization by movements promising alleviation of the individual's difficulties. Erich Fromm described this susceptibility as a desire to "escape from freedom":

Modern man, freed from the bonds of preindividualistic society, which simultaneously gave him security and limited him, has not yet gained freedom in the positive sense of the realization of his individual self; that is, the expression of his intellectual, emotional, and sensuous potentialities. Freedom, though it has brought him independence and rationality, has made him isolated and, thereby, anxious and powerless. This isolation is unbearable and the alternatives he is confronted with are either to escape from the burden of this freedom into new dependencies and submission, or to advance to the full realization of positive freedom which is based upon the uniqueness and individuality of man.[17]

The response to isolation may, as Fromm notes, follow a course toward self-fulfillment; at the other extreme it may result in utter submission to a totalitarian movement. Kornhauser asserts[18] that in time of crisis a greater proportion of those people with few close social ties will resort to mass or totalitarian behavior than of those with extensive social relationships.*

This concentration upon the social nonattachment of mass man implies an acceptance on my part of the pluralist sociological interpretation of democracy. The primary assertion of this interpretation is that a wide network of overlapping secondary social relationships and associations—none of which makes total demands upon the loyalty of its members—provides the firmest social foundation for democratic political systems. Scholars hold various views of these relationships, but all of these writers agree that a network of strong secondary groups, neither totally inclusive (with respect to their members) nor exclusive (regarding one another), interposed between the individual and the state is a valuable social resource in any democratic system.[19]

The effects of such a network are several. It has been suggested that

---

* The concept of nonattachment used here is close to Durkheim's idea of "anomie" as a state of normlessness. In the absence of a strong set of thoroughly internal norms, lack of social connections means fewer group sources of norms; and the proportion of a person's normative system that is not at least indirectly group-derived is probably near zero. Subjective nonattachment is in fact anomie in that no identification with any social groups as normative systems is felt. Parsons would go further: objective nonattachment, a lack of "integration with stable institutional patterns," is also anomie. See Merton, p. 135, and Parsons, *Essays*, p. 125.

The extended meanings of anomie offered by Merton, Srole, Riesman, and De-Grazia closely approximate the idea of "alienation" that I shall use in this work. These writers go considerably beyond Durkheim's original use of the term anomie to denote a nonnormative condition. See Merton, pp. 164–65; Srole in Lane, *Life*, pp. 167–68; Riesman, *Crowd*, pp. 243–44; DeGrazia, pp. 71–72.

membership in secondary groups correlates with the member's perceptions of his own ability to influence the political system and with his commitment to that system or to abstract democratic values.[20] Intermediate groups, if autonomous, serve to insulate the people from the direct impact of the state, and vice versa. And, insofar as they pursue political activity, intermediate groups serve to personalize a political system that in modern society seems increasingly distant from the common man.[21]

The pluralist interpretation of democracy's social basis has especial significance in the case of Japan. Whatever the alacrity with which Japan has taken to democracy since World War II, the Japanese have never taken to crosscutting group affiliations. The sociologist Nakane Chie sees Japan as not a plural but a "unilateral" society, where individuals are members either of a single secondary group, of several such groups with largely identical memberships, or of several groups of which one is the predominant focus of loyalty.[22] Neither the attenuation of traditional patterns of group inclusivity and exclusivity nor the development of voluntary groups on a Western model has progressed enough that Japanese democracy could be described as having a pluralistic social base.[23] Insofar as this base is lacking I believe that Japanese democracy has its unstable aspects.

One such aspect may be the Sōkagakkai, impressionistically described as a conglomeration of lower social elements—the working class, the less educated, the low in status—that tend to be least closely attached to society.[24] The members of any organization have, ipso facto, social relationships; some writers have suggested that Gakkai members will have few, if any, relationships that are not consequent upon their membership in the Society. From the standpoint of the pluralist interpretation of democracy, such a limited pattern of social relationships is nondemocratic. This nondemocratic behavior stems not only from nonattachment, but also from alienation, the second mark of mass man.

Three facets of alienation are considered here: alienation from self, from society *qua* mankind, and from concrete political and social systems. Self-alienation is described by Fromm as

a mode of experience in which the person experiences himself as an alien. He has become ... estranged from himself. He does not experience himself as the center of his world, as the creator of his own acts—but his acts and their consequences have become his masters, whom he obeys, or whom he may even worship. The alienated person is out of touch with himself as he is out of touch with any other person.[25]

Self-alienation is manifested in a sense of futility and impotence, a nonacceptance of oneself, and a low opinion of one's value, abilities, and potentialities. The contemporary obsession with quantification and scientism and the "specialization, functionalization, standardization, anonymization" of modern techniques of organization, communication, and marketing render all men equal and equally interchangeable. The effect is to erode, first, the individual's uniqueness, then his worth as an individual, and finally his evaluation of himself as an individual.[26] Alienation is described by Fromm, Karl Mannheim, and Erich Kahler as a psychological type modal to certain types of societies, notably capitalist, modern, or mass society, depending upon the writer. As used here self-alienation is a less sweeping concept, applicable not to any society as a whole, but to those in any society who feel a high degree of futility, impotence, and nonacceptance of self.

Human alienation—alienation from one's fellow men, both individually and collectively—is also often seen as a concomitant of modern society. Diffuse distrust of people in general, antipathy or jealousy toward certain social groups, and an inability to cooperate or communicate with other people are characteristics of the human alienate.[27] And the obverse of distrust is intense partisanship.[28] Basically alienated people who have become members of some group— whether village, political party, religion, social class, or ethnic category—tend to draw sharp lines between their fellow members and outsiders.[29]

Systemic alienation, i.e., alienation from particular social and political structures, has two ingredients. First is disaffection from one's concrete social, economic, and political context. This can take the form of dissatisfaction with one's own ability to influence the system, with the performance of the system as a provider of values, or with the system as a whole.[30] Second is alienation from the more abstract "rules of the game,"[31] which are equivalent, in my interpretation of them, to Lipset's "democratic formula" (see Note 1).

More detached from society, the lower social strata are also more prone to alienation. Feelings of futility and impotence and predilections for simplistic and irrational belief systems are most common among the lower classes, as are more specifically undemocratic traits.[32] One cross-national study indicated that in several countries lower social elements had less commitment to democratic institutions, processes, and values than did their fellow nationals as a whole.[33] Empirical examples of deviant political movements also demonstrate the connection with the lower classes. The nineteenth-century "urban mobs" examined by Hobsbawm were composed of "little people . . . the unclassifiable urban poor."[34] Similar social elements more recently formed the nuclei of a series of movements that explicitly apotheosized direct action—European fascism.[35]

Little education, marginal status, mobility and instability in job and life pattern, and frustration in efforts to better one's position all conduce to disaffection with self, neighbors, and system. Education in particular has important implications: the less educated appear to tend more toward "rigid and intolerant" political views, narrow ranges of opinion, and extreme and simplistic thought patterns.[36] They are, moreover, less trusting of other people, less confident vis-à-vis their social environment, and less inclined to talk freely about politics with a wide range of people.[37] One study suggests quite simply that alienation from the political system varies inversely with education.[38] The heuristic relevance of these tendencies for the present study is apparent from the ostensible social composition of the Sōka-gakkai.

According to Lipset, the lower classes' predisposition toward rigid and intolerant thought patterns is manifested not only in their political views, but also in their religious outlook and activities.[39] Ties between lower-class religious groups and undemocratic political movements have sometimes been unmistakable. In America in particular, "not only is the entire right-wing movement infused at the mass level with the fundamentalist style of mind, but the place in its ranks of fundamentalist preachers, ex-preachers, and sons of preachers is so prominent as to underline the mutual congeniality of thought."[40] An inclination toward types of religious belief potentially disruptive of political order may be inferred from studies showing the millenarian proclivities of the lower-middle and lower classes in both medieval and modern Europe.[41] Whether such proclivities exist across cultures is not known; the Gakkai may be a worthy subject for study in this regard.

MASS BEHAVIOR AND MASS MOVEMENTS

Kornhauser has characterized mass behavior as unstable, focused on remote objects, and direct. Given a political orientation, such behavior becomes destructive of democratic systems. The remoteness of focus allows action to be mobilized toward utopian goals, and direct action, unmediated by formally sanctioned channels of political behavior or by intervening social relationships, denies the democratic political process.[42] This sort of action by large numbers of people could have lethal effects on a democratic system.

Individuals with the attributes we have ascribed to mass man probably exist in every society. In most societies, however, they do not constitute the modal personality type nor are they likely to be in any way organized. But simply because they are not dominant does not mean they do not exist in considerable numbers. Bell denies the reality of the mass society specter by pointing out that the United States, the most highly developed of all nations, is not subject to large-scale social disorder and pervasive anomie.[43] However, the periodic reappearance during American history of movements such as the Know-Nothings, the Ku Klux Klan, the Minutemen, and a whole spectrum of splinter religious sects, suggests that in this nation, as in any other, there are enough nonattached and alienated to create a potential for mass behavior.

Two key elements are essential to the emergence of a mass movement. First, the proportion of mass men in the society must pass some critical threshold (and some means of communication must exist among them). Second, an organizing catalyst—whether man, institution, or social condition—must precipitate the movement.[44] An "escape from freedom" can take one of two forms: submission to a leader, or compulsive conformity to some set of norms.[45] In either case the mass man has found a mooring. If the mooring is purposeful and sustained mass behavior organized around a program, a mass movement exists.[46]

The internal structure of mass movements is analogous to that of the mass society described above. Non-elites have a high degree of influence over the selection of elites,[47] and the intermediate groups are noninclusive and weak. These groups can be traditionally and culturally weak; they can be weakened by cumulative changes in their environment; or they can be intentionally weakened or kept weak by the elite, as they are in totalitarian movements.[48]

The belief systems of mass movements parallel the psychological patterns of mass men. The belief systems of mass men are characterized stylistically by simplism, unreality, and irrationality, and substantively by assertions of the impotence and futility of the individual. Doctrinal distrust of outsiders is central. Accordingly, the beliefs of mass movements show an alienation both from the socioeconomic and political systems within which they exist and from the more abstract attitudinal "formula" necessary to the existence of stable and effective democracy.

The Sōkagakkai, in organizing several millions of Japanese, has drawn upon those social elements that according to our arguments are most likely to support undemocratic, especially mass, movements. The Gakkai can be examined by focusing either on its members, to determine how closely they approximate the model of mass man, or on the Society as an organization, to determine from official doctrines and activities how closely it approximates the model of mass movement. Kornhauser implies that one will mirror the other. But he neglects the possibility of contradiction and conflict between the official, formal precepts and activities of the organization and the unofficial, informal attitudes and behavior of the rank and file. In this study it is assumed that such contradictions and conflicts may exist within an organization; and that the degree and kind of resolution found for them will have crucial significance for the relationship of the organization as a whole to its environment. Only when one can see the movement in question as a totality of the psychological, doctrinal, programmatic, and behavioral attributes of both its leaders and the rank and file, within the framework of its official and unofficial structures and processes, is one able to understand the relationship of the movement to its environment.

FOCUS OF INQUIRY

The Sōkagakkai has parallels with many movements—religious, political, social—of other times and places. By examining the Gakkai on various levels of abstraction, one can compare its development and present state with those of such diverse social phenomena as the millenarian religious movements of medieval Europe and the religious revivals of medieval Japan;[49] the "totalitarian democracy," "political messianism," and urban "mobs" of nineteenth-century Europe;[50] the "value-oriented movements," splinter religious groups, and deviant political phenomena (Poujadism, McCarthyism, and the like) of the twentieth century;[51] the "revitalization movements" and the new religions of developing areas;[52] and the great totalitarian movements of the right and left, both Eastern and Western.[53]

My concern in this study, although intended as a basis for such comparisons, is more limited. In Part I, I examine the development and present state of the Sōkagakkai; in the first three chapters I make use of Neil Smelser's analysis of emerging social movements, and chapters 4, 5, and 6 are organized in terms of Parsons' functional approach.[54] In Part II, I compare the psychological, attitudinal, and behavioral attributes of Gakkai members with those of Kornhauser's mass man and go on to ask whether the officially espoused beliefs, practices, and structures of the Gakkai approximate those of the mass movement as envisioned by Kornhauser. The interaction of the members' attitudes and actions with the Society's official standards for such thought and activity is discussed in Chapter 11, and out of this analytic process come conclusions about the propositions dependent on these data—conclusions, that is, about the relationships of the Gakkai as a whole to mass movements in the abstract and to the Society's Japanese environment. *Is* the Gakkai a mass movement, with all the behavioral implications thereof? And what, in any case, is its significance for present Japanese political, religious, and social systems?

The final part of the study considers, in its conclusions, the possibility that the Sōkagakkai, though not approximating a mass movement, might yet have destructive consequences for the formally democratic Japanese political system. The dangers to democratic regimes do not issue from mass movements alone. Although the mass movement model was chosen for this study because of its initially perceived parallels with the Gakkai, a movement such as the Gakkai may have undemocratic aspects completely unassociated with its points of congruence with this model.

A related problem of congruence concerns intramodel consistency. Kornhauser's model provides no mensurative aids for the student; nor does it stipulate which of the many attributes of mass men and mass movements are most important in determining whether a person or an organization is "mass." The model provides no measurable threshold for any single attribute: just how alienated one must be to be a mass man is unclear. Nor does one know just how many of the attributes of mass men or movements must be present in the organization studied—and in what strength—before "massness" can be inferred. Moreover, the model offers little help in facing the possibility that an organization that is indubitably mass in structure may be an unequivocal supporter of democratic values, institutions, and processes in both ideal and actual behavior.

A major subjective element will of course intrude itself into the treatment of these problems. All the data obtained on the Society and its members will be presented as they pertain to each characteristic of mass man and mass movement, these characteristics being treated as a syndrome—most of whose components must be present before any conclusion of massness may be drawn. Furthermore, the attributes of the population as a whole and of other movements will be taken into account in an effort to establish the relative proximity of the Gakkai to the mass model. The data so presented may lead different observers to different conclusions. Ultimately, judgment of the Sōkagakkai as mass or not, undemocratic or not, must rest on the interpretation by each observer of the available data. By providing as broad a spectrum of data as possible I hope to furnish an empirical basis from which others, using different models and approaches, may draw their own conclusions.

I have gathered and ordered these data through a process as wide-ranging and unbiased as I could make it. But in any analysis, the personal values of the observer play a role. Values of mine that may be relevant to this study derive primarily from an upbringing in a Western, Judeo-Christian culture. And beyond that caveat, I must add that the authorities of the Gakkai, and members on every level, were extremely helpful in all phases of this study and were congenial at all times; thus, if there are subjective influences on the interpretation of the data they may be in the direction of excessive sympathy toward the Society.

PART I

ORIGINS, STRUCTURE, AND POLITICS

CHAPTER 1

Social Structure and Social Strain

THE SŌKAGAKKAI is but one manifestation of a broad social, psychological, and religious current known as the "new religions" (*shinkō shūkyō*) of Japan.[1] Very difficult to define or delimit—some are hardly new, and some are only generously termed religions—the new religions comprise over one thousand incorporated religious entities claiming over fifteen million believers: some 15 per cent of the total population.[2] Often characterized as "crisis religions," these new groups have arisen largely in reaction to over one hundred years of endemic social crisis, the penalty paid by Japan in her drive to attain, first, modernity, then Asian hegemony, and, finally, reconstruction.[3] But social crisis, though a major factor in the rise of new religions, does not completely account for the appearance of new sects. In his analysis of emerging social movements, Neil Smelser[4] distinguishes six contributing factors:

(1) The "structural conduciveness" of a given social system to certain kinds of behavior, e.g. religious activity.

(2) "Structural strains": "ambiguities, deprivations, conflicts, and discrepancies" in the social structure.

(3) The "growth and spread of a generalized belief" that identifies the origin of strain and prescribes appropriate responses.

(4) "Precipitating factors": for instance, some "dramatic event."

(5) The "mobilization of the participants [believers] for action."

(6) The "operation of social controls," i.e., forces that prevent, deflect, interrupt, or inhibit the foregoing elements; these forces may be either institutional or noninstitutional.*

Each of these factors can exist in society long before a fortuitous

---

* These six factors will serve as the basis for Chapters 1–3.

constellation of the other factors draws it into the production of a new sect.[5] The key to the influence of these factors is the manner in which all six combine: whether the end product is religiously oriented or not, what part of society it appeals to, what sort of organization it develops—in short, its form and character—are determined by the sequence and proportions in which the causative factors all combine.

No close correlation is likely between the form of any of the contributing factors and the resulting movement, since each movement is determined by its own combination of structure, strain, belief, precipitation, mobilization, and control. The influences of all the factors are crucial to the final product.[6] And because the component factors "continuously combine and recombine" through time,[7] this sect development is only theoretically divisible into separate causes. In fact, any one of the new sects is in constant flux. Each factor receives feedback from its interaction with other factors, with each momentary state of the developing product, and with the total environment. A similar feedback characterizes the relationship between the endproduct sect and its environment.

The circumstances that have given rise to the new religions in Japan have undergone changes with the passing years; certain factors have dominated the scene for a time, to be displaced after a while by other factors. Such permutations and shifts in importance among the causes are responsible for the differences among the resulting sects. But parallels among all of the postwar religious movements are also discernible. Thus, in examining the appearance and development of the Gakkai, we shall treat both its shared aspects (why another new religion?) and its unique aspects (why this particular new religion?).

STRUCTURAL CONDUCIVENESS

Four aspects of social structure conduce to the emergence of religious movements such as the Sōkagakkai:

(1) The degree of differentiation of a society's value system from the other components of action, i.e., the extent to which values are distinct from norms. Religious movements tend to appear only when religion is a dominant interest; where a society's world view is couched in primarily religious terms, protest will also be defined in those terms.

(2) The availability of alternative means for expressing grievances and reconstructing the social system.

(3) The social and political environment, especially those institu-

tions and attitudes relevant to tolerance or intolerance of such movements.

(4) The communications facilities available to such movements.[8]

Differentiation of religious values and norms. Religious values in the broadest sense have traditionally been strong in Japan, and are so still; they also have long been related to the political value system. For centuries Japanese rulers have invoked and inculcated religious principles, a practice that underlay the formation of State Shintō, the religious foundation of the Japanese political system from the Meiji period until Japan's defeat in 1945. Nor have religious institutions themselves eschewed intimate ties to political power; for over two hundred years of Tokugawa rule Buddhist temples served, in certain ways, as branches of the governmental apparatus.

From a popular standpoint, recourse to religion has been one of few alternatives open to the Japanese people in times of stress. Historically, denying the people political articulation and participation retarded the secularization of the popular outlook on the world; thus, when the people "have sought aid and security in the resources closest to them, their most accessible resource has been their religious tradition."[9] Politically relevant religious movements are to be found through much of Japan's history.* And below the level of such movements one can discern the historical role of religion in the basic patterns of Japanese social life. Shintō accommodated in its divine pantheon almost every manifestation of nature. Moreover, the shrines—which, with their resident deities and their attendant rituals, played such an important role in the premodern community—have nearly all had both religious and political significance.

All these factors culminated in the State Shintō system of Japan before 1945. The Shintō mythology was used to marshal the people for the great task of modernization, to unite them behind a divinely ordained political system centered upon the God-Emperor. Later, Shintō was used to mobilize them for the realization of Japan's divine mission in East Asia. Thus, even as modernization progressed in much of society, atavism characterized the ethical and religious value system. Differentiation, secularization, and rationalization were impeded, while belief in living gods and in religion's centrality in social and political life was part of the scholastic training of generations of children. But though Shintō was retained as the core of the

---

* Examples are the reformist sects of thirteenth- and fourteenth-century Japan (see Kasahara, *Kakumei no Shūkyō*); the Shimabara Rebellion of 1637; the nineteenth-century Tenrikyō sect; and today's Sōkagakkai.

official value system, Japan was changing. By 1945 Japan already had fifty-five years' experience with parliamentary political institutions, and the people had become well aware of these institutions through the educational system. Opportunities and abilities for political participation were thus developing, and the possibility that popular unrest would flow through secular channels was increasing.

The term that perhaps best describes the present religious orientation of the Japanese is "irreligious religiosity." Of the population as a whole, only about one third admit belief in any religion; and among certain subgroups, notably students, the division is nearer one tenth.[10] In one survey, 30 per cent of those who professed belief gave as a reason "family custom," while another 30 per cent didn't know why they believed.[11] For centuries the Japanese have impressed observers as being apathetic toward all forms of religious observance, aside from memorial services for departed ancestors and perfunctory obeisances at shrines and temples visited in the course of sightseeing trips. In recent times R. P. Dore, in his *City Life in Japan*, reported a "general lack of contact with Buddhist teachings" in the community he studied: of one hundred adults, only nine (of whom two were Christians) had heard a sermon within the previous year.[12]

But Dore also noted the religious side of this irreligiosity. Many of the same people who ignored religious teaching regularly worshiped their ancestors and participated in celebrations at shrines and temples.[13] In addition, Dore perceived "a generalized attitude of religious humility—a sense of the individual's dependence on and insignificance in the face of what may be described as Nature, the Universe, or the whole abstract world of the noumenal."[14] Empirical data corroborate his position: in several polls, up to two-thirds of those questioned, including the extremely irreligious students, responded that they thought religion is important to life or important in the education of children.[15] And the plain fact of the burgeoning of religious groups after World War II, when new sects sprang up "like bamboo shoots after the rain," attests to a religious questing by large numbers of Japanese.

That the Japanese religious orientation is still politically relevant is evident in the persistence of intimate ties between daily life and religion. Kamishima Jirō goes so far as to call this view of the unity of gods and men "the fundamental concept subliminally determining the life of the masses."[16] Although secular political channels for the articulation of demands are far more numerous and more open than in the past, the numbers of people who seek economic, social, and physical benefit from divine sources demonstrate that traditional orientations are still strong. And politics, as a phase of life more open to the common people now than ever before, thus necessarily has its still unsecularized aspects.

The Sōkagakkai, unquestionably the largest and most powerful of all the new religions, may in fact epitomize the present state of Japanese culture as reflected in the level of differentiation of the Japanese value system. In a society where secular politics is highly developed but where traditional religious values remain strong, the Gakkai's unique blend of politics and religion may be the key to its success.

Availability of alternative channels of articulation. There are three alternative channels—the narrowly social, the political, and the conventionally religious—through which those who join the new religions might otherwise articulate their discontent with and demands upon the social system.*

Such observers as Suzuki Eitarō and R. P. Dore see in the cities the development of stable social relationships through which individuals realize a sense of belonging and security, and through which they become attached indirectly to the larger society.[17] Family, community, school, place of work, and personal interests form the bases for such relationships. Suzuki claims that up to 99 per cent of the urban population participate in such primary and secondary relationships, which impart stability and order to their lives.[18]

But despite the purported discovery by Suzuki and others of little *gemeinschaften* all over the cities, the fact remains that the Gakkai has perhaps four hundred thousand member families in Tokyo. Moreover, several other new religions are centered there, indicating that if fulfilling social relationships are in fact as commonplace as supposed, they still are not fulfilling the social and spiritual needs of a sizable portion of the populace. As Dore and Nakane point out, the Japanese do not tend to join multiple, mutually separate voluntary associations.[19] To Dore, "the Japanese are not great joiners," although limited face-to-face groups are pervasive.[20] Voluntary associations were relatively few in the neighborhood Dore studied, and were usually coincidental with some other (e.g. community-centered) organization.[21] In addition, physical mobility has disintegrative effects upon both primary and secondary relationships—and the social strata upon which the Gakkai and other new religions draw are among the most mobile. Wives are particularly penalized: lacking even their hus-

---

* Since the Gakkai and most of the other postwar sects have arisen in the cities, only those means available to the urban dweller will be treated.

bands' opportunities for social intercourse, they are very much at loose ends, and the female majorities in many of the new religions (including the Gakkai) demonstrate their lack of alternative structures.

One other potential alternative social structure through which urbanites might find satisfying relationships is the labor union. But unions benefit only those in union shops, and the great majority of small enterprises in Japan are not unionized. (This type of establishment—one, that is, with under one hundred employees—accounts for approximately half the work force and constitutes over half of the total number of business enterprises.)[22] In any case, the unions themselves are dubious sources of satisfying social relations. Organizational materialism and politicization often supersede members' interests, and venal factionalism and impersonal bureaucratism have plagued the unions throughout the postwar period.[23]

An absence of alternative political channels for a large stratum of the population is often cited as the major element in the rise of the Sōkagakkai. The Society is pictured by Japanese journalists as a voice for the voiceless, an advocate for the urban lower classes who until now have been largely excluded from the political process. Whether or not the Gakkai is such a voice remains an open question; but it is a fact that the government and the established political parties could, if they chose, take considerable initiative in extending the scope of political expression. The Gakkai's size alone indicates a lack of alternatives; moreover, the Society's electoral gains have been primarily at the expense of the established parties.[24] Other, less overtly political, new religions do not necessarily denote a lack of political outlets; the Gakkai, which has achieved its most striking growth since it entered politics, does, for its constituency is just those social elements that journalists claim have no direct representation in the other major political parties.

The new religions as a collective phenomenon indicate that religious sentiment as many Japanese perceive it cannot be expressed or fulfilled through the orthodox religious channels. The same is true in other societies. Splinter religious groups in America "originate mainly among the religiously neglected poor, who find the conventional religion of their day unsuited to their social and psychological needs."[25] In Japan the traditional faiths are just that—the repositories of traditions, of abstruse philosophy and sterile theology far removed from the daily life of the common people. Shintō, as a unifying spiritual system, has not recovered from the blow dealt it by military defeat and subsequent discredit. The established Buddhist sects have never regained the vitality they demonstrated in the fourteenth century. And Christianity, which had had a genuine impact when it was introduced in the sixteenth century, became, after its readmittance in the Meiji era, no more than an imported theological system dispensed by foreigners—attractive to intellectuals but unappealing to the masses.[26] In fact, if one seeks living religion in contemporary Japan, there are very few places to look for it outside of the new religions.

Because all of the new religions benefit from the lack of religious alternatives, it would seem that the key to the peculiar success of the Sōkagakkai lies elsewhere. But whether the Gakkai's primary functions are social, political, or religious, it is clear that some lack of structural alternatives in Japanese society is a major factor in the Society's growth. A point made repeatedly in a series of case studies of Gakkai members was the felt need for some kind of psychological armor with which to gird oneself against the world.[27] Some subjects explicitly recognized the possibility that functions fulfilled for them through Gakkai membership could be fulfilled by other social structures; but they had found, nonetheless, that only the Gakkai did in fact satisfy their needs.

The social and political environment. The new religions are generally quite harmonious with their cultural context. They are more or less a part of the Japanese religious tradition: tolerant, eclectic, attentive to everyday life, and vague as regards the border between the natural and the supernatural.[28] They are singularly amenable to the materialistic trends of postwar Japanese society; economic gain is a commonly promised fruit of faith. Health is another: faith cures are a prominent part of the activities of many of the new sects. This of course is not to say that the appeal of the new faiths is universal. Certain characteristics of both the sects and their believers are disdained by the more educated, and their attraction is in fact limited to less sophisticated social elements. But it is clear that the new religions do not constitute any marked break with the Japanese religious tradition.

The Sōkagakkai is another matter. Intolerant and exclusive, it contravenes major features of its environment. It does, however, have the secular relevance (termed materialism by its detractors) of the other new religions. And it has another feature of great importance: a strong group orientation. The Japanese incline almost instinctively toward group-oriented life, and their components of social behavior have traditionally been groups, not individuals. The individual finds identity as a member of a group, significant in relation to a limited and specific social connection and subordinate to that connection.[29] This group orientation pervades even religious life—the "Japanese thought that to propagate Buddhism was to profit their particular human nexus."[30] Groups, in turn, have tended to be very diffuse and inclusive toward their members, influencing members in practically all phases of their behavior.

This group orientation on the part of the Japanese has been referred to as an "octopus-pot mentality" (*tako-tsubo konjō*), a phrase that implies a desire to crawl into a safe, cozy refuge (composed, in this case, of close, satisfying social relationships).[31] This psychological feature of the Japanese has weakened with modernization, but it is still strong, and the new religions, particularly the Gakkai, minister to it. The cellular organization common to many of the new sects offers a tako-tsubo wherein the isolated urban dweller may find psychic haven, and millions of Japanese have apparently found the offering attractive. The basic unit of the Gakkai, the *kumi* or group, is essentially of this tako-tsubo type. How effective the Gakkai's particular form of this structure is will be seen when we examine the Society's overall organization.

Communications facilities. Universal literacy, an open political system, and an economic affluence permitting general access to radio, television, and written communication of all types: these components form the basis of contemporary Japan's communications system. From this base have sprung a comprehensive network of national and local newspapers, a huge publishing industry, and massive television, radio, and cinematic operations; and ideas of all kinds are therefore disseminated easily and rapidly. Many of the new religions have devoted great efforts to mass communications, and none more than the Sōkagakkai. But the communications of the Gakkai, in common with those of the other new sects, serve more internal than external purposes. Gakkai publications are used in proselyting, of course; data suggest, however, that converts are drawn primarily by personal communication, and it is in small groups that personal communication is most often effected. Here too, then, one sees the importance to the Gakkai's development of the tako-tsubo mentality of the Japanese. One could argue that this mentality, in a context deficient in means of need-satisfaction and social, political, and religious communication, has in fact been the dominant factor in Japanese society conducing to the emergence and growth of the Sōkagakkai.

STRUCTURAL STRAINS

A social structure, even though hospitable to new forms of religion, yet may not witness the appearance of any such sects if the extant value system continues to suffice for the needs of the society's members. When, however, "a way of living which has long been taken for granted is called in question, invalidated or simply rendered impracticable, a situation of peculiar strain is created."[32] Norman Cohn, in his examination of medieval European millenarian sects, saw in such strains the immediate preconditions for radical new forms of religious behavior. When (1) social and economic horizons expand beyond the possibility of satisfaction, or (2) traditional social groups (especially kin groups) disintegrate until people find themselves without their accustomed emotional and material supports, or (3) rapid changes in relative status and economic position of different social classes occur, or (4) society as a whole loses its independence and is subjugated, or (5) traditional authority ceases to fulfill its supposedly proper functions, or (6) supreme authority is discredited or disintegrates altogether, or (7) contact with alien cultures shakes a previously unquestioned world view, then the cohesion and stability of society decrease and the impact of additional calamitous events on social patterns is magnified.[33] In the years since the mid-nineteenth century Japan has undergone all of these forms of social strain, and the appearance of novel religious phenomena has been a continuous occurrence.* But because the Gakkai in its present form is a postwar phenomenon, only the period since World War II will be treated here.

The strains in Japanese society after the war which have facilitated the appearance and flourishing of new religious groups stem primarily from two sources—military defeat and the subsequent process of recovery and rapid socioeconomic change. Following Smelser's typology we shall examine three forms of conducive strains: those related to normative and value disorder; those related to the expectation-deprivation ratio in society; and those related to the inadequacy of old techniques or knowledge in new situations.[34]

---

* The most salient forms of strain have differed at different times and any comprehensive study of the new religions should cover at least the last century. Examples of such periodization can be found in Saki and Oguchi, pp. 34–38, and in McFarland, *Rush Hour,* pp. 54 *et seq.*

Normative and value chaos. The normative and value strains in postwar Japanese society result from the introduction of new elements of Western normative and value systems; from the accretion of more general norms and values that may be thought of as concomitants of modernization; and from the collapse of the officially sanctioned and assiduously inculcated pre-1945 system of values.[35] The influx of foreign ideas began on a major scale in the mid-nineteenth century. Egalitarianism, liberalism, individualism, Marxism—all the major philosophical currents of the West became the common property of the Japanese. But before the Second World War, the State often sanctioned these foreign influences selectively, in order to minimize disruptive effects upon the established morality. In contrast, the postwar political system formally incorporated liberal democratic values and a democratic normative structure that were in diametric contradiction to indigenous social norms and values, with their hierarchical, authoritarian roots. And although Japan now appears to be a relatively stable democratic system, the contradiction is not yet resolved; in many phases of life the traditional values still determine behavior.

Overlapping the strains caused by the introduction of foreign ideas are those strains, dealt with extensively in the literature of the social sciences, that result from the new normative and value patterns accompanying modernization wherever and however it occurs. The development of new principles of social relationship dates from long before World War II. Amid the ultramodern aspects of much of Japanese society, it continues today; and yet "many features of the system of social relations prevailing in the Tokugawa village are still preserved in the city."[36] Standardized criteria for recruitment and advancement, emotionally neutral and functionally specific relationships, and highly rationalized procedures do not sit well with the Japanese in many instances. But strong pressure to abide such criteria, relationships, and procedures is exerted by the processes of social, economic, and political modernization. The tensions resulting from these contradictions are felt by many Japanese; an illuminating study by Robert Jay Lifton of the personality conflicts in Japanese youth points this up clearly.[37]

The most dramatic case of normative and value disorder came in 1945, when the national polity suffered military defeat for the first time in its history. The official value system, already popularly discredited by its failure to lead to victory, was formally abolished by the Occupation authorities. And the agencies of socialization that had transmitted this system lost much of their power when the legal preeminence of the family over its members was ended and the educational system decentralized. Thus, not only had the old normative and value system been largely destroyed, but the difficulty of implanting any new patterns of values and norms had been increased.

In the sense that not only norms, but values too, were missing, the mood of the early postwar period exceeded even Durkheim's description of anomie. Few agencies existed that could offer viable alternatives to the now defunct prewar orientations. The resurrected Communist Party was one; the new religions were another. Both provided ultimate values that gave life meaning and immediate norms by which to regulate social intercourse. Considering the level of secularization of Japan's culture, it may be that a religious solution to normative chaos is still most attractive to the Japanese; the adherents of the new religions, in fact, far outnumber those of the Japan Communist Party. Provision of some sort of normative and value system is a common feature of all of the new religions. It is without doubt one of the most important elements in the sects' rise as a group.

Expectation and deprivation. That deprivation is a major factor in the gravitation of Japanese to the new religions is undebatable. Almost all the reasons given by believers for joining the new sects can be subsumed under the headings of economic, physical, and psychological deprivation. Physical and psychological deprivations are always felt by the old and the ill, but in times of social stress their plight may be greater, and others may also fall prey to such distresses. Economic deprivation, by definition, is poverty; when society in certain of its parts or as a whole is becoming more prosperous, this poverty becomes much harder to bear. The three forms of deprivation often overlap, of course, more so in times of stress; what if, in addition, there is little hope of assistance from secular sources? There is room then for belief systems that either redefine the whole value system and thus eliminate the feeling of deprivation, or promise to fulfill expectations through nonsecular means, or both. This is precisely what the new sects have done in Japan.

World War II and its aftermath paved the way for the new religions. The war's devastation brought severe deprivation to the entire nation, a deprivation that was absolute, affecting everyone. Some of the major psychological deprivations of the period were mentioned in the discussion of normative chaos; economic losses were staggering, and food shortages and disruption of administrative processes meant greatly increased health problems. Surrender accentuated the problem of economic deprivation. Hundreds of thousands of demobilized soldiers returned to Japan; more hundreds of thousands of evacuees poured back into the desolated cities. Inflation wiped out much of whatever savings had been preserved, and food, shelter, and clothing shortages reached emergency proportions in the winter of 1945–46. Remedial Occupation measures staved off crisis, but economic uncertainty was a fact of life for countless families for several years. Some of the Occupation's remedies for the general situation even intensified the deprivations of many Japanese; implementation in 1949 of the Dodge Plan, designed to end inflation, resulted in the dismissal of 300,000 laborers and 260,000 government workers.[38]

Into this situation moved the new religions, promising "instant benefit in this life."[39] One of the primary controls upon the rise of such movements, the ability of the government to respond to strain by reducing its causes, was largely lacking. The new sects, however, were unhindered by such secular limitations; anything and everything could come to those who would believe.

As the nation rebuilt, another source of discontent appeared. With the repudiation of the prewar ideology, the official sanction of asceticism was removed, and acquisitive inclinations became as marked in Japan as in other industrializing nations. At the same time, the high rate of economic growth attained by Japan in the mid-1950's spread prosperity throughout much of the nation. Some families, however, never regained their prewar economic or social status; many more saw their fellows rising more quickly than they on the tide of prosperity. As a result, relative deprivation has become the major contributory factor to the growth of the new religions.

Psychological deprivation, of the sort attributed to members of a mass society, hit many of those who had escaped economic or even relative deprivation after the war. This psychological lack characterized early postwar Japanese society; and it has evidently survived among the newly affluent.[40] That such deprivation exists today is apparent in any of Japan's ubiquitous *pachinko* parlors:

Pachinko [it is a form of pinball game] is the most depressing symptom of the loss of bearings of at least a part of the Japanese people in recent years. . . . You press a lever which releases a small steel ball; if the ball enters the hole you win a small prize; ninety-nine times out of a hundred the ball does not enter the hole. . . . As money prizes are forbidden by law, winners get such things as sweets, fruit, toys, shaving soap, etc., etc. After 1948 *pachinko* establishments spread prodigiously throughout the whole of Japan. At first they were humble affairs in fairgrounds, but then the small, medium, and big sharks of Japanese business life got hold of them, and *pachinko* arcades *de luxe* invaded the principal streets and became one of the characteristics of contemporary Japan.[41]

According to recent statistics, there are roughly ten thousand pachinko parlors in all Japan, with some one million machines—in other words, there is one machine for every ten persons, including women and children.[42] "The characteristic *pachinko* noise [is] rather like that of a factory or printing works, a factory in which nothing is made, a printing works in which nothing is printed."[43] The scene inside is reminiscent of nothing so much as a Las Vegas slot machine emporium: rows of hypnotized players numbly, repetitively pulling the levers, each player depending for success on the chance roll of a ball independent of his will or power. Each is starkly impotent and alone, and well aware that, mathematically, he is destined to lose.

It is difficult to understand its fascination. It is obviously a flight from reality, a drug. . . . Poor Jirō Yamada, a clerk earning [seventy-five dollars] a month, with a wife and three children to keep, bored by his work and a life that has nothing to offer him . . . finds a kind of narcotic salvation in the crazy, endless, absurd, repetitive movement. . . . A people spiritually reduced to zero, which has suffered destruction even in the secret places of the heart, faced with the huge task of finding new reasons for hoping and living, responds like an army of automata to these calls of the unconscious.[44]

Sizable sectors of urban Japanese society have, in effect, been living since 1945 in a giant, interminable pachinko game. If something appears that offers hope and meaning, they are ready to leap hungrily at it. One might refer metaphorically to the social strata that feed the Gakkai as the pachinko players in Japanese society, a group that (like the pachinko phenomenon itself) has dwindled but not vanished with economic recovery.

Relative deprivation of certain social elements, as opposed to absolute deprivation of major portions of the society, is the context of Gakkai growth,[45] and the Gakkai has, in fact, attained its giant size during the period of economic boom. (See Appendix B.) Those who predicted the decline of the new religions with the advent of national prosperity have been confounded by this fact. This unexpected response to affluence by a movement born in times of deprivation indicates either that society's control mechanisms for alleviating the strains conducive to such movements are still incomplete, or that certain forms of deprivation are beyond the reach of such controls, or, possibly, both.

Old knowledge in new situations. Prior to the Meiji era very few Japanese ever faced a "new" situation; the techniques and knowledge acquired from one's family, schooling (if any), and peers had always sufficed to enable one to cope. One of the most momentous consequences of modernization was the institutionalization of the uncertain future, in which increasing numbers of Japanese became involved in new life patterns that their previous socialization had not prepared them to expect, much less to adjust to smoothly. This institutionalization was at first limited by the retention of a traditionalistic value system that dictated proper modes of behavior, modes supposedly valid in all situations. But even among the peasantry, the most tradition-oriented class, the old knowledge was gradually invalidated. Even the officially approved habits of diligence and frugality proved useless in the face of depressions that began elsewhere and came upon the farmers as disembodied, inexplicable disasters.

In 1945 the official value system, the explicatory framework for all situations, was simply swept away. The legal centrality of the family, the model for social groups on all levels of collective behavior, was ended. Deprived of the old framework, the old dictates, those who were faced with new situations felt even more uncertain—and growing urbanization was increasing the frequency of novel experiences.

Urbanization took place on all levels of society, and assumed three forms. The first of these, physical urbanization, the move to the city (see Table 1), resulted in unprecedented numbers of inexperienced, anxious new urbanites. A second form, objective urbanization, saw the manifest adoption everywhere of urban life styles and appurtenances. Great expansions in the mass media and in transportation

TABLE 1

Shifts in Urban and Nonurban Population

Year	Urban (*shibu*) Population: Per Cent of Total	Nonurban (*gunbu*) Population: Per Cent of Total
1930	21.1%	75.9%
1935	32.9	67.1
1940	37.9	62.1
1947	33.1	66.9
1950	37.5	62.5
1955	56.3	43.7
1960	63.5	36.5

SOURCE: Ikado Fujio, *Tōyō Bunka Kenkyū-jo Kiyō*, March 1964, p. 125.

facilitated this spread of the material aspects of urban life. The third form, subjective urbanization, involved changing attitudes. New knowledge required new forms of social interaction, and vice versa; these new patterns of thought and social organization spread to the country along with the television sets and automobiles.

The role of the new religions in the new situations is evident. Ever since the Tenrikyō sect provided a solution for Meiji peasants caught up by economic forces beyond their comprehension, the sects have explained away, sublimated, or otherwise tranquilized the anxieties of many Japanese in new and unaccustomed social contexts. It was in the resolution of the normative and value problems posed by postwar situations that the new religions played their greatest role. But in addition, by providing new knowledge and techniques, the sects have eased the passage of their members into new social structures. The theological interpretations of reality that the new religions offer are occasionally bizarre, as are their techniques—dances, offerings, devotions, or simply self-fulfilling daily life—for adjusting to reality. But it is clear that they do enable many believers to cope with new situations and thus have an attraction for other potential followers.

Along with the other postwar strains conducing to the rise of the new religions, physical and economic deprivation played a role in the Sōkagakkai's development—the Society unquestionably drew upon the ill and the economically disadvantaged in the early postwar period, and does today. But the Gakkai's failure to emerge as a major religious movement until after absolute, general deprivation had eased considerably suggests that relative deprivation has had a greater hand in the Gakkai's remarkable growth. Similarly, that its greatest success came after poverty and health had ceased to be major problems suggests that the economic and physical aftermath of defeat, though a source of Gakkai growth, has been overshadowed by the longer-lasting psychological consequences—normative chaos, psychological deprivation, and the invalidation of old knowledge in new situations.

CHAPTER 2

Sōkagakkai Beliefs

THE BELIEF SYSTEMS forming the doctrinal basis of the new religions, including the Sōkagakkai, are more or less organized sets of ideas that define the world and the proper ends and manners of social and religious behavior.[1] These systems vary in scope from those that seek only personal salvation for a small elect to those, like the Gakkai, that aspire to convert the entire human race and reconstitute all of the world's social structures and values in their own image. Almost all the new sects rely on supernatural agents in their plans for redefinition and reconstitution.*

By and large the same strains have given rise to all the new religions and have given direction to their beliefs; as a result, the new sects show considerable similarities in their doctrines.[2] They are worldly and practical: they stress benefit in this life, set forth concrete (often bluntly materialistic) goals, and in most cases emphasize social relevance and conscience. In the achievement of their goals, however, the sects rely heavily on miracles. Indeed, they rely on divine benefits of all kinds, both concrete and intangible, an attitude that expresses their disillusionment with ordinary politics. They are concerned with social reform in the sense of relieving material deprivations and economic strains. But their main purpose is to establish moral and normative guidelines for human behavior. Such guide-

---

* Religion, as used in this paper, is "the service and adoration of [a supreme being or beings or supernatural force or forces] as expressed . . . in obedience to divine commands, especially as found in accepted sacred writings or as declared by recognized teachers and in the pursuit of a way of life regarded as incumbent on true believers." (*Webster's New International Dictionary of the English Language,* second edition.) Some of the Japanese new religions that perhaps more closely approximate ethical systems are included in the grouping "new religions" owing only to popular usage—hence the qualification "almost all."

lines usually gain added authority in being presented as divine revelation, often by religious leaders who are themselves divine beings
or the representatives of divine agents or forces. The feature of doctrinal simplicity, common to all the new sects, reflects the low level
of sophistication of most believers and suggests the urgency of the
needs for which converts seek satisfaction. That the new sects respond
for the most part to the same cultural influences is apparent from the
tolerance, syncretism, inclusivity, and eclecticism of their doctrines,
and from their nearly universal acceptance of ancestor worship.

The Sōkagakkai shares many, but not all, of these common features.
It is eminently practical and worldly in its orientation. Divine benefit
in daily experience is the core of its appeal: the twin themes of *genze
riyaku* (benefit in this world) and *kudoku* (divine reward) recur incessantly in Gakkai literature and in the testimonials of members.
However, the more spectacular forms of miracles are eschewed by the
Society. Incremental rather than sudden and massive change is the
rule, and through its political activities the Gakkai accords a major
role to secular procedures.

Though the Society denies prescribing any formal system of commandments beyond specified devotional practices, it does in fact provide criteria in more or less concrete form for proper behavior in
one's place of work, in school and family, in Gakkai contexts, and in
society at large. Some of the values and norms incorporated in the
Gakkai's belief system are of divine origin. The writings of the thirteenth-century Buddhist monk Nichiren (revered by the Gakkai as
the True and Universal Buddha) constitute the basic scriptures. But
because these writings must be given contemporary relevance, elaborate interpretations have been made by Gakkai leaders. These exe-
getic additions, though justified by their reference to scripture, do not
in themselves have any divine quality. Nor have the Society's leaders
and exegetes affected any divine qualities; the Gakkai is an organization of lay believers, and its presidents have in turn described themselves as simply fellow worshipers and teachers.

Simplicity of doctrine, in the sense that the number of ideas the
average member must actually understand is minimal, is characteristic of the Society. But the complete theological system of Nichiren
Shōshū, the Gakkai's parent sect, is extensive and extremely complex,
and the Gakkai's intense emphasis upon study suggests that its members probably know more of the teachings of their church than is
usual among the followers of a new sect. The Gakkai also diverges
from the other new sects in the cultural incongruity of its beliefs.

Although the Society's present creed is an amalgam of influences from Nichiren, his successors, and the three Gakkai presidents, the Society emphatically denies any suggestion of syncretism and is intolerant and exclusive of the beliefs of other faiths, including ancestor worship. This cultural dissonance helps make the Gakkai *sui generis* not only among the new religions, but in Japan's entire religious history. That history has indeed included an undercurrent of militance; and it may be that the Society is simply the only contemporary religious group tapping the militant stream. Nevertheless, a traditional dominant religious attitude of the Japanese has been tolerance, and there are signs that the Gakkai itself is cognizant of limits upon its growth as a church militant.

The teachings of the Sōkagakkai are a still-dynamic blend of several elements.[3] Their basic source is the writings of Nichiren (1222–82) as handed down through the Nichiren Shō Sect and rendered into their present state by Nikkan (1665–1726), a high priest of the sect. These writings were taken by Makiguchi Tsunesaburō, founder and first president of the Sōka Kyōiku Gakkai (which in 1946 became the Sōkagakkai), and grafted onto his own "Theory of Value" to form the core of Gakkai ideology. This admixture was reinterpreted by the second president, Toda Jōsei, and further reinterpreted by the third and current president, Ikeda Daisaku.

Because the Gakkai is nominally only a lay organization of the faithful of the Nichiren Shō Sect, it may sound strange to speak of its teachings; but the extent to which Gakkai leaders have redefined Nichiren Shōshū precepts justifies the phrase. In fact, it is more to the point to subsume the Shō Sect under the title Sōkagakkai. Although, in the *Rules of the Sōkagakkai*, the Society appears as a proselyting arm of the Shō Sect,[4] in reality "the Gakkai has intruded into Nichiren Shōshū and the Head Temple has completely lost its autonomy, having become the Religious Affairs Section of the Gakkai."[5] Thus in discussions of theology no distinction will be made here between the present belief systems of the Gakkai and Nichiren Shōshū.

As offered by the Society, Gakkai beliefs often have little apparent organization. I have therefore departed from the Society's outline of its tenets in the following presentation, which thus becomes artificial to the extent that perhaps neither the leaders nor the rank and file of the Gakkai see their beliefs in this order—or are even familiar with all of the elements listed here. What follows, then, is a summary of the important points of Gakkai doctrine as inferred from emphases in official publications. (One final note: I do not essay philosophical and theological criticism; only those facets of belief that have political significance or that bear on the further development of the Gakkai are treated in any detail.)

The theology developed by Nichiren rests on four main points.[6] The first is his acceptance of the Lotus Sutra as the highest and only valid scripture in our age—i.e., in the Latter Day of the Law (*Mappō*), when the true teachings of the Buddha have fallen into general decay. Associated with the Lotus Sutra is the creed that it is the only effective means of salvation; that faith in this sutra alone leads to liberation. The second point, based on this scripture, is Nichiren's postulation of an omnipotent, omnipresent, and eternal Buddha. Third, this Buddha is immanent in every aspect of reality: all beings possess the Buddha-nature and are thus equally able to attain salvation. And fourth, as the means by which salvation is to be achieved, Nichiren set out the "Three Great Secret Laws" (*San Dai Hihō*). The first is the *gohonzon*, or object of worship, a mandala or symbolic representation of the universal, eternal Buddha, inscribed by Nichiren himself. The second is the *daimoku*, or formula, the words *Namu Myōhō Renge Kyō* ("Adoration be to the Sutra of the Lotus of the Wondrous Law"). Reciting the daimoku brings divine blessings upon the believer. Third is the *kaidan*, or high sanctuary. Once all Japan has been converted to Nichiren's religion, a sanctuary symbolizing this achievement—and the country's salvation—will be established, where the rulers of the nation will come to worship.

Nichiren introduced several novel elements into Japanese religious life, beginning with intolerance. He asserted unequivocally that his was the only true and efficacious religion for his day and that all other faiths would lead only to damnation: "Nembutsu is Hell; the Zen are devils; Shingon is national ruin; Ritsu are traitors."[7] All misfortune—social, political, economic, and natural—is the result of heretical religion, and universal acceptance of Nichiren's beliefs (and the elimination of all others) is the only way to avoid calamity. Next, Nichiren advocated a highly aggressive form of proselytism called *shakubuku* (literally, "to break and flatten"), which he considered the only effective method for breaking through the depravity of mankind in the Mappō period. Furthermore, for a religious figure his political orientation was unprecedented. Social calamity as well as personal grief was the result of heretical beliefs; Nichiren's vision of a high sanctuary, therefore, was of a national, not merely a sectarian, shrine. Thus it was imperative that the nation's rulers adopt his precepts as their philosophy of government, and to this end Nichiren brought numerous petitions before the governing authorities of his day, in his customary intolerant and aggressive fashion. (The authorities responded with harsh repressions, exile, and last a commuted death sentence.) Finally, Nichiren had a singularly national outlook. He predicted that his Buddhism would spread from Japan to cover the world and that the Japanese had thus a propagative mission to fulfill. He was not a nationalist in any modern sense; only the chance of his own birth there accounted for the preeminence of Japan in his thinking. Nevertheless, the peculiarly political and ethnocentric elements of his thought have provided a theological basis for many later Japanese nationalists.[8]

Shortly after Nichiren's death the Nichiren Shō Sect split off from the initial Nichiren Sect. Claiming to be the orthodox succession, the Shō Sect moved from the original Head Temple, taking with them what they now assert is the only genuine gohonzon. They retained Nichiren's basic ideas, but in the eighteenth century the high priest Nikkan systematized the doctrine and incorporated the "Nichiren Honbutsu Setsu," the idea that Nichiren himself was an incarnation of the eternal Buddha—a claim never made by the monk himself. Nikkan postulated a mystic unity of Nichiren the man, his mandala, the daimoku, and the universal Buddha of the Lotus Sutra. It is this conception of Nichiren that has become officially enshrined in the teachings of the Sōkagakkai.

The heart of Gakkai ideology is the view the sect takes of life. The entire universe is a single flow of life, eternal and eternally in flux; any given being, at a given moment, is but the present manifestation of a continuous current of life that also has simultaneous past and future manifestations (*ichinen-sanzen*, or "three thousand worlds in a single moment"). Successive forms of life are determined through the workings of karma. But because each form of being possesses a spark of the highest form—Buddhahood—release from the wheel of karma is possible. Man, as a being, is fundamentally neither bad nor good but simply potential; karmic influences work upon him, but since he possesses all possible manifestations of existence within himself, such forces do not determine his future unalterably.

In this flow of existence, subject to these influences and possessing these potentialities, what is the proper aim of man? According to the Gakkai it is happiness.* This goal is assumed to be natural, universal, and self-evident; and owing to the universality of the Buddha-nature,

* This idea was introduced by President Makiguchi.

it is equally attainable by all. With the goal of human life established, the question arises of the means to this end. Here the Gakkai introduces its concept of value: human life is simply a process of creating and maximizing certain values and thereby attaining happiness. President Makiguchi propounded the idea of value, describing three types of value and their respective opposites, or antivalues: in increasing order of importance, beauty and ugliness, gain and loss, and good and evil. But, in fact, gain (*riyaku*, which becomes *goriyaku*, the divine benefit of Gakkai theology) is the most prized value. Gain of itself is an individually achieved value; good is simply collective gain. Thus gain, in its collective aspect, takes precedence over all other goals of human endeavor.

The connection between Makiguchi's value theory and Nichiren Shōshū theology developed in response to the question of just how these values are to be created and their opposites avoided. The answer was explicit: solely through the practice of the True Religion. Not only does the Society claim this exclusive efficacy, it also retains the traditional Nichirenite intolerance of other doctrines. Economic distress, ill health, domestic discord, juvenile delinquency, corrupt politics, earthquakes, and train wrecks have been traced to the pernicious effects of heresy. In recent years the Gakkai has markedly softened its attacks upon other faiths and has made the linking of evil with heresy a much more abstract process. But false religions remain the ultimate culprit, and only universal practice of the principles of Nichiren Shōshū can wipe evil and misery from the earth.

To put these principles of value creation into action the believer must perform a prescribed worship service morning and evening before a copy of the gohonzon enshrined in his home. In addition, he must recite the daimoku as often as possible. By these professions of faith he will derive benefit, both tangible and intangible. Wives will cease their nagging, corns will disappear, business will improve, the weight of misfortunes will be lightened, and one's happiness will increase as bad karma is changed to good and good karma is magnified.

The ultimate stage of the value-creation process is enlightenment (*jōbutsu*). From the traditional Buddhist conception of enlightenment as a breaking away from the wheel of karma into a state of nonbeing, the Gakkai has moved to an interpretation of jōbutsu as a state of absolute happiness to be achieved in this life and enjoyed in endless future lives. The Gakkai calls the winning of jōbutsu in this life "human revolution" (*ningen kakumei*), the realization of personal bliss through religious faith.

A believer's personal happiness, however, even though absolute, is incomplete by itself. The ultimate goal of the Sōkagakkai is not a selfish happiness enjoyed in solitude by the faithful, unmindful of the miseries of the rest of the world. No man's happiness is complete until every man's is; thus individual human revolution must be expanded into universal revolution. Every Gakkai member bears the responsibility for propagating the faith, and the immensity of this task justifies the aggressive tactics (a spiritual inheritance from Nichiren) he is expected to employ. The goal is *kōsen-rufu*, conversion of the entire world, and its attainment will usher in the millennium.

Political activity is indispensable to such intentions. In the Nichirenite tradition of remonstration with national leadership, the Gakkai pursues its objective of winning the government over to the True Religion by participating in the political system. By sending its own representatives into government the Society can work for the good (i.e. the collective benefit) of the nation while striving to establish the principles of Nichiren Shōshū as the proper foundation for political behavior. The Gakkai expects its efforts to result in *ōbutsu-myōgō*, "fusion of Buddhism and politics"—actually, the fusion of Buddhist beliefs with every phase of secular behavior, the veritable reconstitution of society on a comprehensive base of religious values and norms.

It is highly unlikely that many members of the Sōkagakkai have internalized their organization's beliefs in any fashion resembling this exposition. For the great majority the most salient articles of faith are without doubt the life goal of personal happiness and the divine rewards accompanying that state. The practical and this-worldly aspects of faith appeal immediately to those in need of economic, physical, or mental assistance; that there is no "rigid or unusually lofty moral code" to adhere to, nor any stringent standards of asceticism or contemplation in worship, makes the pursuit of practical value through faith relatively simple.[9] Simple also is the Gakkai's comprehensive explanation of the universe and all the good and evil therein.[10]

But the appeal of the Gakkai's teachings is not only for those with narrow, personal goals. The Society's doctrines are, in fact, a series of dual premises offering something to almost everyone. This skillful broadening of appeal may be the most significant contribution of the Gakkai belief system toward the Society's expansion. The first in this series of premises is the creed's combination of the spiritual ("the more you believe . . .") and the material (". . . the more you will receive").[11]

Second is its distinction between the relative and the absolute. Values are relative. The value of any object or action is determined by the extent to which it is relevant to the needs of its perceiver. Because political behavior is also relative, the merits of any political act are judged according to the resulting benefit to the total environment. The function of religion, on the contrary, is to provide ultimate standards of good and evil: even heretics may, and should, be included in the beneficial political measures enacted for all society, but in the absolute sphere heretical beliefs remain the source of evil, and according to religious and spiritual conviction are to be overcome. Thus the Gakkai emphasizes that relative and absolute spheres must be kept distinct; the struggle to eliminate false religions must be restricted to debate, education, and prayer, and must never degenerate into physical, social, or political pressure.[12]

A third strength of the Gakkai is its capacity for blending egoism with altruism. One is offered an opportunity to benefit not only oneself but also one's fellow man. In fact, such a blend is incumbent on the true believer, for propagation, or shakubuku, combines these elements. In performing shakubuku one not only obtains divine blessings for himself but contributes to the universal goal of kōsen-rufu.

Fourth, the Gakkai offers both security and adventure: a comprehensive frame of reference is provided for believers, but those who have achieved security are urged to move outward, to participate in the great adventure of world proselytism.

Fifth, the Gakkai appeals both to reason and to emotion. It accepts the advances and the beneficial influences of modern science and medicine, but also emphasizes their limitations. Science is incomplete at best, and catastrophic at worst, without a proper guiding philosophy; moreover, there are social and natural phenomena which even science is at a loss to explain, but which the Gakkai claims to understand with the aid of its theology. Medicine, too, is efficacious, but there are diseases that defy modern medical science; since heresy is the ultimate cause of disease, such sicknesses can and must be attacked through faith.

A sixth duality is that the Sōkagakkai beliefs are a blend of old and new. The roots of Nichiren Shōshū are in the thirteenth century, affording believers a tie with their national heritage. At the same time, the Gakkai claims contemporary, "scientific" validity for its precepts. Thousands of members have attested that the Theory of Value is empirically efficacious, and the Society's modern phraseology —"neo-socialism," "third civilization," and so on—conveys an impression of current and even avant-garde thought. In Japan, where old and new are often in intimate juxtaposition, this feature may be especially prepossessing.

The last of these broad appeals is the Gakkai's merging of nationalism with internationalism. The Nichiren tradition is indigenous; Nichiren himself was the most nationally oriented of Japan's great religious leaders, and the Japanese are at all times a very nationally conscious people. The Society, in establishing universal goals, tends to project feelings of national superiority or altruism outward, thus accommodating in its ranks those who have transcended a national orientation as well as those with a parochial outlook. With this final appeal, and with the rest of its wide-ranging premises, the Sōkagakkai has infused the simple, historically rooted religious creed we have examined with a relevance to the contemporary world that many Japanese find superior to the offerings of any other new religion.

CHAPTER 3

Precipitation and Mobilization

WE SHALL now examine the process by which a society's conducive structures and strains become linked to a generalized belief system to produce a new social movement. The structures and strains considered are of course those of Japanese society, as examined in Chapter 1; the belief system is that of the Sōkagakkai, as examined in Chapter 2.

PRECIPITATION

For Norman Cohn the key precipitating factor in the production of a new movement is catastrophe:

> When the existing structure of a society is undermined or devalued, the members of that society become less able to face calamity. This process is a cumulative one; and if after it has gone at all far some major catastrophe strikes the lower and more exposed strata of the population, the way to revolutionary chiliasm may lie wide open.[1]

Catastrophes or catalytic events, e.g., a sudden collective deprivation (economic, social, or political), create or intensify structural conduciveness or strain.[2] (Another sort of catalyst is the appearance of a charismatic or otherwise extraordinarily able leader.) In the case of the medieval European millenarian movements investigated by Cohn, the catalytic factors tended to be plagues, protracted civil disorders, and natural disasters. In a context of disintegrating normative and value systems and decaying traditional organizations and institutions, the effects of these events were magnified until they set off "an outburst of paranoia, a sudden, collective and fanatical pursuit of the Millennium."[3] In more recent times, the rise of Nazism exhibited all the elements tending to precipitate social movements.[4] Economic deprivation, national shame and outrage, and a political system that had neither won popular acceptance nor responded effectively to certain crucial issues became fuel for the flames kindled by a charismatic leader.

In the rise of the new religions in postwar Japan, the key precipitating elements were the changes in the Japanese psychological climate and political structure occasioned by defeat and Occupation. The all-embracing official value system, in any case a source of disillusionment since the Allied victory, was formally abolished by the Occupation authorities. So were its restrictions on all unofficial forms of religion. Whereas the prewar constitution permitted religious freedom only insofar as it did not interfere with the subject's obligations to his emperor, the 1947 Constitution unconditionally guaranteed freedom of religion to all. The effect of this guarantee was to render almost impossible any control over the propagation of any ideology claiming religious status; and such status was very broadly defined.[5] Without these changes it is highly doubtful that, even with military defeat, many of the new sects (and especially the Gakkai) would ever have appeared.

But the Sōkagakkai itself provided a specific precipitating factor that led directly to the Society's emergence as the most prominent of the new sects. This was the Shakubuku Dai-Kōshin, or Great Propagation Drive, launched in July 1951. From a membership of about three thousand persons in April 1951, the Gakkai grew to 5,728 families* by the end of the year, 22,324 families by the end of 1952, and 70,000 families in late 1953.[6]

MOBILIZATION

Although the Sōkagakkai was established in 1930, it is inaccurate to speak of "mobilization" in any real sense until 1951, the year of the Great Propagation Drive. The prewar Gakkai, which never numbered more than a few thousand members, was concerned primarily with questions of education and with the creation of a pedagogical system based upon Makiguchi Tsunesaburō's Theory of Value. Makiguchi and his protégé Toda had joined Nichiren Shōshū in 1928; but during the prewar years the influence of religion upon the Sōka Kyōiku Gakkai (or Value-Creation Education Academic Society, as the organization was first named) was minor.[7] The religious element became more pronounced after the formal founding of the Society in 1937 with Makiguchi as first president and Toda as general director. In the

---

* The Gakkai estimates from two to three members to a family.

late 1930's and early 1940's, as the government became more restrictive toward religious behavior, exclusive groups such as Nichiren Shōshū came under pressure. Amalgamation and conformity were the order of the day, and the Gakkai's obstinacy brought on police surveillance and harassment. In 1943 the Gakkai refused to obey a governmental order that Shintō paper offerings (*kamifuda*) be received and worshipped by all members; in July the twenty-two top leaders of the Gakkai were imprisoned and the Society dissolved. In November 1944, Makiguchi died in prison; Toda was released shortly before surrender came.

The years 1945–50 were a rebuilding period.[8] Toda reassembled as many of the prewar members as he could, renamed the organization the Sōkagakkai (to signify a larger relevance), and began limited propagation. At the same time he started to build the infrastructure for later expansion—encouraging selected leaders, providing the membership with a strong ideological weaponry, developing a sturdy organizational structure, and systematizing the proselyting technique.

In May 1951, Toda was inaugurated as second president of the Gakkai; his Great Propagation Drive was launched in July and spearheaded by the Youth Division, a 1946 Toda creation. The success of this drive was largely due to the Gakkai's organization. Well-equipped with doctrinal arguments, members aggressively presented their teachings to those who were unsure of themselves, their beliefs, and their future, who were at least relatively aware of calamity or crisis and a sense of lacking reliable support, whether material or spiritual. The entire program—the proselyting style, the choice of target social strata, and the emphasis on appropriate doctrines—was conceived and managed by President Toda. With the help of both scripture and shrewd social observation he outlined what was needed and succeeded in creating a militant, vigorous, proselyting movement.[9] As a result, the years 1951–58 were a period of rapid growth as the shakubuku campaign proved a success; the religious coloring of the Gakkai intensified and the Theory of Value was reduced to secondary status. In 1955 the Society made its political debut: fifty-three members, running as independents, were elected to local assemblies throughout the nation. By the time of Toda's death, in April 1958, the Society had grown to almost nine hundred thousand families and held fifty-six legislative seats, including three in the 250-seat Upper House of the National Diet (see Appendix B, Table B.1; Appendix C, Fig. C.1).

With the death of Toda, the organizer and guiding spirit of the

Gakkai, many observers expected the Society to decline. But even during the 1958–60 interregnum the membership grew, and by May 1960, when Ikeda Daisaku took office as third president, the Gakkai claimed almost one and a half million member families and boasted 281 legislative assembly seats, nine in the Upper House.

Ikeda's tenure has been termed the "period of the religious political party."[10] Although the teachings of Nichiren have been accorded unquestioned predominance within the Gakkai's belief system, political activities have expanded many times over. The creation of a specialized and nominally autonomous political arm in 1961 was followed by the formation of a full-fledged political party, the Kōmeitō (Clean Government Party), in November 1964. Through the new party the Gakkai entered its first Lower House election; it emerged as the fourth largest force in that body. At present the Gakkai maintains its political and religious structural dualism, having become the third strongest political force in Japan (almost two thousand legislative assembly seats) and one of the largest postwar sects (claiming six and a half million families).

Thus it is the years after 1951 that are of interest to this study; only then did the Gakkai become a mass organization in any sense. These years may be periodized and analyzed in many ways; we shall examine the mobilization process through its five principal aspects:

(1) Leadership and its role in the mobilization process—notably charismatic leadership, a common element in movements oriented toward reconstitution or revitalization of entire societal value systems.

(2) Real goals of the movement (those originally perceived) and derived goals (those introduced by different social elements later attracted to the movement).

(3) Success or failure of specific tactics, and strategic or tactical change brought about by trial and error.

(4) The process of routinization or institutionalization.

(5) Problems and instability developing during the routinization process (appearance of new types of leaders, increasing social heterogeneity of the organization, strategic and tactical changes, and the problem of adaptation to the environment).[11]

LEADERSHIP

Strong leadership roles are a common feature of social movements in general and the Japanese new religions in particular. In mass movements "it is the leader who makes the crowd last over a longer period" and makes possible the organization of the masses.[12] Quite often such men are marginal intellectuals: frustrated aspirants to roles of prestige, achievement, and self-realization in education, the arts, or the professions, who do not possess sufficient talent or connections to enable them to succeed.

The role of a central leadership figure is traditionally important in Japanese Buddhism.

> It might not be going too far to say that it is generally true of Japanese Buddhism that the general conception of the tie uniting the members of a given sect is [not so much] that they share certain doctrinal views in common as that they share the characteristic of being all the followers of a certain sect founder.[13]

True to this tradition, the new religions almost without exception are built around an outstanding leader—often divine—who represents his religion's ideals in his own life.[14]

The Sōkagakkai is no exception to these predications. Makiguchi Tsunesaburō (1871–1944) was a frustrated academic who wrote one well-received book but, because of his novel pedagogical notions, could not penetrate the highly centralized and bureaucratized educational establishment of his day.[15] He moved through a succession of jobs in textbook publishing and elementary school administration, always deeply critical of prevalent educational approaches, convinced that education should be pragmatic and creative of value, not stiff, formal, and archaic. Makiguchi's academic nature strongly influenced the Sōka Kyōiku Gakkai. He was a scholar and pedagogue, not an organizer or orator—his protégé Toda Jōsei often handled the lecturing chores.[16] Makiguchi was largely unconcerned with organizational expansion; had he lived longer the Gakkai might well have remained a small discussion circle.

Toda Jōsei (1900–1958) was quite another type of man.[17] Like Makiguchi he came to Tokyo from Hokkaido. In Tokyo he began a teaching career during which he met Makiguchi and was so impressed by him that he virtually became his disciple. But he gave it up in 1923 to try his hand at, in turn, selling insurance, running a school, writing, printing, and publishing. Prosperity eluded him and in 1924 his child died, followed in 1926 by his wife. He tried Christianity without success, and in 1928 entered Nichiren Shōshū along with his mentor. In the Sōka Kyōiku Gakkai, Toda was concerned with organization and finance. He was little learned in the articles of faith until his imprisonment, when he pored over the scriptures, developed his sense of resolution and mission, and reportedly recited the daimoku two million times.[18] Upon his release from prison Toda set to work to resurrect the Gakkai, and as it developed he was an ideal man for the task.

In contrast to Makiguchi the scholar, methodical, steady, persuasive, austere in his personal habits, meditative and speculative, Toda was a hard-sell pitchman for his faith—frank, vigorous, often rude, talkative, fond of tobacco and alcohol in quantity, impulsive, and activist.[19] He much preferred speaking to writing. This was evident from his propagational style; he could beat down, win over, and inspire his adversaries much in the tradition of his predecessor Nichiren. He was also an organizational innovator; the interlocking horizontal and vertical dual structure to which the Society today owes much of its cohesion was established during his tenure.

The incumbent president of the Gakkai, Ikeda Daisaku (born 1928), was, like Toda, a fortuitous addition to the Gakkai at a turning point in its history. At the time he met Toda and was won over to the Gakkai, Ikeda was nineteen, a sickly youth whose family had suffered intensely from the war. His rise in the organization was swift.[20] He was a charter member of the executive staff of the Youth Division, established in 1951, and in 1954 became Chief of Staff of the Division, thus becoming in substance the operational head of the shakubuku program. This indication that he was being groomed for the succession was strengthened when he added to this role that of General Administrator in 1958, just after Toda's death. Upon his election to the presidency in 1960 Ikeda became sole head of the Society.

Although an extremely able manager, as was Toda, Ikeda is also an "organization man." Smooth and urbane, persuasive rather than vituperative, he has been described quite accurately by one Western journalist as "remarkably unassuming ... forceful ... calmly authoritative and ... extremely self-possessed," a man of "abiding patience and consideration."[21] More subtle and flexible, less open and ideological in style than Toda, he is very much the image of the leader of an organization that has arrived and feels secure and confident.

And the Sōkagakkai has arrived. Ikeda inherited an organization of almost one million families, a viable religious and political concern. His tasks have been to keep the Society intact (no small job, in faction-ridden Japan); to prevent lethargy and preserve proselyting vigor; to enable the Gakkai to expand further by making it more versatile in function and appeal; and to consolidate past and present gains by strengthening the internal agencies of indoctrination. Talents more administrative than evangelical are required, and

Ikeda has them in abundance, as the continued growth and stability of the Gakkai show. But at the same time he is definitely an activist; decisive, and intolerant of quibbling and hesitation, he is always impatient to translate thought into action. A man of strong habits, tastes, and preferences, he has impressed his own personality upon the Gakkai perhaps more than either of his predecessors had. With Ikeda, the element of charisma has appeared for the first time in the Gakkai's history.

Makiguchi was devoid of charisma. Toda may have possessed the quality to a degree, but it was not a major factor in his leadership. To the Youth Division in particular he was the great master, the transmitter of the teachings, the commander and guide; but he was not idolized.[22] Ikeda, on the contrary, is without doubt idolized and most probably deified by some of the Gakkai members. The awe and respect in the voices of believers when they speak of him is impressive; the rapture with which they listen to one describe a conversation with him is intimidating. The sight of him at large gatherings moves many to tears. His interpretations of scripture and his writings on guidance are considered equal to the works of Nichiren himself as repositories of truth.[23]

REAL AND DERIVED GOALS

The original ultimate goals of the postwar Sōkagakkai were jōbutsu and kōsen-rufu—personal enlightenment and world conversion. Jōbutsu is within the reach of all members; divine benefits, which both accompany and provide proof of jōbutsu, have always been one of the most important doctrinal points in mobilizing converts. Kōsen-rufu, on the contrary, has remained beyond reach; with time it has become a very vague goal, and partial, short-term, and intermediate goals have been devised to fill in the foreseeable future.[24] One additional concept derived from scripture to make kōsen-rufu a more plausible goal is that of *Shae no san'oku* ("the three hundred million people of Shae"). According to this idea (first publicized in the early 1960's), when one-third of the population of an area has accepted Buddhism, one-third is sympathetic but unconverted, and one-third is yet ignorant of the faith, kōsen-rufu of that area may be considered complete. On this principle the Gakkai has set up numerous partial kōsen-rufu goals: the Japanese student population, Tokyo, Japan. Other, more concrete, short-term goals have also been provided to keep spirits from lagging. In 1966 Ikeda set forth a series of seven seven-year periods, each period with its own set of goals.[25] At the beginning of each year a new set of annual goals is published;[26] and in addition, monthly propagation goals and hortative slogans are presented.

But the Gakkai action program's most important derivatives are its political goals. This political aspect of the Sōkagakkai also includes ultimate and short-range objectives: ōbutsu-myōgō (fusion of Buddhism with politics, itself a derived goal) is the final aim, but meanwhile the Kōmeitō restricts itself to such targets as seat increases in successive elections, vigorous campaigns, and the realization of its policies in legislation.

The concrete, immediate goals of divine reward and electoral success—the one real, the other derived—could well be the formal aspects of the Gakkai most responsible for the mobilization of several million believers to date. There is also an informal (and real, in that it dates from the Gakkai's earliest postwar beginnings) aspect that is probably of equal importance: the feeling of belonging. The quality of the Society as a psychological and interpersonal tako-tsubo that provides a system of values and norms for the socially distressed, and the simple fact of membership, are likely to be at least as important to mobilization as are any of the principles or objectives formally adopted by the organization.

SPECIFIC TACTICS AND STRATEGIES

Since the Society's inception, changes in presidential personality, organizational size, and social context have produced changes in Gakkai strategies and tactics. Many of the constant factors of Gakkai tactics, though, are shared with the other new religions.[27] One such factor is structure: the new sects tend to have simple and highly centralized organizations. The complexity of the Gakkai's structure is a difference of degree, not of kind; the Society has reached a more advanced stage of differentiation. Another shared factor is finance: the new faiths put little compulsory financial burden upon their members, but derive their revenues from other sources (see Chapter 6, section on Gakkai finance).

A third factor is activity and energy. As a rule the new sects are proselyting groups, eager to demonstrate their virtues to the world. Religious gatherings feature testimonial stories of blessings enjoyed; mass assemblies convey a strong impression of unity, enthusiasm, and power to believer and nonbeliever alike. This demonstrative proclivity is directed both outward and inward. Within the Gakkai, for example, vertical leader-follower instruction, guidance, and counseling and horizontal small-group interaction are highly developed. The believer's superiors are exemplars of faith with whom to identify; his cellular worship group is a reference group and *gemeinschaft* from within which he can cope with the outside world.

All the new sects also handle construction projects in much the same way. Many of the new religions have extensive real estate holdings and elaborate headquarters. The Sōkagakkai has contributed great sums to the Taisekiji, the Head Temple of Nichiren Shōshū at the foot of Mount Fuji, and now huge ferroconcrete edifices for worship and the accommodation of pilgrims tower over the original, centuries-old temples, archways, and pagoda. The Gakkai's administrative headquarters in Tokyo dominates the local skyline; new multistory buildings in ultramodern style house the Gakkai, the Seikyō Publishing Company, the Kōmeitō, and the Sōka Cultural Hall. The impression (doubtless intended) made by all this architecture is one of great affluence and financial power, of a very *au courant* philosophy with the solid and devoted backing of its adherents.

A final common factor is the approach to propagation. The new religions are extremely rational, tailoring their beliefs and approaches to the social structures and strains that are potentially fruitful, and aiming their efforts at the most deprived, yet expectant, social strata.* Nearly all of the new religions offer immediate concrete benefit along with group membership. The Gakkai, in addition, offers channels to the political system, where increasing numbers of Japanese see the possibility of benefit. Moreover, the Gakkai ties the new member into the Japanese religious tradition and the currents of national pride by means of its connection with Nichiren.

Unlike the other new sects, the Society makes explicit tactical appeal to the anomic elements in Japanese society.[28] The Gakkai accepts the notion of an atomized, alienated mass society and claims that its philosophy alone makes restoration of man to himself possible, through the organizing and coordinating agency of the Gakkai itself.

The changes the Sōkagakkai has made in its strategies and tactics, although not entirely due to leadership, can best be described in terms of the Society's three presidential regimes: Makiguchi's academic period, Toda's more religious, mobilizing era, and Ikeda's political phase. During the Makiguchi period the Gakkai's strategy—if there was one—was simply the dissemination of its pedagogical ideas;

---

* An example of such tailored appeals is the remark of one Gakkai leader to a deprived but hopeful young American scholar: "Going into teaching, are you? Join the Gakkai—you'll have tenure before you know it."

its tactics—if it had any—were those of a small study group interested in neither organizational growth nor efficiency. What proselyting was done was carried on largely through preaching, and the tactical style was relatively passive.[29]

Under Toda the Gakkai's strategy became the achievement of religious goals through social mobilization on a vast scale. Though tactical elements were the same as before, the tactical style became belligerent, activist, and ideological. In the years 1945–51 Toda armed the lukewarm followers from the Makiguchi period with his own brand of activist theory, replacing *Theory of Value* with a new *Propagation Handbook* (first edition November 1951) as the principal guide to action. He also organized a new shock troop of proselyters, the Youth Division; and he redefined the relationship between the Gakkai and Nichiren Shōshū, arrogating to the Society substantive operational supremacy.[30] Thus during Toda's presidency the religious nature of the Sōkagakkai grew stronger. Toda drew extensively on the writings of Nichiren to justify both general strategy and specific tactics, and relegated the teachings of Makiguchi to a tertiary role after his own instructions and interpretations. The latter were embodied in numerous speeches, in the *Shakubuku Handbook*, and in two hortatory works aimed at the Youth Division, *Injunctions to Youth* and *Injunctions to Patriots*. In the last of these works he urged youth to become "the pillar, the eyes, the great vessel of Japan," as Nichiren had claimed to be.[31]

Two examples of the activism typical of Toda's strategy are the Otaru Debate and the Tanrō Controversy. In March 1955 the Sōkagakkai challenged the original Nichiren Sect, Nichiren Shū, to a theological debate in the Hokkaido city of Otaru. The Nichiren Sect sent priests as its representatives, but at the hall they were met by a packed house (mainly Gakkai supporters) and a battery of skilled debaters brought from the Sōkagakkai Study Department in Tokyo. The priests resorted to involuted, philosophical arguments, the very language of which is difficult for the average Japanese to understand. The Gakkai forces accused Nichiren Shū of worshiping snakes and foxes and of pursuing contributions more fervently than converts. The hall was soon in an uproar; the Nichiren Shū priests, recognizing the futility of further talk, withdrew. The Gakkai deemed this a signal victory for the faith and has since enshrined the incident in its chronology of achievements.[32]

The Sōkagakkai came into conflict with Tanrō, the Japanese coal miners' union, in the mid-1950's.[33] In Yūbari, a Hokkaido coal city, local Gakkai membership climbed from 3,800 families to 15,000 in 1956 and to 25,000 families in 1957. By 1957 there were Gakkai groups in all seventy-five Tanrō locals and proselytism was proceeding apace. The Gakkai's approach was to stress the efficacy of faith over union membership in the achievement of higher wages and better working conditions; the Society also emphasized a cooperative, mutually beneficial relationship between labor and management that was anathema to the Marxist union leaders. At first nonplussed by the Gakkai offensive and sharply restricted in their reaction by the laws guaranteeing religious freedom, the union mounted a program of counter-education, which, along with informal, on-the-job pressure, eventually proved successful in halting the Gakkai drive. Nevertheless, today Hokkaido is one of the Gakkai's secondary power centers, and the Tanrō incident has become a widely cited precedent in the Gakkai's self-proclaimed record of resistance against religious repression.

Although a process of thaw began in the late 1950's, the moderate Sōkagakkai image is associated primarily with the tenure of President Ikeda. The aggressive shakubuku practices of the more zealous members of Toda's Youth Division sometimes constituted intimidation or invasion of privacy and occasionally led to violence. The belligerence with which priests of other faiths were set upon and badgered created an extremely negative impression in the public mind that still exists. Meanwhile, the Gakkai had begun to pursue political goals; to increase its electoral strength a broadening of appeal was necessary, and moderation thus became a more advisable tactic than continued militance and combativeness. And after all, the environment was changing. The tensions and widespread dislocations of the Occupation and early post-Occupation years were giving way to increasing social stability, economic affluence, and expanding popular perspectives.

In this new context the tactics and strategies of Ikeda Daisaku have proved admirably successful. In 1966 he wrote:

The Sōkagakkai was once able to rush forward at a speed of 100 miles per hour, on a wide-open field. However, almost everyone knows about the Sōkagakkai now. Thus, today conditions are changed, as if [we were] driving a car in the city of Tokyo.

To drive at 100 miles per hour in a place as crowded as Tokyo would cause terrible accidents. Therefore, I think a method of *shakubuku* based on a realization of the present environs, wherein everyone is coming to be quite conscious of Nichiren Shōshū and the Sōkagakkai, would be best for the attainment of [our] goals.[34]

A general abatement of the previous climate of permanent mobilization was part of Ikeda's moderation program. The adoption of the Shae no san'oku concept and an expanded program of nonreligious cultural activities characterized this strategy. The spirit of shakubuku has become more "Do your utmost!" than "Attack!"; and the goals of propagation drives have been revised downward since the early 1960's. In fact, the tactical atmosphere of the Gakkai is now one of "three steps forward, one step back."[35] One to three months of shakubuku activity are followed by a month of study, guidance, and counseling to consolidate the gains. Ikeda's speeches turn upon such themes as these, plus mention of short-term goals proposed and attained, and the necessity of long-term belief that is calm and rhythmic, rather than unstable and fiery, before any spectacular benefits can be expected.[36]

The outlook of the Japanese people changed during the late 1950's. With personal security achieved, people could afford to look beyond narrow individual interests; as Japan attained political and economic stability it began to move tentatively into a role in the international community. President Ikeda's doctrinal emphases have mirrored this trend and in some cases anticipated it. Where Toda stressed individual gain, national development, and racial salvation, Ikeda dwells upon altruistic self-exertion for society's benefit, a spirit of community with all the world, and the ultimate happiness of all mankind.[37] Ikeda's peripatetic habits—he has visited North America and Europe several times since his inauguration—reinforce the internationalist impression.

The internal workings of the Sōkagakkai are not sufficiently open to the nonmember observer to permit judgment of the relative degree to which the strategic and tactical consistencies and changes described above are the outcome of personality, organizational size, or environmental influences. The president, throughout Gakkai history, has appeared to be a nearly absolute ruler; certainly, the outward aspect of the Society has mirrored in turn the behavioral and stylistic traits of the three presidents. This constitutes, I feel, a prima facie case for the primacy of the presidential personality.

ROUTINIZATION

As one would expect, the Sōkagakkai has undergone routinization since it began to mobilize.[38] Functional specialization has been extensive. (See Appendix C, Fig. C.3, and Appendix D, Figs. D.1 and D.2.) Roles have been well developed; since most of the top leaders hold several positions at once, individual specialization is limited, but any impression of the Gakkai as an unstructured, fluid, social conglomerate would be totally inaccurate. An excellent example of the degree to which internal processes have stabilized is the succession of Ikeda Daisaku to the presidency of the Gakkai.

With Toda's death in 1958 the disintegration of the Gakkai was widely predicted.[39] However, the uninterrupted growth and expansion of political power during the 1958–60 interregnum indicate that the leadership gap was structural and not functional. This can be seen in the matter of the succession. According to one Gakkai leader, Akiya Einosuke, all of those at the top of the Society had known for some years that Toda favored young Ikeda. The matter had, Akiya says, already been settled by the time of Toda's death. As proof he offers the fact that Ikeda was appointed General Administrator only months after Toda's death.

The point remains that the interregnum did last two years; perhaps it took that long to "settle" everyone's thinking. Although the *Rules of the Sōkagakkai* stipulates procedures for selection of presidents, Akiya reminds us that these rules are codified in order to obtain permission from the public authorities to incorporate as a juridical person. Accordingly, they should not be regarded as an exact model of the Gakkai's internal workings.[40] Whatever the case, succession problems can be among the very knottiest for social movements. The fact that this particular one was solved without either significant discontinuity in organizational behavior or visible internal division is strong indication that the Sōkagakkai has established a stable modus operandi.

The behavioral routinization of the Gakkai is demonstrated by the relative relaxation of the Society under President Ikeda and the development of a stable pattern of activities. (The development of a patterned sequence of short-term goals also betokens routinization.) The easing of intensity was to some extent dictated by the Gakkai's changing environment; it is not, however, a wholly beneficial development in the eyes of the leadership. That many members are becoming slovenly in their faith is shown by repeated exhortations in the *Seikyō Shimbun* (*Holy Teaching News*) to "return to the spirit of the early days," and at all costs to avoid complacency and inertia in one's organizational role.

In direct contradiction to this overall process of routinization is a possible trend toward idolatry of the president. The "routinization of charisma" that Max Weber attributed to social movements appears to be working in reverse in the Gakkai. An idolizing tendency is found at the lowest level of the Society in the remarks of the faithful, and, although explicitly inveighed against by Ikeda, it is probably enhanced by the increasing prominence given to his teachings in the total Gakkai ideology. This reverse development of charisma is one of the elements of fluidity and flux that should prevent us calling the Gakkai a "church" or "denomination."[41] The Gakkai is no longer an amorphous mass nor an unstable group with intermittent structures; it has a highly developed organizational framework, very sophisticated operational strategies, and stabilized patterns of action. But it is still somewhere near the middle of any continuum leading from "sect" to "church."

CHANGE AND INSTABILITY

In a social context so given to factionalism and a religious context so characterized by division and fragmentation, the cohesion and apparent freedom from instabilities that have accompanied the growth of the Sōkagakkai are incredible. Leaders have changed, the membership has become increasingly heterogeneous, tactics and strategies have evolved, and a tentative process of harmonization with the environment has begun, all without significant disruptive influences on the organization. Therefore, problems of instability associated with the Gakkai's growth and routinization will come under discussion farther on, when possible future developments are considered. In this chapter I shall cite only a few past and present matters.

Two facts smoothed the way for the change in leadership from Makiguchi to Toda: Toda was Makiguchi's recognized protégé, and he was also one of only three prewar leaders who did not recant after the arrests and repression of 1943.* During the early postwar years Toda gathered together the old believers,[42] and at the same time created the Youth Division as a source of future leaders. It is also alleged that during this period Toda exerted pressure upon the Nichiren Shōshū hierarchy to accept the new role of the Sōkagakkai vis-à-vis the sect. Apparently this new, upstart organization was not accepted by all of the priesthood, and a number of priests were "purged" and driven from the Taisekiji by the Gakkai.[43]

By the late 1950's two groups were distinguishable in the elite of

---

* Nineteen leaders recanted and were released from prison, Makiguchi died, and Toda and Yajima Shūhei—the latter now a Shōshū priest—remained steadfast until their release in 1945.

the Gakkai: the older Makiguchi converts and the younger Toda followers. It would seem that a détente was reached in 1960, when Ikeda became president and Harashima Kōji, a "Makiguchi man," was named General Director immediately below him.[44] The appointment of Izumi Satoru, another prewar convert, to the post of General Director after the death of Harashima in 1964 supports this interpretation. One suspects, however, that these two supposed factions may be more analytical (or even fanciful) than actual. Every member of the Gakkai can be categorized according to the period of his conversion. But factions—in the sense of relatively stable intraorganizational groups espousing differing policies or serving different interests, even where such positions may be destructive of the common good—have never been apparent in any documentable form. This is so even now that a third group, the Ikeda followers, can be distinguished analytically.

According to Takase Hiroi,[45] an experienced observer of the Gakkai, while Ikeda was still Chief of Staff of the Youth Division he began to attract his own followers, whose first loyalties were with him rather than President Toda. Many of them are now reaching prominence in the Kōmeitō. But as in the case of the Makiguchi-Toda "division" a substantive split between Toda's and Ikeda's followers on any issue of religion or politics has yet to be shown.

The changes in strategy and tactics from which schism in the Society could most easily have resulted have been those connected, first, with supersession—of Makiguchi by Toda, of Toda by Ikeda, of Nichiren Shōshū by the Sōkagakkai—and second, with the Society's politicization. The eclipse of Makiguchi and his stress on the Theory of Value has been recounted in Chapter 2. Doctrinally, Toda never occupied as central a place in the Gakkai as Makiguchi had; it may be misleading, therefore, to speak of Toda's "eclipse." In any case, the stylistic characteristics of the Toda period, summed up in the bluntly intolerant *Shakubuku Handbook*, have been replaced by the easy, confident tone of Ikeda's *Guidance Memo*, which counsels rhythm, consistency and constancy, sociability, and moderation.[46]

The eclipse of Nichiren Shōshū by the Sōkagakkai is actually part of the politicization process of the Gakkai.[47] The intolerant spirit of Nichiren was also that of Toda; its categorical denial by Ikeda's Gakkai ("We're not anti-Christian, we're just un-Christian") runs counter to the spiritual core of Nichiren Shōshū. A recent article by Ikeda in the doctrinal journal *Dai Byaku Renge* (*Great White Lotus*) leaves little question that the Gakkai has assumed this central position itself. While mentioning the Shō Sect once (as part of the full name of the Society—Nichiren Shōshū-Sōkagakkai), Ikeda declared that "It is clear, in light of the Sacred Teachings [of Nichiren], that, apart from the Sōkagakkai, neither the true exaltation of Buddhism, nor the tranquillity of the nation, nor a peaceful world is possible."[48]

Such changes in emphasis as these could well have led to schism between leaders and followers, within the elite, or among the rank and file. There are today leaders definitely oriented more toward religion than toward politics, and vice versa. And there are members who can be identified temporally with each president and therefore possibly with his ideas. But, again, no division has been seen. Perhaps the sense of common purpose has been too strong, or the Gakkai ideology too pervasive. It may well have been the personalities of the last two presidents. In any case, the Gakkai have certainly been successful. This may have enabled them to survive post facto doctrinal changes. On the elites' level all of these factors are influential; among the members at large one suspects that presidential personality and success have been most crucial. In addition, a considerable number of believers find the primary gratifications obtained through membership in the Gakkai cellular group most important, and see ideology, organizational goals, and even charisma as minor factors.

Throughout its period of mobilization, the Sōkagakkai has exhibited a combination of growth and cohesion unparalleled in Japanese history. The leadership tandem of Toda the builder and Ikeda the maintainer, a pair of organizational and inspirational wizards, has put the Gakkai far ahead of the other new religions. And as I have noted, other facets of the Gakkai movement have also affected its growth significantly, especially the original doctrine of divine reward, the derived goal of electoral success, and the original though unstipulated ability to provide primary gratification in the small, face-to-face group. But both in the evolution of strategy and tactics and in the routinization process the presidents' crucial role is evident. It has been largely through the influence of strong and inspiring presidential personalities that factional activity in the Gakkai has been forestalled. Of course, as Weber points out, charisma depends on success. Although the Gakkai's presidents helped shape the doctrine and structure that have proved so appealing, the Society's evolution was, as with any other new sect, a complex process of interaction between Japanese social structures, prevailing social strains, the Gakkai's own belief system, certain precipitating factors, and, finally, actual mobilization. And at all stages of this process the presence or absence of social controls was critical.

Having looked at some length at the process by which the Sōkagakkai appeared on the Japanese scene and grew to its present size, we may address ourselves once again to the questions posed in Chapter 1: Why another new religion? And why this particular new religion? The social system within which the new sects arose exhibited four characteristics constituting fertile soil for such movements: first, a relatively low degree of cultural differentiation, i.e., religious orientations were still central to the culture; second, the absence of adequate alternative structures through which basic religious and social needs could be satisfied; third, the acute desire of Japanese for a psychic tako-tsubo, a framework of stable and intimate social relationships established within a small-group context; and fourth, the related need that such a framework also be an extremely effective communication structure. Two peculiarities of the social structure especially conducive to the Gakkai's growth were, first, the stage of secularization and differentiation that Japanese culture had reached, a stage where the populace had become politically conscious, thus creating a potential audience for the Gakkai's political appeals; and second, the corollary feeling on the part of a sizable element of society that open and responsive structures for political articulation were lacking.

The social strains that contributed to the "rush hour of the gods" after World War II stemmed from defeat and subsequent reconstruction/hyperdevelopment under Occupation and after. Of these strains, the most relevant to the new religions were normative chaos and absolute and relative deprivations, and the Gakkai battened on the many people suffering from such strains. The Society's expansion after the initial postwar crisis, however, indicates that the Gakkai responded more successfully than the other new sects to the relative (and psychological) deprivations that later appeared. The responses of Gakkai members to questions on the subject support this view; a further piece of evidence, in light of the Gakkai's present prosperity, is the fact that the salient form of deprivation in Japanese society today is a relative sense of want.

All of the new religions reacted to structural characteristics and strains with certain common doctrinal points, the most important being provision of normative and value systems purportedly valid in contemporary society and the promise of divine benefits as the immediate, tangible fruit of faith. The Gakkai's theories of happiness and divine reward (*kōfuku-ron* and *kudoku-ron*), and its rituals and (often tacit) behavioral guidance, are examples of this response in belief systems. In addition, the singularly national flavor of the Gakkai's doctrinal heritage, and the consummate skill with which it blends seemingly contradictory qualities, have helped elevate the Society among the new sects.

Earlier we traced the mass appearance of the new religions to specific precipitants—military defeat and occupation. The Sōkagakkai's exclusive rise to prominence, however, was a direct result of the Great Propagation Drive of 1951, masterminded by Toda Jōsei. Great leaders, especially charismatic ones, have been central figures in the upsurgence of most of the new sects in Japan; but in no case have they been as vital as in that of the Gakkai.

In its mobilizing efforts the Gakkai has marshaled its forces with many of the same tactics and strategies developed in other sects. Its focus upon lower socioeconomic strata and its patterns of internal and external communication are not unique. But whereas the problems of altering strategy and coping with routinization have brought schism and decline to many of the new religions, the Gakkai flourishes. Why? The Society owes its extraordinarily successful development to the quality of its leadership and to two products of that superior administration—politicization and success. And apparently nothing succeeds like success. This very situation has had a feedback effect upon both the Gakkai and its environment, which so far has proved singularly beneficial for its continued growth and stability.

CHAPTER 4

The Membership

WE HAVE looked briefly at the belief system of the Sōkagakkai and at its history of organization and growth. The efforts of the Society to attract adherents and to mold a stable, active membership should be considered more closely; but first the membership itself merits study. How large is the Gakkai? Who has swelled its ranks? And who, in light of the Society's present composition, will respond to the movement's message in the years to come?

NUMBERS

All observers of the Sōkagakkai agree that its growth has been breathtaking, but estimates of the actual number of Gakkai members vary considerably, and whether the membership's rate of change remains positive is also a matter for dispute. The Society itself tends to exaggerate its numbers. At the beginning of 1968 it claimed approximately 6.5 million member families; in computing total members it has variously doubled or tripled this figure, thus arriving at a range of anything from 13 million to 19 million members. Year-end statistics for 1964, furnished by the Head Temple for the *Religion Yearbook* of the Ministry of Education, gave Nichiren Shōshū about 15 million adherents, a figure that corroborated the Gakkai's generous self-estimates.[1]

Other indexes of Gakkai membership contradict these figures, however. Two nationwide surveys indicate the degree of discrepancy. In 1963 the Gakkai had, by its own declaration, just below 3.5 million families. At a charitable two believers per family, the Society should have comprised some 7 million members, or 7 per cent of the total population. But in a survey run that year, only 3.5 per cent of the respondents affirmed membership.[2] A more recent survey, conducted in late 1966, supported this smaller membership figure: though the Gakkai claimed 6 million families, or at least 12 million individuals— about 12 per cent of the population—only 4.1 per cent of the survey sample listed themselves as Gakkai members.[3] Furthermore, various surveys inferring Gakkai membership through questions about political party preference have also reflected discrepancies of this sort (see Appendix D, Figs. D.2, D.3).[4]

The Sōkagakkai-Kōmeitō vote offers another clue to the organization's size, as an index of members who are electorally mobilized (and of politically sympathetic members). The Diet Upper House elections from the national constituency afford the Gakkai its only opportunity to put up candidates in every electoral district; hence, voting figures from these elections constitute the most accurate base for calculating the Society's national electoral strength. Table D.3, in Appendix D, shows that the Gakkai vote from the national constituency in the last five Upper House elections has been consistently greater than membership figures deduced from the survey responses (by 3.5 per cent, 8.5 per cent, 11.5 per cent, 13.7 per cent, and 15.5 per cent). Until 1965 the vote was even greater than the number of member families claimed by the Gakkai. But in comparing claimed total membership at election times with the vote, one finds that the vote has been less than what even a generous estimate of voters per family would imply. The results of the 1956 election suggested a ratio of 2.5 votes per claimed family; in 1959 this ratio had decreased to 2.1, in 1962 to 1.5, and in 1965 to .96.[5] (The 1968 election showed a slight rise in the ratio to 1 vote per family.)

A final measurement of Gakkai membership used by some observers is the circulation of the *Seikyō Shimbun*, which at one subscription per family suggests that the organization contains 3 million families, perhaps as many as 6 million readers. Since many members do not subscribe to the paper and many others buy several copies for use in shakubuku,[6] these figures suffer from a liability similar to that of the voting statistics, whose usefulness is impaired by the existence of nonmember supporters.

We have, then, five more or less conflicting indexes of the size of the Sōkagakkai. First, there are the Gakkai's own figures: 6.5 million families, i.e. some 16 million persons, 15 per cent of the population. Second, there are the numbers committed to the Society in survey responses: approximately 1.6 million families by the usual Gakkai manner of calculating (2.5 members per family), i.e. 4 million persons,

4 per cent of the population. Third, there are those who are politically committed in their survey responses: very roughly, about 1.6 million families or 4 million persons, again something like 4 per cent of the population. Fourth, there is the voting record of the politically mobilized members: 6.6 million persons in the 1968 Upper House election from the national constituency, i.e., 15.5 per cent of the 43 million Japanese who voted. And fifth, there is the readership of the *Seikyō Shimbun*: 3 million families, possibly 6 million persons.

The official Gakkai reckoning is, at least, precise—it is simply the total number of gohonzon distributed, 6.5 million, at one per family.[7] (Changes, such as births and intrafamilial conversions on the one hand and deaths and defections on the other, are ignored.) Other available data indicate that this figure is considerably exaggerated. The second largest measure, the votes won in the Upper House national constituency elections, may be taken as the upper limit of a consciously committed membership. If one considers that the 6.6 million votes polled by the Kōmeitō in the 1965 Upper House election represented mobilized, politicized Gakkai members, one will conclude that the total membership, including less active adherents, is well above 6.6 million. But of course a certain number of persons outside the Gakkai also vote for Kōmeitō candidates.[8] Their exact number is impossible to calculate; the fact that they support the Kōmeitō without joining the Gakkai suggests reservations about the Society itself, and such uncommitted voters may be reticent about supporting the Kōmeitō. More important, since such voters are not likely to be habitual Kōmeitō supporters, the surveys, which nearly always phrase their questions in terms of customary party support, are not apt to indicate their numbers.

Surveys aimed at measuring either religious or political party affiliation suggest that the verbally committed membership is approximately 4 per cent of the population, or about 4 million persons. However, where both types of questions are included in one survey, professed Gakkai members outnumber Kōmeitō supporters.[9] This supports the assumption that many members are politically apathetic, an assumption that seems intuitively valid, since Kōmeitō members are—verbally, at least—the politically mobilized members of the Gakkai. The great majority of Gakkai members enter the Society primarily for nonpolitical reasons, and politicization seems to follow later.

In estimating the Gakkai's size one must rely heavily upon intuition, inference, and the estimates of those conversant with the movement. Opinion survey data seem to be the most accurate indicator, recording the response of those persons who have received the gohonzon in their families and still consider themselves believers. *Seikyō Shimbun* data, though of limited usefulness, serve to reinforce the impression that an interested membership is somewhere in the range of 3 to 5 million persons. This is the closest approximation I feel entitled to make.

As regards rate of change, according to the Gakkai's own published figures (see Appendix B, Table B.1) the Society has increased in size each year since 1951. But the rate of growth in 1966/67 and 1967/68— 13 per cent and 6 per cent—suggests that the organization may be approaching peak membership, although at its present size an increase of only a few per cent is, in absolute numbers, quite large. The slowdown in the growth rate after 1965 visible in Appendix B, Table B.1, reflects President Ikeda's announcement in early 1966 that, although total shakubuku figures accounted for almost 6 million families, an estimated half-million families had deserted the faith.[10] If one attempts to prorate the half-million decrease in members over the three preceding years, a drop in the 1965 rate of increase is still apparent. Even though we are relying on extremely generalized estimates of membership, it is apparent that the Gakkai, which should, by its own conversion figures, possess at least 13 million members, has effectively lost two-thirds of the number converted.

Thus reality seems not to bear out the Gakkai's claims; however, as a political movement and, particularly, as a possible mass movement, the reality of several million believers is more significant than the weakness underlying the organization's exaggerated claims. And even more significant is the proportion of Gakkai members that may be termed "active"—i.e., most likely to take part in the sort of direct political behavior that Kornhauser sees as typifying mass movements. Gakkai activism can be measured in two ways: by participation in organizational activities and by officeholding. Surveys indicate that approximately half of those who aver their membership can be considered active in terms of the frequency with which they perform the worship service, attend meetings, and practice shakubuku.[11] If the membership is somewhere between 3 and 5 million, this means 1.5 to 2.5 million activists. Statistics on officeholding strongly second this deduction.[12] Narrowing the focus a bit further, one can try to estimate the size of the hard core of Gakkai activists, i.e., members who hold high office or who participate in every phase of Gakkai activities; if the indications of several surveys are correct, 10 to 20 per cent of the self-declared members (i.e., 20 to 40 per cent of the activists) belong to this group.[13] On the basis of calculations for participatory and officeholding activists, one would posit a hard core of from 300,000 to 1 million members. In June 1967 President Ikeda stated in effect that there were 100,000 unspecified "top leaders" in the Gakkai; this suggests that the best estimate of the Society's activist nucleus is closer to the lower limit of what is possible. I find 500,000 persons an intuitively attractive figure, although it is an extremely rough estimate.[14]

COMPOSITION

Impressionistic descriptions of the social composition of the Gakkai's membership prompt one to draw parallels between this giant politico-religious movement and other historical movements. The Gakkai has been termed a "lower-class urban" phenomenon, its members uneducated, poor, and concentrated in low-status occupations.[15] They are the mobile, the deprived, the voiceless; the ones who suffered in defeat and struggled unsuccessfully during reconstruction, and who have failed to win a share of the new affluence.[16] Theirs are lives of frustration and irrelevancy, enlivened—or escaped from—only through pachinko and similar diversions.

The part such "little people" play in mass movements was touched on in the Introduction to this study. The only point to be made here is, again, that the lower-class and less-educated tend to constitute the bulk of mass movements. The characteristics of mass man—nonattachment and alienation—are likely to be more common among these sectors of society; this has been found in generalizing from historical examples of mass movements and from broad studies of unorganized population groups. No evidence exists to justify an assumption that simply because the members of the Gakkai are less affluent and less well-educated than the Japanese norm, they form, ipso facto, a mass movement. But sociological data do have heuristic value, and a glance toward the sociological bases of other social movements may strengthen the comparative framework within which one can analyze the Gakkai.

For each of the socioeconomic factors dealt with below from five to ten nationwide surveys were used, and in some cases local surveys were drawn upon. The sociological composition of the Gakkai is still an open question, however, and the data presented here would best be considered as indicating modal qualities of the membership, not as defining exact proportions.

Sex. The majority of Japanese who profess belief in a religion are women. They are the majority of the believers in both the traditional religions and the new sects, and the Sōkagakkai is no exception.[17] In nine nationwide surveys conducted between 1963 and 1967 the majority of professed Gakkai members or Kōmeitō supporters were women, and in all the surveys but one the proportion of men in the Gakkai sample was smaller than the proportion of men in the total sample.[18] The mean proportions for the Gakkai membership in the nine surveys were 42 per cent men, 58 per cent women; the mean proportions for the nine national samples as a whole were 49 per cent men, 51 per cent women.

There are more men among the Gakkai activists, however, than among the membership as a whole. (Since the national surveys used here take Kōmeitō supporters to represent Gakkai members, we are dealing with a relatively activist element, likely to include more men than the norm; thus the Gakkai membership as a whole may be even more heavily female than these data indicate.) In three surveys of activists (two local and one national) the numbers of men and women were approximately equal.[19] These findings reinforce the impression one gets from an examination of the upper ranks of the Gakkai; of the top hundred leaders, only one, General Administrator Kashiwabara Yasu, is a woman.

Age. The Gakkai commonly claims that it is an organization of the young. With respect to the total Japanese population and the urban sector, this is true; it also holds relative to the other Japanese religions, new and old.[20] The Kōmeitō, however, compared to the other political parties, attracts what tends to be the second oldest group of party supporters (after the followers of the conservative Liberal Democrats) in terms of its proportion of professed supporters in their twenties and thirties.[21]

A 1963 nationwide survey offers a picture of relative age distribution of the Gakkai and the general population that is paralleled by ten similar polls[22] covering the years 1963–67:

	Percentages of Sample, by Age Groups				
	20–29	30–39	40–49	50–59	Over 60
Sōkagakkai members	24%	24%	27%	13%	8%
National sample	26	26	19	15	14

On the basis of all eleven surveys, one can posit a relative concentration of Gakkai members in the 20–49 age group, greater representation in the 30–49 age group, and the heaviest concentration in the 40–49 age group. If we consider the term youth in a stricter sense, as those under 40 years of age, we find that the Gakkai is no younger than the general population and is certainly older than the urban population. However, the segment of the Gakkai's membership that is under fifty clearly exceeds the national proportion even in the cities where the population is younger than the national average.

But the age groups of greatest interest to this study are the thirties and forties. In each of the surveys mentioned the proportion of Gakkai members in their forties exceeds the proportion of 40-year-olds in the general population; the same is true of the combined thirties-forties age group in ten of the eleven surveys. These are the age groups that took the full psychic brunt of war and defeat. Old enough to have received their education in whole or in part under the prewar system but not old enough to have completed the most intense period of their socialization before defeat came, many of today's 30- and 40-year-olds are the survivors of the generation that provided the bulk of the Japanese military; late in the war many others became young labor conscripts, mobilized in an education-disrupting effort to boost production. The Japanese who were in their teens or early twenties during the war years 1937–45 underwent the most severe psychological deprivation and dislocation—so much so that the Japanese have come to describe this disoriented generation as the "wandering thirties." The fact that the Gakkai draws a disproportionately large following from this generation lends credence to the assertion that one of the Society's important functions is to provide psychological stabilization for its members.

Though the general age distribution of the Gakkai is not notably skewed toward youth, younger people are most evident in the active element of the Society. Two polls of Gakkai activists support this impression, the under-40 age group constituting 62 per cent of one sample and 75 per cent of the other.[23] Still, however, in the urban areas covered by the surveys the Gakkai does not exceed the general population in percentage of members under forty.

Education. In many societies, and at many points in time, the less educated social strata have provided fertile ground for the spread of extremist political and religious ideas. They have also most often predominated in the followings of mass movements and other types of undemocratic organizations.[24] Lipset considers that in modernized societies the extremist movements he describes as "fascist" have most often drawn their principal following from the less educated.[25] The case of Japan bears him out: the fascist trends of the 1930's drew their broadest backing from these sectors of society. In contrast, the Japanese extreme left has traditionally been stronger among the more educated strata.[26] (A study of ex-Communists in the United States, England, France, and Italy supports this tradition; a full 40 per cent of the subjects of the study had received some higher education.[27])

From extended contact with the Gakkai one gains the impression of a relatively little-educated membership. Members who have risen in the organization without benefit of much formal education seem proud of the fact. Gakkai publications are lavish in their use of *furigana,* a notational aid in pronouncing characters that is inserted between the lines of Japanese text; one might conclude that the Gakkai is conscious of the relatively low educational level of its followers.

TABLE 2

Education in the Nation, the Sōkagakkai, and Five Political Parties

	Extent of Education			
Sample[a]	Elementary School (6 years or less)	Junior High School (7–9 years)	High School (10–12 years)	College (13 years or more)
(First Survey)				
National Sample	21%	41%	29%	8%
Sōkagakkai Members	19	55	18	4
(Second Survey)	(9 years or less)			
National Sample	56.4	34.4	8.7	
Liberal Democratic Party	60.5	31.1	8.4	
Japan Socialist Party	47.1	41.3	11.6	
Democratic Socialist Party	53.3	36.0	10.7	
Japan Communist Party	55.6	25.9	18.5	
Kōmei Party	65.5	34.5	—	

SOURCES: Nihonjin no Kokuminsei data; data from *Yomiuri Shimbun,* January 1967 survey.
[a] Several samples total less than 100 per cent; "not applicable" and "don't know" responses make up the difference.

Survey data amply confirm this impression. In each of ten nationwide surveys conducted during the years 1963–67, the percentage of Gakkai members or Kōmeitō supporters with no more than nine years' education exceeded the national percentage, regardless of what demographic or socioeconomic controls one applies.[28] In addition, Kōmeitō supporters were found to be less educated than the followers of any of the four major parties. Two of these surveys, presented in Table 2, suffice to indicate the pattern. In the ten surveys taken as a whole, the proportion of Sōkagakkai-Kōmeitō affiliates who had received nine years of schooling or less averaged 70 per cent (over a range of 62 to 80 per cent); the proportion for the national samples was 59 per cent (over a range of 55 to 63 per cent). Five local surveys[29] reflect the same pattern.*

However few the well-educated may be in the Gakkai, they apparently have occupied a disproportionately large number of leadership roles. One critic estimates that 70 per cent of the younger leaders are college graduates. Fifteen members of the twenty-five-man Kōmeitō contingent in the Lower House in 1968 had completed thirteen years or more of schooling; so had eleven of the fourteen Kōmeitō candidates in the Upper House election of July 1968.[30] Two groups of activists in the Tokyo area illustrate a similar tendency: whereas the membership's overall average of persons with college educations is 1–3 per cent, members with thirteen years or more of schooling comprised 17 per cent and 19 per cent of the two activist samples.[31] Again, if one assumes that Kōmeitō supporters are more likely to be activists than those people who articulate Sōkagakkai membership alone, then the inclusion of Kōmeitō supporters as typical Gakkai members in the general educational picture of the Gakkai may exaggerate the educational level of the membership as a whole.

Geographic distribution. The Gakkai is a predominantly urban phenomenon. A gross examination of survey data shows that Gakkai-member respondents are relatively concentrated in the Kantō, the region containing the cities of Tokyo and Yokohama.[32] Areas of secondary concentration are the Kinki, where Kyoto, Osaka, and Kōbe are located, and the Chūbu, where Nagoya is the chief city.

Gakkai members are most numerous in large cities in these and other areas. In six nationwide surveys run during the years 1963–67, an average of 77 per cent of the Gakkai-Kōmeitō respondents (with a range of 73 to 82 per cent) were in urban areas (*shibu*).[33] The average for the national samples in these surveys was 68 per cent, with a range of ±2 per cent. An average of 27 per cent of the Gakkai members lived in the seven largest cities alone; an average of only 19 per cent of the national samples lived in these cities. Among the political parties surveyed the Kōmeitō was usually the second most urbanized,

---

* The constant asseveration of the Society that university students are flocking to join it seems to conflict with these findings. According to the *Seikyō Shimbun* of August 7 and 25, 1967, the Sōkagakkai [university] Student Division had acquired two hundred thousand members out of the slightly more than one million college students in the nation—roughly 18 per cent. But a 1966 survey of six thousand university students in the Tokyo area turned up only fifty-two professed Gakkai members, less than 1 per cent of the respondents. See Basabe, pp. 53, 125 *et seq.*

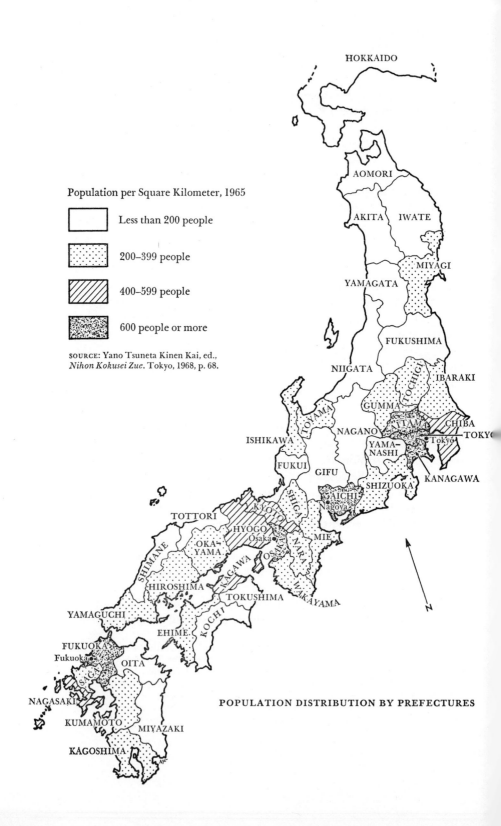

Population per Square Kilometer, 1965

Less than 200 people

200–399 people

400–599 people

600 people or more

SOURCE: Yano Tsuneta Kinen Kai, ed.,
Nihon Kokusei Zue. Tokyo, 1968, p. 68.

HOKKAIDO

AOMORI

AKITA   IWATE

MIYAGI

YAMAGATA

FUKUSHIMA

NIIGATA

IBARAKI

TOCHIGI

GUMMA

TOYAMA

NAGANO

SAITAMA

CHIBA

ISHIKAWA

YAMA-
NASHI

TOKYO

Tokyo

FUKUI

GIFU

SHIZUOKA

KANAGAWA

AICHI

Nagoya

TOTTORI

KYOTO

SHIGA

SHIMANE

HYOGO

Osaka

NARA

MIE

OKA-
YAMA

OSAKA

KAGAWA

WAKAYAMA

HIROSHIMA

TOKUSHIMA

YAMAGUCHI

KOCHI

EHIME

FUKUOKA

Fukuoka

OITA

SAGA

NAGASAKI

KUMAMOTO

MIYAZAKI

KAGOSHIMA

N

POPULATION DISTRIBUTION BY PREFECTURES

TABLE 3

Geographic Distribution of Supporters of the Major
Japanese Political Parties

Place of Residence	Party					National Sample
	Liberal Democratic	Socialist	Democratic Socialist	Communist	Kōmei	
Seven large cities	14%	22%	22%	35%	30%	19%
Other cities	49	49	48	41	43	49
Rural areas (*gunbu*)	37	29	30	24	27	32

following only the Japan Communist Party. The data in Table 3, from a survey by the *Mainichi Shimbun* in May 1966, are typical.

Statistics from the national constituency elections for the House of Councillors (the Upper House of the Diet) agree with these data on urbanity: the absolute vote polled by the Gakkai is greatest in the urban Pacific coast prefectures, and absolute growth in Gakkai electoral strength since 1956 has been greatest there (see Appendix D, Table D.1). True, among the ten prefectures that led the nation in percentage growth of absolute Gakkai vote between the 1962 and 1965 elections, seven were rural ones;* but in many cases such high percentages are of such small absolute voting totals that the increase is of little importance nationally or locally. Thus, among these ten prefectures Ishikawa, Shiga, Shimane, and Tottori were also among the ten prefectures having the lowest absolute Kōmeitō vote in 1965; and furthermore, Ishikawa, Shiga, and Shimane were among the ten prefectures lowest in the Kōmeitō's percentage of the total vote.

Outside the Pacific belt a number of local power centers have appeared (centers where the Kōmeitō draws over 15 per cent of the local vote; see Appendix D, Table D.3). The Kōmeitō's current strength (relative to other parties) in such urban prefectures as Tokyo, Osaka, Okayama, Kanagawa, Chiba, and Saitama is matched in Kōchi, Kagawa, Wakayama, Ibaraki, Ehime, Mie, and Tokushima; moreover, since 1959 these relatively nonurban prefectures, along with Gifu, Tottori, and Yamaguchi, have enjoyed the greatest absolute increases in the Gakkai's share of the total vote.

Appendix D, Table D.2, shows the Gakkai becoming more reliant over time upon the urban Pacific belt prefectures, a trend seen in the distribution of the Kōmeitō vote among the various prefectures (1968 may have marked a reversal of this trend). The greatest intra-Gakkai

* Ishikawa, Shiga, Shimane, Mie, Ehime, Tokushima, and Tottori.

power centers (in 1968, Tokyo, Osaka, Kanagawa, Hyōgo, Hokkaido, Aichi, Fukuoka, Saitama, Shizuoka, and Chiba in that order) have increasingly become the urban power centers (Hokkaido is the lone exception), and since 1959 the Gakkai has come more and more to rely on them. (These prefectures produced 49.8 per cent of the Kōmeitō vote in 1959, 50.7 per cent in 1962, and 52.6 per cent in 1965, but 52.2 per cent in 1968.) Nevertheless, if one measures by change in each prefecture's share of the total Kōmeitō vote, a few rural prefectures are among the fastest-growing areas of intra-Gakkai power. Between 1965 and 1968 the Gakkai's fastest growing power centers included such relatively nonurban prefectures as Ishikawa, Niigata, Miyagi, Saga, Toyama, Fukui, Yamanashi, Nagano, Tokushima, Kagawa, Ehime, Kōchi, and Oita. But, again, these were often cases of the high relative growth of a small absolute figure; the weakest areas in absolute share of total Kōmeitō vote in 1968 still included Toyama, Fukui, Ishikawa, Saga, and Yamanashi.

The trends visible in these voting statistics indicate that the Gakkai is strongest in urban areas and that it has become increasingly concentrated in the cities. Relative to overall population shifts, however, the Gakkai may be—and the Kōmeitō's electoral support certainly is—becoming less urban. Appendix D, Table D.4, shows that from 1956 to 1968 the proportion of the general electorate concentrated in twelve prefectures of the Pacific belt area increased 16.6 per cent (from 45.2 per cent of the total electorate to about 52.7 per cent); the proportion of the total vote coming from these prefectures increased 23.6 per cent (from 40.7 per cent of the total vote to 50.3 per cent) during the same period. The proportion of the Gakkai vote coming from these prefectures decreased 6.6 per cent (from 59.3 per cent of the Gakkai total to 55.4 per cent) at first. From 1959 to 1968 the proportion of the Gakkai vote from this area increased 4.1 per cent (from 53.2 to 55.4 per cent); but the proportion of the electorate in the area also increased—by 13.6 per cent—during this nine-year period. Whether this relative expansion into the countryside represents rural religious acceptance of the Gakkai or political acceptance of the Kōmeitō is unclear; in either case it implies the Gakkai's ability to broaden its appeal beyond the cities, an ability whose implications for the future are dealt with in a later chapter.

The distribution of Gakkai members within cities reflects the national distribution pattern. In Tokyo, for example, both survey and electoral data show that the Gakkai is strongest in the downtown inner-core wards of Adachi, Katsushika, Edogawa, Kita, Itabashi,

Kōtō, Arakawa, and Sumida, with a secondary concentration in the southern industrial wards of Shinagawa and Ōta.[34] These inner and industrial areas are characterized by industry—much of it nonunionized and very small-scale—and by great congestion and relatively low living standards. But recently a trend toward other sections of Tokyo has begun to appear. The vote won by the Kōmeitō in the Tokyo second election district (Shinagawa and Ōta wards) in the January 1967 general election was slightly less than the vote won there in the 1965 Upper House election.[35] In the sixth district (Sumida, Kōtō, and Arakawa wards) there was a slight increase; while in the uptown fifth district (Toshima and Nerima wards) and the more suburban seventh district (Santama), both residential areas, the Kōmeitō enjoyed a great increase in vote. Two recent surveys show an increase in Sōkagakkai-Kōmeitō strength in the seventh electoral district and in an area that includes the uptown wards of Nakano, Suginami, Toshima, and Nerima, as well as the more downtown Itabashi and Kita wards.[36]

Living standards are relatively higher in the uptown and Santama areas, which suggests that the Gakkai is diversifying its appeal. The latter area is particularly worth noting; the seventeen cities and three counties of the Santama district are the focal points of the present trend toward giant impersonal apartment complexes (*danchi*), where thousands of persons (primarily white-collar families) are housed in buildings that suggest concrete ant farms. The ties of kin, locality, and voluntary association are relatively weak in the danchi; the atomized life style is a new phenomenon in Japanese society and often gives rise to acute loneliness, especially in wives whose husbands commute to central Tokyo.[37] Spatially proximate tako-tsubo for the residents of the danchi are relatively rare; the Gakkai is in a position to remedy this lack, and polls and voting statistics suggest that it does.

Occupational distribution. The Gakkai claims to be a microcosm of Japanese society, and many Gakkai gatherings seem to substantiate this assertion. Bar girls and bank clerks, students and teachers, shop owners and day laborers, factory workers and housewives are all in evidence. However, a closer inspection reveals that some occupational groups are heavily overrepresented in the Society.

Nine national surveys indicate that housewives and laborers of all types are extraordinarily numerous in the Gakkai, while official, managerial, professional, and technical personnel, white-collar workers, students, and persons engaged in agriculture, forestry, and fishing

TABLE 4

Occupational Distribution in the Sōkagakkai and in Japan

Mode of Employment	Occupation	Gakkai Members	National Sample
Self-employed at home	Agriculture/forestry/fishing	4.9%	9.5%
	Trade/manufacturing/ service/professional	2.9	3.5
Self-employed elsewhere	Agriculture/forestry/fishing	5.4	11.9
	Trade/manufacturing/service	13.2	9.0
	Professional	.6	1.3
Employed by other	Managerial	—	1.7
	Technical	1.1	3.2
	White collar	6.3	10.0
	Labor	22.4	14.8
Unemployed	Student	—[a]	1.1
	Housewife and other	43.2[b]	34.1
Total		100.0%	100.0%

[a] No members of the Student Division appeared in this sample, which corroborates other indications that Gakkai estimates of their numbers are inflated.

[b] Housewives 33.8%
Others 9.4

are by contrast rare.[38] The data in Table 4, taken from a 1965 survey, are representative (aside from the high incidence of persons engaged in trade and services, which is not reflected in most of the other nationwide data compiled).[39]

Survey data on the occupational distribution of Gakkai members in particular urban localities generally pattern the national distribution of the membership. Again, housewives and laborers are overrepresented. So are those who engage in medium- to small-scale and self-owned commercial and industrial enterprises, especially shops, and in sales and services of all kinds (such members may be recent migrants from the country, unskilled and unfamiliar with the requirements of the modern, urban economic sector).[40] At the national level the frequency of shopkeepers, shop workers, and personnel from smaller businesses among the Gakkai membership parallels the general distribution of the population, but in the local surveys — in Tokyo, Fukuoka, and the Kansai (the Kyoto-Osaka-Kōbe region) — these workers on the periphery of the modern economy were overrepresented. The local data, as well, find the professions, technology, managment, and white-collar sectors underrepresented.

The geographical distribution of the Gakkai membership within

Tokyo corroborates these surveys. Statistics for 1959 indicate that in the downtown areas, where the Gakkai is strongest, there is a relatively high incidence of workers in transport, labor, and crafts; in contrast, the uptown district shows a much higher frequency of persons employed in the professions, management, and white-collar occupations.[41]

Since the Gakkai is increasing its numbers in the suburban areas one may surmise that, although isolated danchi housewives may be the most receptive audience, the Society is also succeeding in attracting more and more white-collar workers, who, though having gained entry into the economically favored sector of society, are nonetheless dissatisfied with life.[42]

Two additional characteristics of the occupational makeup of the Gakkai's general membership should be noted. First, Gakkai members, though largely laborers, tend to be nonunion laborers. This suggests that the unions, were they to make the effort, could provide a satisfying social nexus for the worker; the Gakkai, which does, is capturing workers' loyalties by default. According to a national survey by the Prime Minister's Office, supporters of the Kōmeitō were 50 per cent more likely to be employed in nonunion enterprises than other employed respondents.[43]

Second, Gakkai members are relatively mobile occupationally. The degree of the Gakkai membership's occupational and physical mobility is still an open question if one takes a methodologically rigorous approach. But two small local studies do indicate mobility and lend credence to the argument that mobility fosters anxiety, normative disorder, and receptivity to the teachings of organizations like the Gakkai. Table 5, taken from a study of Gakkai members in Fukuoka City by Suzuki Hiroshi,* shows considerable mobility among members, both occupational and physical.[44] One should note that the agrarian origins reported by 40.67 per cent of the sample suggest migration from the country to the city of Fukuoka. Suzuki shows that in fact 34.7 per cent of his sample were countryborn, 81 per cent were born outside of Fukuoka, and at the time of the study almost none were living in the neighborhood of their birth.[45] A Tokyo study shows a similar pattern: a sample of thirty-five Gakkai members consisted of twenty migrants from outside Tokyo and fourteen natives, only eight of whom were living in the wards where they were born.[46]

---

* One shortcoming of the Suzuki data is that no non-Gakkai control sample was included in the study; therefore these data are relevant only for an analysis of internal characteristics of the Gakkai and not for comparison of Gakkai members with nonmembers.

TABLE 5

1963 Occupational Distribution of Sōkagakkai Members in Fukuoka City as a Function of Occupations in Family Background

Occupation of Respondent's Natural Family	Respondent's Occupational Position								
	Salaried or Managerial	Owner of Enterprise, Employer	Owner, No Employees	Work in Own Home	Public Employee	Employee in Private Enterprise	Part-time or Temporary Employee	Other	Total
Agriculture, forestry, fishing	.75%	3.73%	8.21%	2.61%	1.49%	15.30%	5.97%	2.61%	40.67%
Self-employed in trade or industry	1.49	3.36	5.60	.37	1.87	11.19	2.24	1.12	27.24
Employee in trade or industry	—	1.12	1.12	.37	.37	4.10	.75	.37	8.21
Employee in transportation	.37	—	1.87	.37	.75	2.61	.37	.75	6.72
Professional	.37	1.12	.75	.37	.75	1.12	—	.37	4.48
Clerical	.37	1.12	1.49	.37	.37	1.87	—	.75	5.60
Managerial or executive	—	.37	—	—	—	—	—	—	.37
Temporary, day, or unskilled labor	—	—	.37	—	—	.75	.75	—	1.87
Other	—	.37	1.49	.37	—	1.49	—	.37	4.48
Indeterminate	—	—	—	—	.37	—	—	.37	.37
Total	3.36%	10.07%	20.89%	5.22%	5.22%	38.43%	10.07%	6.72%	100.00%

NOTE: Owing to typographical errors in the survey from which this table is drawn, several totals do not add up correctly; however, none of the errors exceeds 1 per cent.

A final specific note on the occupational patterns of Gakkai activists: according to a single small survey in the Tokyo area, Gakkai activists, despite their relatively high educational level, were with inordinate frequency self-employed and engaged in small enterprises.[47] This discrepancy between background and current situation might easily produce frustration and a sense of relative—and unjust—deprivation.

Income. The data on occupations suggest, at least relatively, that the Gakkai membership draws on the lower-income sectors of Japanese society. Voting statistics also lead to this inference: in the Tokyo local constituency for the 1962 Upper House election, the Kōmeitō returns were proportionately larger in wards where a sizable segment of the population was on welfare.[48] Survey data provide more explicit information. Gakkai members are indeed relatively low on the income scale, though not overwhelmingly so; and although the absolute economic position of the membership is improving, there is no real sign that the Society is becoming more like a microcosm of Japanese society.

In a representative national survey in 1960 the average income per family among Gakkai members was very roughly 30,000 yen, about $80, per month; the average income of a laborer's family at the time was 30 per cent higher (38,900 yen, or about $108 per month).[49] By 1965 the average income of Gakkai families, as indicated in a nationwide survey, had climbed to 39,000 yen, about $108, per month; in 1966, however, the income of the average urban laborer's family was almost 40 per cent higher (56,515 yen or about $157).[50] Even if one assumes that this average was somewhat lower in 1965, it seems likely that the increase in the average Gakkai family's income over five years (about 30 per cent) was matched by the increase in the national average. And local surveys have produced similar data.[51]

The argument has been advanced that Gakkai members tend to be younger than the overall population of a society where seniority, and therefore age, is the major determinant of income; if this is so, a collectivity of the young in these circumstances will inevitably appear as an economically depressed group.[52] The point is doubtless valid; but the concentration of Gakkai members in lower-class neighborhoods and lower-class occupations, and their rather lower-class appearance, indicate that age alone is not the explanation of discrepancy in incomes.

The more activist Gakkai members may have generally higher incomes than the membership as a whole. In one survey, conducted in

July 1965, a full 67.4 per cent of a sample of Tokyo activists reported incomes of over 50,000 yen, about $140, per month; 20.2 per cent reported making between 70,000 and 100,000 yen (between $195 and $280) per month, and 20.2 per cent claimed incomes of over 100,000 yen per month.[53] This apparent relative affluence can be interpreted variously. One's faith is undoubtedly reinforced to some degree by increased income, i.e. by divine benefit. Another study, however, found a positive correlation between activism and age; and if activists are the older members one would expect them, in a seniority-oriented society, to have higher incomes for that reason.[54] In any case, one could surmise that since activists are relatively affluent, they might be less prone to frustration and anxiety than the discrepancy between their educational and occupational levels noted above suggests. But we shall see in Part II that this is not so; for several reasons activists are, if anything, more alienated and frustrated than the membership as a whole.

Turning to class mobility, another aspect of income, we find that the data for Gakkai members are inconclusive, as Table 5 above illustrates. A large proportion of the families in agriculture/forestry/fishing and self-employed in commerce and manufacturing—a full 68 per cent of all the families represented in the sample—were certainly self-employed. In contrast, 57 per cent of the sample reported that they themselves were employees in either public or private enterprises. Thus perhaps 40 per cent of this sample had undergone the transition from a self-employed to an employed condition. On the other hand, of the 31 per cent of the respondents who classified themselves as self-employed about one-third came from employed families and thus had managed to establish an enterprise of their own. No generalizations are possible about the subjective status consequences of either transition, but we may assume that psychological strain accompanies both, especially where migration to the city is a concomitant factor. One could guess that exchanging independence for employment is more often negative social mobility than is the reverse, but nothing is known about the feelings within the classes from which Gakkai members come; those members moving to the city, even into employee status, may have found a welcome escape from rural poverty. And the possibility of their experiencing upward mobility through urban occupations cannot be entirely dismissed.

Political background. Available data do not enable us to determine just what the voting behavior of Gakkai members may have been prior to their conversion. The Gakkai could be attracting people who had previously been politically inactive. Koya Azumi's study of activists (made in July 1966), based on a small sample of Gakkai members in the Tokyo area, points to politicization's taking place in the Society: 35 per cent of Azumi's sample reported that until joining the Gakkai they had voted occasionally or not at all, whereas 98 per cent reported voting in the 1965 House of Councillors election.[55] Of course, since the study was made at Gakkai meetings the subjects may well have felt constrained to present themselves in the most orthodox (in this case active) light possible.

However, if rather than drawing on political inactives the Gakkai is attracting voters away from the other political parties, from which one does it draw its strength? Certain data suggest a consonance with the views of the right: in a nationwide survey of 1963, of the Gakkai members who did not support the Kōseiren (the predecessor of the Kōmeitō), 22 per cent supported the conservative Liberal Democrats and 10 per cent supported the parties of the left.[56] A local poll in Tokyo's Itabashi ward shows a similar pattern: about 60 per cent of the Gakkai members reported having conservative leanings prior to their entry, and the rest had been supporters of the socialist parties.[57] In the Azumi survey of activists, out of those who had not voted for Kōmeitō candidates before conversion 57 per cent had voted for parties of the right and 37 per cent for parties of the left.[58] In addition, when respondents were asked toward which parties, if any, they felt a particular aversion, 66 per cent of the sample named leftist parties, whereas only 3 per cent specified parties of the right.*

There are conflicting data. A survey of Kōmeitō supporters' voting behavior in Lower House elections in the years before that party began to put up candidates for the Lower House showed roughly equal numbers of respondents voting for parties of the left and of the right. And a local poll in Fukuoka City indicated that 60 per cent of the Kōmeitō's backers there were former leftists, whereas only 40 per cent had come from the right.[59]

The samples in all of these surveys were in any case too small to warrant our reaching useful conclusions about the former political

* This anti-leftism varies with commitment and politicization, according to data collected by Sidney Verba and his associates in 1966. Gakkai members who supported the Kōmeitō strongly were more anti-left than those who simply supported the party, who were in turn more anti-left than Gakkai members who considered their faith "important," who were in turn more anti-leftist than the average Gakkai member.

coloration of Gakkai members. But the evidence suggesting rightist roots is more persuasive, especially in light of the demographic and socioeconomic parallels between the members of the Gakkai and the supporters of social movements on the political right.[60]

The modal member of the Sōkagakkai is (1) a woman who (2) is in her thirties or forties, (3) has less than a high school education, (4) lives in a city, (5) is a housewife (if a man, he is a laborer or is engaged in some commercial or service enterprise and is not a member of any labor union), (6) receives a family income of 40,000 yen (about $111) per month or less, (7) was brought into the Gakkai by a relative or neighbor (or, if a man, possibly by a friend or co-worker), (8) was motivated to join primarily by problems of mental or social conflict and secondarily by problems of economics and health, and (9) was to a certain degree unconcerned with any specific Gakkai doctrines.

The activist element in the Society differs from the general membership in several respects.* The typical activist is (1) a man who (2) is in his twenties or thirties, (3) is much more likely to have a high school or college education—though nine years or less is still modal, (4) also lives in a city, (5) is a laborer or is engaged in some commercial or service enterprise and is not a member of any labor union, and (6) earns between 50,000 and 70,000 yen (about $140–195) per month.

For the years surveyed a few changes in the composition of the Gakkai can be tentatively inferred. The proportion of women in the Society may be increasing; and so may the proportion of members who are in their twenties.[61] As we have seen, the Society is increasing and concentrating its absolute power in the cities. But at the same time it is perhaps coming to rely upon urban centers relatively less for electoral strength; a number of rural power centers have appeared that the Gakkai may be able to parlay into seats in the Lower House of the Diet. Relative to the general populace the Society is becoming less urban;[62] even within the cities a shift toward the suburbs seems to be taking place that is reflected in the increased frequency of white-collar members, who enjoy higher status than does the membership as a whole.[63]

The urban concentration of the Gakkai membership nonetheless throws the Society into sharp contrast with several other social movements to which it otherwise bears thought-provoking likenesses. Several studies have concluded that Nazism, for example, drew its greatest strength from small cities and rural areas;[64] the French Poujadist

---

* Owing to the sparseness of aggregate demographic data available, only the two types of member can be described with any accuracy.

movement, too, was strongest in the provincial cities and the country-side.[65] This contrast extends to religious movements as well. Charles Braden has shown, for example, that American splinter sects have gained their greatest following in the less urban areas of this country.[66] One might assume—and many have—that most urban Gakkai members are recently arrived from the country and thus qualitatively similar to adherents of all these movements. Data on migration are sketchy; but the social movement to which the Gakkai shows the greatest geographical resemblance is Communism. (In other, equally significant ways, however, the two movements differ—a subject I shall return to shortly.)

At many points the occupational, educational, and income/class distributions of the Gakkai membership fit the pattern of late-nine-teenth-century and twentieth-century social movements on the European right. One such movement comprised the anti-Semitic groups of late-nineteenth-century Germany and Austria.[67] The lower middle classes—tradespeople, artisans, low-ranking officials, medium- and small-scale entrepreneurs and their employees—were heavily repre-sented in this movement, which, like the Gakkai, had both political and religious aspects. (Its specific political content, where there was any, was often a variant of the Christian democracy that had devel-oped from the encyclicals of Pope Leo XIII.) The National Socialist German Workers' Party (Nationalsozialistische Deutsche Arbeiter-partei, or NSDAP), the culmination of the European anti-Semitic tradition, drew on two occupational groups that are mainstays of the Gakkai—workers and housewives.[68] Also bringing to mind the Gak-kai is the fact that the NSDAP apparently possessed an especial attrac-tion for secondary school teachers; they became the "best represented of all professional groups composing the Nazi party." By 1940, 97 per cent of the teachers in Germany were members of the Party or one of its affiliated groups.[69] One wonders if their careers correspond to the abortive pedagogical undertakings of Gakkai presidents Makiguchi and Toda.

The prewar extreme right in Japan also relied heavily upon some of the social elements that now support the Gakkai. Maruyama Masao has characterized the major social backing of Japanese "fascism" as "pseudo-intellectuals": teachers, low-level official functionaries, inde-pendent farmers and small landlords, artisans, and owners of small factories and shops, who, with no great education, knowledge, or in-sight were nevertheless self-styled interpreters and expositors of ideol-ogy.[70] Barrington Moore describes fascism, in both its Japanese and

German variations, as right-wing radicalism buttressed by the peasantry and petty bourgeoisie who were suffering from the dislocations and strains brought on by the advance of capitalism.[71] In contemporary Japan the peasantry, though not completely happy with its lot, is kept in an artifically prosperous state by a program of governmental price supports; and owing to the Occupation's land reform it is relatively free of landlordism or tenantry, sources of considerable agrarian unrest in other societies. But the petty bourgeoisie does constitute the primary support of the Gakkai. The middle class does not at present flock to the Society's banner; nor did it turn to the NSDAP until German society was faced with economic disaster. "Only when the storm engulfed them did any port seem good"; until that time the lower middle class was the Nazis' principal socioeconomic pillar.[72]

The Poujadist movement, too, as its title—the Union for the Defense of Merchants and Artisans—indicates, was consciously and formally founded in just those social strata in which the Gakkai finds its greatest support.[73] Stanley Hoffmann, in his study of the Poujadists, describes the membership as being of the *classes moyennes*; but his middle classes are roughly equivalent to the lower middle classes from which the Gakkai takes its strength. Stemming from the provincial lower middle class and the peasantry, the movement was, in fact, strongest in those *départements* where per capita production and revenue are lowest.[74] Thus the socioeconomic similarity of the Poujadists and Nazis to the members of the Gakkai is established, even though the former, in the early stages of their activity at least, found most of their support in the provinces whereas the latter grew up in the major cities. This similarity suggests that though certain forms of political expression may correlate positively with geographical distribution, the more significant variables are the social, the economic, and the occupational. In the provincial areas of Germany in the 'twenties and 'thirties and of France in the 'fifties, the types of deprivation, the social discontinuities, and the stresses felt when values began to come under attack may have been similar to the postwar strains that have been experienced in Japanese cities since the 'fifties (especially where those affected are emigrants from the rural areas of Japan).

Finally, the social elements in the United States that are most readily drawn into apparent "mass" right-wing movements are again the lower classes. Joseph McCarthy counted the lower classes among his strongest supporters; and his support was socioeconomically on a higher level than that of his ideological predecessor, Father Coughlin.[75] A more recent movement, the Christian Anti-Communist Crusade, has been shown to command support from social elements better educated, more affluent, and of higher status. Of course, since the study from which these data issued was made at a meeting of the Crusaders, those involved are perhaps specifically comparable to Gakkai activists.[76]

In at least one case, certainly, likenesses can be traced beyond general memberships to elements within the memberships. The Nazi elite shared prominent sociological characteristics with its Gakkai counterpart.[77] The deprived, "resentful intellectuals" who made up "perhaps the single most important element in the Fascist elite" are not present in the Gakkai in great numbers, but they make up a disproportionately large segment of the Gakkai elite. One might draw parallels between the "new middle class" white-collar Nazis, who suffered from the sharp discrepancy between their social and economic statuses, and the underpaid but highly educated young Japanese office workers belonging to the Gakkai, residents of the danchi, who are trapped in a seniority-oriented system of questionable legitimacy. In short, when one considers the relatively high educational and income levels of the Gakkai activists and the disproportionately large number of teachers among them, one is reminded of Daniel Lerner's description of the "twentieth century revolutionary elite" who emerged from the "middle-income skill groups"—"the frustrated and vengeful middle groups that had experienced some upward social mobility, gained some economic rewards, and wanted political power."[78]

Up to this point we have been occupied with linking the Society to movements on the right. On the left, in the Communist movement at least, one finds that the contrasts are more noticeable than the similarities. As regards occupational distribution, the Japan Communist Party draws more students, organized workers, and intelligentsia than the Gakkai. Moreover, a cross-national study of ex-Communists revealed a high frequency of skilled workmen, professionals, and students, accompanied by a relative paucity of small entrepreneurs and unskilled workmen.[79] The elites of Communist states and movements include such "plebian" elements as constitute the core of the Gakkai; but they also include a much higher frequency of persons with professional and intellectual backgrounds.[80] The best that the Gakkai can boast in this area is an overrepresentation of primary and secondary teachers in its ranks, especially in its elite. The Communists' rank-and-file supporters also tend to be better educated than the Society's and, at least in Tokyo, more concentrated in the higher-class uptown area. (See Chapter 8.) And in comparison to extremists on the left the Gakkai's members appear to be relatively lower-class. In Gabriel Almond's cross-national study of ex-Communists, almost 60 per cent of the respondents reported that their parents' income had been average or high.[81] Had the respondents experienced downward social mobility, which several studies cited as a factor in the development of extremist attitudes? Apparently not; only 16 per cent of the sample reported that their own socioeconomic status was below their parents', and 23 per cent claimed to have risen in status.[82] In addition, only a minority—29 per cent—reported that at the time they entered the party they felt dissatisfied with career prospects relative to aspirations.[83]

Interesting to note are the different reactions of the Society and the Party to unions: whereas the Gakkai is relatively strong in the non-unionized small-business sector of the economy, the militant left anchors its power in unionized labor. This relationship of unions and Communism suggests the possibility that the unions and the Communist Party may serve as viable structures for satisfying the social and political needs of the more psychologically modern sectors of the Japanese working class. The degree to which one retains traditional cultural elements in one's thinking may determine the relative attractiveness, in times of stress, of sacred versus secular solutions.

Finally, the two movements seem to differ in the degree of alienation felt. In numerous opinion surveys Communist Party supporters invariably seemed to feel far more alienated from themselves, from their fellow citizens, and from the social and political systems than supporters of the Gakkai or Kōmeitō did. However, the question of alienation is not, strictly speaking, part of an analysis of the Gakkai's sociological composition. We shall come to that question in Part II. All we can say at this point is that Sōkagakkai members share certain sociological characteristics with the followers of historical mass movements and with those social elements, found cross-nationally, in which the unattachment, alienation, and political behavior of mass man are prevalent.

CHAPTER 5

Recruitment and Indoctrination

CHAPTER 4 described the size and the sources of the membership of the Sōkagakkai; this chapter will deal with the two steps by which potential members are turned into true adherents of the Society. These steps are the practical basis of the organization's growth and stability.

RECRUITMENT

The Gakkai perpetuates itself through a three-phase recruitment process involving propagation tactics, the congruence of these tactics and the Gakkai message with the needs of the potential convert, and actual conversion to Nichiren Shōshū and entry into the Gakkai.

Tactics. The Gakkai is a proselyting organization: in its view, any faith that makes no attempt to proselyte, to take issue with other religions, or to reform the world (which in this Mappō era is characterized by glaring injustice, rampant evil, and general moral decay) is by definition a dead religion.[1] Propagation is not simply a natural feature of any real religion; it is the epitome of the proper relationship of religion and society. And the exigencies of our age demand the shakubuku approach. In these chaotic days heretical religious thought is rampant, befogging the minds of the people and necessitating a drastic tactical approach that can forcibly root out mistaken modes of thought. The duty to proselyte is accordingly impressed upon the Gakkai members. Shakubuku is not only "one's natural duty as a member of society," but "one's essential activity as a Gakkai member";[2] propagation is thus "the marrow of the Gakkai spirit."[3]

The Gakkai's propagation tactics center on shakubuku, especially as it is practiced in the *zadankai*, or discussion meeting, the gathering of the lowest-level subunits of the Gakkai. As time passes, the Society's new members will more and more often be drawn in naturally, through family socialization. But for the present, the preponderance of new members are brought in through the propagation process. Shakubuku is defined by the Gakkai as "the merciful deed of saving those who are troubled with various kinds of misfortunes arising from heretical religions."[4] In practice it is most often a technique of determining the dominant problem troubling the prospective convert and offering him the ideas of happiness and divine benefit as the solution to the problem.

Although this tactic is defined as an "act of mercy" emanating from the compassionate heart of the propagator, in the past it has often been rhetorically (and sometimes physically) a violent matter. The Gakkai disavows all violence but acknowledges that pressure may be necessary: shakubuku is "forceful urging, as in the case where a child may be about to fall off a precipice or into a river. At that point one does not worry about niceties, but out of zeal to save the individual puts all his force into his appeal and literally commands."[5] However that may be, the spiritual motivation of shakubuku is always compassion. This feeling, *jihi*, is akin to the Western notion of *agape*; it is neither *eros* (the Gakkai denounces the conflict and misery attending Christian passion) nor love (which the Gakkai sees as meaningful only in relation to hate) but rather "the absolute, highest manifestation of life," which springs from realization of the unity of all forms of life in the Buddha.[6]

Until the early 1960's the literal translation of shakubuku, "to break and flatten," was a reasonably accurate description of the proselyting process. On occasion Gakkai members would surround a home and make noise until one family member agreed to join. Or they would belabor a mark with argument and exhortation for hours on end.[7] Sometimes threats of divine punishment were used: dire injuries and calamities might be predicted as the cost of resistance to the True Religion; a child's illness or death might be traced to the parents' heretical beliefs.[8] In such instances the "fear of punishment [instilled] in a mind weakened and made receptive by hours of pressure" could lead to the collapse of the subject's critical faculties and intellectual defenses, and to his acquiescing in the demands of the proselyters.[9]

Much of the Gakkai's reputation as a fanatical, ultramilitant band of religious zealots derives from this earlier style of shakubuku. One of President Ikeda's major concerns has been to institute a gentler form of propagation that would help to improve the Gakkai's image.

Ikeda advocates a more reasonable approach to shakubuku,[10] stressing conversion by example:

(1) The member should first build a united, harmonious, and happy family circle worthy of admiration and respect by all; thus (a) familial discord and late hours are to be avoided, and (b) neighbors are to be treated with respect and consideration regardless of their religious beliefs.
(2) The member should endeavor to make himself the most trusted and respected person at his place of work.
(3) Specific shakubuku activity should be bright, enjoyable, and relaxed.[11]

In fact, shakubuku has largely lost its aggressive quality and has begun to approximate Nichiren's other propagation technique, *shōju*.

Shōju is best described as soft-sell shakubuku; according to the Gakkai it is to "introduce the True Buddhism [to another] without denying the sect to which the other man belongs."[12] It is much more explanatory than shakubuku, much less combative and imperative. Shōju has received major emphasis only since early 1964;[13] since that time, however, the entire propagation program has tacitly assumed its attributes.

As the style of propagation has shifted from hard sell to soft sell, so the primary recruitment medium has changed from confrontation in the streets or in the target person's home to discussion in the zadankai. This trend began in the latter half of the 1950's, and by 1960 the shift was clear.[14] The advantages of zadankai proselytism are many. A nonmember's voluntary attendance at meetings is quite different from virtual incarceration in his own home; the whole situation is less intimidating. The visitor can observe a congenial gathering of a few dozen kindred spirits who have established mutual trust and an enviable rapport. In a gathering of this size, probably at least one of the members present will either be plagued by or will through faith already have overcome problems similar to any that may be bothering the visitor; such shared problems facilitate a feeling of empathy and familiarity. The zadankai format permits collective attack where such a tactic may be considered necessary, but it also enables the Gakkai leadership to control the shakubuku campaign, thus reducing the chance that overzealous believers will depart from officially sanctioned tactical methods. It is firmly asserted by the Gakkai—and generally the assertion seems justified—that whatever excesses were committed in the past were unsanctioned and uncondoned. The major role of the zadankai today can certainly be interpreted as an effort to avoid damaging publicity in the future.

Another recruiting agency that has developed during the last few years is the Kōmei Party. Ostensibly independent of the Gakkai, the Kōmeitō assiduously cultivates a secular image. The party newspaper, the *Kōmei Shimbun*, seldom mentions either religious goals or principles, although, since Kōmeitō leaders are also Gakkai members, all of the policies it presents issue from the Gakkai. The Kōmeitō strives to attract votes outside the Gakkai membership; its policies are calculated to appeal to almost every social group. But the Kōmeitō's significance as a recruitment structure is difficult to assess. Even though considerable numbers of non-Gakkai voters apparently succumb to secular Kōmeitō appeals, probably very few converts are drawn solely by political means. However, the Gakkai uses political arguments in its propagation activities, and these arguments no doubt contribute to the persuasiveness of shakubuku efforts.

The pace of the proselyting program, like its style, has changed with time. In the early stages of the Great Propagation Drive, mobilization was constant and the Gakkai increased geometrically (see Appendix D, Fig. D.1). With time the rate of growth began to decline (see Appendix B, Table B.1) and the earlier pace of mobilization became an unrealistic goal; in the mid-1960's the Society seems to have settled upon a conversion strategy of "one family per *han*"* in its propagation drives.[15] This was the goal in the May, July, and August 1967 conversion campaigns; the converts in these three periods totalled 174,197, 133,333, and 165,938 families, respectively.[16]

But despite the continued success that absolute figures show, problems have arisen in the program. As the rate of increase of the membership declines, the pressure upon each han to convert one new family during each drive has become considerable. One backslider told of a member under pressure to find converts who offered a taxi driver 3,000 yen (about eight dollars) to accompany him to a temple and join nominally.[17] Another member spoke to me about the anxiety he felt when he discovered that he had approached every one of his relatives and acquaintances. The importance of his statement is seen in an examination of the relationship of proselyters and converts. Hardly anyone, it appears, is subjected to shakubuku by a stranger. In a number of surveys, Gakkai members have indicated that they were won over by friends (average of three surveys, 33.3 per cent), neighbors (30 per cent), co-workers (22.3 per cent), or relatives (average of five surveys, 24.4 per cent).[18] The popular image of Sōkagakkai members scouring the streets accosting strangers is inaccurate; in the

---

* A Gakkai organizational subunit of fifty to one hundred families.

five surveys cited here the proportion of respondents who named strangers as their converters averaged 4 per cent.

A tentative distinction on the basis of sex can be made from these data. Male Gakkai members tend to have been converted by relatives, friends, or co-workers; female members are more often brought in by relatives and neighbors.[19] Given the stay-at-home life pattern of Japanese wives and the considerable time spent away from home by working Japanese men, one intuitively agrees with this distinction.[20] Once conversion has been accomplished, a Gakkai member becomes responsible for the spiritual fidelity and maturation of his proselyte. Thus the absence of geographical ties between many converts—especially men—and their converters is potentially damaging to organizational unity. As we shall see later, the Gakkai has taken steps to compensate for this problem.

Entry motives: congruence of tactics and conditions. To win over a new convert to the teachings of the Sōkagakkai, the proselyter must bring to bear tactics that touch the concerns and mental condition of his target. The answers of Gakkai members to the question "Why did you join?" indicate that this contact most often occurs when the Gakkai's doctrines of happiness and divine benefit are seen in relation to the subject's personal problems. Motives for entry into the Gakkai have been impressionistically grouped into three main categories: illness (*byō*), poverty (*hin*), and conflict (*sō*). Empirical data support this description of the motives bringing new members into the Gakkai, although they do not provide a direct explanation of whether the motive force is social (a search for sympathy or other human assistance) or religious (a quest for divine blessing). The importance of social motivating forces can at least be inferred from such data as the following.

In five surveys of Gakkai members, the proportion of respondents who gave illness as the major motive for entry varied from 13 to 28 per cent, with a mean of 20 per cent.[21] The popular impression of the Sōkagakkai, "fattening on the hopelessness of the poor,"[22] is apparently belied by the responses in the same five surveys about economic motives for joining: only 4 to 27 per cent of the respondents (mean, 14 per cent) gave economic reasons for their entry. Conflict, by contrast, seems to be a very important factor. This category is loosely defined to include all kinds of interpersonal friction and miscellaneous problems of human relations. The proportion of members placing themselves in this classification ranged from 11 to 61 per cent, with a mean of 29 per cent. This suggests that social causes have figured largely in the growth of the Gakkai. Though it is possible that converts expect their social relationships to be transformed through divine assistance, it is also quite possible that they are not concerned with doctrine at all but are searching for a satisfying social nexus, a search that is fulfilled in the act of conversion. The total proportion of Gakkai members whose motives for entry fell under these three headings in the five surveys cited above ranged from 38 to 80 per cent, with a mean of 63 per cent. The remaining respondents were divided among a great many other motives, no one of which seemed to account for a significant sector of the Gakkai membership.

More intensive data parallel the aggregates presented above. A study of testimonials in the *Seikyō Shimbun* apportioned motives for entry to reasons of health, family, and economics in the ratio 4:3:3.[23] Three examples illustrate these motives:

Miss Satō Yoshiko (22 years old) suffered from dermatitis; a red rash broke out all over her face and initial itching gave way to pain. With hospitalization she improved but, after her release, she still suffered from the rash and redness. Ashamed, she avoided her friends. Upon seeing her thus, one of her co-workers spoke to her of the faith of Nichiren Shōshū.... By the time a week had passed, Miss Satō had enshrined her *gohonzon* and, sitting properly before it, recited her prayers in a small voice.

Until I entered the faith three years ago, my desk was full of stomach and liver remedies, which I treated like valuables. Medicine was everywhere; the drawers of my wife's mirror-stand were full. Every day, even at dinner—which should be enjoyable—I gulped down medicine while listening to my wife hysterically complaining about the misery of life.

Now, only three years later, clippings from the *Seikyō Shimbun* have taken the place of the medicine in my desk, and once again, after 25 years of marriage, it is as it was when we were newly wed, with ordinary cosmetics neatly arranged on my wife's mirror-stand (Mr. Aoki Kōji, 53 years old).

The P. Clothing Store of Miss Iga Kazue (34 years old) is extremely busy with orders for summer wear, and every day she is furiously at work. "We're so busy, so busy; it's like year-end all year long. It's got to the point where I have to turn customers away."—With happy cries of despair, Miss Iga works away at her sewing machine.

For Miss Iga, too, who has been with her needles for 15 years, her earnest wish since the time she entered the faith has been fulfilled; since last July she has owned a shop—a small shop, but her own.[24]

Entry motives appear to differ from one sector of the Gakkai membership to the next. The reasons given by the younger believers center more on social and spiritual needs, on altruistic and universal goals, and on specifically doctrinal orientations.[25] The dullness, decadence, or disorder of life and the search for a significant, meaningful mode of existence often direct youth to the Gakkai. A more specific element in their motivation is the extreme pressure of secondary school—especially over preparation for college entrance examinations—that Japanese children experience.[26] Illness is also a factor among young people. President Ikeda, Vice President Akiya Einosuke, Student Division Chief Shinohara Makoto, and other top leaders offer physical disability as a major cause in their having accepted the faith.[27] Health problems, though, are more likely to draw older people to the Gakkai. Financial and family difficulties, along with other concrete everyday problems, are given more often by older Gakkai members as reasons for their conversion than by young ones, and more often by women than by men.[28] Men tend to be slightly more altruistic and, expectably, more concerned with job problems than women are.

People are not impelled toward the Gakkai only by these external forces, however. The Gakkai's own internal teachings, relating as they do to these external problems, provide a link between external cause and the acceptance of faith. And there are still other causal elements influencing the decision to join. In a survey run by the Gakkai itself, 29 per cent of the respondents asserted that they had been attracted "by the zeal of the proselyter."[29] Akin to this group are the respondents in two other surveys—25 per cent in one and 37 per cent in the other—who averred that they entered because they "were persuaded to" or "were advised to."[30] Some converts are attracted simply by the atmosphere of the zadankai, where the sharing of talk and advice is a basic activity.[31]

The establishment of secure social relationships, and the possibility that such relationships may be yearned for, sought, and achieved by conversion without the proselyte's having internalized the Gakkai beliefs, has also been discussed. Similarly, the confidence and new sense of orientation that are part of the internalization of Sōkagakkai teachings can also be gained, it would seem, independently of these doctrines. In answer to a question about the possibility of benefiting from divine reward without the Gakkai, one member replied, "I think that even if you don't join the Gakkai, if you have self-confidence you can receive benefit. In everything, having confidence in oneself is most important of all."[32] In this member's case such self-confidence is no doubt created in some measure by absorption of Gakkai teachings, since he presumably had been unable to acquire confidence outside the Society. But his nonchalance regarding the absolute and exclusive efficacy of Gakkai tenets suggests that here, again, membership per se may be attractive.

Conversion and entry. Whatever factors may have led to a person's commitment, and however secular they may be, his actual entry into the Sōkagakkai is a religious act: it has become integral with the act of formal conversion to Nichiren Shōshū. The *gojukai*, or act of receiving one's own copy of the gohonzon, signifies both acceptance of the faith and acceptance into the Gakkai.[33] But at this point the average convert, who has taken this step in response to coaxing or to social obligations, has only the vaguest notion of the whole Gakkai belief system, the most tenuous commitment to its teachings, and the weakest of expectations.[34] Thus the Society must rely upon post-entry indoctrination to transform the new believer into the true believer. The key figure in this inculcation of beliefs is the converter, the person who brought the new member to the temple. He must be constantly the mentor and the source of help and guidance, and he must see to it that the new believer attends meetings and participates in Gakkai activities; he is the critical link between the uncertain convert and a host of supplementary socializing agencies.[35] That this socialization process is effective is borne out by the number of converts the Gakkai manages to retain.

INDOCTRINATION

Owing to the almost involuntary manner in which most persons enter the Sōkagakkai, the process of socialization by which the norms, ideals, and ideology of the sect are firmly implanted in new converts is of crucial importance. In Japan, where religious belief is traditionally casual and simultaneous profession by one person to two or more faiths is common, the implantation of an exclusivist view of religion is no mean task. The Gakkai has responded to the challenge with a proliferation of carefully designed indoctrinating agencies.

There are three major types of structures in the Gakkai performing principally socializing functions: the "vertical line," peer groups, and functional groups. Supporting them are miscellaneous other agencies (see Appendix C, Fig. C.2)[36] as well as the family. One may assume that with the passing of time the family's role as an agent for religious socialization will steadily expand; such a trend is already apparent in the case of recruitment. But at present most new believers are those already beyond the stage of childhood socialization, and artificial structures must bear the burden of maintaining orthodox patterns of thought and action. The various structures in which the individual Gakkai member is involved overlap and interlock and are based upon different organizing principles—e.g., age, sex, knowledge of the faith, place of residence, occupation, and leisure-time interests—so as to bring into play almost every type of human relationship and to be able to satisfy practically any social need. I have considered these agencies singly in order to analyze the whole indoctrination process; but the mutually reinforcing relationships that they provide act upon each Gakkai member's thoughts and behavior in ways that such dissection cannot reflect. (All of these agencies also serve the Society for other purposes besides indoctrination.)

Of course, successful socialization of members demands more than a structure of interlocking agencies. Of equal importance is what we might call operational style: the skill used in expounding doctrine and applying it to the concrete problems of individual members, the degree to which formal channels of advancement and communication are kept open, and the diligence, sincerity, and responsiveness of those in the upper echelons in interacting with those below. If the diffuse social needs of converts were not fulfilled, no genuine commitment to the Gakkai could be achieved; and without that commitment the Society's efforts to instill and maintain certain ideas would be in vain.

The vertical line. Vertical line is a term that describes the basic socializing hierarchy. The type of small face-to-face group that characterizes the Gakkai's vertical line was referred to in Chapter 1 as playing an important role in the organization of a person's social existence. If such organizing structures do not exist in a society—especially in one characterized by the tako-tsubo mentality many Japanese evince—people will endeavor to establish them wherever they can.[37] By providing a comprehensive network of such groups, the Gakkai capitalizes upon both the general cultural tako-tsubo element and the particular social stresses that tend to diminish the number of available face-to-face groups.

The vertical line (see Appendix C, Fig. C.2) consists of the unit (*kumi*), up to ten families (twenty adults); the group (*han*), five to ten units, or fifty to one hundred families; the district (*chiku*), five to ten groups, or five hundred to one thousand families; the chapter (*shibu*), five to ten districts, or five thousand to ten thousand families; the general chapter (*sō-shibu*), an unspecified number of chapters; the headquarters (*honbu*), several general chapters; and the joint headquarters (*sōgō honbu*), several headquarters. A number of joint headquarters form the common apex of both the vertical line and the horizontal line.* As of late 1967 the vertical line consisted of 53 joint headquarters, 194 headquarters, and 3,500 chapters.[38] The data on

* The horizontal line, a geographically organized hierarchy that functions for the most part as an administrative organ, will be examined in Chapter 6.

shakubuku targets set and attained indicate that there are roughly one hundred fifty thousand han in the Gakkai.[39] (There are no firm figures for units, groups, or districts.)

Each level on the vertical line multiplies regularly; i.e., the lowest level, the kumi, is never allowed to grow so large that intensive face-to-face communication becomes impossible. Upon conversion the new Gakkai member becomes a member of his converter's kumi. When a converter has brought in approximately four families he becomes a unit chief (*kumi-chō*). If one of the new believers converts several families himself, he in turn establishes his own kumi. A kumi that has become too large is simply subdivided into several new kumi and becomes itself a han, with the old kumi-chō as the new group chief (*han-chō*). In the same way, the han grow until they become chiku, and so on. As a member rises in position in the vertical line he maintains his role (though not the title) of kumi-chō, staying in touch with those whom he personally converted and looking after their continuing socialization.

The strength of the vertical line lies in its personal connections. Each member is in a teacher-follower relationship that approximates the "parent-child" relationship characterizing so much of social interaction in Japan.[40] He is at once both the follower of his own converter and the teacher of those he himself has converted. This vertical interaction, resting on transmission of faith, is constantly stressed; the converter is entrusted not only with instructing the new member in specific articles of faith, but also with ushering him into a diffuse pattern of interaction that increases his social ties to the Gakkai and thus, hopefully, his receptivity to its socializing efforts.

The vertical line's weakness is its nongeographical basis. A Gakkai member from Hokkaido visiting in Tokyo may make a convert; the latter is then ideally obliged to attend his converter's kumi meetings regularly in Hokkaido, an unrealistic obligation. The members of a chapter are seldom this geographically divided, but tend to be concentrated in one area so that districts, chapters, and the higher substructures can be organized on a regional basis. The members of a kumi can still, however, be spread throughout a city, making administration difficult. It was to remedy such situations that a geographically oriented horizontal line was established.

Meetings take place on each level of the Gakkai vertical line. On the kumi, han, and chiku levels all the members gather for zadankai, which each substructure schedules independently. These meetings are the primary socialization situations, and the leader bears heavy responsibility for the progress of each of his protégés.[41] On the district level, the zadankai are supplemented by lecture meetings, which are usually concerned with announcements, scriptural exegesis, and exhortation. At this level and at all higher levels leaders' meetings are also held. At the higher levels, these gatherings become increasingly administrative, although the administrative measures they produce are concerned largely with the structure and process of socialization at the lower levels.

Whether on the kumi, han, or chiku level, the zadankai affords members an opportunity to escape the obligations and discriminations of secular society and enter a setting of equality, free intercourse, and self-expression. The meeting is structured, but not excessively; the agenda is established by the leaders along general guidelines for the month's activities, but considerable autonomy remains. Typical programs include official announcements, short explanations of articles of faith, shakubuku of visitors (which is often more of an earnest but persistent exchange than the vituperative attack of the past), discussion of common problems in light of scripture, political planning and discussion, and personal testimonials and professions of faith.

The cardinal elements of the meeting are participation and dialogue. According to President Ikeda, "all attendants should be conscious that they are essential members of the meeting."[42] He criticizes the one-way communication of the mass media and stresses that at the zadankai all are equally to be heard. Meeting leaders who make the "grandstand play" are excoriated, for their responsibility is to draw participants into the discussion. The dialogue thus fostered is not as integral to the zadankai as the Gakkai would have it, however. Questions are answered, problems are interpreted, and encouragement is given, but the only real dialogue occurs during shakubuku. For the most part, the zadankai is a vehicle for self-expression. Every participant has a chance to unburden himself before a sympathetic audience. Such self-revelation has never been characteristic of the "inscrutable" Japanese, but in the zadankai believers describe their own intimate problems and show open concern for the difficulties of others. That the Japanese are as capable of self-revelation as any other people is nowhere so strikingly obvious as in the zadankai.[43]

The testimonial aspect of the zadankai has been compared to self-criticism on the Chinese Communist model, and its shakubuku and prayer to brainwashing. Group therapy is a much better analogy; speakers are not assailed by harsh criticism, nor must they make abject confessions of guilt. The whole process is positive. The unison chanting of prayer and the vigorous affirmative response to the leader's rhetorical questions during zadankai suggest the inducement of a state of suspended consciousness or even, at times, of trance. But such periods are usually brief, and the observations of relatively unbiased outsiders suggest the brainwashing metaphor is hyperbolic.

But brainwashing in the sense of unremitting socialization is unquestionably a purpose of the zadankai. The primary purpose of zadankai socialization is to strengthen the believer's faith in the efficacy of the True Religion in solving human problems. The testimonials all turn on the same point: faith creates value; pray and you shall receive. The divine benefits thus received vary—a high school student has passed his college entrance examinations, a husband has stopped his carousing, a young girl has become the talk of her shop through her diligence. Aside from such material attainments, active Gakkai members find that the zadankai context itself alters their lives. Its enveloping atmosphere of intimacy, enthusiasm, and trust, in which the participant shares his problems with other believers, generates a sense of security. The participant gains in self-expression and self-confidence. He is reassured of his significance as a person, and of a well-marked path through the maze of modern urban life.

A final socialization strategy realized in the vertical line is shakubuku. One observer has said that the zadankai's primary function is simply to propagate, and that the problems of members are of secondary importance.[44] But propagation does not serve simply to attract and to convert; it is a means of disciplining and strengthening the faith of the members. The obligation to proselyte pressures members to internalize Gakkai theology if they are to present Nichiren Shōshū persuasively. And since shakubuku is another form of devotion, it too will produce divine reward. The story of Mr. Okayama Takeo (50 years old), of Katsushika ward, Tokyo, illustrates this point. This account appeared in the *Seikyō Shimbun* under the title "Springtime in the Family Through Shakubuku."[45]

June 1964 . . . the leaders' meeting held that month became the great turning point for Okayama Takeo. The Edogawa Public Hall was choking with heat and stuffiness.

"No matter how hard a time you may have, you must not be distracted," ran the guidance of the diligent senior member.

Okayama, seated quietly, recalled the panorama of his life until that time. He had drunk liquor by the quart and become riotous. He had not worked and had spent like water the money that his wife and children had earned with their own sweat. And to complete the misery, he had fought incessantly with Masae, his wife. Naturally, the events in such a family had subtly influenced his adolescent daughters. He had even been told by his eldest daughter's elementary school teacher that "Noriko has good manners, but she can't express her own opinions and doesn't know how to be comfortable with people. Is there some problem in the family . . . ?"

Okayama suddenly remembered this event. "Noriko, I'm sorry. Even at school you're ashamed. From now on your father, too, will work hard at his faith. I'll achieve a wonderful human revolution!" From then on, Okayama went about his shakubuku assiduously, winning finally the nickname "Proselyting Okayama." Once he debated fiercely with a young man for five hours and at last brought his adversary to conversion.

Struggles like this led Okayama gradually to find himself. As his senior, General Chapter Chief Ishikura, says, "That one has matured through shakubuku; he has admirably and brightly matured." Says Noriko, beaming, "Nowadays Father is really reliable."

Today, the Okayama family, with father as the center, is in good health and is devoting all its energies to its work. Even the family restaurant is prospering.

It is the example a believer sets as the manifestation of a living faith that is crucial in shakubuku.[46] The Society stresses that doctrinal proficiency, though desirable, does not of itself suffice; indeed, sheer force of conviction can substitute successfully for theological argument. The proselyter is also encouraged in the knowledge that he accrues divine benefit whether or not he succeeds in converting anyone. The Gakkai posits two forms of shakubuku: *monpō geshu*, bringing knowledge of the True Religion to another, and *hosshin geshu*, bringing another to accept the True Religion.[47] Both produce blessings; all that is required of the proselyting Gakkai member is that he make the earnest effort.

PEER GROUPS

According to the Gakkai, peer groups are the "pillars" of the organization.[48] Whereas the vertical line arrangement addresses itself primarily to members' individual social and psychological needs, the peer groups deal mainly in the intercommunication and mobilization of the membership. Basically, the peer-group structure has three branches: the Men's Division, the Women's Division, and the Youth Division. But two subgroups of the Youth Division, the Young Men's Division and the Young Women's Division, have become increasingly influential, and the Gakkai now usually speaks of the "unity of the four." In addition to the YMD and the YWD, the Youth Division has elaborated a Student Division for university students, a High School Division, a Junior High School Division, and a Boys' and Girls' Division. Every Gakkai member automatically belongs to a peer group.

The Youth Division was established by Toda in 1951 for single Gakkai members between the ages of eighteen and thirty. By 1963 over half the Gakkai Board of Directors were ex-Youth Division members.[49] The Division now claims more than four million members, including nearly a half million in the YMD, one and a half million in the YWD, two hundred thousand in the Student Division, one hundred fifty thousand in the secondary school divisions, and nearly one hundred thousand in the Boys' and Girls' Division.[50] The Youth Division's structural terminology—corps, company, squad—has a military flavor. The corps (*butai*) of the YMD and YWD, like their vertical line equivalent, the chapters, each receive their own banners from the president. A sense of fellowship is also stimulated by the frequent addresses of senior leaders. "You are the well," they say, "from which the future motive forces of the Gakkai and of the nation will be drawn; therefore, be proud and diligent in study and activity." Thus adjured, the Youth Division is the peer group most thoroughly acquainted with orthodox patterns of belief.

Appendix C, Fig. C.2, shows the parallel construction of the vertical line and the peer groups; the relationship is clearest in the YMD and the YWD. (These two groups also have their own internal elite groups, the men's Suiko Club and the women's Kayō Club, which permit even more intensive socialization.[51]) Members of the "four" are all customarily present in the lower levels of the vertical line— the han, the chiku, and, when possible, the kumi. But the peer groups, though associated with the vertical line, are independent, individually responsible to the Board of Directors. Each has its own rallies, goals, and activities, and in cooperative endeavors such as shakubuku there is a peer-group *esprit* that arouses competitiveness in the vertical line efforts to win converts.

The YMD, YWD, Men's Division, and Student Division all function as socializing agencies, but have been assigned distinctly differing roles. To the YMD and YWD the admonition now seems to be: "Apply yourselves!" President Ikeda has called on them to "be revolutionary youths, unsparing of body and life. . . . I want you to exert yourselves to the utmost in the time of your youth. . . . You must not be distracted by such things as school record, position, wealth, honor, or titles."[52] Gone are the Todaesque injunctions to take command, to lead, to become the nucleus of the organization. The leading role appears to have devolved upon the Men's Division, which is, according to Vice President Hōjō Hiroshi, the "backbone," the "pillar," and the "mainstay" of the Gakkai.[53] In the speech just quoted, President Ikeda declared to the Men's Division, "You are the Gakkai's backbone, you are its nucleus, you are its foundation. . . . Take command brilliantly, as renowned leaders."

Ikeda has at times described quite pointedly the new division of labor among the peer groups. The Men's Division is encouraged to see itself as the present leader, whereas the Student Division is admonished to develop the capacities for future leadership of the Gakkai. (The less educated sectors of the Youth Division are presumably left with the less demanding tasks.) The students are the "axis" of the Gakkai and, as its "heirs," must "carry the future of the Society."[54] They must "be the power source and brains of the bloodless revolution" and the future leaders of the nation and the world.[55]

To prepare for their future role, students are adjured to master the doctrines of Nichiren Shōshū, for, in addition to becoming the administrative leaders of the Gakkai, they will be expected to form the "nucleus of the theoretical struggle."[56] To this end the Student Division is strengthening its position on university campuses with philosophical and theological study clubs. Where there are few Gakkai members, informal discussion circles are organized.[57] Some of the major institutions in Japan having Gakkai student organizations are Tokyo University, Tokyo Institute of Technology, Meiji University, Keiō University, Kansai Gakuin University, and Ochanomizu Women's University. The Division has also spawned its own internal elite group, the Ushio Club.

As mentioned above, the Student Division presently claims over two hundred thousand members. The ostensible rate of growth (see Appendix B, Table B.1) has been remarkable. Extrapolating from this growth, the Gakkai predicts that by 1972, 400,000 of a total of 1.2 million university students will be Gakkai members. On the basis of the Shae-no-san'oku principle this would constitute substantive kōsen-rufu of the student world.[58] A survey of university students indicated that the Society's share of the student world is nearer to 1 per cent than to the 15 per cent claimed.[59] Nevertheless, the Sōkagakkai Student Division probably has more activist members than any other student organization in Japan, including the better known Zengakuren.* And members of the Division can retain symbolic ties

---

* On October 10, 1969, the Gakkai announced the inauguration of a new organization within the Student Division, the New Student League (Shin Gakusei Dōmei or Shingakudō), headed by Tsuda Takaaki, a graduate student at Tokyo University. Claiming 120,000 members on 368 campuses, Shingakudō sees itself as a "third road" in two senses, steering between the "right" and "left" extremes of the present student movements and between the "violence and lethargy" that typify

with it after graduation through the Student Division Alumni Division.[60]

The final peer groups, the Women's Division and the Boys' and Girls' Division, though structurally independent, are undoubtedly interrelated. The majority of Gakkai members are women, and a great number of them are married; thus the establishment of the Women's Division created both a means of mobilizing a large group for various Gakkai activities and a natural agency for family socialization. Japanese mothers play a far greater role in the socialization of children than American mothers do.[61] In some situations the child becomes a virtual extension of the mother's ego; in general the child tends to be "more receptive" to instruction by the mother than by the father. "Until late adolescence, the child is a part of the mother's world."[62] In these circumstances the Gakkai's attention to the housewife is an indirect—but certainly not unconscious—strategem of considerable perspicacity for maintaining orthodox belief patterns. And the growth of the Boys' and Girls' Division, whose members (drawn from the first through sixth grades) are too young to have been "converted" in any meaningful sense, attests to a successful integration of Gakkai indoctrination and basic familial socialization.

FUNCTIONAL GROUPS

The peer groups and the vertical line are explicitly multipurpose. Two other structures, the Study Department and the Culture Bureau, have been designed to perform specifically socializing functions. Both are charged with defining, interpreting, and articulating the patterns of thought and behavior that the Gakkai wishes to perpetuate. The Study Department, moreover, handles a large-scale educational program designed both to instill Gakkai creed in the common members and to provide intensive doctrinal training for the future leaders.

This department, established in 1951, grew out of Toda's disillusionment with the original Gakkai leaders, almost all of whom recanted upon incarceration by the prewar Japanese government. In Ikeda's words, "it was clearly proved that faith had not been proportionate to office."[63] Toda believed, as does Ikeda, that everyone can find at least two or three leisure hours each day in which to read

---

the Japanese college student population as a whole. It is too soon to know whether Shingakudō will in fact hew to this middle course; one suspects that it will pursue a course rather to the left of the Kōmeitō. See *Japan Times Weekly*, October 25, 1969.

and reflect. The Gakkai is vehement on this point. In each zadankai, time is devoted to study; frequent lecture meetings at various levels of the vertical line are part of the doctrinal study program. Members are also encouraged to subscribe to the *Seikyō Shimbun* and to read as many of the other official publications as possible. But paradoxically, despite this stress on the members' study, learning is not of paramount importance. The Gakkai draws a sharp line between academic knowledge and true wisdom, which is living knowledge enlightened by faith. Of the three elements of wisdom—faith, action, and knowledge—the last often seems the least important to the Society. Faith is supreme; living faith, i.e. belief put into action, is acceptable even without knowledge. However, knowledge is essential to sustained faith, and to effective action like shakubuku—hence the great emphasis on the Society's formal study program.

Personal achievement in the study program is an important element in the indoctrination and socialization of the individual Gakkai member. At present the Study Department has six ranks, from assistant lecturer to full professor (see page 98). In Japanese society, where academic standing is prestigious, these titles contribute greatly to self-esteem. Many Gakkai members have had little formal schooling, and to attain the grade of professor despite this handicap is a major victory. Such standing, coupled with the Gakkai emphasis on wisdom over knowledge, contributes to the feelings of superiority befitting adherents of the one and only True Religion. Thus academic accomplishment within the Gakkai study structure increases a member's sense of competence vis-à-vis both his peers and the secular society that may have disparaged or ignored him. That the Gakkai does not ignore such members, but rather fosters and recognizes their achievements, tends to increase their commitment to the Society without reference to specific doctrines—though the commitment can be expected to spur members to internalize the doctrines.

The Study Department sets study standards for every level of the academic achievement in the Gakkai. The general membership is encouraged to read at least the *Seikyō Shimbun* and *Dai Byaku Renge*, and if one aspires to an academic position the requirements become increasingly difficult. Examinations begin at the Junior High School Division level; fifty thousand people turned out for the 1967 JHSD test.[64] This examination, for admission to the Study Department, presupposes a greater familiarity with scriptural material and the *Shakubuku Handbook* than the general membership possesses, and knowledge of certain articles from *Dai Byaku Renge*.

Preparation for admission and for each succeeding rank in the Study Department is not easy—the classical Japanese used in the scriptures is exceedingly difficult to read and, in contrast to the rote-learning procedures that typify the formal Japanese educational system, Gakkai members must be able to interpret their beliefs and apply them to everyday life situations. Nor are the examinations themselves a simple affair. The would-be professor faces twenty questions ranging from abstruse points of pure theology to demands such as:

Discuss Feuerbach's critique of Hegelian philosophy.
Briefly discuss, and criticize from the Buddhist point of view, Jaspers' "reason" and "reality" and Sartre's "existence" and "emptiness."
Discuss the theft of Tendai's concept of *ichinen-sanzen* by the Kegon Sect and the Shingon Sect.[65]

The annual advent of examination time rouses many members to a tremendous outpouring of energy. One sees them reading Gakkai publications in coffee shops and subways and on the streets. In the May–June 1967 series of tests, well over one million members took examinations and seven hundred thousand of them passed.[66] Of these, some had taken makeup examinations, and many on the professorial level had taken the required periodic in-service examinations. But the 1967 test results still increased the membership of the Study Department to approximately one and a half million persons, up from a little over one million the previous year and only 3,131 in 1957 (the cutoff point for available data).[67] This membership is distributed* as follows:

Professors	1,000
Associate professors	8,000
Assistant professors	50,000
Subassistant professors	200,000
Lecturers	400,000
Assistant lecturers	900,000
Total Study Department membership	1,559,000[68]

The Culture Bureau's part in the Gakkai indoctrination program is less obvious than is that of the Study Department, but it is perhaps equally important. The current branches of the Bureau are the Economics Department, the Education Department, the Public Opinion Department (official translation, *Genron-bu*), the Art Department, and the Science Department.[69] Each of these organs is engaged in de-

---

* This is a crudely proportional representation; different official Gakkai figures are contradictory.

fining and explicating the official Gakkai policies relating to its field, primarily as a method of indoctrination; secondarily as another tactic for conversion. Until 1961 the Culture Bureau also included a Politics Department, which managed all of the Gakkai's political operations under the rubric "cultural activities." But in November of that year the League of Fair Statesmen was established, and assumed the tasks of forming and disseminating policies and of managing election campaigns. Since then the vertical line has handled general political socialization, and the horizontal line has been the primary medium for internal electoral publicity and mobilization.

Some of the defining and communicating of doctrines required for the Gakkai's socialization program have devolved upon the newer Theory Department, formed in April 1967. This department is headed by Tada Shōgo, who at 37 is the youngest of the general administrators, already a Member of Parliament, and perhaps one of the three top-ranking theoreticians in the Gakkai.* The Theory Department, which has assumed the Study Department's policy-making role, studies political, economic, philosophical, and social problems from a Buddhist viewpoint and accounts for them in terms of the Gakkai theological framework. And it concerns itself particularly with refuting "mistaken" perceptions and criticisms of the Society.[70] The department is divided into eight branches, whose names reflect the department's preoccupation with contemporary problems and with the Japanese communications media's treatment of the Gakkai. These divisions are the Oriental-Occidental Philosophy Study Club, the Contemporary Thought Conference, the Modern Mass Communications Comrades' Club, the Political Reform Discussion Group, the Middle-of-the-Road Politics Study Club, the Welfare Economy Study Club, the Contemporary Mass Communications Study Club, and the Pearl Pen Club.

A fourth functional group in the Society is the Pilgrimage Department. This department manages the trips of over three million believers each year to the Taisekiji, the Head Temple of Nichiren Shōshū. A pilgrimage is a brief period, sometimes just overnight, of intensive socialization—both overt and implicit. The pilgrims attend a midnight prayer service, where the mass chanting of scripture creates a trancelike atmosphere; this preparation is then followed up with small seminars and with lectures on theology. In the less obvious

* The supreme theoretician is, of course, President Ikeda, followed, probably, by Kodaira Yoshihei—a Toda convert, Member of Parliament, General Administrator, and the head of the Study Department.

phase of the socialization program, the pilgrims are conducted around the precincts of the temple to draw their own conclusions from what they see. Here they view the results of building projects furthered by their own sacrifices. The massive buildings, towering out of the cypress groves, "provide a vision of splendor for people whose everyday lives are drab." The scope of the whole Taisekiji compound is enormous; seated dramatically at the foot of Mount Fuji and thronged with the faithful, the shrine and its compound are an impressive sight. It cannot fail to impress the pilgrims with a sense of awe at the magnitude, affluence, and power of the Sōkagakkai.[71]

The organization responsible for managing the pilgrimage program is the Yusōhan or guide group. Members of the Yusōhan are chosen for their enthusiastic faith, honesty, and diligence, with the understanding that their sole function is to manage this program.[72] Zealous and rather aggressive, they have a tightly regimented system for organizing the pilgrims and making sure they attend every scheduled event. Japanese pilgrims do not seem to mind, but American pilgrims have objected on occasion to so much discipline and so little freedom of movement. Some Japanese critics of the Gakkai have in fact called the Yusōhan a storm troop.[73] But the Gakkai stoutly denies this characterization and asserts that without a certain degree of regimentation the Taisekiji, receiving as it does over ten thousand visitors daily, would be chaos.

OTHER SOCIALIZING AGENCIES

The remaining Gakkai structures involved in manifest or latent indoctrination are various interest groups; several Gakkai publications; a recently established educational complex, the Sōka Schools; and the Society's mass meetings. Gakkai interest groups, such as the Democratic Music Association and the Democratic Drama Association, perform socializing functions only indirectly, for the most part; their activities are largely nonsectarian, and nonmembers are admitted. Nevertheless, these interest groups are still collectivities of Gakkai members, accessible to Gakkai influence. Thus faith will sometimes be referred to explicitly: a member of the Fuji Symphony Orchestra may be advised to practice more, but he may also be counseled to pray oftener before the gohonzon. In the same vein, a good performance, especially at a Gakkai function, is considered a sign of divine assistance and reward, and will be capitalized on to reinforce belief in the Society's doctrine of happiness.

The Sōkagakkai and its various subsidiaries* produce three types of publications: exoteric materials, i.e., materials oriented primarily toward the larger society; intermediate socializing materials aimed at the general membership; and esoteric materials, i.e., doctrinal classics and more sophisticated and theoretical journals directed toward familiarizing top leaders in the Gakkai with the more complex patterns of the official belief system.[74]

The fully exoteric publications of the Gakkai are few: *Ushio* (a nonpartisan monthly), *Shūkan Genron* (a magazine of current events), the political journal *Kōmei*, and various nonsectarian books published by the Ushio Publishing Company, a Gakkai subsidiary. One could call the flashy weekly *Seikyō Graphic* exoteric, though it serves also as a colorful socialization tool for members. The *Graphic* is devoted to religious criticism, testimonials, and Gakkai activities; a 1960–61 content analysis showed that these three areas accounted for 76 per cent of the total page makeup, and advertisements for another 14 per cent.[75]

The *Seikyō Shimbun*, the Society's daily newspaper, is an intermediate organ. One might call it exoteric but for the fact that it can be obtained only through Gakkai members or directly from Gakkai headquarters. Evidently the membership is its primary audience—although the Society encourages members to use it in shakubuku. The *Seikyō Shimbun* deals less with Gakkai activities and criticism than the *Graphic*, though a current analysis would probably reveal an increased stress on criticism and politics.[76] Articles by members of the Theory Department are now frequently printed, and since the early 1960's the coverage of elections and of the Kōmeitō's parliamentary activities has become quite extensive. Its many advertisements (27 per cent of total page makeup) indicate that the *Seikyō Shimbun* is a money-maker.

The Study Department examination system blurs the distinction between intermediate and esoteric communications media. Perhaps the only texts not studied by the membership are Nichiren's writings and Makiguchi's *Theory of Value*. And it is unlikely that leaders spend much time with these works, either. Neither of these texts really serves as much more than a convenient fund of concepts for explaining every occasion and every change of doctrinal strategy. The Gakkai's living corpus of beliefs is contained in the *Shakubuku Handbook* and, even more, in the writings of President Ikeda.

The *Shakubuku Handbook* forgoes all of the niceties indulged

* Gakkai publishing activities are described further in Chapter 6.

in by the more theoretical and exoteric Gakkai media. Until the 1967 edition appeared it completely ignored such shibboleths as democracy, tolerance, and freedom of religion. Its concern is with the concrete tactics of propagation—criticism, condemnation, attack, and vilification. The primary themes of the book are (1) why Nichiren Shōshū is the one absolute True Religion; (2) why all other religions are evil; and (3) how to attack heresies. The 1967 edition contained a new section on freedom of religion that extended copious guarantees and assurances, discussed and supported constitutional references to religion, and stressed that politics belongs to the realm of relativity, where compromise is the guiding principle.[77] But the balance of the book remains substantively unchanged. A nonmember reading the *Handbook* is not likely to escape the conclusion that prolonged socialization in the book's behavioral imperatives would be profoundly subversive of a democratic political system. It may well be, however, that the *Propagation Handbook* is undergoing de-emphasis; references to texts most useful in shakubuku show that the *Seikyō Shimbun* is now preferred over the *Handbook*. And in other areas of doctrine, *Dai Byaku Renge* and the presidents' writings are evidently of greater importance.

The theoretical monthly, *Dai Byaku Renge*, is the closest the Society comes to a thoroughly esoteric journal. It prints a good deal of doctrine and criticism, few testimonials, and no advertisements.[78] Nevertheless, 31 per cent of the magazine is devoted to didactic stories, fictionalized historical excerpts from scripture, and "reader interest" articles. These indicate that the journal is not solely a leadership aid; it also serves as an important educational source for the rank and file. As mentioned above, *Dai Byaku Renge* is required reading for the Study Department examinations. It is interesting to note that, like the *Seikyō Shimbun* and the *Seikyō Graphic*, this central source of theory makes virtually no reference to Makiguchi's Theory of Value as such.

The only Gakkai president, in fact, whose output is currently considered important is Ikeda. Makiguchi's *Theory of Value* is an unread classic; Toda's speeches are often quoted, but his writings are rather too extreme to suit the Gakkai's new, moderate image. The books of President Ikeda convey the substance of this image. *Politics and Religion* is an exposition of the Society's political philosophy; but it also includes a survey of the history of political thought in both the East and the West, emphasizing the evolution of secular, liberal

European democracy. Ikeda has obviously read widely; he cites with approval Locke, Montesquieu, Jefferson, Paine, the *Declaration of the Rights of Man and Citizen*, the Mills, and Bentham, among others.

His single major work to date is the *Lectures on the Risshō Ankoku Ron*, a commentary on Nichiren's memorial to the thirteenth-century rulers of Japan on the necessity of adopting his faith as the official religion. In the course of this long book Ikeda sets forth the entire Gakkai belief system, including current political policies. Many passages cover the same ground as the *Shakubuku Handbook* and *Politics and Religion*. In general, *Lectures* plays down Nichiren's intemperate tone. Probably few people have read this work in its entirety; still, it is a valuable compendium of Ikeda's thoughts, the only book in which all of his ideas are brought together.

A more readable and exoteric, albeit equally repetitious, work is *Human Revolution*, Ikeda's fictionalized biography of President Toda. Excerpts from this biography (of the ten volumes planned, four have been completed) are often read at zadankai and cited in speeches and *Seikyō Shimbun* articles; the book is "the Sōkagakkai made easy." It contains Gakkai history, Japanese history, Nichiren Shōshū teachings (with Gakkai additions), and "how to" sections on leadership, shakubuku, methods of study, and proper zadankai forms. With its intellectually less pretentious tone and its biographical rather than documentary format, *Human Revolution* may turn out to be the most widely read Gakkai work. In the Gakkai's educational program, at least, it will probably be the most significant of Ikeda's works.

In the spring of 1968, the Sōka Junior and Senior High Schools opened in the Tokyo suburb of Kodaira City, with a combined enrollment of 500 students. Sōka University is scheduled to open in the suburb of Hachiōji City in 1972.[79] All are part of the Sōka Gakuen, the Gakkai's new school system, a socializing agency with converting potential. True, Vice President Hōjō Hiroshi denies that the Sōka Gakuen will be a Gakkai socialization structure. He asserts that the socialization structures of the Sōkagakkai are the zadankai and the family, and that the Society neither needs nor intends to utilize the schools as well.[80] But although the schools will provide a standard curriculum in accordance with law, they will further attempt to nurture talent, to develop each student to his fullest potential, and to emphasize "humanism"; all these concerns are features of Makiguchi's "value-creation education" system and of the Gakkai's pedagogical philosophy. Evidently, the ingredients of Gakkai socialization will be present in the Sōka Gakuen's curriculum.[81] And the possibility of the Sōka Schools' producing converts is strengthened by the fact that enrollment is not limited to Gakkai members.

To date the faculty are all Society members; but according to Hōjō, this is simply because the number of qualified teachers in the Gakkai's ranks presently exceeds the school's needs.[82] No religious restriction is intended, however.* For the students, Vice President and Director of the Sōka Gakuen Morita Kazuya has stated that the admission process will be an impartial one, based on previous academic record and an entrance examination. There will be no "free pass" for the children of Gakkai members.[83] Once enrolled, nonmember students will not be pressured in any way to accept Gakkai ideas. In Morita's words, "there will be absolutely nothing special. In particular, we are not even thinking of religious education. . . . In teaching history we won't deny or ignore other religious sects."[84] It seems evident, though, that whether the Sōka Gakuen create new Gakkai members or just sympathizers impressed by the Society's doctrines or the liberal, nondoctrinal nature of the schools, they will indeed perform some function of conversion.

The final socializing agency of the Gakkai is the mass meeting. The Gakkai holds dozens every year: national and regional general meetings, chapter meetings, peer group rallies, gatherings of leaders on every level. These meetings exert a greater socializing influence upon the leaders who actually participate than upon the rank and file, but all members can enjoy such spectacles vicariously through the Society's communications media (which include motion pictures).

At mass meetings the medium is the message, and the message is enthusiasm, power, and unity.[85] Rhythmic clapping and singing literally shake the hall, lustily delivered speeches arouse thunderous applause, and the spectator finds it difficult to refrain from joining in. A parallel that has occurred immediately to many observers is the Nuremberg rallies of the Nazis. Although the socializing effect was probably similar, the content and atmosphere were so different that the analogy is misleading and invidious. Darkness and hatred were part of the staging and the content of the Nazi rallies; neither enters into the overwhelmingly positive message of Gakkai mass meetings.

The most striking mass meeting in Gakkai history was the Tokyo Culture Festival held in October 1967. For the previous three months

* The author can attest to the nonsectarian criteria for hiring—in the case of foreigners, at least—as he was offered a position at Sōka University.

preparations for this spectacular pageant had claimed the spare time of some 60,000 members. The result was an impressive demonstration of mass dancing and gymnastic exercises, synchronized with symphonic music and a constant succession of vivid, animated scenes created by a 40,000-member card section spread across one side of the stadium. Dancers symbolized Gakkai ideals. The more explicit themes were quite secular, especially that of the finale: "World Peace" was spelled out by the card section in fifteen different languages, interspersed with panoramic views of famous scenes from fifteen corresponding countries.

The program represented a tremendous investment of time and energy by the participants, but the psychic rewards were apparently worth it. Participating members questioned by the author responded with stories of gratitude, joy, and pride; and as all the participants passed before President Ikeda in the reviewing stand, enthusiasm and happiness radiated forth. Letters to the *Seikyō Shimbun* expressed the same feelings, in a more reflective vein.

In this, the Culture Festival of the century, I handsomely fulfilled my duty. Before Ikeda *sensei* I displayed my strength to the utmost.

I don't know why it was, but after the program ended tears began to flow and I couldn't stop them. It was the first time in my life I had been so moved. Thinking upon it, I realized that it had been three months of practice. The faces of my father and mother and of my seniors who urged me on in everything during that time floated into view. I wish to say "thank you" from my heart.

Until I participated in the practice for the Culture Festival I couldn't do *gongyō* [prayer before the gohonzon] satisfactorily. Now it is different; with hope for the future, I am filled with a feeling of wanting to grow up into a truly pure-hearted man of talent who is of service to society.

—Terazono Tatsuzō, high school student, 15.

I was able to participate in the long-wished-for Tokyo Culture Festival and to revolutionize my life wonderfully.

As I marched around the ground [at the finale] wrapped in the applause of the spectators, events from the time of the 1964 Tokyo Culture Festival floated vividly into view. At that time I was working in a laundry; I was opposed in various matters by the boss, and worried constantly about working hours. Moreover, the pay was low, so that economically, too, it was an impossible situation. In such conditions, I—at the time a *han-chō*—was encouraged by my seniors and, setting my teeth, kept on practicing and participated.

At that time I resolved, "I'll participate in the next Culture Festival in more relaxed circumstances, for sure," and from then on prayed continuously. As a result, I was able to get a job as a cook at the T. Construction

Company and to solve my time and money problems at the same time. Thus, today I could participate in the Tokyo Culture Festival in good spirits.

As I marched around the stadium my breast filled with emotion. I could not help feeling from the bottom of my heart "By believing, I have succeeded."

—Yamada Yōko, cook, 25.[86]

This identification of medium with message is a salient aspect of the Gakkai's socialization program. In this program the Society attempts to encompass all the social relationships of its members. This sort of inclusivity is achieved by setting up multiple, reinforcing channels of communication between the organization and its members—peer and interest groups, the examination system, and mass media—supplemented by person-to-person contact. But despite the magnitude of the system, the member does not feel himself the prisoner of an oppressive indoctrination apparatus. The Society has managed to keep the apparatus humanized through the intimate links built into the vertical line substructures. Indeed, the Gakkai's program is humanized through the very medium of communication and socialization, be it a convivial zadankai, a friendly peer or interest group, a towering building at the Taisekiji, or a mass meeting pulsating with an energy born of faith.

CHAPTER 6

Goals and Internal Government

A NUMBER of factors bear upon the goal-attainment processes of the Sōkagakkai: how goals are determined; where the Society finds the financial and public support to sustain its efforts; what role the Gakkai elite plays in setting goals and mobilizing members; and why the Gakkai seems able to pursue its aims with little of the internal dissension that often plagues the ambitions of social and political movements. All warrant close attention, and all shed light on the nature of the Society's internal government.

PROJECTING AND REACHING GOALS

The ways in which the Gakkai formulates objectives and then goes about achieving them are not always open to outside observation. One might envision the process as a flow upward, from all branches of the Gakkai toward the highest leaders, of interests, proposals, and demands that may be turned into official policy, and a subsequent flow downward of binding decisions designed to realize the policy goals set by the top leaders. One perceives with relative clarity the downward process; the upward flow, however, must be largely surmised.[1]

The first move toward eventual attainment of some goal is often made by President Ikeda himself, who instructs an appropriate organ, such as the Planning Department of the General Executive Bureau or the Executive Staff of the Youth Division, to draw up concrete proposals concerning a particular problem.[2] These plans are then taken up at the vice-general directors' meeting, where a preliminary decision is reached. In important matters the full Board of Directors convenes before the president for thorough discussion, with the aim of unanimity. (The Board of Directors customarily convenes monthly.) When a consensus is apparent the president states it as a decision; if unanimity cannot be reached, the president may, on the basis of the viewpoints advanced, reach a decision on his own and present it as the official ruling.[3]

The Planning Department and Youth Division Executive Staff may themselves generate policy proposals, as may the vertical line, the various branches of the Culture Bureau, and the leaders of other peer groups. The leaders of all of these structures are directors, and therefore can bring any interests that develop in their divisions directly before the Board of Directors' meetings. The most noteworthy channel of interest articulation from the standpoint of organizational stability is the vertical line. It would seem that the president solicits the rank-and-file viewpoint in some matters, through the mediation of leaders on each level; in any event, the vertical line acts as a sounding board through which current problems and opinions are carried upward toward the elite.

Another channel for the articulation of interests that may influence policies and objectives is the Citizens' Livelihood Discussion Centers, the Kōmeitō grass-roots communication system. This system, to be discussed more fully in Chapter 8 as an adjunct of the Kōmeitō, consists of offices throughout Japan where any citizen may voice demands, complaints, or political opinions. The consequence of these discussion centers and of the vertical-line system has been that Gakkai members in general perceive an open communication channel linking them with the top echelons of the Society. One of the virtues of the Society customarily mentioned by members is that leaders care— that they visit meetings on the kumi level and are receptive to the views of the rank and file. Whatever the original source of the ideas ultimately articulated by President Ikeda as official Gakkai objectives, members seem persuaded that they themselves have a role in formulating these goals.

Once policy has been framed at the Gakkai summit it is relayed to the head leaders' meeting, at which leaders from all branches of the Society are present.[4] From this point on, two patterns of policy implementation exist, one overt, the other tacit. In the first case, slogans and goals for the coming month (or year) are announced on the basis of decisions reached in the monthly meetings of the Board of Directors. Then begins a succession of gatherings, recorded in the *Seikyō Shimbun*: headquarters leaders' meetings, headquarters general meetings, leaders' meetings of all subordinate organizations (vertical, horizontal, peer, and functional), general meetings of the members of these organs, and finally sequential gatherings of suborgans down to the minor block* and kumi level. At each meeting the directives from above are presented and explained, and hortatory phrases based on the higher-level slogans are declared to be the suborgan's action policies for the period in question. Thus by the time a kumi holds its zadankai the members are generally aware of the new goals.

The give-and-take of the zadankai clarifies, and so reinforces, the messages already received through the mass media. Overt disagreement with official policy at this level is unheard of, or at least never admitted. In time, however, certain policies may prove beyond the energy or ability of the members, who may report great difficulty in achieving goals, or may even defect when certain activities are insisted on. Such signs alert lower-level leaders to problems in attaining set goals, and these leaders are expected to pass word up to the higher goal-setting echelons of the Society.

The less overt pattern of implementation can be discovered in such far-reaching policy changes as the gradual displacement of President Makiguchi's teachings, the moderation of the shakubuku program, and the increasing politicization of the Gakkai. Such developments may spread downward along lines roughly similar to those taken by expressed policies, although leaders' meetings probably supersede general assemblages as the agents of communication. The outsider's means of discovering such changes, of course, are the Gakkai's mass media and observed shifts in the behavioral patterns of the Society, from which changes in strategy can be inferred. In the realization of either manifest or undeclared programs, however, to the average Gakkai member the key agents are probably the vertical and horizontal lines. And of these, the vertical line primarily converts and socializes, while the horizontal line, basically a mechanism for attaining goals, efficiently disseminates information and mobilizes the membership toward the realization of policy.

The block system of the horizontal line, established in 1955, was designed to overcome the inherent weakness of the vertical line: its nongeographical basis. A geographically oriented structure lent itself to more efficient administration, and unification of geographically proximate members brought another type of social relationship—neighborhood acquaintances—within the organizing scope of the Gakkai.[5] Since its inception the horizontal line has assumed several

* The basic unit of the horizontal line: a small organization based on a geographic area to which all Gakkai members in that area automatically belong.

charges: it is the system through which the *Seikyō Shimbun* is distributed; it is the vehicle for an extensive program of lectures and for the voicing of local problems; and perhaps most important of all, it is the crucial electoral structure.

In all elections except those for the national constituency of the Upper House, seats are won through local concentrations of electoral power. Thus, if the Gakkai wishes to translate its numbers into assembly seats it must be able to mobilize localized groups of Gakkai members. It is impossible to organize election campaigns through the vertical line. The members of a single kumi may be spread throughout a large city like Tokyo, and the candidate each must be familiar with is not the one campaigning where the unit chief resides, but the Gakkai-supported candidate from the member's own district. The Gakkai, in order to reckon its electoral strength in each district (and thus to decide whether or not it will put up a candidate), must have some structure through which it can gather statistics on geographically based power. As the political efforts of the Gakkai have multiplied, the horizontal line has been elaborated; in 1957 the general block system was established in Tokyo, and in 1961 the present national net of joint blocks was set up. The Gakkai's success in calculating its electoral strength accurately and attaining its electoral goals attests to the skill with which the Society has developed this structure.

FINANCE AND PUBLIC RELATIONS

In order to maintain itself and ultimately to accomplish the mission of Nichiren Shōshū, the Gakkai requires money—as well as a favorable climate of public opinion (a subject we shall return to in the pages that follow). Whether or not the Gakkai is borne up by faith as it claims, no organization of its magnitude, with such a multifaceted program of activities, can continue long without a solid financial base. The Gakkai publishes no accounts of its financial activities, a policy that has touched off numerous rumors, which are eagerly exploited by the Society's opponents, concerning its sources of funds. One recent estimate placed the regular expenses of the Gakkai at $28 million, with income exceeding outgo.[6] According to President Ikeda, income—apart from the Gakkai's publishing activities—comprises contributions from the members of the Financial Department and money raised in special donation drives among the whole membership. There are no regular assessments levied upon the members aside from the obligation to buy certain publications. Ninety per cent of the Society's income is donated to the Taisekiji and the construc-

TABLE 6

Sōkagakkai Journals and Newspapers, 1966

Publication	Circulation	Monthly Rate Yen	Cents
Seikyō Shimbun			
(Holy Teachings News)	3,000,000/dy.	300	80
Seikyō Gurafu			
(Holy Teachings Graphic)	1,100,000/wk.	160	40
Dai Byaku Renge			
(Great White Lotus)	1,500,000/mo.	50	15
Tōdai (Lighthouse)	50,000/mo.	50	15
Kibō no Tomo (Friends of Hope)	350,000/mo.	130	35
Ushio (The Tide)	430,000/mo.	120	33
Shūkan Genron (Weekly Forum)	500,000/wk.	160	40
Kōmei Shimbun			
(Clean Government News)	1,300,000/dy.	200	55
Dai San Bummei (Third			
Civilization) and others	200,000/mo.	150	42

SOURCE: Yui Hiromichi, *Datō Sōkagakkai* (*Down with the Sōkagakkai*), p. 17.

tion of local Nichiren Shōshū temples; the balance, plus publishing profits, goes into construction and maintenance of Gakkai headquarters buildings and local halls.[7]

The Financial Department is something of an elite group within the Gakkai. Membership is voluntary and selective: if applicants demonstrate firm belief and solid theological knowledge, their financial situation is investigated and they are interviewed by leaders; if all is satisfactory, appointment by Gakkai Headquarters follows.[8] Upon appointment the member receives a distinctive gold Gakkai lapel badge, in contrast to the lead badge worn by the rest of the members. Members of the Financial Department are obliged to contribute a minimum sum to the Gakkai annually. At present this sum is 8,000 yen (about $22); since there are an estimated two million persons in the department, the annual income from this source is at least $40 million.[9]

Slightly less profitable (once overhead has been deducted) is the Sōkagakkai's publishing empire. The Gakkai pours forth a flood of written material, from Nichiren's works and exegeses thereof to children's picture magazines. Table 6 shows only the Society's periodical literature as of 1966; even if one excludes the *Kōmei Shimbun*, the Kōmeitō party paper, the Gakkai's income remains an estimated $45 million per year. In addition, the Seikyō Press, Ushio Publishing Company, and other Gakkai subsidiaries offer over one hundred titles, including the collected lectures and writings of presidents Toda and Ikeda and a number of works by nonmembers that are unrelated to the Gakkai. The figures in Table 6 were compiled for an anti-Gakkai book, and may have been inflated to emphasize the financial magnitude of this supposedly religious organization. They do, however, reflect the partial statistics available from scattered sources. Taken as a gross representation of the Gakkai's publishing enterprises, the figures indicate that the Gakkai's annual income from its periodicals is roughly 19 billion yen, or $54 million.

In addition to the revenue these publishing activities bring in, they conserve manpower. Since Gakkai leaders receive no pay at all for their roles in the organization, on lower levels of the Society the leaders must hold fulltime outside jobs; but many of the top-echelon leaders, including President Ikeda, hold salaried positions in the Seikyō Publishing Company and other commercial Gakkai subsidiaries, sinecures that allow them to devote their full energies to the Gakkai. The Society also conserves on certain membership apparatus and activities. Gohonzon, prayer beads, and badges must be bought upon entry (total cost, about two dollars), and everyone is expected to subscribe to the *Seikyō Shimbun*. Periodic pilgrimages to the Taisekiji are also expected; although more a privilege than an onerous duty, these create more costs that are borne by the individual members. Any travel expenses a rank-and-file member incurs in the course of his Gakkai activities must be paid out of his own pocket. But because participation in these activities brings divine blessings, the expense is rarely begrudged by the members; and such indirect levies upon the members are themselves a blessing for the Society, enabling it to avoid what would otherwise be a great cash drain.

In fact, the most spectacular source of Gakkai financial backing is neither the Financial Department nor the publishing business, but rather the members. As mentioned above, no regular levies are imposed upon the members; but the dramatic and paradoxical examples of financial commitment seen in the lower-class religious groups of other countries are also found in the Gakkai.[10] The most striking example of giving is the donation drive. Such drives are staged for the benefit of special construction projects, but the financial response is such that the costs of the project involved are invariably surpassed, thus providing the Gakkai with additional working capital.

In 1961 the Gakkai held a four-day contribution drive to finance the construction of the Grand Reception Hall at the Taisekiji. The goal was one billion yen (close to $2.8 million); the faithful donated almost 3.2 billion yen (about $8.9 million).[11] In 1965 another drive was held to benefit the projected Main Hall of Worship at the temple. This time the goal was five billion yen (about $14 million). Again the campaign lasted four days; in this period the Gakkai claimed that over eight million of the faithful participated, giving an average of 4,500 yen ($12.50) apiece, for the astonishing total of 35.5 billion yen —almost $100 million.[12]

Besides supplying vital income, the publishing activities of the Society form one of several agencies designed to shape the relationship of the organization to the rest of Japanese society. The Gakkai's publications, especially its periodicals, depict the Society as an assemblage of happy, brotherly fellow citizens at work for the salvation of their entire nation and all mankind. The *Seikyō Shimbun*, which is used extensively in shakubuku, and the *Seikyō Graphic*, a slick and colorful magazine along the lines of *Life* and *Look*, are instrumental in this regard.

The Ushio Publishing Company plays a less obvious role among the publishing enterprises of the Society. This nominally independent firm publishes *Ushio*, a nonsectarian monthly that carries articles of general interest, including pieces by such external figures as Imperial Prince Mikasa and Edwin O. Reischauer. The magazine's circulation compares favorably with that of other magazines of the same type. For although most of its buyers are probably Gakkai members, *Ushio* presents an unbiased, nonpartisan picture. The Ushio New Books series, which includes such titles as *Mao Tse-Tung and Liu Shao-Chi*, *Gladstone*, and *The Japanese in Brazil*, is also nonsectarian.

The Ushio Publishing Company is but one of a number of organizations helping to improve the Society's public relations. These organizations, coordinated with the Sōkagakkai's Culture Bureau, promote activities of a largely or completely nonsectarian nature, and are open to nonmembers "who approve of the Society's ideals."[13] These front groups (see Appendix C, Fig. C.2) include: the Institute of Buddhist Philosophy (Buppō Tetsugaku Kenkyū-jo); the Institute of Occidental and Oriental Thought (Seiyō Tōyō Shisō Kenkyū-jo); the Institute of Politics and Economics (Seiji Keizai Kenkyū-jo); the Institute of Oriental Science (Tōyō Gakujutsu Kenkyū-jo); the Asian People's Association (Ajia Minzoku Kyōkai); the Institute of Asian Culture (Ajia Bunka Kenkyū-jo); the Democratic Music Association (Minshu Ongaku Kyōkai or Min'on); the Democratic Drama Association (Minshu Engeki Kyōkai or Min'en); and the Fuji Symphonic

Orchestra (Fuji Suisō Gakudan). The most noteworthy of these groups are Min'on and Min'en: each provides opportunities for participation in musical and dramatic activities and a slate of performances for audiences of all ages. Min'on supports a host of small local musical groups, and in 1967 claimed a membership of one million (of which an estimated 20 per cent were not Gakkai members).[14] In the same year the Association also sponsored tours to Japan by the Novosibirsk Ballet and the Twentieth Century Ballet company of Belgium. On a smaller scale, it stages Sunday concerts in the danchi. Other front organizations include the Kōmeitō and the Gakkai's projected labor union. The Kōmeitō is important enough to be treated separately in the chapters that follow; at this writing the labor union is still in the early planning stages and may be considered a future development.

The final, obviously important structure for enhancing the public image of the Society is the Sōkagakkai Public Relations Bureau. Under the direct supervision of the Board of Directors, its formal duty is the betterment of relations between the Gakkai and its environment. The author has had very little contact with this organ; however, if the Bureau's output is proportionally greater than that of the Overseas Bureau's own public relations division—which turns out quantities of press releases, reprints of Gakkai publications and related articles, and general informative material—it is indeed active in linking the Society with its surroundings.

THE ROLE OF THE GAKKAI ELITE

The formal capacity of the president of the Sōkagakkai, in the words of President Ikeda, is as the "representative of the believers."[15] He is the chief officer of the Gakkai, the chief supporter of Nichiren Shōshū, the chief guide in matters of faith.[16] He is teacher, father, brother, comrade; to some members he is probably the Buddha as well. His title does not do justice to his stature in the organization. Formal roles, as Vice President Akiya Einosuke explains, do not necessarily reflect accurately the operational realities of the Gakkai.[17] Nevertheless, an examination of three versions of the *Rules of the Religious Juridical Person "Sōkagakkai,"* dated 1957, 1962, and 1966, indicates how Ikeda's role within the Society has expanded.[18]

According to the 1957 *Rules,*

(1) The president of the Gakkai is one of seven "responsible officials."
(2) These officials are elected by the Board of Directors.
(3) The president is elected by the responsible officials.

(4) He is dismissable by the Board of Directors.
(5) He is appointed for life except as stipulated in (4).

By 1962 the number of responsible officials had grown to thirty-one.
The *Rules* now stipulated that

(1) The president is also the "official representative" of the Gakkai.
(2) He is one of the responsible officials and is elected by them; they, in
turn, are elected by the Board of Directors.
(3) He is dismissable by the Board of Directors.
(4) His term is limited to four years.
(5) He convokes the Board of Directors and chairs the board meetings.

These last two points limit the efficacy of the provision for the president's dismissal; but the specification of a term of office appears decisive. For those who choose to view the interregnum between the
tenure of Toda and Ikeda as a period when various groups were vying
for power, the limitation on tenure may be considered as a check
imposed upon Ikeda by his competitors. Be that as it may, the current set of *Rules* under which the Gakkai ostensibly operates leaves
no question concerning the ascendancy of Ikeda, and is in vivid contrast to the 1962 version. In sum,

(1) The president is also the "official representative" of the Gakkai.
(2) He is manager of all its affairs.
(3) He has the power to convoke the Leaders' Meeting (of all twenty-one
responsible officials).
(4) He appoints and dismisses all of the other responsible officials.
(5) He appoints and dismisses all of the vice-general directors, the directors, and all "other necessary officials."
(6) He holds office for life.
(7) He chooses his own successor.

The responsible officials of this latest set of *Rules* are apparently
the general director and the general administrators. The position of
general administrator is a comparatively new one, created in February
1966. The previous top administration had consisted of the president,
the general director, the vice-general directors, and the directors. It is
probable that this group became unwieldly (by early 1967 the entire
Board of Directors totalled almost eight hundred persons), for in
1966 when Director Izumi Satoru became general director, a General
Affairs Committee of six general administrators was created below
him.[19]

At the same time, Izumi became head of the newly instituted Men's
Division. The net effect of these changes was a relative weakening of
the Youth Division, since of the six new general administrators only

three had notable records in the Youth Division, and the general directorship of the Gakkai was transferred from former Youth Division leader Hōjō Hiroshi to Izumi, leader of the Men's Division and a Makiguchi convert. Ikeda seemed to have taken supreme command, with Izumi as a link with the past and Takeiri Yoshikatsu, one of Ikeda's protégés and chairman of the Kōmeitō, as a concrete illustration of his power and a symbol of the Gakkai's politicization.[20]

In 1966, then, the Gakkai elite consisted of:

President: Ikeda Daisaku.

General Director: Izumi Satoru. Born 1911, entered the Gakkai 1940; a Makiguchi convert. Military Police warrant officer during the war; Member of Parliament until 1968. Administrative head of the Gakkai, but still looks more like a noncommissioned officer—beefy, brusque, and uncomplicated.

General Administrators: Hōjō Hiroshi. Born 1923, entered 1951; a Toda convert. Member of the aristocratic Hōjō family; nephew of Hōjō Shumpachi (exmember, prewar House of Peers, and former Kōmeitō Member of Parliament); educated at the Peers' School. Became Gakkai General Director in 1954 upon death of Harashima Kōji and held that office until February 1966. Now Member of Parliament. Serene and Buddha-like of countenance, a calmly confident man. Vice President since January 1970.

Tsuji Takehisa. Born 1918, entered during Makiguchi period. Longtime head of the Youth Division and public relations functionary. Committee Chairman of the Kōmeitō from the death of Harashima Kōji until replaced by Takeiri Yoshikatsu in February 1967; former Member of Parliament. Short and round, but conveys an impression of sharpness.

Morita Kazuya. Born 1926, entered 1942. Son of a Gakkai member; educated at Chūō University. In charge of Gakkai administration and, like Hōjō, occasionally rumored to be the top General Administrator; head of Sōka Schools. No political activity. Vice President since January 1970.

Shiraki Giichirō. Born 1919, entered before the war. Graduated from Keiō Higher School. Led expansion of Gakkai in the Kansai (Osaka-Kōbe-Kyoto) area. As General Administrator has regional responsibility for this area. Member of Parliament. A former professional baseball player, he still has an athlete's build and a broad, open approach.

Kodaira Yoshihei. Born 1921, entered during Makiguchi period. Graduate of Chūō University. His sphere as General Administrator is theory and study. Head of the Study Department. Member of Parliament.

Takeiri Yoshikatsu. Born 1926, entered 1953; a real Ikeda protégé. Schooling ended at the Army Air Force Officers' School. Formal political chief of the Gakkai; Member of Parliament and Chairman of the Kōmeitō.[21]

Since then the number of general administrators has increased to eighty-four. Some of the noteworthy additions are Akiya Einosuke, articulate and scholarly Waseda University graduate and head of the *Seikyō Shimbun*; stolid Tōhoku University graduate and Member of

Parliament Tada Shōgo; Yamada Tetsuichi, specialist in economic affairs and organizer of the Gakkai in the Nagoya area; and Meiji University graduate Ishida Kōshirō, former head of the Youth Division, Member of Parliament, and brother of an earlier leader of the YD (now invalided), Ishida Tsugio. Two young but very promising vice-general directors might also be mentioned: stocky, forthright, and positive Kuroyanagi Akira, Waseda graduate, Member of Parliament, and one of the Kōmeitō's chief hatchetmen whenever the party has a new scandal with which to belabor its parliamentary opponents; and Shinohara Makoto, Tokyo University graduate, editor of *Dai Byaku Renge*, and head of the Student Division.

One aspect of the topmost Gakkai elite that several observers have noted is the frequency of intermarriages and other kinship ties. None of the children or other relatives of either Makiguchi or Toda hold office in the Gakkai, though the Society asserts that they are all believers. But the relationship of the Ishida brothers has already been pointed out, and that of the Hōjōs, uncle and nephew. The fathers of Morita Kazuya and of the wives of Ikeda and Kuroyanagi Akira—Morita Teiji, Shiraki Kunji, and Imaizumi Tarō—are all vice-general directors.[22] Furthermore, the wives of Vice-General Director Fujiwara Yukimasa and Director Watanabe Jōkoku are sisters, and Akiya Einosuke is married to the sister of Ishida Tsugio.[23] And the wife of Abe Ken'ichi, Kōmeitō candidate for the governorship of Tokyo in 1967, is the elder sister of Hōjō Hiroshi.[24] It is possible that all these ties among the Gakkai elite bear on the fact that the Gakkai has not suffered from any noticeable internal divisions.

Below the level of the general administrators is the Board of Directors, which as of January 1970 had 2,291 members.[25] This figure includes the general director and the eighty-four general administrators, as well as 183 vice-general directors, and 2,023 directors. When added to the leaders of approximately 3,500 chapters throughout the country, this makes a total of roughly 5,700 high-level leaders in the Society.[26]

The total number of leaders, though indeterminate, is in the vicinity of 1.5 to 2.5 million.[27] No fixed information is available concerning the duties of the lower-level leaders, which appear to be considerable and diffuse. Leaders of blocks and minor blocks must see to it that lecture meetings are held, newspapers are delivered, and the vote is mobilized for elections. Chiku, han, and kumi chiefs are responsible for the sustained faith of their respective flocks and for attaining shakubuku goals.

No lower-level leader possesses any inherent power whatsoever; all powers are delegated from above, and responsibilities are emphasized far more than prerogatives. Leaders without specific powers are supported in their efforts to mobilize followers by two constraints operating on Gakkai members. The first of these is allegiance. The frequency of defections from the Society suggests that the members are largely a voluntary group with an internalized commitment. This commitment is partly to the Gakkai as a religion and partly to the Gakkai as a human group; once made, it bolsters an inclination to obey instructions from above. The second constraint is obligation: Gakkai members are usually the relatives, neighbors, friends, co-workers, or employees of other Gakkai members, and considerable social obligation may have been involved in their initial decision to join. After entry, the same obligations or social bonds contribute to sustained membership.

ELEVATION TO LEADERSHIP

One important Gakkai practice in attaining goals is internal promotion, which provides goal-attainment organs with the personnel they need. The primary consideration in the promotion scheme is personal achievement; the usual technique is co-optation. The usual sequence is promotion followed by training rather than the reverse. Ikeda admits that this sequence may result in temporary instability and substandard leadership, but insists that it is the best way to "cultivate men of talent."[28] In responding to the need for more skilled personnel, Ikeda himself is apparently differentiating between peer groups in the promotion process by cultivating "an intellectual class of ex-members of the Student Division."[29]

There are important exceptions to co-optation. Membership in the Finance Department is voluntary and depends on personal financial solvency and strength of faith. The Study Department is open to all members and rank is determined through competitive examination. Promotion along the vertical line follows from one's shakubuku performance and is largely automatic. But for positions in the horizontal line, in administration and the top leadership, and in the various functional groups, co-optation is the rule.

Of course the promotional processes overlap. Organizational mobility and flexibility is increased by the fact that the vertical line both creates and fills new status roles without adding to the tasks of the top echelons of the organization.[30] However, prospective kumi, han, and chiku chiefs must also meet standards of faith, peer-group respect, and emotional and behavioral stability.[31] Similarly, when new horizontal-line units are created, locally resident vertical-line officers are quite likely to be named as leaders.[32] In addition, Study Department rank is taken into consideration. Formal advancement is similar in the vertical and horizontal lines, and is bestowed from above. The offices of han-chō and below are handled by the chapter chief; district chiefs and above are named by the president. When a new chapter is formed the chief receives the chapter flag from the president personally. Block and minor block chiefs are appointed by the head of their general block; the president appoints chiefs of major blocks and above.[33]

The manner in which top leaders are recruited is unclear. According to the most recent version of the *Rules of the Sōkagakkai* all posts from the rank of director on up, plus all "other necessary officials," are filled and vacated at the discretion of the president.[34] The vague criteria of promotion are described by Gakkai officials in terms of strength of faith, leadership qualities, specific skills, and human attributes. And once in office, a leader is not exempt from the continuing selection process. In late 1966 President Ikeda announced that senior leaders and Study Department members would be periodically tested; those who failed twice in succession would be demoted one rank.[35] As for the president himself, the 1966 *Rules* firmly establish an apostolic succession. (To criticism of the undemocratic nature of this selection process the Gakkai responds that neither were Christ's disciples chosen by ballot.) In the event a successor is not designated, the presidency is to be filled by vote in the Leaders' Meeting.

Succession is one of the crucial processes in the development of a social movement. Braden cites several American religious sects that have disintegrated upon the death of the founder or seem likely to do so.[36] Cohn notes a similar propensity in the millenarian sects of medieval Europe.[37] The fragmentation of Nichiren's own sect shortly after his death illustrates the difficulty of establishing a stable succession pattern.

Toda Jōsei, despite having been second in command in the prewar Sōka Kyōiku Gakkai, succeeded to the presidency partly by default. According to Saki Akio and Oguchi Iichi he was chosen following the circulation of a petition among the members at large.[38] The Gakkai itself is vague regarding the actual mechanics of Toda's succession and seems to feel that his general aura of diffuse legitimacy—the result of prior service and imprisonment—was the only important factor.

In Ikeda's case the exact process of succession is again unclear, and again the mantle of legitimacy thrown over him by his predecessor appears to have been the major consideration. He was clearly the protégé of Toda, who, though never actually naming a successor, went so far as to state that the next president should be from the Youth Division (of which Ikeda became chief of staff in 1954).[39] According to Nakaba Tadakuni, a sympathetic and privileged observer, the leaders were generally aware of the relationship between Ikeda and Toda and, as the late General Director Harashima Kōji put it, that any other should have been chosen president was "unthinkable."[40]

According to Ikeda, the group that chose him was the Board of Directors;[41] he was subsequently presented to the annual meeting of the Society and approved by acclaim. At forty, he has perhaps another thirty years of leadership ahead of him. However, he believes that the president must be young, original, and energetic, which suggests that perhaps he will select the next president only some ten or twenty years hence. As yet, no one figure has emerged as Ikeda's protégé and possible successor.

INTERNAL COHESION

As we have seen, up to this time the Society has not been shaken by presidential succession; nor has it, throughout its history, experienced any noteworthy instances of integrative crisis. The cohesion or integration of a social organization rests on a pattern of behavior that permits relations between the component units of the collectivity to be adjusted, ensuring that all parts will contribute to the desired order of the whole. In collectivities such as the Gakkai, integration may be thought of as a process of internal control, and the Society's controls are built into the various structures we have already surveyed. It does not have at its command the material and physical controls available to some organizations; leaders do not draw any remuneration that could be increased or withheld to pressure them, and dissidents can defect without fear of coercion.* What the Gakkai does have is an intercommunicating pyramidal power structure with the president at its apex and an elaborate system of indoctrination and socialization.

The Gakkai has developed a communication system of the type that Elihu Katz and Paul Lazarsfeld consider to be the most effective: a system of mass media supplemented by personal communication at each level of the organization, and also by frequent interlevel com-

---

* See Etzioni, *Organizations* and "Structure," on this subject.

munication. Personal relationships, as the Society evidently is well aware, are crucial to effective communication. A strong case can be built for Katz and Lazarsfeld's position that "the movement of ideas in what might be called the 'lesser concepts' or 'everyday life' problems is more horizontal than vertical"; ideas in general "often penetrate the public as a whole slowly and—even more important—very often by interaction of neighbor on neighbor without any apparent influence of the mass media."[42] The Gakkai communication network minimizes the distortion of messages communicated in this way, since the Society can reach each member with the same message through several simultaneously functioning channels of communication (the vertical line, the horizontal line, a peer group, a newspaper or magazine). Furthermore, the presence of top leaders at zadankai and low-level lectures ensures direct links between the rank and file and the supreme elite. Thus the communication system, with its accessibility and responsiveness to any member, is a basic point to remember in considering the Society's measures to maintain an integrated organization.

In the indoctrination process, and of the various organizational levels, the zadankai is probably the most important integrative organ. It copes with tension on the most personal terms: the counseling of the kumi-chō may be the single factor determining a believer's continued membership or his defection. Lacking material controls (though where one member is employed by another the economic pressure can be considerable), the leader of the zadankai may apply symbolic-normative controls by invoking doctrine or the personal charisma of President Ikeda. He may also exert another important form of influence, ecological control—i.e., the indirect control of a person through changes in his environment.[43] If we assume that the zadankai is a social environment satisfying to its participants—and observation shows that it is indeed a special, if not the primary, focus of the loyalties of members—it follows that the zadankai leader's ability to manipulate the environment of each individual in an approving or condemnatory direction increases the integrative capacity of the organization as a whole.

But although the zadankai is certainly one of the Society's sources of integrative strength, it can also be a disintegrative force in certain respects.

An important element in the internal strength of large organizations is their ability to capitalize on loyalties that are generated toward smaller groups within the organization. It is often the small face-to-face group that commands the deepest loyalties. . . . One of the problems of large organizations is that it is difficult to keep large purposes before the minds of small people. Consequently, organizations frequently devise a system of minor goals for individuals and smaller groups which altogether may fit into the larger purpose but which are close enough to the individual and to his levels of aspiration to be powerful as motivators.[44]

The Gakkai has certainly created its system of minor goals and groups. It must be careful, however, that these groups do not develop excessive autonomy.[45] Certainly, the possibility that another center of legitimate power might appear seems remote; the High Priest, who might be its logical focal point, is sequestered at the Taisekiji, and issues forth only for ceremonial occasions. Individual rival claims to power are in general weakened by the absence of revelatory pronouncements on doctrine or policy in the Gakkai—no member can claim divine legitimacy directly from Buddha and hope for general acceptance. A more probable locus of future competitive power is the Kōmeitō; as it becomes more established it could become a source of pragmatic political interests running counter to the religious goals of the Gakkai.

Possibly in an effort to forestall the appearance of groups at intermediate organizational levels that might develop into competing sources of interests, goals, or even power, the Gakkai discourages spontaneous horizontal gatherings of leaders on any level, in the Kōmeitō as well as the Society.[46] There seems to be a conscious policy of disapproval of any such gathering not held under higher Gakkai auspices and thus within official control; this policy hinders the possible collusion of intermediate groups in contravening official goals, and prevents the growth of any sizable interference between the elite and the members to be mobilized. A further restraint on possible factionalism is the role the president plays in the Society's operation. He alone defines all theological, political, and organizational problems and gives the final clarification of all goals. However his autonomy may be limited in reality, he appears from outside the Society to be a total, absolute ruler. Presumably he takes full cognizance of the differing views that may arise in the leaders' meetings, but the degree of opposition that he feels free to override is totally unknown to outside observers.

The Society's restraints and integrative controls to some extent explain its quiet history; but it is important to recognize, too, that those who object strongly to the integrative efforts of the Gakkai simply defect. They go quietly, but they do go. The large number of defectors (approximately two-thirds of those "converted") and the frequent notices in the *Seikyō Shimbun* that "the following persons are released from office:" indicate basic integrative failure. One reason for this failure is undoubtedly the nonselectivity of the Gakkai in its recruitment. When initial symbolic commitment is low and means of physical and material control are largely lacking, a staggering burden is placed upon the socializing agencies responsible for creating symbolically committed believers. Where active membership requires behavior (e.g. shakubuku) regarded as deviant by general society and, moreover, puts a strain on the believer in terms of the time and effort expected of him, the intensity of belief that must be instilled by the indoctrinating structures is all the greater.

Aware of this integrative problem, the Gakkai has periodically instituted remedial innovations. The Superintendent's Department (official translation of Tōkan-bu) was established to check up on former backsliders who have since rejoined, and to investigate reportedly opportunist members and doubting Thomases.[47] As the Society grew in geometric progression during the mid- and late 1950's, the horizontal line was developed to increase central control; high executives were appointed from Tokyo as regional headquarters chiefs, albeit with regional recommendation.[48] And relaxing the propagation drive and moderating the propagating style have probably also had integrative implications—although whether integrative concerns influenced these changes is not known.

It is the interaction of all of the structures mentioned in Chapters 5 and 6, and more, that constitutes the organizational entity known as the Sōkagakkai. The most significant characteristics of this entity as it performs the functions necessary to its continued existence and further growth are its peculiar inclusivity, its humanization, and a communication pattern in which, although content is important, the medium is almost equally as important as any message.

First, as has been pointed out, the inclusivity of the Gakkai's relationship with its members has important consequences for the organization's socialization, goal-attainment, and integration. In fact, if Gakkai-related groups can encompass within their activities almost all of the social experiences of Gakkai members, the mutually reinforcing influences thus brought to bear amount to constant socialization in the behavior patterns needed to achieve the Society's objectives. The incorporation of intimate human relationships and more functionally specific relationships into the formal organizational structure through the creation of the dual vertical-horizontal hierarchy, and the combination of line and staff roles for each member, both figure in the integrative process. And if, as some critics say, entry into the Gakkai can be best understood as an "escape from freedom," then this high degree of inclusivity may also be an important factor in recruitment.

Second, despite its mammoth size and elaborate organization, the movement has nevertheless managed to retain a human touch. Groups such as the Communists totally submerge the individual in the organization; all relationships are stringently commanding-hierarchical, and ties are impersonal. The Gakkai stresses individual happiness and self-expression; the teaching-paternal vertical line constitutes the core relationship structure, and its ties are diffuse and intimate. The elite express constant concern, care, and responsibility toward the rank and file, and the membership feels and responds to this sympathy and awareness. The humanistic element is a strong selling point in a society where such structures are lacking, and therefore, in order to strengthen his sense of security and belonging, a member may develop a receptivity to the official norms and goals of this gratifying social nexus. The member who feels satisfied in a human way, who benefits from a lowered level of interpersonal tension and sees his membership as one major cause of his well-being, is more likely to be a well-integrated member of the organization, which in turn finds all its tasks made easier as a result of its efforts at humanization.

Third, the Gakkai's communication system has important implications for all of the Gakkai's functions. The blanketing effect of the system certainly aids efforts at indoctrination; the personal channels in particular are crucial in the propagation process. Mobilization of the membership in the pursuit of any goal would be impossible without an effective intraorganizational communication system. The perceived responsiveness of the communication system and its accessibility to any member certainly aid integration, as does the constant stream of instructions to lower-level leaders concerning ways to increase the integration of one's own unit members with each other and of the unit with the larger organizational context. The content of the Gakkai's message to both members and prospective converts has been examined above; what should be reiterated here is the importance of the very media that carry the message. The congeniality, warmth, and happiness of the zadankai; the pulsating power and concentrated numerical strength of the mass meetings; the tranquilizing, mesmerizing effect of chanting the daimoku in unison; the impression of affluence and magnificence received at the Taisekiji; the youthful energy, devotion, and achievement symbolized by President Ikeda himself— all have a significance for the members far beyond their specific, overt message. The phenomenon of media as message is characteristic of most of the major structures of the Gakkai, and contributes to the efficient performance of all the functions requisite for its furtherance.

CHAPTER 7

The Sōkagakkai and Politics

THE ULTIMATE goal of the Sōkagakkai, as described in Chapter 2, is ōbutsu-myōgō (fusion of Buddhism and politics), actually the adoption of the principles of Nichiren Shōshū in all phases of human thought and behavior. While the Gakkai pursues human revolution, a sort of micro-ōbutsu-myōgō, the Kōmeitō works toward effecting the structural changes in society that will produce a social, economic, and political environment in which Nichiren Shōshū can be fully accepted.

Such structural changes are essentially of a synthesizing nature, for as the Buddha-nature is immanent in all worldly phenomena, so are the seeds of the ideal contained in all of the world's existing social, political, and economic systems. Each system, however, is flawed by undesirable aspects. The freedom of capitalism is subverted by its inequalities, and the equality of socialism is vitiated by its restrictions on free behavior. The spiritual self-fulfillment possible in Western "idealist" culture is offset by its otherworldliness, whereas the extreme worldly pragmatism of Marxist materialist culture obstructs the development of the spirit. Western liberal democracy, though admirably free, degenerates into license; Communist people's democracy, though more orderly and egalitarian, is repressive. Finally, although the modern nation-state offers unparalleled opportunities for social development, it has also led to the emergence of aggressive xenophobia and expansionism. Internationalism, by contrast, symbolizes the true unity of all mankind, but as yet this unity is insufficiently realized to allow states to dispense with military power in maintaining the security of peoples.

The Kōmeitō works toward the resolution of these four dichotomies, seeking to develop the virtues of each into four new systems: "neo-socialism" (shin shakaishugi), a "third civilization" (dai san *bummei*), "buddhist democracy" (*buppō minshushugi*), and "global nationalism" (*gurobaru nashonarizumu*), respectively. Obutsu-myōgō is the overall descriptive term for a world organized into these systems; however, since January 1967 the Kōmeitō has adopted the more secular term "middle-of-the-road politics" (*chūdō seiji*) to describe its methods and goals.[1]

The essence of middle-of-the-road politics, according to President Ikeda—who originally elaborated the phrase in the *Kōmei Shimbun* of January 1, 1967—is strict respect for human life and for humanitarian means in the treatment of people. Middle-of-the-road politics, he claims, is the framework within which the happiness of each individual and the prosperity of the entire society can be realized simultaneously. It is also the only road by which man can achieve a world without war. Politics itself, as the Gakkai perceives it, is the organization through the organs of public authority (the formal political structure) of all of society's oppositions and differences, and their direction, in cooperation, toward set goals.[2] Politics is thus an intermediary, a technician, an organizer that sets and achieves goals, thereby realizing ideal social conditions. President Ikeda, applying the concepts of chūdō seiji, says that the state should strive to achieve its goals without the use of power; the goals of the state are peace, happiness, and respect for life, and power is inherently incompatible with these objectives.[3]

The proper focus of politics, then, is the people—both as individuals to be treated equally and with the dignity befitting their basic humanity, and as a collectivity that can benefit from the adoption of humanitarian policies. The proper objective of politics is the unity of personal happiness and social prosperity. And its proper spirit is the respect for the human that springs from a deep sense of compassion. For a polity to be constituted in accord with these standards of focus, objective, and spirit, the people who live under it must hold a view of man (*ningen-kan* or *menschenbild*) characterized by an appreciation of the self as a free and autonomous being possessed of the competence to act as the subject, not simply the object, of social and political phenomena. The concomitant of this sense of "subjective competence" and freedom is a recognition[4] of the equality of others.[5]

But how is man to develop the respect for life that is requisite to truly democratic political systems? President Ikeda attributes the development of humanistic philosophies in the West to Christianity in general and Protestantism in particular.[6] But, as Ikeda sees it, there is no comparable philosophical foundation in Japan; consequently, Japan's new democratic institutions are like "a castle built on the sand."[7] Therefore, the most urgent task facing Japan is the establishment of popular attitudes toward mankind that will reinforce the nation's formally democratic political system.[8]

Japan's problems reflect those of the world—the established political forces are uniformly corrupt. The Socialists are guilty of sectarian parochialism: they represent not even the entire labor movement but only the organized workers as "agents of the labor aristocracy."[9] As for Communism, its record of bloody revolution and great human sacrifice is abhorrent, and in Japan the Communists are, in Ikeda's words, "the most irresponsible" party of all.[10] Complementing the street demonstrations of the left as a threat to parliamentary democracy is the one-party tyranny exercised in the National Diet by the conservative Liberal Democratic Party. The LDP is as partial as the Socialists, representing only the interests of finance and big business at home and toadying to the purposes of the United States in its foreign policy.[11] And in the center, the Democratic Socialist Party, although sharing numerous policies with the Kōmeitō, is far from satisfactory. Whereas the Kōmeitō has a firm philosophical backing for its policies, the DSP is vacillating, vague, and opportunistic; it has no consistent position and appears to stand in the center simply by reacting to either the Socialists or the LDP.[12] In fact, it is something of a "second LDP."

POLITICAL BUDDHISM

In theory, neither the Kōmeitō nor even Nichiren Shōshū need be present to restore the people's faith in government and to cause the formal polity to operate along the lines originally intended.[13] The essence of Buddhism can permeate politics "regardless of whether or not the men who engage in politics know Buddhism," for it is more a natural development of the "workings of the heart" than a form of religious discipline.[14] "Concretely, a politics that aims at mass welfare is itself congruent with the spirit of compassion. Even if one is not especially conscious of Buddhism, if he engages in politics with mass welfare as his aim, cannot we say that this itself is linked to the true meaning of Buddhism and is equatable with *ōbutsu-myōgō*?"[15] But in the degenerate age of Mappō such a spontaneous application of Buddhist principles is hardly to be expected. Thus the presence of the Kōmeitō becomes crucial. Only its philosophy "has immanent power to guide politics, economics, education, and culture, . . . [to] instruct all aspects of society and life and lead them toward the highest stage [of development]."[16] Only the Kōmeitō, which has secured a broad, grass-roots electoral base, can speak for the whole people. And among Japanese political parties, only the Kōmeitō has the special cultural integrity that stems from the indigenous roots of its beliefs and its origin among the Japanese masses.[17]

The idea of a religiously based political party attempting to instill faith in the populace has proved repugnant to many Japanese, however. The Gakkai and the Kōmeitō have been accused repeatedly of planning a state religion or of intending to limit, if not abolish, freedom of belief. Their denials have been myriad and vehement: Nichiren Shōshū is too vast, too magnificent in scope to be designated the state religion of one nation; to limit the eternal laws of the True Buddhism through a changeable constitutional sanction would be "degrading."[18] The Kōmeitō asserts that it will never restrict freedom of religion; nor does it even intend to draw its policies straight from scripture. According to President Ikeda, policy should be determined to suit the times and the people's welfare; although the Kōmeitō has entered the Lower House of the National Diet, the site of legislative power, "We are not in any way thinking of taking religious philosophy or religious teachings into the world of politics just as they are."[19] The Gakkai feels that the key to its political attitude is the distinction it makes between absolute and relative levels of existence.[20] Religion is on the plane of absolute, immutable, eternal truths. As the True Religion, Nichiren Shōshū can never compromise with heresy or accept misguided religious spirit. However, humans live most of their lives in a transient, unsubstantial world where judgments of good and evil are relative, made in light of the position and pursuits of the one judging. Politics is of this world; it operates, at best, in a context of compromise, tolerance, and principled expedience. Thus the Kōmeitō can enact secular legislation that benefits everyone, including heretics, and can protect the religious rights of everyone, even of heretical clerics, without fear of divine punishment.

But such pragmatism is not to be construed as restricting the relevance of Buddhism to only the spiritual plane. For, after all, the roots of contemporary political corruption, scandal, and even of natural calamities lie in the antagonism that some feel toward Buddhism; and conversely, "The reason a nation prospers is because it has the Law."[21] But to have the Law does not mean having clergy in government, a divine ruler, or papal control of secular government.[22] It means, rather, being blessed with statesmen who have assimilated religious principles and as a result are impelled to serve selflessly in the popular interest and to recognize the equality and freedom of all beings.

Still, many Japanese react with distrust. In self-defense, the Kō-meitō cites examples of religiously based political parties in other nations that do not appear to contradict the democratic process.[23] They frequently refer to the Christian Democratic Union of West Germany, the French Democratic Center, and the Italian Christian Democrats, and point out that the two major parties in both the United States and Britain are indirectly linked to pervasive cultural influences that have resulted largely from religious traditions. Not all of the protestations of the Society are accepted at face value by all observers, but insofar as official Gakkai doctrine is any indication, ōbutsu-myōgō seems to be no more dangerous to democracy than the concept of Christian democracy, which has proved in practice to be compatible with the democratic process.*

As the Gakkai envisions it, the democratic process wells up from below. Obutsu-myōgō can be achieved by converting the political leaders of a given state, or by converting the people, who then elect enlightened men as their representatives—the result in either case being the reconstruction of government along ideal lines. Nichiren attempted the first method; today the second is more suitable. Working with the populace is more efficacious, in the Gakkai's estimation, because ours is an age of "mass democracy": every citizen above a certain age has an equal right to political participation as a voter.[24] Because the masses can vote whom they wish in or out of office, and because the Gakkai defines the masses indiscriminately as "all of the people who constitute the present society," the Society's primary focus of activity is shakubuku on all levels of society.[25] Through shakubuku more and more people can experience human revolution and thereby join the enlightened mass that truly democratic institutions require for their base. Only thus can real ōbutsu-myōgō be achieved.

If human revolution and political change do not progress concurrently, the political system will be unstable. President Ikeda emphasizes that formal political structures must embrace popular political culture—i.e., the totality of the attitudes and orientations of a society

---

* In fact, on the surface at least, the Gakkai's proposed politico-religious relationship is more compatible with liberal democratic processes than was the Christian democracy presented in the encyclicals of Pope Leo XIII. See Gilson, pp. 142–46, 164–65, 188 *et seq.*, 205 *et seq.*, 222, 315 *et seq.*; and Pius XI, pp. 5, 10–11, 15, 20–21, 29, 38.

toward political behavior.[26] For a democratic system in a modern state to be stable, the people must be aware of their rights, duties, and obligations; if they are not, politicians will not feel constrained either to be responsive or to be honest.[27]

The dangers attendant on establishing democratic institutions on a base of popular ignorance are clearly noted by the Gakkai: "Democratic politics run by an ignorant mass will inevitably sink into ochlocracy. Freedom and equality, given to an ignorant, irresponsible, unaware mass, are only invitations to license, disorder, corruption, and chaos."[28] Nevertheless, the Gakkai and Kōmeitō profess a basic trust in the masses and their "capacity for reason."[29] "The masses are wise," and any leaders who treat them as if they were stupid will eventually be deserted by them.[30]

Though at present only a portion of the electorate (i.e. the Kōmeitō's supporters) may be sufficiently aware to form a foundation for democracy, the Kōmeitō hews steadfastly to the ideal of representing the whole people.[31] The party sees itself as assembling myriad popular interests and articulating them in the formal political system, thus becoming the representative of the will of the masses: "A political party, in its true sense, should harmonize the political interests of the people through its policies. For that purpose, political parties should be closely connected with the demands of the public."[32] And the other Japanese parties represent only fractional interests; they aggregate no varied interests nor do they care to.

At the governmental level, Buddhist democracy entails reestablishing the proper focus, objective, and spirit of politics. All the political ideals that have been mentioned in this study are to be achieved through Buddhist democracy: compassion, humanism, freedom, equality, trust, cooperation, and harmony between men; responsiveness and honesty in government; responsible political behavior among the people. Because democracy as the Gakkai defines it is a set of attitudes, rather than structures, it can be realized under any formal political, social, or economic system, whether capitalist, precapitalist, or communist.[33] But there is an optimal economic basis for Buddhist democracy, which the Kōmeitō calls *ningensei shakaishugi*, or "humanistic socialism" (also called "neo-socialism" and "mass welfare economy").

Humanistic socialism aims at the unification of social and individual welfare.[34] Exactly how this is to be achieved is not clear, but the process will be primarily redistributive and revisionist. (The policies of the Kōmeitō, to be discussed below, will give some suggestion of the process.) First, private ownership per se is not considered evil; values, however, must be redistributed sufficiently to correct injustice and gross inequalities.[35] Material equality is not equality of values: different people see different values in the same material goods. The goal of a humanistic socialist economy is to maximize the value position of each member of society; redistribution of values and materials is conducted toward this end.[36]

Second, neo-socialism intends to revise the capitalist system, not abolish it. Many features of the capitalist economy stand to be "corrected," says Tsuji Takehisa; free enterprise will not be prohibited, but "we will move in the direction of nationalization of basic industries" (e.g., coal, electricity, and other power sources).[37] A mixed economy will be constructed gradually; "we will not pursue any radical reform, and we flatly reject revolution by force."[38] Furthermore, decisions to nationalize particular enterprises will be made not on *a priori*, ideological grounds but pragmatically, by representatives of all classes, taking into account the interests of the populace, governmental bureaucracy, and owners.[39]

Similarly, parochial interests should not predominate in the international system. The Kōmeitō claims that it takes its foreign policy stance from the "absolute pacifism" of Nichiren (how the party arrives at this rather surprising interpretation of the generally contentious monk is not clear).[40] Today the world may have peace, but it is a fragile thing, propped up by fear and armaments.[41] The only solution to this dangerous situation will be an all-encompassing, pluralistic international community in which all nations can enjoy peace and prosperity without one people's happiness being sacrificed to any other's, and in which all cooperate toward mutual development and benefit.[42] At present, international conditions are such that unilateral disarmament would be unrealistic. As a first step toward reduction of tension, then, all peoples should come to understand that all men are one through their common possession of the Buddhanature. And they should know that, owing to the development of weapons that threaten the entire world, mankind has already become a single "community of fate"—a state of affairs that further enjoins nations to an awareness of a community of brotherhood.[43]

POLITICAL PARTIES OF THE GAKKAI

Nichiren, the spiritual predecessor of the Gakkai, had strong political views; as a result, his belief system included such specifically political ideas as ōbutsu-myōgō, the kaidan (see Chapter 2, page 33), and the

Utoku-O (the Virtuous Ruler, a national leader who would secure the faith from the incursions of evil priests and their secular henchmen). But Nichiren had no concrete ideas to offer regarding the form the state should take after kōsen-rufu had been achieved. He envisioned only the adoption of his teachings by rulers and people, and assumed that from this one circumstance would flow all of the changes necessary to the realization of utopia.

The pre-World War II offshoot of Nichiren Shōshū, the Sōka Kyōiku Gakkai, was also almost completely apolitical at first. The antiwar, antigovernment stand of the Gakkai in the early 1940's was taken in reaction to the actions of the authorities. And at the war's end Toda Jōsei was still apolitical.[44] But by early 1949, President Ikeda claims, Toda recognized that the time would inevitably arrive when the Gakkai would have to enter the political world, or kōsen-rufu would never be possible.[45] A more detached observer, Takase Hiroi, maintains that Toda knew any political efforts would be in vain, even suicidal, during the initial period of Gakkai growth, and he therefore limited himself to a simple religious emphasis on happiness versus unhappiness and gain versus loss.*

Whatever the case, the Sōkagakkai did make its political debut in the nationwide series of local elections held in April 1955.† It put up fifty-four candidates, who ran as independents, for seats in various local assemblies; fifty-three were elected and the Gakkai's amazing record of electoral success was begun (see Appendix D, Tables D.5–D.11). Since that time the Gakkai's share of the total electorate has swelled to over 10 per cent, and as of early 1970 it holds some two thousand seats in national and local assemblies, making it the third strongest political party in Japan by this index.

The Culture Department, which carried out as one of its functions the planning and administration of political operations, had been established in November 1954.[46] From then until 1961 the Gakkai was in the process of building its horizontal line and consolidating and politicizing the great numbers of new converts made since the beginning of the Great Shakubuku Drive in 1951. Political efforts were still somewhat tentative; platforms were modest, and candidates were nominally independent. But in 1961 the Culture Department was elevated in status to the Culture Bureau, and within it was created a new Political Department. In November of that year the Kōmei Seiji Remmei or Kōseiren (official translation: League of Fair States-

---

* For the reasoning behind the delay, see Takase, *Kōmeitō*, pp. 83–85.
† For the background of the decision to enter politics, see *ibid.*

men) was established, as an ostensibly independent political organization that would form its own policies and nominate its own candidates for public office. In this fashion the Gakkai divorced itself formally from politics; the relationship between the Society and its political arm was evident to any observer, but the Gakkai nevertheless insisted upon their separateness.[47]

Throughout their history the political structures of the Gakkai have been multifunctional. Most prominently, they have been designed for the attainment of those goals of the Gakkai that are amenable to secular interpretations and realization. The Gakkai's political subsystem is only a minor agent in the socialization of believers; the great majority of Gakkai members are socialized into the Society and then, as one part of this socialization process, politicized. Still, the political structures serve to occupy one more sphere of the daily life of the members, rendering the Gakkai's ideal relationship with the individual member even more inclusive, and providing additional channels of communication through which to bombard the member. It may also be inferred that the creation of an elaborate political substructure in the Gakkai has helped to integrate the Society internally. This, however, is only speculation. It is quite possible that structural change within the Gakkai has resulted from divisions of opinion and has been carried out in order to reestablish consensus. But the argument that such steps as the formation of Kōseiren or Kōmeitō have forestalled major dissension that could break out at any time over organizational ends or means lacks substantive evidence.

According to President Ikeda, the unprecedentedly chaotic conditions of contemporary Japanese politics called for the appearance of the Kōseiren: "There has never been a period in which, while democracy is preached, people and politics have been so isolated as in the case of present-day Japan."[48] Domestic party politics had degenerated into factional strife that ignored the interests of the people; international politics had been reduced to hostility and deadlock, posing the incessant threat that mankind would be annihilated in one nuclear cataclysm.

The result of this shameful condition was that honest people had withdrawn from the hopelessly corrupt and corrupting, misdirected, and irresponsible political system and had left it to the ever freer depredations of self-seeking, parochial, and venal party politicians.[49] International politics seemed beyond the comprehension, much less the control, of either statesmen or common citizens, and was drawing ever further away. Some new political force was needed that could arouse the people to the evils being perpetrated in the political world;

provide a new ideology that would define the situation and prescribe remedies; and introduce into the political system statesmen with high ideals and practical skills.

The Kōseiren, of course, was to be this new force. The Gakkai, feeling the sense of obligation instilled by Nichiren's teachings to serve one's fellowmen and ultimately lead them all to salvation, would "present its candidates to purify the political world and achieve the state of ōbutsu-myōgō."[50] It would do so not for its own sake, but in order that, through the enlightenment of Nichiren Shōshū, politics might be conducted "solely for the sake of the Japanese race and world peace."[51]

In one respect even the Gakkai's critics could agree that the Kōseiren was unmatched: its platform was nebulous to the point of vacuity. The program of the League of Fair Statesmen was ambiguous and contradictory, and embraced a mélange of proposals of the motherhood-flag-apple-pie variety, calculated to appeal to practically the entire population.[52] The League opposed revision, by conservative forces desiring rearmament, of the 1946 "Peace" Constitution; nuclear weapons; war; income taxes; and the tax burden borne by medium- and small-scale entrepreneurs. Among the measures it advocated were fair elections; recognition of Communist China; restoration to Japan of Okinawa and of the northern territories occupied by the U.S.S.R.; establishment of several new ministries and government bureaus; greatly expanded programs of aid, incentive, and subsidy to small enterprise and agriculture; increased public housing measures; and expansion of social security and other welfare programs.

How provisions for a drastically narrowed tax base and for bureaucratic proliferation and increased welfare were to be reconciled was a problem that bothered many observers. It was no doubt the result in part of simple political immaturity and naiveté. The Gakkai acknowledged its inexperience in the political arena, but promised to study diligently and to draw upon all available sources of information in order to overcome this shortcoming.[53]

Nevertheless, in the early 1960's, at least, the Gakkai-Kōseiren platform was still a conglomeration of oversimplification, overgeneralization, platitudes, and pie in the sky. Gakkai legislators were consistently in the minority and were neither feared nor respected by their colleagues; they could not enact any of their policies nor could they convince many people that the Kōseiren was a viable political force with a future. Meanwhile, in the Gakkai's opinion, the condition of the political system, at home and abroad, continued to deteriorate.

In July 1962, the Society created the Kōmeikai, or Fair Council, its members being the representatives of the Kōseiren in the Upper House.[54] The Kōmeikai was to be a nonpartisan liaison group in the Diet; but the Gakkai still pictured itself as an independent agent that would not stoop to becoming a partisan force in the Lower House. In April 1963 Kōseiren leader Ryū Toshimitsu could say "We are at present not in the least interested in running for the Lower House."[55] But one year later, in May 1964, the Society announced that it would put up thirty-two candidates in the next general election for the House of Representatives. This step marked a turning point in the Gakkai's political history.

The decision to enter the Lower House appeared as part of a statement entitled "Demands of the Times and of the People," in which the Society called for the creation of a new party, one that would clean up politics.[56] The statement defined the international situation as one wherein a highly mechanized civilization had combined fearsome weapons and political incompetence to produce a "balance of fear" between two fragmented and unstable blocs of nations, whose guiding ideologies were obsolete, mistaken, and so contradictory as to render détente impossible.[57] Rampant nationalism and racism aggravated the situation. In addition, particular conditions within Japan necessitated the emergence of a revolutionary new party. According to the "Demands," these conditions were:

(1) The poverty of politics and the isolation of the masses.

(2) The political distrust and apathy of the people.

(3) The confusion and diversity of thought.

(4) The ideological bankruptcy of youth, stemming from egoism and an appetite-oriented view of values.

(5) The essential collapse of the bicameral system and the stalemate in government brought on by the opposition of the two major parties.

(6) The corruption of the power structure brought on by factional politics.

(7) The constraints of national restrictions on the resolution of problems by local government.

(8) The urgings of the press and of the intelligentsia—the necessity of a third party and the expectation of politics with a religious sense.

(9) The heightened political capability of the Kōseiren.

(10) The increased rate of abstention of Gakkai members from Lower House elections (for the reason that there are no parties or men worth voting for).

(11) The wishes of the members of the Sōkagakkai Youth Division.[58]

The corruption and pettiness of all of the existing parties, and thus of the party system itself, were the primary targets of the Gakkai's attack.[59] In fact, according to Ikeda, Japanese democracy was still a facade. The new institutions were not built on any ideological or philosophical basis—the old feudal and authoritarian political habits were simply operating within the new structures to negate their intended functions.[60] To fill the philosophical void and thus give substance to Japan's democratic promise, a new political party was a historical necessity.

Accordingly, in November 1964 the Kōmeitō was founded.* The commitment to seek representation in the Lower House, which in Japan as in Great Britain is the only real seat of parliamentary power, marked the Society's full assumption of a political role. It was the first open admission that the Gakkai's political activity aimed at political takeover through the machinery of the parliamentary system.

KŌMEITŌ STRUCTURE

The Kōmeitō has stressed from its inception that it is a party of all the people. One need not be a Gakkai member in order to join (although since one should be in agreement with the principles and policies of the party, most nonbelievers are effectively ruled out); the recommendations of two party members suffice.[61] By early 1967 the reputed membership of the Kōmeitō was 200,000 persons.[62]

The Sōkagakkai is quite adamant about distinguishing between the Society itself and the Kōmeitō. According to one Gakkai publication the Kōmeitō is simply another political party supported by a nonpolitical organization, just as the Democratic Socialists are supported by the Dōmei labor federation and the Socialists by the Sōhyō labor federation.[63] The Society also draws a distinction in objectives; as Ikeda says, "the Gakkai is faith; the Kōmeitō is action."[64] The Kōmeitō is but one aspect of the Society's overall scheme of world conversion. The Gakkai, by disseminating the teachings of the True Buddhism, strives to achieve human revolution in every member of the human race, eradicating in each the heretical sources of unhappiness. The Kōmeitō, by contrast, strives for a revolution through the ballot box, the elimination of social and political contradictions, of injustice, and of collective poverty and misery.

But in reality, the Gakkai and the Kōmeitō are one and the same. According to President Ikeda, their coexistence is analogous to a single human viewed in his religious and political roles; the Gakkai and the party are "a single body with different names. . . . The Kōmeitō is strictly a religious political party . . . apart from the Sōka-

* And the Kōmeikai was dissolved.

gakkai there is no Kōmeitō."[65] All of the Kōmeitō's Central Executive Committee members hold vice-general directorships or some higher post in the Gakkai; looking from the other direction, one finds Ikeda recognized as "the creator of the Kōmeitō, the doctrinal leader."[66] There is, moreover, an almost complete overlap in general memberships[67] between the two organizations—which is not surprising, since Ikeda has stipulated that all Kōmeitō leaders and representatives must be "revolutionized" men, i.e. believers.[68]

This structural overlap is crucial to the Kōmeitō's conduct of electoral campaigns. The secret to the amazing record of electoral success compiled by the Kōmeitō and its predecessors is the block system of the Gakkai. The Kōmeitō has a more highly developed grass-roots organization than any other political party in Japan; nevertheless, the horizontal line of the Gakkai permits direct access to a far larger proportion of the electorate than could ever be achieved through either the Livelihood Discussion Centers or the street-corner speeches at campaign time. In addition, candidates and incumbent representatives visit local zadankai regularly; this contact with the rank and file is an opportunity both for vertical intercommunication and for intensive presentation of party policies.

The effectiveness of the Gakkai's communication system can be seen in the highly disciplined vote the Society turns out in the national constituency elections for the House of Councillors (see Appendix D). Gakkai mass media have nationwide coverage; thus each Kōmeitō candidate can carve out with considerable precision a region with enough Gakkai members and sympathizers to guarantee his own election, without drawing off an appreciable number of votes from the other Kōmeitō candidates in the national constituency. Another index of the effectiveness of Gakkai person-to-person communication is a 1965 survey on voting behavior in which the question was asked, "How do you decide what candidate to vote for in the national constituency election?"[69] As the distribution of responses shows (see Table 7), personal communication channels (friend's request; acquaintance) were far more important to the Kōmeitō than to any of the other parties.

The structure of the Kōmeitō is highly differentiated; however, the fact that its leaders all hold several offices suggests that a small number of persons at the top exercise general control. The nominal apex of the Kōmeitō organization is the party convention (see Appendix C, Fig. C.3), which is held annually with occasional "extraordinary conventions" falling between; but the party convention is actually more of a "policy announcement meeting" than a policy-mak-

TABLE 7

Vote-Deciding Factors in the 1965 National Constituency Election

| Deciding Factors | Respondents by Party | | | | National Sample as a Whole |
	Liberal Democrats	Socialists	Democratic Socialists	Kōmei	
Radio, television, press	53%	60%	47%	29%	51%
Official party bulletins	35	44	37	15	33
Speeches heard	15	23	11	17	15
Friend's request	8	8	3	15	7
Acquaintance with candidate	11	7	16	40	9
Nothing in particular	12	5	16	10	17
Total	134%	147%	132%	126%	132%

NOTE: Total percentages are the result of multiple responses.

ing or nominating convention.[70] At the February 1967 convention, for example, new appointments in accord with previous decisions of the Central Executive Committee were announced. Then one of the vice-committee chairmen, Hōjō Hiroshi, announced that Abe Ken'-ichi would be the Kōmeitō candidate in the forthcoming Tokyo gubernatorial election. Various speakers presented the party platform for the April series of local elections. And then the convention was adjourned, having taken only a few hours.[71]

There was no move–second–vote procedure, nor any debate. But to doubts about the democratic nature of the convention the Kōmeitō replies that, owing to extensive debate at lower levels of the party, by the time the convention is held all variances have been resolved. And, in fact, in neither the content of the policies nor the reception of the candidates presented at these conventions does one find any suggestion that measures are taken "by high-handed leadership without regard for the choices of the rank and file."[72]

Supreme party power is de facto in the hands of the Central Executive Committee and the Secretariat. The first Committee chairman, Harashima Kōji, died in December 1964 and was succeeded by present Gakkai General Administrator Tsuji Takehisa, a member until 1968 of the Upper House. In February 1967 Tsuji was replaced by General Administrator Takeiri Yoshikatsu, a member of the Lower House—a change that reflected the new importance of the Lower House in the Gakkai's political scheme. The Central Executive Committee, under the guidance of its chairman, specifically controls policy and strategy; and the Secretariat, next in order of importance, supervises the organizational structure and all its activities. Heading the CEC under Takeiri is vice-chairman Shiraki Giichirō. The whole Committee is composed of forty persons (as of February 1970), of whom thirteen are general executives of the Society; all are important Gakkai leaders.[73]

The members of the CEC are co-opted; the Committee also fills all other party offices.[74] And although it calls on an extensive array of policy-making committees and subcommittees, according to Chairman Takeiri the decisive word on any matter rests with a few top members of the CEC.[75]

There are two sources of interests that provide material for policy proposals. The first, seldom noted openly by the party, is the Sōkagakkai. It is certain that determinations made at the top of the Society on doctrinal interpretations, religious goals, and problems from the Gakkai rank and file will all be articulated through the Kōmeitō if the Gakkai leaders favor a secular solution. The second source is the hierarchy of the Kōmeitō itself. The party has a dual structure. One branch connects the various levels of legislative assembly to one another; the Kōmeitō representatives in each level of assembly are members of this substructure. The other branch, the Organization Bureau, links the regional party headquarters to the Assembly Leagues in each prefecture,* and thence to the local branches, the basic units of the party organization. (It is through these branches that the Citizens' Livelihood Discussion Centers are organized.)

Once each month all of the Kōmeitō members serving in the nation's legislative assemblies meet at their different levels to debate activities and policies and to report upward their recommendations on these matters.[76] The entire policy-making process, in the words of Chairman Takeiri, is as follows:

All policies originate from activities carried on in close contact with masses and are decided after repeated, thorough discussion. At the center of the policy process are the local assembly members and, through the livelihood discussions . . . problems pertaining to the livelihood of the people are drawn upward and passed through the Assembly Leagues. The party Executive Committee meets once a month; here these problems are studied with an eye to policy. Then we reach down to the local level again and solicit opinions. In this fashion, as regards, for example, the single case of the Security Treaty question, which took about a year, we consolidate the basic attitude of the party.[77]

Candidates are probably chosen in the same way as party leaders, i.e. by co-optation, but the mechanics of selection remain obscure. The candidates selected can be considered representatives of the party

* Each League is composed of the Kōmeitō members in the prefectural legislative assembly.

elite; as such they are a distinct element within the Gakkai leadership. They are generally young: the eight Kōmeitō candidates standing from districts in Tokyo for the general election of January 1967 averaged 43 years of age, whereas the average age of all the candidates from Tokyo was 55.[78] Kōmeitō candidates are not as well educated as the average representative: of the twenty-five Kōmeitō members elected in the 1967 general election, 60 per cent had received some higher education, as against 74 per cent of all 486 candidates who were elected.[79] However, they are much better educated than the Gakkai membership as a whole. Occupationally, Kōmeitō candidates are also superior to the general membership. Five of the twenty-five Kōmeitō Lower House members elected in 1967 had managerial backgrounds and five were ex-government employees (this last is a broad category, however—Chairman Takeiri is a former ticket puncher on the national railway); four were also holding posts as functionaries in the party or in other Gakkai subsidiary organizations. The number also included a former lathe operator, cosmetics shop clerk, and milkman, but the overall occupational pattern reflects a socioeconomic status considerably higher than that of the Gakkai rank and file.[80]

To those candidates who are successful the Kōmeitō addresses a number of injunctions. Do not be carried away by prospects of honor and wealth, but fight unrelentingly for the happiness of the masses. Never cooperate with dishonest politicians. Be truly international in outlook.[81] Above all, do not become involved in factionalism. At the founding convention, CEC Chairman Harashima Kōji declared, "If factions appear we will dissolve the party immediately."[82]

The fact that the Kōmeitō does not represent a diversity of specialized political interests simplifies the task of preventing factionalism. No leader is permitted to acquire a following of his own, for to do so would be a divisive incursion into President Ikeda's prerogatives as supreme leader. No Kōmeitō member is allowed to develop an independent following or financial base (known as a *kaban* or money satchel), both of which constitute extra-party bases of power for members of other Japanese political parties. Local personally controlled power centers are nonexistent since the party assigns candidates to electoral districts; personal popularity is submerged in party loyalty. And pork-barreling for local constituencies (a politician's *rieki* or "benefit" function) is handled by the party, e.g., through the Livelihood Discussion Centers.[83]

In addition to facilitating policy-making and smooth internal government, the structure of the Kōmeitō is designed to provide for three fundamental resources—new members, votes, and finance. The agencies for recruiting party members do not actually function within the Kōmeitō, but are part of the socialization structure of the parent organization, the Gakkai. The way in which Gakkai members are drawn to the political party is unknown, but it probably involves the members' own personal interest, effort, and achievement. The business of attracting votes is also conducted primarily by the Society, since the vast majority of the Kōmeitō's electoral support comes from Gakkai members. There are indications, however, that the Kōmeitō is beginning to exercise an appeal of its own.[84]

In the matter of finance the Kōmeitō is independent of the Gakkai, maintaining itself entirely through membership dues (100 yen per year, or 28 cents) and revenues from publishing. According to figures published by the Japanese government the Kōmeitō's total income in 1966 was 471,312,816 yen (about $1.31 million), an amount that placed it third among Japanese political parties (after the Liberal Democrats and Socialists) in declared income.[85] As these figures suggest, the Kōmeitō has an impressive publishing establishment. The principal Kōmeitō media are the *Kōmei Shimbun* (*Kōmei News*), with a circulation of approximately one and a half million; *Kōmei*, a monthly covering political events; and *Kōmei Gurafu* (*Kōmei Graphic*), a pictorial dealing with the activities of the party. The most important of these publications is the *Kōmei Shimbun*, a thoroughly secular and energetic muckraker. This newspaper deals almost exclusively with party activities (both in and out of legislative bodies), party achievements (new parks, roads, housing, all presented as party victories), political scandals and bad social conditions, and international news, in that order.

One final aspect of the Kōmeitō structure is worthy of note—a projected labor union. On November 19, 1967, President Ikeda declared that the Kōmeitō needed an affiliated labor union that would truly reflect the will of the Japanese workers, those pawns in the self-seeking strategems of the major political parties and the established unions.[86] Such a union would "breathe fresh air into union activities," said Ikeda, and would offer protection especially to the thousands of unorganized workers.[87] In a press release the same day, the Kōmeitō stated that "no religious activity [would] be brought into the labor movement," and that unions ought to protect all the workers' basic rights, including freedom of political party choice.[88] Thus the intended union seems to be planned as a nonpartisan body. However, assuming that it attracts principally Gakkai members, one can expect that it may well become simply an additional structure for socializing and mobilizing the Gakkai's laboring members, i.e., an occupational group to supplement the peer and interest groups. And even if it does draw only Gakkai members, the new union could be a disruptive force in organized labor. It is estimated that some 630,000 Gakkai believers are now enrolled in unions; the threat of their defections would almost certainly provoke some conflict.[89]

THE KŌMEITŌ PLATFORM

In the earlier years of the Gakkai's political career, the organization made few concrete policy proposals. Those it did advance tended to be either largely negative criticisms of Japanese politics or artless platitudes on the advisability of multiplying administrative bureaus, reducing taxes, and increasing welfare measures. Gakkai policies on international affairs revolved about pacifism, disarmament, and world federation.[90] Recently, particularly since the establishment of the Kōmeitō, the policy formulations of the Gakkai have become increasingly specific.[91] The Kōmeitō is an important participant in numerous local assemblies, and the process of actually operationalizing Gakkai policy as legislation has progressed furthest on the local level. But development is also visible on a national and an international plane. The increased definition of the Kōmeitō's platform, brought about through the party's legislative activity, sets the Gakkai apart from the authoritarian movements in other countries with which it has occasionally been compared. In Hannah Arendt's words, "totalitarian movements, each in its own way, have done their utmost to get rid of the party programs which specified concrete content."[92] The Gakkai, while trying to appeal to as many people as possible, has developed its platforms in the opposite direction.

Except for becoming more concrete, the local policies of the Kōmeitō have changed little over the last several years.[93] Many public opinion surveys have shown that the vast majority of Japanese, like electors in other countries, are far more interested in immediate, domestic issues than in ideological bickering and distant international problems;[94] Kōmeitō policies reflect a shrewd decision to concentrate upon salient internal issues at both local and national levels. For the nationwide series of local elections held in April 1967 the Kōmeitō presented a ten-point general platform; to this it added specific policies for specific localities. The ten points were:

(1) The firm establishment of local politics for the sake of local residents.
(2) Sound financial administration and the lightening of financial burdens upon the residents.
(3) A "warm" social security system.

(4) Stable prices.

(5) Construction of public kindergartens and nurseries and the elimination of parents' financial responsibility for them.

(6) Achievement through public aid of a ratio of one family per dwelling.

(7) Elimination of public hazards and traffic problems.

(8) Prevention of accidents and creation of a hospitable local environment.

(9) Increased credit for and promotion of the modernization of medium- and small-scale business.

(10) Promotion of a prosperous agricultural, forestry, and fisheries industry.[95]

The added policies for Tokyo included these:

(1) Measures to counter the overconcentration of Tokyo.

(2) Creation of a net of concentric circular highways and communications circuits.

(3) Unification of all metropolitan transit systems.

(4) Establishment of a secondary urban center (*fuku-toshin*).

(5) Elimination of administrative inequalities between the suburban Santama district and the twenty-five wards of Tokyo to standardize metropolitan government.

(6) Demand for additional economic privileges for Tokyo from the national government.

(7) Measures for youth and children: parks, playgrounds, libraries, halls.

(8) Increased welfare administration: more facilities for children's care, first aid, maternal care, and care of the handicapped.

(9) Construction of pedestrian safety facilities.

(10) Additional medical welfare measures.

(11) Elimination of waste-collection fees; higher wages for sanitation workers.

(12) Creation of additional sources of water supply.

(13) Expanded sewage-disposal facilities.

(14) For water for industrial use, diffusion of extraction points to prevent sinking of land.

(15) Reduction of urban hazards by requiring antismog devices on cars, smoke controls on factories, limits on noise and on disposal of industrial wastes.

(16) Establishment of public parks and green belts.

(17) Riparian works.

(18) Construction of dikes and sewage pumps for lowland areas.

(19) Development of harbor facilities for the port of Tokyo.

(20) Acceleration of the social and economic development of the peripheral Santama area.[96]

One can easily recognize in such policies the basis of the Kōmeitō's appeal to the electorate. What one will probably also note is that the Kōmeitō's quite specific plans for renovating the city of Tokyo make no mention of how this vast undertaking is to be financed. At a press conference the then chief of the Policy Bureau, Suzuki Kazuhiro, spoke of higher taxes on large corporations, greater frugality in government spending (including abolition of customary *enkai seiji*—lavish entertainment for political purposes), and elimination of unnecessary *gaikaku dantai*, the quasi-governmental organizations that are attached to almost all administrative bureaus.[97] Although such measures would make considerable funds available, money on the fantastic scale needed to realize the Kōmeitō's vision is simply not to be seen.

The platform of the Kōmeitō in national elections is fully as elaborate as the party's proposals in local elections. It embodies the same characteristic puzzle—grandiose plans for public expenditures without correspondingly large-scale proposals for increased public funds. And on the national level one again finds the Kōmeitō tending to focus on the domestic and foreign issues that will appeal to the broadest possible sector of the Japanese public. In a pamphlet prepared for the January 1967 general election, the Kōmeitō presented ten "major policies" (with numerous subdivisions); of these, six dealt with the economic issues of housing, aid to small business, price stabilization, antiaccident and antipoverty measures, and promotion of primary industries.[98] The ten policies were based on the following points:

(1) Realization of clean elections and of parliamentary politics "for the people."
(2) Establishment of an independent foreign policy.
(3) Defense for the sake of peace.
(4) Establishment of a welfare economy.
(5) Elimination of housing and traffic problems.
(6) Banishment of accidents and poverty.
(7) Establishment of labor policies that protect the workers.
(8) Promotion of prosperous agricultural, forestry, and fishing industries.
(9) Protection of medium- and small-scale business.
(10) Opposition to revision of the constitution and to establishment of a small-electoral-district system.

Several points in the above platform require explanation. In the matter of clean elections, the Kōmeitō has been the only consistent proponent of strict limits on political contributions and heavier penalties for violation of laws concerned with the control of political funds. Prime Minister Satō, who has also called for such legislation, has been unable to push these measures through his own Liberal Democratic Party. In regard to foreign policy, the Kōmeitō has often spoken out against the excessive reliance of Japan upon the United States—economic, military, and diplomatic. Tsuji Takehisa has remarked that "the subservience [of the Satō cabinet] is rather a wonder."[99] The Kōmeitō holds that Japan can best serve its own interests through an autonomous foreign policy emphasizing relations with and aid to the other developing nations of Asia, including Communist countries.[100]

As for Vietnam, the Kōmeitō may still be in the process of hardening its stand. In 1962 the Gakkai spoke of the "aggressive invasion" of South Vietnam from the North; by the mid-1960's its position had become one of neutrality. "We strongly advise that Japan propose to all of the nations involved that all foreign military forces should be withdrawn unconditionally, that peace be maintained by a United Nations armed force, and that a conference be held immediately on the basis of the Geneva Accords."[101] The Gakkai's advocacy of a bilateral ceasefire,[102] and hence the Kōmeitō's, was withdrawn abruptly in August 1967, when President Ikeda outlined a new Vietnam policy: a cessation of bombing of the North, a cessation of all fighting in and troop movements into South Vietnam, a conference of concerned nations, including the Viet Cong, in Tokyo, and a mutual agreement leading to the withdrawal of all American military forces from Vietnam.[103]

To read into this policy statement a cooling of Gakkai attitudes toward the American effort in Southeast Asia may be unjustified. The Kōmeitō may simply have been staking out its own distinctive position on the Vietnam issue. Gakkai officials insist that the statement signified no change whatsoever in their policy toward either Vietnam or the United States.[104] Nevertheless, the August statements did mark a new, unprecedentedly positive position on the Vietnam issue.

In the same speech President Ikeda raised the question of Okinawa. Restoration of the island had long been a plank in the Sōkagakkai's platform, but on this occasion the point was made with a new intensity; Ikeda declared, "I hereby strongly advocate immediate, complete restoration by the American military government in Okinawa and Okinawa's restitution to Japan." In addition, he called for immediate dismantling of all nuclear bases on the island and the removal of all military installations within five years of restoration.[105] It is possible that the Kōmeitō, in its own eyes, was again simply clarifying rather than changing its policy; but the statement was made in a context of rising national sentiment concerning Okinawa. In October a national survey by the newspaper *Asahi Shimbun* found 85 per cent of the respondents favoring restitution of Okinawa to Japan; 81 per cent wanted restoration as soon as possible and 57 per cent wanted it returned free of all nuclear weapons (only 15 per cent accepted the idea of reversion with nuclear bases intact).[106] The sensitivity of the Kōmeitō to popular opinion suggests that the Kōmeitō was trying either to mount a possible "return-Okinawa" bandwagon or to lead what it perceived to be a possible nascent trend of opinion; the party's juxtaposition of time with message does not seem to be coincidental.

Regarding "defense for the sake of peace" and disarmament, the Kōmeitō opines that military alliances create more instability and danger than they suppress; in particular, American bases make Japan a top-priority target for anyone planning to attack the United States.[107] The party would much prefer protection from a United Nations police force. Initially the Gakkai was ambivalent about the Self-Defense Forces. But Ikeda has emphasized that since Japan in her constitution renounces war entirely as an instrument of foreign policy, "we ought not to have the right of self-defense."[108] Hence the Kōmeitō currently feels that the SDF is "unconstitutional" and should be disbanded.

Abolition of American bases in Japan and unilateral Japanese disarmament immediately would be unrealistic, however. Thus until recently the Gakkai has had little to say about the Japan–United States Mutual Security Treaty, treating it simply as a *fait accompli*.[109] Present Kōmeitō policy advocates its abrogation, but since "there is no guarantee that we absolutely will not be aggressed against," the party suggests abrogation should take the form of gradual dissolution (over ten or more years) through a flexible process.[110]

One of the primary factors contributing to international tension and to the necessity for military pacts is the status of China. The Gakkai has always advocated increased trade with, diplomatic recognition of, and United Nations membership for Communist China.[111] It also hopes for unification of China, as it does for Vietnam and all other states subject to partition (a condition that contravenes the principles of One-Worldism).[112]

The one point in the Kōmeitō's foreign policy that does not ring true in its general tone of humanitarianism is the provision that users of nuclear weapons be executed for violating the right of mankind to exist. This provision is a legacy from President Toda that the Gakkai has retained; it becomes increasingly incongruous as the Society moves toward a greater emphasis on humanism.[113]

In the domestic economy, one of the Kōmeitō's main interests is rising prices. To counter the rising cost of living the party advocates not a restriction of demand, but an increase in supply, to be achieved by lowering interest rates (and thus lowering production costs) and by putting ceilings on land prices and rents.[114] The Kōmeitō suggests few new sources of governmental revenue: it opposes the sale of public bonds, which it sees as inflationary; it favors the abolition of taxes on earned income; and it puts great emphasis on the expansion of trade in order to increase the general prosperity.[115] It also proposes higher taxes on corporations, but their application remains unclear.[116]

Looking at the country's economic structure as a whole, the Kō-meitō urges reform of the double nature of the system. Great discrepancies in size, capitalization, wage scales, and modernity of equipment and practices exist within each Japanese industry; the Kōmeitō seeks equalization or at least coordination of the various sectors.[117] Sufficient controls should operate on free competition to ward off its major concomitant evils. The Kōmeitō's objective is a "controlled market structure" based on "effective competition"—many Gakkai leaders suggest the British mixed economy as a model for their own policies.[118]

And finally, education, small enterprise, and constitutional and electoral-system revision are additional domestic problems claiming the Kōmeitō's attention. For instance, the party has grandiose intentions of building numerous educational facilities, renovating the generally dilapidated rural schools, and extending aid to institutions of higher learning. But the most important change it proposes is one in attitude, in the whole Japanese orientation toward education. The present system is overcentralized, and educational authorities spend far too much time in squabbles with the leftist Japan Teachers' Union. Instead, a pedagogical system should be adopted that emphasizes individual development and achievement.[119] The Sōka Schools, the Gakkai asserts, will demonstrate this method.

The Kōmeitō's interest in medium and small business reflects the support that the Gakkai receives from employees in this sector of the economy. The party suggests that a Medium- and Small-Scale Business Ministry be established through which the spheres of large and small enterprise can be coordinated to minimize unnecessary competition, duplication, and waste. The Ministry would also abolish exploitation: it could protect the countless small subcontracting firms through laws requiring quick payment of subcontract bills and assist them with loans not requiring collateral.[120]

In the late 1950's the Gakkai was reticent on the subject of constitutional revision; now, however, it has a comprehensive policy concerning the constitution, based on a single premise: no revision.[121] The position of the Emperor as no more than the symbol of the state is suitable "because it meets the sentimental emotional needs of the people and because at present it does not disturb the smooth operation of politics."[122] Article IX, the clause renouncing war, should be logically extended into a Japanese foreign policy that actively advocates worldwide disarmament and the universal renunciation of war. The Kōmeitō approves the present form of the National Diet, the cabinet system, and the judiciary despite the factionalism, corruption, and violations of election laws so common today.[123] Local governments, however, should be protected against the interference of the central authorities in their affairs.[124]

The duties of the citizenry are limited to a single point: the dictum to refrain from infringing upon the rights of any other person.[125] No incursions whatsoever may be permitted into the rights of the citizenry; it is the duty of the state to protect to the utmost the freedoms guaranteed by the constitution. The Kōmeitō, therefore, takes pains to refute accusations that it plans a National High Sanctuary (the Gakkai Kaidan)—since for it to build such a temple with state funds would be unconstitutional. The party points out that the Grand Main Hall presently under construction at the Taisekiji *is* the High Sanctuary, and that it is being built wholly through the contributions of Gakkai members. "The fact speaks for itself. Thus the groundless rumor of the National Sanctuary has been completely repudiated."[126]

Revision of the electoral system into single-member districts on the British model, which members of the Liberal Democrats have proposed, is a particular focus of Kōmeitō attacks, for the simple reason that the change would wipe the Kōmeitō out of nearly all legislative assemblies in the nation.[127] A study of the 1963 Japanese general election by Nishihira Shigeki of the Institute of Statistical Mathematics backs up the party's apprehension.[128] According to Nishihira's calculations, if the election had been held according to the British single-member-constituency system instead of the Japanese variant of proportional representation, the Liberal Democrats would have won 403 seats (86.3 per cent of the total of 467) with their 54.6 per cent of the popular vote, instead of the 283 seats (61 per cent) they did win. The Socialist Party would have won 57 seats (12.2 per cent) with its 29 per cent of the vote, instead of 144 seats (31 per cent). The Democratic Socialists would have won only 7 seats (1.5 per cent) with their 7.4 per cent of the vote, instead of 23 seats (5 per cent). The Communist Party and all other candidates, who won 17 seats (4 per cent) with 9 per cent of the popular vote, would have been completely unrepresented under the British system. In short, regardless of the abstract relative merits of two-party or multiparty systems, the adoption of a single-member electoral system in Japan would greatly enhance the parliamentary power of the ruling party and very likely end the career of the Kōmeitō in parliament.[129]

The overall platform of the Kōmeitō has been attacked as a collection of progressive policies stolen from the parties of the left; the Gakkai has been cast as "a second Democratic Socialist Party wearing clerical robes and existing in the gap between the conservatives and the reformers."[130] The Kōmeitō acknowledges the superficial similarity between its policies—especially its welfare measures—and those of the Socialists and Democratic Socialists, but insists that its proposals are sincere, unlike the cynically tactical welfarism of the Socialists.[131] Hōjō Hiroshi has even suggested a relative proximity to the Liberal Democrats: "The Kōmeitō really leans a little toward conservatism. . . . But in Japan, a new party must appeal to a very wide range of voters. We must attract people from all points of the spectrum."[132] In fact, Kōmeitō policies do parallel Tory stands on many issues. One study found that Kōmeitō positions on fourteen of sixteen issues coincided with the Liberal Democratic stands on those issues. The Kōmeitō and Democratic Socialist Party agreed on fifteen issues, the Kōmeitō and the Socialist Party on nine, and the Kōmeitō and the Communist Party on one.[133] In general, though, one cannot pin the Kōmeitō's whole platform to a single spot on the political spectrum. Welfarism, pacifism, quasi-socialism, and pro-China and anti-constitutional-revision stands suggest leftist leanings; these, however, must be balanced against conditional acceptance of the Mutual Security Treaty and the Self-Defense Forces, and less programmatic but perhaps more significant statements like Hōjō's.

There are two conclusions one can reach after examining the Kōmeitō's political policies. First, the social reconstruction and welfare measures planned by the party continue to demonstrate a large measure of fiscal irresponsibility. Second, one receives the inescapable impression that, underlying the policies of the Kōmeitō, there is a broader political philosophy involving sincere formal adherence to democratic values and processes. Many of the Kōmeitō's ideas are vague; and many points at which religion and politics intersect could become sources of sacred-secular conflict that could destroy democratic politics; but when one questions Gakkai officials, their explanations are clear and, unless they are examples of studied and towering duplicity, quite sincere. There are exceptions—President Toda's prescription of the death penalty for nuclear warfare is one—but such exceptions are increasingly rare.* If one reads widely and regularly in Gakkai and Kōmeitō publications one must conclude that although the Society still exhibits a degree of political naiveté, it has made a strong and formal commitment to secular parliamentary democracy.

* The Toda quotation, for instance, was seen by the author in only two documents: the English-language *Seikyō News* of August 15, 1962, and a 1966 Kōmeitō policy statement, *Kōmeitō no Jūten Seisaku.* The possible implications of such exceptions cannot be ignored, of course, and a number of similar statements will be cited in the analysis of formal Gakkai ideology in Chapters 10 and 11.

CHAPTER 8

The Kōmeitō in Action

JAPANESE religious organizations have managed on occasion to seat members in local or national assemblies; usually, however, these representatives have operated as members of the established parties.[1] The Kōmeitō, in contrast, entered the political arena as an independent entity with a comprehensive set of political philosophies and policies and the professed aim of realizing its theological premises through the existing political system. And for the Kōmeitō, even more than for the established parties, tactics on every level of political life are determined by overarching strategic considerations.

For example, party image is extremely important to the Kōmeitō, which styles itself the true friend and representative of the masses. It enters local elections largely for the sake of public relations: winning a seat in a new area means gaining a stage from which to address all the local residents. Through speeches and by exemplary behavior, the Kōmeitō representative in the area builds a broader base of support for future elections.[2] Because votes are, after all, cast at the local level, the Kōmeitō considers the activities of its members in local assemblies more important than its National Diet[3] operations.

In addition to this basic strategic consideration, several nonstrategic idiosyncracies also distinguish the operations of the Kōmeitō. One of these is vacillation between the parties of the right and left in legislative situations (variously attributed to flexibility or opportunism); another is a popular view of politics, an approach not found in any of the established parties; a third is concentration on a program of grass-roots extraparliamentary activities, a program unmatched by any other political force in Japan.

PARLIAMENTARY PERFORMANCE AND POPULAR ACTIVITY

In the National Diet. The Kōmeitō's record in the National Diet has been one of cooperation with the right drifting toward limited, unstable coalitions with various elements of the left. Because of the party's minority status, it has seldom been able to realize any of its policies; but this has not kept it from loudly proclaiming the Kōmeitō's virtues, broadly criticizing its opposition, and taking credit for any legislation that happens to be congruent with Kōmeitō policy.

Until the mid-1960's the Gakkai's politics were still in a formative stage; its representatives had little experience and probably no operational code of parliamentary behavior. The Kōmeitō appeared to be cooperating closely with the Liberal Democrats in the Diet, while condemning them in public.[4] Indeed, the Society had emphasized from the outset that diehard opposition on every minor issue was not nearly as important as the endeavor to reconstruct (through "human revolution") the system empowered to deal with these issues.[5]

But in the early 1960's a movement to disengage from the Liberal Democratic Party was under way. In comparison to the 96.8 per cent of government-sponsored bills that Gakkai Upper House members assented to in the 1960 session of the Diet, the proportion approved decreased to 94.2 per cent in 1961, 92.8 per cent in 1962, 88.9 per cent in 1963, and 86.5 per cent in 1964.[6] (By contrast, in 1964 the Democratic Socialists approved 88.8 per cent of the LDP's legislation.) The Kōmeitō opposed the government-backed Japan-Korea Treaty of 1965,* and more recently has joined with the Socialists and Communists in backing a resolution to reiterate Japan's refusal to permit nuclear armaments on Japanese territory, clamored for the resignation of an LDP cabinet minister who suggested that Japan play a greater role in her own defense, and contested firmly the visit to Japan of the American aircraft carrier *Enterprise*.[7] Such opposition to LDP policies has prompted some observers to deduce a Kōmeitō drift to the left.

The Kōmeitō, however, flatly denied any leftist tendencies in the party's activities.[8] And it is probable that the Kōmeitō was sincere in these protestations, although they have since ceased;[9] the party is not leaning to the left, but rather trying to establish a distinctive position on several issues. Any position at variance with the ruling party's has in common with the stands of the other opposition parties reaction, if nothing else. If this opposition is intense enough it can cause the reacting parties to cooperate even though their positions on an issue may vary greatly.

This is in fact what has happened in the case of the Kōmeitō, a minority that wishes to influence legislation without becoming a satellite of the ruling party. Since taking its place in the Lower House the Kō-

---

* Using in the process the obstructionist technique of walking very slowly up to the speaker's rostrum to vote (*ushi-aruki*).

meitō has ceaselessly advocated opposition coalitions as the most effective means of opposing the LDP.[10] In February 1967 the Socialists, the Democratic Socialists, and the Kōmeitō joined in a budget proposal. In April 1967 they called on Prime Minister Eisaku Satō for stringent legislation to restrict political contributions.[11] The Communist Party joined the triumvirate to create a solid front voicing dissatisfaction with the proposed Nuclear Non-Proliferation Treaty of 1967.[12]

The Kōmeitō's efforts to form alliances on other issues, however, have met with mixed success.[13] No coalition, of course, can stop the LDP when that party is thoroughly determined to pass a measure. But since the fall of Prime Minister Kishi, owing mainly to his high-handed manner of forcing bills through the Diet, the ruling party has been relatively circumspect. A completely united opposition front would give the conservatives pause in the exploitation of their parliamentary majority.

Ad hoc coalition has often proved possible, but one wonders whether the Kōmeitō's drive for individuality and integrity will permit close identification with any other single party. The evidence presented by Azumi and by Sidney Verba and his associates of much stronger antileftist than antirightist feelings among Gakkai activists suggests that prolonged identification with parties on the left perhaps would have a deleterious effect on the unity of the Gakkai.[14] Nevertheless, the party has evidently concluded that to become recognized as a viable political actor it must sever certain old relationships with the LDP and chance any internal tensions that may result.

Even when in coalition the Kōmeitō is in the minority; by itself it is far too small to push through legislation of its own. Therefore its substantive, autonomous achievements have been few. Instead, the primary functions of the Kōmeitō in parliament to date have been as a muckraker, a self-appointed guardian of the public interest, drawing attention with nonpartisan zeal to political irregularities of all kinds. This role underlies the vacillation of the Kōmeitō between the two major parties. The party decides each political issue according to the Kōmeitō conception of popular welfare, and then supports whichever party seems to best represent the people's interests on that issue.

The Kōmeitō's "cleanup of the political world" in the Diet focuses on "normalization of procedure."[15] (Contrary to "normal procedures" are the unilateral forcing through of legislation by the LDP and the obstructionism of the leftists.) Since every act of the Kōmeitō contributes ipso facto to normalization—even, one is left to suppose, the party's occasional use of obstructionist tactics—the party takes credit for the orderly settlement of all intraparliamentary conflicts. It also helps to purify politics by pointing out irregularities. The *Kōmei Shimbun* carries extensive accounts of the attacks of Kōmeitō legislators on alleged scandals, on inconsistent policies or performance, and on political infringements of the public interest. The Kōmeitō holds up its muckraking record as basic evidence of its concern for the masses. Recent catalogs of the "injustices" attacked by Kōmeitō Diet members included the following:

May 7, 1965: Ninomiya Bunzō attacks the improper sale of Toranomon Public Park and the lease of the property of the former Army Administration School. (Upper House Accounting Committee.)

October 17, 1966: Tada Shōgo brings up the question of Defense Agency chief Kanbayashiyama's parade in his home town at public expense and calls for the resignation of the cabinet minister at fault. (Upper House Cabinet Committee.)

November 17, 1966: Kuroyanagi Akira points out that the LDP, DSP, and Socialists have all accepted political contributions from the Kyōwa Sugar interests, already implicated in a political scandal. (Upper House Accounting Committee.)

March 23, 1967: Kōmeitō Secretary-General Yano Jun'ya assails the LDP's Diet expenditures, suggesting that the party made payoffs to opposition party members to influence them toward support of the government-sponsored treaty with Korea, and calls for the LDP to publicize its disbursement records. (Lower House Budget Committee.)[16]

It is clear from this brief list and from further entries in the Kōmeitō's inventories that the party's allegations tend often to be no more than suggestions. Some, such as the Kanbayashiyama incident and the Kyōwa Sugar scandal, were merely facets of already uncovered irregularities. The question of LDP payoffs to other parties disrupted the proceedings of the Budget Committee for a few days but the LDP refused to open its records and no further investigation followed. Never, in fact, has specific legislation resulted from the Kōmeitō's efforts to publicize scandal. Nonetheless, many of the Kōmeitō's attacks receive attention in the popular press, and the party's failure to achieve concrete results has not detracted from its efficacy in the eyes of its supporters. I found from conversations with Gakkai members that the Kōmeitō is accepted as a serious, able, admirably honest group using its position in the Diet to work ceaselessly for the people's welfare. The following letters to the *Kōmei Shimbun* exemplify this view.

"As opposed to the established parties' backstage dealings and opportunist connivance, the Kōmeitō followed decisively and clearly its predetermined basic line of 'reject the bill' . . . . This party of 25 men has managed to move the 'adult' established parties adroitly. The recent decision was formally reached according to the established pattern, but one should probably consider the style of the Kōmeitō as qualitatively different, a third force in the face of the wheeler-dealer style in which party interests and strategems take precedence." *Mainichi Shimbun*, August 6, 1967.

It was in this fashion that the newspapers evaluated the activities of the Kōmeitō amid the disorders that attended the Diet deliberations on the proposed Special Temporary Health Insurance Law; as I read these articles I remember how my heart stirred. I was unable to refrain from applauding them inwardly, thinking: they're still working for us.

I had heard that the backstage dealings in the Diet were really like "a bunch of crooks cheating each other," but with the entry upon the stage of the Kōmeitō one doesn't hear of the old kind of humbug any more; the thieves' masks have been skilfully torn off by the Kōmeitō. The shameful conduct displayed by the Socialists has led even to intraparty chaos. The work of the Kōmeitō, so diametrically opposed to this, is, I am sure, something that can gradually win the hearts of conscientious citizens.

—Mr. Yamada Mitsuru, company employee, 32.

I send my heartfelt applause for the fact that, as of August 1, the compensation provided under automobile liability insurance went from 1.5 million yen to 3 million yen; this is the fruit of the extraordinary activity of the Kōmeitō.

Some time ago, on an afternoon TV show, this matter was brought up; but even though the views of each party were presented in informal conversation, they didn't show me any satisfying, concrete answers. Only the Kōmeitō gave a clear policy. At that time they explained that their initial goal was 3 million yen, but when I saw it realized today, I again marveled at the Kōmeitō's great power of execution.

In these days, when auto accidents increase year by year, I have great hopes for the Kōmeitō's traffic accident policy.

—Miss Omori Sumie, public servant, 36.[17]

In local assemblies. Many of the trends visible in the Kōmeitō's National Diet proceedings are reflected in its activities in the local assemblies. A close approximation of Liberal Democratic attitudes has given way to a clearly independent stand, at least in principle.[18] It is much clearer on the local level than on the national that the party is moving toward broad opposition, not a narrowly leftist stance. In the Tokyo Metropolitan Assembly left-wing forces hold more seats than the Tories. Here, although opposition could entail cooperation with the conservatives, the Kōmeitō has recently become something of an opposition party.

The oppositionist trend has been most marked in the Tokyo Metropolitan Assembly since a Socialist, Minobe Ryōkichi, was elected governor. The Kōmeitō vetoed two of the three men whom Minobe nominated for lieutenant governors, although its reasons for the veto were weak. The party turned down one nominee, the former head of the Metropolitan Sanitation Bureau, saying, "We conclude from his record that he is not up to the heavy responsibilities of the post." Of the other, previously chief of the Statistical Standards Bureau in the Prime Minister's Agency, the party stated, "We haven't heard of any national achievements and don't know him well and therefore can't expect much of him."[19] The press read in the Kōmeitō–Liberal Democrat coalition that voted down these two nominees a "long hostility" to the Socialist-Communist alliance that had backed Minobe's campaign. It interpreted the veto as an attempt to obstruct Minobe's administration before it could get under way.[20]

At the local level, as at the national, the Kōmeitō is still in every case a minority. However, its performance in the 1967 municipal assembly elections for Japan's five largest cities indicates that the party possesses considerable leverage in some locales. As a result, the testimony of Gakkai members to the efficacy of the party on the local level has a more convincing foundation in fact than have accounts of party performance in the Diet. In local politics, where the populace is more directly involved, the Kōmeitō's microscopic approach to politics is more clearly seen.

The party itself, never reticent, has published an account of its activities in the Tokyo Assembly that takes credit for the recall of the scandal-ridden Tokyo Assembly in 1965, and for more effective measures against peculation of tax moneys; dishonesties in the purchase and sale of public property and in bidding for metropolitan contracts; shoddy construction in public buildings; and lavish expenditures of public funds on politically motivated entertainment.[21] More positively, the Kōmeitō cites among its accomplishments yearly increases in appropriations for school equipment; an increased number of playgrounds, parks, traffic lights, and pedestrian overpasses; more public housing, better in quality and in administration; and more loan funds for medium-sized and small businesses. Such measures frequently epitomize microscopic politics. Perhaps a neighborhood demand for a guardrail on a dangerous street corner comes to the attention of a Kōmeitō representative; he introduces the demand in the local assembly as Kōmeitō policy, and if the guardrail is ever built the Kōmeitō, as initial articulator of the interest, takes the credit. At this level, outsiders recognize the justice of many of the Kōmeitō's claims, especially since its successes are often tangible (e.g., parks, playgrounds, and traffic safety facilities) and observable by local residents.[22]

The following letters to the *Kōmei Shimbun* suggest the response such local legislation generates. The writers of these letters are probably all Gakkai believers, but the measures they describe have been witnessed by the entire electorate.

Tokyo's Kōtō ward, where we live, is famous for flooding and sinking land; but owing to the activity of the Kōmeitō during the last several years, levee construction is nearing completion and sewage drainage projects are also progressing. Also (and this too is in accord with the position of the Kōmeitō assemblymen), since the pumping-up of water for industrial use has been prohibited, land sinkage has ceased. Thanks to this, high-rise public housing units have been built in great numbers.

Ten years ago, tired of the flooding, I was looking for somewhere else to live. Today I even feel pride in being a resident of Kōtō ward. From now on, I want to work for the construction of an even better society, in support of the Kōmeitō legislators.

—Mrs. Takayasu Mutsuko, housewife.

The last day of the school term ended and the children came racing home. "Mama, tomorrow we can go swimming in the new pool!"

This pool is one example of the fruition of the "pool in every elementary school" policy emphasized by the Kōmeitō in the ward assembly. The pool was opened without difficulties on the 19th; just as summer vacation begins the children can use it.

Here in the Nishi-Sugamo area the traffic problem is terrific and the houses are crowded together; until three years ago, when, through the efforts of the Kōmeitō, a playground was opened at the school, there wasn't a single place for the children to play. For this reason, when summer used to come parents would worry themselves sick trying to figure how to keep their children occupied through the month-long summer vacation.

This year, when I think that I can let my children play without any worries, my heart is full of joy.

—Mrs. Yasui Kiyo, housewife, 46.

The other day Mr. Y., who was elected to the city assembly in the April local elections, visited our home. "In thanks for the support of all of you, isn't there anything you want from the city government that I can try to obtain?" he said. Contrasting him to assemblymen from other parties, who bob their heads concernedly until elected, whereupon they cease to think of us at all, I was deeply impressed by this remarkable sincerity.

Quickly, we asked him that the bridge near our house, which was narrow and had been the scene of many auto accidents, be widened. Before a month had passed we heard the happy news that an appropriation had been made. Isn't this the style of the true legislator, anxious to hear even the smallest request of the people?

—Mrs. Tōyama Junko, housewife, 24.[23]

Outside the parliamentary arena. Outside of the legislative arena the Kōmeitō shows none of the left-right vacillation that characterizes its parliamentary practices. Its extraparliamentary activity is also microscopic, primarily involving "livelihood discussion" and investigatory action.

The system of Citizens' Livelihood Discussion Centers was established after the local elections of 1963, with a center in every region where the Kōseiren held assembly seats. Although each of the centers offers free legal aid, their primary function is political: to gather complaints and demands about the immediate concerns of the citizenry. The Kōmeitō describes the system as a "warm hand stretched out to those people discarded by politics." Probably the centers do provide a unique opportunity to articulate grievances.[24] The Kōmeitō relays these popular appeals to appropriate public offices or, if necessary, introduces them in local assemblies.[25] Party members are adjured to promote local awareness of the centers—and always to inform those presenting grievances of the final disposition of their cases.[26]

Just how many of the cases heard are successfully settled is not clear. In 1964 the Kōmeikai claimed that of 2,084 cases heard by centers in Tokyo, 1,875 were resolved.[27] Year by year the volume of cases received has increased, from a nationwide total of 131,908 cases in 1963 to 178,712 in 1964, 215,362 in 1965, and 238,628 in 1966, by which time there were 7,200 discussion centers throughout the nation.[28] The 10,866 cases heard by seven urban centers in July 1967 present the following pattern of popular complaints: social security, 22 per cent of the cases heard; housing, 20 per cent; sanitation and general environmental wholesomeness, 15 per cent; roads and traffic, 9 per cent; livelihood and welfare, 8 per cent; education, 7 per cent; medical, 4 per cent; taxes, 3 per cent; other, 12 per cent.[29] The Kōmeitō is the only Japanese political party to produce such an effective, functionally specific structure for tapping public opinion at its discontented source. The discussion center system enables the Kōmeitō to steal a march on the other parties in developing policies likely to meet with popular approval.

Tied to the discussion center system are the Kōmeitō's extraparliamentary investigative operations, its muckraking activities. In the discussion centers the party hears rumors of political irregularities, which trigger investigations by Kōmeitō members. Meetings with citizens and surveys of residents in problem areas supplement the data these members gain from official sources and through the discussion centers. Such thorough efforts serve to promote the party's image as watchdog over each and every citizen's welfare.

The Kōmeitō also takes advantage of natural catastrophes to make its presence felt by the electorate at large.[30] The following letter to the *Kōmei Shimbun* describes the party's response to a flood in south-western Japan:

The activities of the Kōmeitō during the recent flood in Imari City were amazing. On seeing these men wearing armbands with "Kōmeitō" written on them in white letters racing to the area to exert themselves to the utmost, I thought, sure enough, just as you'd expect, it's the Kōmeitō.

Due to the heavy rain, a muddy deluge some six feet deep had poured through the city's main streets, which were a sea of mud. Amid these conditions the police, who should have been looking to the security and protection of the people, were engaged throughout in clearing out of their police boxes the water that had flooded into them.

In contrast to this, the activity of Kōmeitō assemblymen and Youth Bureau members was so impressive as to defy description. Going into muddy floodwaters up to the chest, delivering emergency messages by hand because the telephone lines were down, taking to safety the victims of the disaster amid the deep darkness brought on by electrical failure, and, in the morning, distributing food they had prepared while ignoring their own empty stomachs—this was the behavior of the Kōmeitō. I saw with my own eyes the true activist style of the Kōmeitō.

My neighbors, too, were deeply impressed: "The Kōmeitō assemblymen carry out their campaign promise to tie politics to the people right on the spot, don't they?"

—Saitō Matsuo, restaurant employee, 52.[31]

There is another form of extraparliamentary political action with a long history in Japan. Direct action—demonstration, riot, and assassination—has from time to time received considerable social sanction.[32] Neither the Gakkai nor its political organs have ever officially espoused direct action of an extreme nature, although individual Gakkai members have frequently broken laws regulating political expression. Gakkai leaders have, however, threatened mass action. Referring to the problem of constitutional revision, President Ikeda stated: "I hope that the time will never come when the Sōka-gakkai and the Kōmeitō must really rise up. But if the national authorities interfere with the party and the Gakkai by prejudicially revising the constitution, we will throw our total organization into the struggle."[33] Gakkai leaders are more explicit on the subject of adopting a single-member electoral system—a far more likely development. In an interview, Hōjō Hiroshi outlined Kōmeitō strategy. The party seeks to prevent such a proposal's ever reaching the Diet, but failing this, it would attempt to kill such a bill in committee; if the government still tried to push the measure through, the party's "inevitable" final step would be to take to the streets.

We have never as yet resorted to ultimate measures. But if a situation arises wherein, in order to obstruct the advance of the Sōkagakkai or the Kōmeitō, the government seriously tries to push through a small-constituency system by force, what then? Shall we not resort to ultimate measures and, calling forth a brilliant and unprecedentedly great mass movement and giant demonstrations, put an end to it?[34]

The intent here is clear, but the word "demonstration" is not. In Japan, the term covers everything from orderly parades of banner-carrying union members, making a symbolic call for American disengagement in Vietnam, to ranks of helmeted left-wing students, armed with staves and bombarding the police with paving stones. Several kinds of political action that can be called "demonstration" are in no way incompatible with the stable functioning of democratic systems. Since the Gakkai has never specified what form of action it might take and has no record of direct action, one cannot justifiably assume that organized Kōmeitō extraparliamentary protest would be violent or excessively disruptive.*

The one example of the party's extraparliamentary action that might be called direct, and which the party described at the time as "mass action," is a series of lecture meetings, held in the city of Sasebo, Organized to protest the visit to that seaport of the American nuclear-powered aircraft carrier *Enterprise* in January 1968, the lectures drew some 18,000 persons to six locations.[35] Some observers described these meetings as "demonstrations," but the *Seikyō Shimbun* emphasized the "stark contrast" of the Kōmeitō meetings to the riotous demonstrations of the Communists and the ultramilitant factions of *Zengakuren*. A Kōmeitō press release described the lectures as "an orderly, systematic, and peaceful gathering of protest," and the pictures that newspapers carried of the meetings bear out this description. In fact, except that they were held out-of-doors, the "Mass Meetings to Protest in Opposition to the Visit of the *Enterprise*" bore a closer resemblance to the Kōmeitō's Current Events Lecture Meetings than to any "demonstration."

The Current Events Lectures complete the picture of the Kōmeitō's extraparliamentary operations. They are held frequently but irregularly, and are conducted by chief Kōmeitō leaders, who give topical speeches on current issues and on the party's policies and activities. In these meetings, as in all the other activities of the Kōmeitō, the

---

* I say "excessively" because in an urban setting even the most orderly large-scale demonstrations must disrupt ordinary pedestrian and traffic patterns.

party image projected is personal, locally oriented, conscientious, and diligent, but not in the least extremist.

Campaign tactics. The Sōkagakkai's campaign strategy, though it has become somewhat more daring in recent years, calls mainly for highly disciplined voters and conservative numbers of candidates. The Gakkai eschewed dark-horse candidates until the Tokyo gubernatorial election of 1967.* In the beginning, the Gakkai itself, as a religious body, was closely identifiable with any of its political endeavors. Thus the Society, thinking of the possible reflection on Nichiren Shōshū's claims to omnipotence, may have tried to hedge its political losses. Its readiness now to endure such losses could signify that it believes members do distinguish between it and the Kōmeitō.

Naturally enough, the Kōmeitō relies heavily on the Gakkai's structure and media in its campaign activities. According to Ishida Ikuo, Gakkai block leaders meet nightly during campaigns to calculate local voting strength.[36] A common campaign strategy calls for "onefor-two"; i.e., for every two Gakkai members campaigning, a new nonmember voter attracted to the Kōmeitō.[37] One result of this strategy is that during campaign time it is difficult to distinguish true shakubuku visits to nonmember homes from outright political activity. According to Saki and Oguchi, longtime observers of the Gakkai, Society members have actually accosted citizens and informed them that good or evil would result from the way their votes were cast.[38] In Japan, however, door-to-door canvassing in elections is illegal, so that shakubuku has earned a doubtful reputation as one of the means by which Gakkai members elicit votes.

Election law violations were a major characteristic of the Gakkai's initial political activities. In the House of Councillors election of 1956, 80 per cent of those arrested for door-to-door solicitation offenses were Sōkagakkai members.[39] Neither the offenders nor the Gakkai conceded guilt: the Society declared that the arrests were "illegal," while the culprits protested that "they were only trying to purify the political world and to correct the distortions of heretical religions."[40] In a special by-election to the House of Councillors in Osaka in 1957 such violations reached a climax. Ninety per cent of all the breaches of election laws involved Gakkai members or support-

---

* Until then the policy had been to run only sure winners, determined on the basis of the recorded Gakkai membership for the electoral district in question.

ers.[41] An apparently unauthorized group of believers who had come down from Tokyo distributed one-hundred-yen notes and cigarettes bearing the name of the Gakkai candidate. In the aftermath of the election the Chief of Staff of the Youth Division, Ikeda Daisaku, was arrested; he was released for lack of proof that he had had any guiding role in the offenses committed, but twenty other Gakkai members were convicted, and seventeen of them had their civil rights suspended for two to three years.[42]

The Gakkai, as it had after the 1956 election, took an indignant stand.[43] But in the years that followed the Society made a distinct effort to avoid election offenses. Since 1957 Gakkai members have rarely violated the election laws, and although the popular image of their illegality persists, actual Gakkai-Kōmeitō campaign practices at the present time are at least as responsible as those of the other major parties.

Present campaign strategy in the Kōmeitō directs attention to the party first and foremost. Whereas the candidates of other parties often campaign on their own local reputations or personal legislative records, Kōmeitō candidates run simply as the party's representatives— it is the party's platform and record that matter. The Kōmeitō also claims that it campaigns entirely on the issues, not on promises to local interest groups or personal appeals. In principle, at least, it is true that the party's campaign strategy is issue-oriented. But if one follows a campaign in the *Kōmei Shimbun,* one finds the party less concerned with issues and policies than with attack and criticism.[44] The evils of the political system in general and of all other political parties in particular are described extensively. Policies are summed up in broad slogans for the most part; it is Kōmeitō philosophies that are stressed, especially the party's assumption of the role of representative and voice of the masses.

The early years. The Sōkagakkai made its political debut in a series of local elections in April 1955, immediately following its "victory" in the Otaru Debate (for data on this and other elections see Appendix D, Tables D.1–D.11). It won 98 per cent of its first election contests. In the Upper House election the following year only three of six Gakkai candidates won; however, the four candidates in the national constituency drew a total of 990,000 votes, versus a claimed Gakkai membership of something less than 400,000 members, for a ratio of roughly 2.4 Gakkai votes per member family (see Appendix D, Fig. D.1).

In the local elections of April 1959 the Gakkai continued its modest advance; a total of 272 out of 304 Gakkai candidates emerged victorious. In the House of Councillors elections that June, all six of the Gakkai's candidates were elected, while the Gakkai vote in the national constituency climbed to 8.5 per cent of the total (see Appendix D, Tables D.1–D.4), as opposed to 3.5 per cent in 1956. However, by 1959 the Gakkai was claiming just under 1.2 million families, and the vote-to-member-family ratio had decreased to 2.32:1.

In the next House of Councillors election, in July 1962, all of the earlier trends continued. The number of seats held by the Gakkai increased, and both the movement's absolute vote and its percentage of the total vote increased. The rate of this increase in the Gakkai's percentage of the vote declined, however—from 143 per cent between 1956 and 1959 to 35 per cent between 1959 and 1962; and the vote-to-member-family ratio decreased to only 1.52:1.

These decreases were first taken up by the Society's critics following the local elections of April 1963. Again, the percentage of winning candidates had been high—98 per cent. In the Tokyo Metropolitan Assembly election the Kōmeitō became the Assembly's third largest force. In the Tokyo ward assembly elections the Kōseiren became the second largest political force after the Liberal Democrats, as well as the second most powerful party in eleven of the twenty-two wards holding elections.[45] But these gains were not what interested political observers.

"In the Tokyo Metropolitan Assembly election Kōseiren candidates in 16 wards drew 413,845 votes, an increase of only 30,380 votes, or 8 per cent, over the 383,465 votes drawn by Kōseiren candidates in the same 16 wards in the July 1962 Upper House election. An increase of 8 per cent in nine months represents an almost negligible growth compared to the usual growth rate claimed by the Sōkagakkai.

In the Tokyo ward assembly elections . . . Kōseiren candidates in these 16 wards attracted only 288,419 votes, a *decrease* of 95,046 votes (ca. 25 per cent) from July 1962 and a drop of 125,426 votes (ca. 30 per cent) in less than two weeks [the Tokyo Metropolitan Assembly election was held on April 17, the ward assembly elections on April 30]. In 22 Tokyo wards Kōseiren candidates polled 335,840 votes, again a decrease of some 25 per cent from the 383,465 votes the same 22 wards yielded in July 1962."[46]

In these partial returns some observers professed to perceive the limits of Gakkai political strength; but their conclusions are open to question. Since in Japan voting rates vary according to the type of election involved, generalizing from one level of elections to another is hazardous. It hardly seems likely that the Gakkai suffered a net loss of 125,000 of its supporters between April 17 and April 30, or even of 95,000 adherents in nine months. A more plausible explanation of the election results lies in comparative voting rates (i.e., their ratio of actual votes to registered voters) and Gakkai campaign strategy.

The voting rates in Upper House and Metropolitan Assembly elections are similar. But whereas in a House of Councillors election every Gakkai supporter in Tokyo could vote for a Kōseiren candidate, in a Metropolitan election only members living in districts where the Kōseiren ran candidates could express their support.[47] Gakkai strategy, of course, provides for candidates only in those districts where success is sure. Thus, in any district the Gakkai's returns are predictably smaller in the local assembly than in the Upper House elections. The voting rate for Tokyo's ward assembly elections is usually below the rate for the Metropolitan Assembly election, a phenomenon not noted by the Gakkai's critics; in 1963 the rates were 59 per cent and 67 per cent, respectively.[48] And again, all the inhabitants of a given ward could vote for that ward's Kōseiren candidate in a Metropolitan Assembly election—but only those living in the ward's smaller ward-assembly districts where Kōseiren candidates were running could vote Kōseiren in ward assembly elections. In other words, from Upper House to Metropolitan Assembly to ward assembly elections, the Gakkai membership's opportunity to express its support of the Kōseiren decreased proportionately.

Even if the local-election results of April 1963 did not constitute a downturn in the Gakkai's political fortunes, though, they did suggest that numerical growth was not what it should be, and that political mobilization was less than complete. The Upper House election of July 1965, the first such test of the new Kōmeitō party, confirmed this. In this election the Gakkai got out the vote as never before—5,097,682 votes from the national constituency, 13.7 per cent of the total—and the Kōmeitō won nine seats from the national constituency. But the party may have been squeezing the absolute maximum number of seats out of its electoral strength. Although all nine candidates from the national constituency were successful, only two of the five standing in local districts were elected. With the eleven new members the Kōmeitō gained a total representation of 20 seats in the House of Councillors. This meant a winning percentage of 79 per cent, not up to the Kōmeitō's standard of growth. The rate of increase in the Kōmeitō's share of the total vote from the national constituency reached a new low, 19.1 per cent, as did the vote-to-membership ratio: 0.96:1.

The Gakkai reacted quickly. Less than a month after the Upper House election a special election was being held for the Tokyo Metropolitan Assembly, which had been dissolved (owing partly to the

TABLE 8

Results of the Tokyo Metropolitan Assembly Election of July 22, 1965

Party	Seats Held Before Dissolution	Seats Held After Election
Liberal Democrats	66	38
Socialists	32	45
Kōmei	17	23
Democratic Socialists	—	4
Communists	2	9
Independents	1	1
Totals	120	120

NOTE: Pre-election total includes two vacancies.

Kōmeitō's efforts) over an internal scandal involving many of the Liberal Democratic assemblymen. The Kōmeitō put up twenty-three candidates, all of whom were elected. The balance of power in the assembly before and after the election is shown in Table 8.[49] As this table makes clear, after the by-election the Kōmeitō held the deciding vote in the new assembly: barring a coalition of Liberal Democrats and Socialists (unlikely on major issues), nothing could pass the assembly without the Kōmeitō's consent. Whichever side could win that party's assistance could dominate the assembly.

The elections of 1967. The Sōkagakkai intended the general election of 1967 to mark the Kōmeitō's entry into the Lower House. Although such a breakthrough is a formidable task for a new political entrant, the Society exuded confidence in the days before the election.[50] A new factor in the electoral system was expected to aid the Gakkai's debut: redistricting had produced five new urban constituencies with nineteen new seats. Table 9 shows the election results.[51]

The contrast between the 1963 and 1967 elections was strongest in Tokyo. There the Liberal Democratic Party's vote fell from 44 per cent of the total to 32 per cent; it lost votes not to the Socialists (whose returns dropped from 36 per cent to 27 per cent) but to the independents (whose share of the vote went up 6 per cent), the Communists and the Democratic Socialists (up 2 to 3 per cent apiece), and especially to the Kōmeitō, which tallied 13 per cent of the total vote.[52] The Kōmeitō's strongest areas were, predictably, the downtown lower-income districts—the tenth (Adachi, Katsushika, and Edogawa wards), where the Kōmeitō polled over 19 per cent of the total vote, and the sixth (Sumida, Kōtō, and Arakawa wards), where the Kōmeitō accounted for almost 18 per cent.[53]

TABLE 9

Results of the Japanese General Elections of 1963 and 1967

Party	Number of Votes	Percentage of Total Vote	Seats Won
NOVEMBER 1963 GENERAL ELECTION			
Liberal Democrats	22,423,915	54.7%	283
Socialists	11,906,766	29.0	144
Democratic Socialists	3,023,302	7.4	23
Communists	1,646,477	4.0	5
Other	59,765	0.1	—
Independents	1,956,313	4.8	12
Totals	41,016,540	100.0%	467
JANUARY 1967 GENERAL ELECTION			
Liberal Democrats	22,447,834	48.8%	277
Socialists	12,826,099	27.9	140
Democratic Socialists	3,404,462	7.4	30
Kōmei	2,472,371	5.4	25
Communists	2,190,563	4.8	5
Other	101,244	0.2	—
Independents	2,553,988	5.5	9
Totals	45,996,561	100.0%	486

Election analyses centered upon two related phenomena: the supposed "emergence of a multiparty system" and the increase in seats held by the Democratic Socialists and the Kōmeitō. From 1958 to 1967 the combined vote for the Liberal Democrats and the Socialists had declined from 90.7 per cent of the total vote to 76.7 per cent, while electoral support for the other parties had increased from 2.6 per cent to 17.6 per cent.[54] The proportion of Lower House seats held by the two major parties shrank from 92 per cent in 1960 to 86 per cent in 1967. However, parliamentary seats constitute power, and the LDP, regardless of losses, still held 57 per cent of the seats after the 1967 election. One commentator observed that election changes would be most appropriately termed a transformation from a one-and-a-half party system to a one-and-seven-eighths party system. And Prime Minister Satō, in a televised interview soon after the election, remarked that what had become "multiparty" was not the whole system but only the opposition.[55]

The Kōmeitō considered its own election performance only "satisfactory."[56] But even though its general election debut may not have been all the Gakkai hoped for, the party did succeed in breaking established voting patterns. The question observers asked was, how did the Kōmeitō win its votes and seats, and at whose expense? The answer seemed to be threefold: efficient organization, mobilization of previous nonvoters, and encroachment upon the electoral base of the Liberal Democratic Party.

A striking example of the Kōmeitō's organizational ability is its winning of a seat in rural Tokushima prefecture, hitherto an LDP stronghold. The Kōmeitō candidate in Tokushima was a stranger to the prefecture and thus could not capitalize on any of the kinship or local ties that count for so much in elections in rural Japan.[57] But through vigorous efforts the Kōmeitō managed to mobilize 49,000 votes—although the Gakkai claimed only 22,000 franchised members in the prefecture.[58] The Kōmeitō votes were spread evenly throughout the prefecture; in a typical instance, whereas the LDP candidate drew all of his votes from his bailiwick of four out of the prefecture's twenty-three districts, the Kōmeitō candidate polled between 9 and 12 per cent of the vote in nine of these twenty-three districts.[59]

In electoral districts where the Kōmeitō ran candidates in the January 1967 election, with one exception the voting rate increased over that of 1963. According to Nishihira Shigeki of the Institute of Statistical Mathematics, this was due partly to intensified activity among those strongly opposed to the Gakkai as well as to an increased turnout by Society members.[60] A study of the election returns by the editorial staff of the *Asahi Journal* corroborated the assumption of increased Gakkai support.[61] Nishihira and the *Asahi Journal* were agreed that most of the seats won by the Kōmeitō were either taken from the LDP or won from among the nineteen newly added seats. Nishihira estimated that the Kōmeitō took ten out of the nineteen new seats, eight seats from the LDP, five from the Socialists, and one apiece from the Democratic Socialists and the Communists.[62] According to the *Asahi Journal* the toll was twelve of the new seats, six LDP seats, and five Socialist seats.[63]

The nationwide series of local elections in April 1967 was held in two rounds. The first, on April 15, included elections for the governor of Tokyo, for the ward assemblies of Tokyo, and for the prefectural assemblies. Kōmeitō performance, though acceptable overall, was marred by the party's first major setback.

In the prefectural assembly elections, at least, eighty-four of the Kōmeitō's ninety-four candidates were successful. The pattern of seat increases reflected previous trends; the greatest gains were made in the urban areas.[64] But in the Tokyo ward elections, the other parties had apparently prepared to meet the Kōmeitō challenge by cutting back on their numbers of candidates; the overall ratio of candidates to seats, 1.47:1, was the lowest since the end of the war.[65] The Kōmeitō, on the contrary, ran over sixty candidates more than it had in 1963. Of its 202 candidates, only 124 were elected; the party lost its second-place standing to the Socialists, who won a total of 170 seats.[66] The Kōmeitō vote did rise 39 per cent; the party emphasized this positive aspect of the election but admitted the magnitude of the defeat.[67] And even more significant than the ward assembly defeat was the Kōmeitō's campaign in the Tokyo gubernatorial contest. For the first time the Kōmeitō had put up a candidate in a single-seat constituency, and for the first time it had entered a race where defeat seemed certain.

In the 1963 gubernatorial election the Sōkagakkai had supported the successful independent conservative candidate, Azuma Ryūtarō, as had the LDP. The reasoning behind the decision to back Azuma was never made clear; critics (especially those on the left) asserted that the Gakkai was simply showing its true reactionary colors.[68] Whatever the grounds for the 1963 strategy, the Kōmeitō's announcement in February 1967 that it would run its own candidate for governor, brought on fresh speculation about the Gakkai's motives. For although the estimated 600,000 votes ascribed to the Gakkai in Tokyo could be of great importance to some party with considerable voting strength of its own, they could hardly be expected to produce a winning candidate in a city of seven million eligible voters.

The Gakkai explained its decision by saying that such a candidacy was only natural for a party of the Kōmeitō's stature; to back another party's candidate again would be "fainthearted."[69] Outsiders varied in their interpretations of the announcement. The *Asahi Shimbun* saw the Gakkai's other alternatives as either alliance with one or more parties, or neutrality, with the members left free to vote as they pleased. The choice the Society had actually made seemed best calculated both to underline the Kōmeitō's active middle-of-the-road stance and to silence accusations that the party was essentially an insubstantial political actor.[70] Another view suggested that for the Kōmeitō to have followed another party again would have hurt its chances in the other local elections. According to this interpretation, the Gakkai sacrificed its gubernatorial candidate in the hope of winning representation in as many local assemblies as possible.[71]

The Kōmeitō's choice of Abe Ken'ichi, a heretofore unknown Gakkai director, as its candidate heightened speculation — which

Abe's campaign tactics did nothing to allay. Abe was indeed an indifferent candidate, who did little more than go through the motions of campaigning ("at my own pace"). His theme was "cleanliness": "Clean elections, clean metropolitan government, and a clean Tokyo."[72] The election-day returns reflected Abe's casual approach: leftist independent Minobe Ryōkichi won with 2,200,389 votes (44.5 per cent of the total), followed by conservative Matsushita Masayoshi with 2,063,752 votes (41.6 per cent); Abe drew 601,527 votes (12.1 per cent).[73]

Two weeks later, on April 28, the second round of elections, for city, town, and village assemblies throughout the nation, was held. Learning from its defeat in the ward elections, the Kōmeitō cut back its slate of candidates. The tactic apparently paid off: 96 per cent of the Kōmeitō candidates in city elections were successful. For town and village elections the reports are contradictory. The Kōmeitō claimed that it had put up 343 candidates and that 326 were elected.[74] According to official government figures, however, no seats were won by Kōmeitō candidates.[75]

The Kōmeitō's own evaluation of the 1967 local elections was mixed. The Tokyo ward elections were described as "a complete tactical mistake."[76] Kōmeitō electoral organization is so efficient that the total Kōmeitō vote is spread very carefully among all Kōmeitō candidates; thus, every election is an all-or-nothing effort and, if votes are divided among barely too many candidates, all may lose.[77] Why so many candidates were put up in the wards is an unanswered question. The party may have misread its strength, but it may also be that the Kōmeitō is falling victim to the same pressures that cause other parties to provide candidates for as many of their supporters as is possible. Of the gubernatorial contest the Kōmeitō said, "it was not necessarily a favorable result."[78] In a negative sense the campaign had been successful; had the Kōmeitō not run its own candidate, the membership of the Gakkai would have become a prize for the other parties to fight over.[79] Then, too, Abe had become well known in Tokyo. When the Kōmeitō named him as a candidate in the July 1968 Upper House election he won easily, with over 800,000 votes.

In all of the April 1967 elections eighty-nine per cent of the Kōmeitō's candidates were successful. The absolute Kōmeitō vote increased in every contest; so also did the party's percentage of the vote. In May, the number of Kōmeitō seats in local legislative bodies (including seats not up for reelection that April) totaled 1,873. By January 1968 that figure had risen, with by-elections, to 1,954.[80]

ELECTORAL PROSPECTS

In any study of the Sōkagakkai, the question is raised of the organization's future expansion. Is the Gakkai actually a viable social, religious, and political actor that can be expected to increase in size and power—or at least to continue to exist—in the foreseeable future? For, as the Gakkai election performance illustrates, the law of diminishing returns seems to be operating on the Gakkai's efforts to build up its numerical and electoral strength. What are the consequences for the Society's political party? Several critics have applied the "limit argument" *(genkaisetsu)* to the current position of the Kōmeitō. They base their interpretation on how the Gakkai fared in the last five Upper House elections (see Table 10); the outcome of the 1963 local elections; the results of the 1967 general elections; the apparent ceiling on Kōmeitō electoral power in Tokyo, the Gakkai's birthplace; and the limitations imposed on the party by its association with the Gakkai.

The Upper House and 1963 election results (indexes of actual party electoral strength) reiterate the message of the Gakkai membership's growth rate (an index of potential Kōmeitō power), tabulated in Appendix B: Gakkai growth is slowing down. Whether this signifies stagnation or stabilization depends upon one's frame of reference. In any case, the Kōmeitō appears to have secured its position as a minority party, in a role roughly equivalent to that of the Democratic Socialists. As for the general election of 1967, the Kōmeitō candidates

TABLE 10

Sōkagakkai Performance in Five Upper House Elections

Year	Seats Held by Gakkai	Total Gakkai Vote (National Constituency)	Percentage of National Vote	Claimed Membership at Election Time (in Families)	Votes Per Family	Increase in Total Gakkai Vote	Percentage Increase in Total Gakkai Vote	Absolute Increase in Percentage of National Vote
1956	3	991,540	3.5%	460,000	2.44			
						+1,495,261	+143%	+5%
1959	9	2,486,801	8.5	1,177,000	2.32			
						+1,637,468	+ 73	+3
1962	15	4,124,269	11.5	2,700,000	1.52			
						+ 937,413	+ 19.1	+2.2
1965	20	5,097,682	13.7	5,300,000	.96			
						+1,558,818	+ 13.1	+1.8
1968	24	6,656,500	15.5	6,600,000	.99			

SOURCE: Sangi-in Jimukyoku, *Sangi-in Giin Senkyo Ichiran*, Nos. 4–7; Kasahara Kazuo, *Seiji to Shūkyō*, p. 290; *Mainichi Shimbun*, July 9, 1968.

who were put up in thirty-two districts polled a total of 2,472,371 votes; in the same districts in the 1965 Upper House election, the party had received a total of 2,058,044 votes.[81] The relatively small increase looks even smaller when one recalls that the voting rate for Upper House elections is slightly lower than that for Lower House elections.[82] The Kōmeitō's percentage of the total returns, in 1967, compared with its proportion of the 1965 Upper House election vote, increased in four of the thirty-two districts and decreased in twenty-four. In five districts the absolute Kōmeitō vote fell below what it had been in 1965.[83]

In the mid-1960's a ceiling on Gakkai electoral strength in Tokyo seems to have developed. Two* of the five districts where absolute vote declined in 1967 had been bastions of Gakkai strength. Earlier, after winning 529,575 votes in the Tokyo district in the 1962 Upper House election and 413,826 in the 1963 Tokyo Metropolitan Assembly election, the Kōmeitō drew 608,235, 506,705, 618,864, and 601,527 votes in the 1965 Upper House election, the 1965 Metropolitan Assembly election, the 1967 Lower House election, and the 1967 Tokyo Gubernatorial election respectively.[84] Tokyo saw the initial growth of the Gakkai after World War II; this apparent leveling-off at the Society's birthplace may foreshadow a similar phenomenon in other urban centers. However, the 831,893 votes won in Tokyo by Abe in the July 1968 Upper House election could mark a new trend: support for the Kōmeitō coming from outside the Gakkai.

The force of the genkaisetsu can best be realized if one visualizes the increases in Gakkai numerical strength and Kōmeitō electoral strength as a pair of curves, with the space separating them representing a time lag (see Fig. 1). The time lag derives from two factors: conversion and politicization are not simultaneous, and politicization may not coincide with an election. A new Gakkai member thus does not necessarily figure as a new Kōmeitō voter immediately upon embracing the faith. "The Present" in Figure 1 shows a probable national pattern; but in areas like Tokyo or Osaka the electoral power of the Kōmeitō as well as the numbers of the Gakkai may already be nearer the maximum.[85]

The limit argument has validity, but one must distinguish between electoral and parliamentary power and not anticipate the future too closely. Kōmeitō electoral power (the total number of votes commanded) may be approaching a limit, as we have seen, but the election

---

* The sixth district (Sumida, Kōtō, and Arakawa wards) and the tenth district (Adachi, Katsushika, and Edogawa wards).

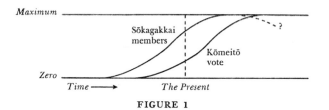

FIGURE 1

record makes it clear that Kōmeitō parliamentary power (the number of seats held) is growing steadily in most areas. Moreover, Figure 1 will be invalidated if the Gakkai or Kōmeitō succeeds in appealing to social elements now essentially outside the Society's radius. In Part II the various social and economic trends that might contribute to a broadened appeal will be considered in relation to the future of the Gakkai as a whole; however, one supposed political trend that might benefit the Kōmeitō directly should be mentioned here.

The "multiparty" trend was referred to in connection with interpretations of the 1967 general election. The source of this tendency appears to be antiestablishment voter sentiment: while traditionally conservative voters in the countryside are beginning to vote for parties of the left and center, the strongly socialist urban areas elected a remarkable number of Democratic Socialists and Kōmeitō representatives.[86] The gradual electoral decline of the LDP over the last decade is an empirical fact; the defeats that party received in the 1965 Tokyo Metropolitan Assembly election and in the urban districts in the 1967 general election indicate a discontent with the ruling party that can be expected to grow.* The Socialist Party, however, is apparently unable to capture the LDP's lost votes, and there is no compelling reason for believing that they will be any more successful in this effort in the future.

Both major parties harbor disaffection in their ranks. The fact that disaffected supporters do not shift their allegiance from one major party to the other is due, according to Nishihira, to the distinctive ideologies of the two main Japanese parties, and to the way these affect their adherents. The ideological distance between the LDP and

* The apparent LDP resurgence in the 1969 general election is largely the result of shrewd candidate selection, not electoral appeal. Although the LDP won 288 seats in the 1969 election (as opposed to 277 in 1967) the LDP's share of the popular vote fell from 48.8% in 1967 to 47.6% in 1969. See *Mainichi Shimbun*, December 29, 1969.

the Socialist Party is so great that to cross over from one to the other is extremely trying psychologically for the Japanese. As a result, when a voter is dissatisfied with his party, he is bound to find a more ideologically familiar minor party preferable to the other major party.[87] Thus the dissatisfied voters are highly accessible to the Kōmeitō, the Democratic Socialist Party, and, to a lesser extent, the Communist Party. Whether the Kōmeitō will be able to take especial advantage of this trend will depend on the attractiveness of the Gakkai's appeal to the discontented elements in the electorate.

ELECTORAL OBJECTIVES

Despite its ceaseless exertions both in and out of parliament, the Kōmeitō finds the world little better today than when the party was founded.[88] The party's objective, therefore, is to redouble its efforts and attain a commanding position in the political system. Its short-term goals are couched in terms of additional legislative seats: in the 1969 general election the party put up seventy-six candidates. In the near future it plans to run candidates in every electoral contest held;[89] within the next seven years the Kōmeitō intends to control the deciding vote in both houses of the National Diet and in legislative assemblies all over the nation.[90]

Political power is the ultimate organizational goal of the Kōmeitō. But the party emphasizes that its measures for welfare and reform can enjoy a large measure of success even while the Kōmeitō is a minority party. Hōjō Hiroshi has said,

I don't think it is so vital for us to become the ruling party in order to attain our purpose. . . .

Our main target is to clean up corrupt politics, to make Japanese politics as it ought to be, and so make Japan a stable and reliable force in Asia for achieving world peace. . . .

The Kōmeitō today is a relatively small party. . . . Even if we want to be the ruling party, we cannot be unless we have the support of more voters. But by and by, as the people acknowledge how we are working for the Japanese nation, they will decide for themselves.

To take power is not our purpose, but rather to sweep away corruption and establish a public-welfare society. If the Japanese people favor this course, however, the Kōmeitō might become the ruling party. . . .

Of course, . . . any party aims at becoming the majority party someday.[91]

Most Japanese observers go to considerable lengths in evaluating the Kōmeitō to assign the party and the Sōkagakkai a place in a left-right political spectrum. As we have seen, the philosophy, policy, and intra- and extraparliamentary action of the Kōmeitō make this no simple task. Furthermore, the same oppositionist tendency that appears leftist in the context of the National Diet seems conservative when expressed in the Tokyo Assembly. Opposition to the visit of the *Enterprise,* to the role of the United States in the Vietnam war, and to American control of Okinawa may all seem leftist. Survey data suggest, however, that such attitudes form part of the ever more self-assertive mainstream of Japanese popular opinion, which one could conceivably term rightist. The Gakkai itself insists that "left" and "right" have become obsolete concepts, that the distinction is a meaningless one. It criticizes everyone impartially but not wholly; past positions never hinder its adoption of new and radically different ones, and the Kōmeitō acts in concert with the Society.

The dissenting trend in the Kōmeitō's policies is calculated to win votes away from the major parties, with which more and more electors are apparently dissatisfied. (One suspects therefore that Kōmeitō opposition—*vide* the veto of Minobe's nominees for lieutenant-governor—is not always as principled as the party would have one believe.) Similarly, the party's new self-assertiveness, paralleling the rise of popular feeling, will probably be to its benefit electorally. The danger here is that if the Kōmeitō forsakes its commitment to Gakkai philosophy in attempting to voice the desires of the masses, the party may become no more than a vehicle for public opinion—a demogogic expositor of popular passions. Nevertheless, this responsiveness of the Kōmeitō to public opinion testifies to the fact that the Gakkai's real significance for Japanese political life lies in its relationship to a democratic political system.

Looking at the Gakkai in this light, I think a continuum ranging from moderate to extreme rather than from left to right more to the point in characterizing the Society's political import. Our survey of Gakkai organization, action, and membership suggests that the best way to locate the Society and its political party on such a continuum will be to examine the Sōkagakkai as an entity and its members as a social collectivity, using the models of mass movement and mass man.

PART II

THE SOKAGAKKAI AND
THE MASS MODEL

CHAPTER 9

The Member as Mass Man

IN PART I, through a comparative examination of the social composition of the Sōkagakkai, I attempted to make a prima facie case
for studying the Gakkai in terms of Kornhauser's model of a mass
movement. In this chapter and in those to come, I shall apply the
mass man and mass movement models to the Society more syste-
matically, analyzing it as a social collectivity and as an organizational
entity. At the beginning of this book, the essential characteristics of
mass man were set down as follows.

(1) Nonattachment characterizes his position in and connection
with society. Theoretically, in comparison with his fellows, he has
fewer ties to social groups, especially to secondary ones; he has access
to fewer sources of information from his environment and receives
less information about it; and he feels a weaker sense of identity with
other social groupings (such as socioeconomic classes) within his society.

(2) Alienation characterizes his psychological patterns. He is, first
of all, alienated from himself. In comparison with his fellows, he feels
relatively impotent and helpless, and he perceives the futility of all
his actions. These feelings lead to a disrespect for his own intellectual
capability, manifested in a desire for simple solutions and explanations and a generalized mistrust of rational intellectual processes.[1]
Another theoretical characteristic of the self-alienated mass man is
the syndrome of psychological attributes known as the "authoritarian
personality,"[2] which is the distinguishing feature of totalitarian man
according to Kornhauser.[3] The Sōkagakkai has been described so frequently as fascist, or otherwise totalitarian, that it is advisable to test
for this property.

Alienation also characterizes his social patterns. He is relatively less trusting of people in general; whatever relationships he does have are highly partisan and exclusive, accentuating the general context of distrust. In addition, although mass man does not have any deep sense of identity with the groups of which he is objectively a member, he envies and feels enmity toward those he senses are better off.

Finally, alienation characterizes his position within the social, economic, and political system. He feels a relatively high sense of frustration and unfulfilled expectation at the way "the system" treats him. More generally, mass man feels less commitment to his society. In Japan, as in any other democratic society, such a lack of commitment by numbers of people bears on whether or not the system will function in a stable manner.[4]

(3) Mass behavior characterizes the activities of mass man. He is relatively apathetic toward his society. When he does act he pursues remote—even utopian—goals, and he acts directly without regard to social norms, rules, or relationships.

The social, psychological, and behavioral characteristics of mass man—especially the behavioral—clearly relate to the stable functioning of a democratic political system, which we take to be

a political system which supplies regular constitutional opportunities for changing the governing officials, and a social mechanism which permits the largest possible part of the population to influence major decisions by choosing among contenders for political office.

This definition . . . implies a number of specific conditions: (1) a "political formula" or body of beliefs specifying which institutions—political parties, a free press, and so forth—are legitimate (accepted as proper by all); (2) one set of political leaders in office; and (3) one or more sets of recognized leaders attempting to gain office.[5]

The concept of a democratic "political formula" has been defined and tested by James Prothro and Charles Grigg. The three features of their "formula" are acceptance of democracy (undefined) as the best form of government; acceptance of the principle of majority rule; and acceptance of the principle of minority rights.[6]

When we speak of a "mass man" or a "mass society" we are speaking hypothetically. There is no exact social or psychological threshold at which an individual is declared to be a mass man. There is, however, a threshold at which the behavior of such individuals and groups becomes politically relevant. Once nonattached and alienated individuals and groups turn to direct political action and thus pose a threat to a stable democratic polity, such individuals and groups may be considered mass men and mass movements.

Clearly any study of this type is limited by the data available.* Although the data assembled here constitute the broadest empirical base used in a study of the Sōkagakkai to date, it must be stated that inevitably the samples used were insufficient. Over two dozen surveys of varied political and sociological foci were collected.[7] Supplementing these surveys were clinical data from several sources[8] and a great number of more informal interviews and conversations with Gakkai members on various levels of the organization.

Survey data necessarily tap only orientations, which are both potential and relative. Unless empirical evidence of direct action or an absolutely clear potential for such action can be proven, we cannot designate mass men or mass movements in Kornhauser's sense. For these reasons the behavioral aspect of the model of mass man is assumed here to be of special importance. If behavior is crucial, one might ask, why bother with the attitudes of all the Gakkai members surveyed, when only the activists really matter? One should note that the most apathetic elements of the Gakkai membership, including apostates, do not appear in the samples, which require, if nothing further, at least a verbalized profession of faith. It is reasonable that any believer willing to admit his faith thus could be mobilized toward Gakkai goals; therefore, his attitudes are relevant to a full understanding of the political behavioral potential of the Gakkai.

Our emphasis on religious faith and its relevance to Japanese politics needs explanation, especially in light of a 1963 nationwide survey that found the most significant factors influencing responses to attitudinal questions to be (in descending order of importance) education, age, occupation, sex, place of residence (by geographical area), political party support, place of residence (urban or rural), and interest in elections.[9] The impact of religious faith was negligible. More specifically, in contrast to the positive relationship between religious belief and intolerance in the West discerned by Lipset and others, a Japanese survey of 1958 yielded the results set out in Table 11.[10] The implication of the data is clear: not only is religious faith likely to prove a relatively unimportant factor in the total pattern of orientations and attitudes among Japanese, but a more specific aspect of

* A discussion of methodology and data-gathering will be found in Appendix A, pp. 299–302.

TABLE 11
Responses to the Statement "All Religions Are Really the Same"

Viewpoints	Respondents			
	Agreeing	Disagreeing	Undecided, No Answer	n
Belief in a religion	74%	11%	15%	320
Lack of belief in religion, but a "religious spirit" considered important	70	13	17	425
Lack of belief; a "religious spirit" considered unimportant	50	21	29	103

religious belief particularly relevant to this study is apparently con-tradicted by Japanese data.

The assumption made in this study, however, is that in the case of the Gakkai, at least, religious faith can bear an important relation-ship to other aspects of one's personality and behavior. If this is true, then the significance of the Gakkai as a faith that already constitutes an exception to the general pattern of religion in Japan in several re-spects is increased.

NONATTACHMENT

One of the primary features of Kornhauser's mass man is a lack of secondary ties to society: "differences in receptivity to mass symbols and leaders are due primarily to the strength of social ties."[11] This connection between social nonattachment and massness (and thus to a susceptibility to mass movements) is corroborated both by other theorists[12] and by empirical example. Kornhauser demonstrates that social elements lacking ties to the larger society are drawn to mass movements, citing the Communists in France, Italy, Russia, Canada, and England; the Poujadists in France; and the Nazis in Germany.[13] America's Moral Rearmament movement attracted many persons of the same type.[14]

The study by Raymond Wolfinger and his colleagues of the sup-porters of the Christian Anti-Communist Crusade who attended meetings indicates that extremists need not be "social isolates"; they may maintain group memberships and participate in community or other nonpolitical activities.[15] However, these Crusaders, by the fact of their attendance at a meeting, appear to be relatively activist. This example does not refute the previous assertion that the followers of mass movements tend to be relatively nonattached to society, but it does suggest that activists in mass movements may differ from the rank and file in their social position and connections.

The inclination to join groups appears to vary culturally and demographically. Gabriel Almond and Sidney Verba found that the proportion of respondents who were members of some secondary voluntary association varied from a high of 57 per cent in the United States through 47 per cent in England, 44 per cent in Germany, and 29 per cent in Italy to a low of 25 per cent in Mexico. In every country, more men than women had joined groups. The tendency to develop a network of secondary ties, and the extent of this network, varied directly with education.[16] A 1966 survey indicates that the Japanese are especially prone to join secondary groups: 75 per cent of the respondents professed membership in at least one such group.[17] Demographic variations parallel the Almond and Verba data.

Since the Gakkai membership is composed primarily of the social elements least likely to participate in secondary groups, one might expect members to have established relatively few voluntary relationships compared to the Japanese norm. This should be the case if members approximate the model of mass man; but survey data contradict this assumption. In one Tokyo University study, Gakkai members in the sample averaged 1.83 organizational relationships each, as opposed to 1.86 per respondent for nonmembers from approximately the same background.[18] Of course, membership in the Gakkai constitutes one such relationship for each Society member. But in addition, 36 per cent of the secondary relationships reported by Gakkai members were with local neighborhood organizations not affiliated with the Society (nonmembers reported 48 per cent). Data on officeholding experience corroborate the impression that Gakkai members are not nonattached. Out of a large sample of Kōmeitō supporters, 9.3 per cent reported such experience (in local or neighborhood government or in unofficial bodies and unions), as opposed to 3.1 per cent of the total national sample.[19] Thus one can conclude that Gakkai members have secondary ties and that these ties are not restricted to Gakkai-related associations.

Since members of the Gakkai are ipso facto attached to a secondary group, what concerns us is the degree to which they confine other secondary relationships to Gakkai-related groups. (This idea is especially important in light of the pluralist assertion that a network of crosscutting intermediate relationships is a more stable foundation for a democratic system than is a multiplicity of mutually exclusive social groups.) In the Tokyo University study cited above, Gakkai members were almost as active as nonmembers in the nonreligious associations to which they belonged, and were much more active (in terms of attendance) in their overall networks of secondary relationships.[20] In another survey, 31 per cent of a sample of Gakkai members reported belonging to other groups besides the Society.[21] This figure is more significant if one notes that only 58 per cent of the sample described themselves as participating members of the Society. The survey did suggest, however, that the degree of exclusivity of the relationship with the Gakkai increases with time. A possible positive correlation exists between duration of membership and the likelihood that one's only secondary relationships will be with religious organizations.

Exclusivity can also be examined in terms of reference groups— those persons to whom one turns in time of trouble. Two surveys (see Tables 12 and 13) suggest a tendency already noted: Gakkai members tend to see the Society as their primary reference group, but only in the case of activist members is the magnitude of isolation or nonattachment that is attributed to the mass man model approximated. Other surveys indicate the same pattern of social attachments.[22] Because Gakkai members do not absolutely lack secondary relationships and because their relationships are not exclusively within the Gakkai, one cannot conclude that the members are nonattached to society.

We have noted that a lack of communication, a deficiency in sources of information, affects mass man's nonattachment to society.

TABLE 12
Relationship of Involvement in the Sōkagakkai to Choice of a Reference Group

Reference Groups (person(s) sought when one is troubled with human problems)	Entire Sōka- gakkai Membership	Members by Degree of Activism (in terms of extent of participation)		
		Attend All Activities	Participate on Occasion	Don't Par- ticipate Much
Gakkai leaders or seniors	41.9%	75%	55.6%	14.3%
Groups of believers at Gakkai meetings	6.5	—	11.1	7.1
The gohonzon (individual worship)	12.9	12.5	11.1	14.3
Family, relatives	6.5	—	—	14.3
Friends	6.5	—	—	14.9
Other	3.2	—	—	6.5
No one in particular	22.6	12.5	22.2	28.6
Total	100.1%	100.0%	100.0%	100.0%

SOURCE: Naikaku Kanbō, *Shinkō Shūkyō*, p. 60.

TABLE 13

Where the Sōkagakkai Member Finds His Most Intimate Friend

Location of Friend	Sōkagakkai Leaders	Nonleader Members
In the Sōkagakkai:	94.56%	45.16%
Outside the Sōkagakkai:	3.36	45.76
Respondent "can't really say"	2.17	2.26
Other, don't know, no answer	—	6.82
Total	100.09%	100.00%

SOURCE: Suzuki Hiroshi, pp. 83–84.

It also influences mass movements, for "the force possessed by totalitarian propaganda . . . lies in its ability to shut the masses off from the real world."[23] A member of a mass movement can be expected to limit communications from society to those that reach him through the channels of the movement.

The sources of information open to members of the Gakkai are so varied that one cannot call the membership as a whole isolated or nonattached to the larger social environment. A small, local survey does indicate that over half of the members obtain their information about elections through media that are or may be connected with the Gakkai. Reliance on such sources seems to increase with length of membership; almost all respondents of over six years' membership reported acquiring their political information through "religious organization(s)."[24] But even though Gakkai-related media are primary, the membership on the whole does not appear to the isolated. In seeking general information, the members combine general dependence on Gakkai media and nonisolation, and even exhibit definite apathy toward Gakkai communication channels.[25] In a survey in Fukuoka City, only 20 per cent of a sample of Gakkai members restricted their newspaper reading to the *Seikyō Shimbun*, although an additional 53 per cent read the *Seikyō* and some other newspaper.[26] A slightly larger number of Gakkai members apparently limit their reading to Society magazines—38 per cent of the sample in the Fukuoka survey. However, 53 per cent reported that they did not read any Gakkai-related magazines.[27] Moreover, fully half of the Gakkai members admitted they had never read any of the Society's four classics (*Shakubuku Handbook, Human Revolution, Nichiren Shōshū–Sōkagakkai,* and *Theory of Value*); only 6 per cent claimed they had read all of them.[28] In general, leaders and those with longer periods of membership showed a marked tendency toward closure of secular communications links with society—whether the medium was newspapers, magazines, or classics—and whereas only 35 per cent of the rank and file were buyers and readers of religious magazines, 80 per cent of the officeholders were.[29]

Kornhauser defines masses in part as "people who are not integrated into any broad social groupings, including classes."[30] Data on the class consciousness of Gakkai members are insufficient to allow any but the most tentative suppositions. It has been asserted that Gakkai members relative to others in their society are not class conscious in the militant unionist sense of that term: despite the preponderance of proletarians in the employed part of the Gakkai membership, one survey indicated that Kōmeitō followers did not favor strikes as much as the supporters of any other party except the Liberal Democrats.[31] Such attitudes, of course, reflect Gakkai teachings, which recommend prayers and hard work, not strikes; one cannot be sure whether working-class members of the Gakkai are unaware of their proper Marxist role, or are just inclined to repeat what they have been told. If available survey data are any indication, Gakkai members do not find it hard to identify with a socioeconomic class. In two small surveys, practically all the Gakkai members in the samples put themselves in a specific class, albeit with some notable cases of discrepancy between subjective and apparent objective class status.[32]

To sum up briefly, then, we find that in general Gakkai members do rely heavily on communications media and persons connected with the Society as points of reference. This reliance seems to vary with the degree of activism, and there may be elements in the Gakkai leadership sufficiently isolated from secular society in terms of human and communications links that they may be described as mass men in this respect. However, Gakkai members, even the more completely socialized Kōmeitō supporters, are involved with secondary groups to an extent inconsistent with the characteristics of mass man.* Thus one cannot conclude on the basis of the data reviewed so far that the members of the Sōkagakkai are "mass men" in Kornhauser's sense.

SELF-ALIENATION

The self-alienation of Sōkagakkai members can be analyzed, with considerable theoretical justification, in terms of their sense of powerlessness and futility and their tendency to seek simple explanations

---

* This involvement is the more notable when one considers that Gakkai members are primarily from those social elements connected, in other countries besides Japan, with a tendency toward noninvolvement.

TABLE 14

Responses to the Question "In This World, Do You Think That If One Works Honestly One Can Save and Thus Stabilize One's Livelihood?"

Viewpoints	Sōkagakkai Members	Whole Sample
Yes	36.5%	45.7%
No	40.4	29.7
Even if something can be saved, no stability will result	11.5	15.9
Not interested in saving	6.0	1.5
Other, don't know, no answer	5.6	7.2

TABLE 15

Expectations of Job Advancement

Responses to Questioning	Sōkagakkai Members	Nonmembers
Promotion to executive thought possible	8.7%	12.4%
Promotion to section chief thought possible	—	8.6
No hope of promotion	17.4	6.7
No interest in promotion	4.3	11.5
Question irrelevant to respondent's hopes	30.4	29.2
Other, don't know, no answer	39.2	31.6

and solutions.[33] According to Kornhauser, the feeling of powerlessness is the primary manifestation of self-alienation.[34] The sense of "political efficacy" or "subjective competence," which may be considered the antithesis of self-alienated subjective impotence,* tends to vary with education and socioeconomic status. Thus one would expect members of the Gakkai to be more liable to feelings of powerlessness and futility than are the Japanese in general,[35] and this appears in some respects to be the case.[36] Table 14 illustrates the attitudes of members of the Gakkai and the general populace who were polled in a survey about the possibility of success.[37] The apparent pessimism of the Gakkai members' responses is ambiguous, since one does not know whether believers really have so little faith in the possibility of success, or if they simply feel that work is of no use unless supplemented with religious belief. Data from another survey (see Table 15) suggest that the members really feel impotent; people were asked about their expectations of job advancement and the possible extent of any advance.[38]

---

* Lane supports the validity of this consideration when he notes a covariance between such a sense of efficacy and a broader sense of mastery of oneself and one's environment (*Life*, pp. 149–55).

Contradicting these data are my observations and the results of several clinical psychological studies.[39] In my contacts with Gakkai members, I found them almost without exception to be outgoing, active (but not agitated), positive, and apparently confident of achieving their goals. Survey data also suggest a feeling among members that people have a certain power or control, at least in the political system; implied is the opinion that people should act to realize this potency.[40] Asked what the causes of political corruption were, 65 per cent of the Kōmeitō supporters as opposed to 46 per cent of a national sample polled in an *Asahi Shimbun* survey cited "insufficient voter awareness." In the same survey 72 per cent of the Kōmeitō supporters, compared to a national average of 60 per cent, agreed with the statement, "If the people would only take more interest in national politics, politics would become better." In a survey conducted by Verba and his associates, Gakkai members were twice as likely as other persons to feel a sense of political potency when asked three questions about local and national politics. The answers to these questions varied with sex, education, and income; the concentration of Gakkai members in female, low-education, and low-income categories thus renders more noteworthy the contrast between their feelings and those of the general population.

The data on the feelings of powerlessness and futility among Gakkai members permit no conclusions. An apparent sense of social impotence and hopelessness is countered by a sense of initiative and a strong feeling of subjective competence (*shutaisei*) in the political framework. It is possible that Gakkai members compartmentalize the socioeconomic and the political in their minds. The Society has demonstrated its effectiveness in the political system, thus possibly giving the membership a vicarious sense of competence, but the social system has remained beyond the manipulations of the Gakkai and so is a sphere in which faith has yet to prove its strength.

The stress under which the mass man lives weakens his tolerance of complexity. He seeks a set of easily understandable beliefs that will render his total environment coherent, whether or not these beliefs coincide with normally elementary criteria of truth or rationality or with "the most obvious rules of common sense."[41] The total theology of the Gakkai, although in reality constituting a highly complex body of doctrine, appears in the responses of members as a blanket explanation of the universe that is not only simple, but inconsistent with the most rudimentary criteria of scientific truth.

Gakkai members, in innumerable testimonials, have claimed relief from infantile paralysis, general debilitation, tuberculosis, hernia, and high blood pressure.[42] Claims regarding the power of faith include such statements as these:

When typhoons came, our family threw itself into devout prayer and was protected from damage . . . wouldn't all Japan also be saved from damage in typhoons as the result of faith?

During the May–June rice-planting period the sun beat down every day. The prayers of the farmers, eyes turned to the sky, were in vain; the fields dried and cracked and now the green shoots are already turning brown.

Strangely, the predictions made by St. Nichiren are coming true, and the "three calamities and seven disasters" (*sanzai-shichinan*) described in the *Risshō Ankoku Ron* are appearing today.

As Typhoon No. 7 dissipated, the low pressure stimulated the rainy-season weather front, bringing record heavy rains to many areas that inflicted great damage and cost in human life. . . . After *kōsen-rufu* this kind of natural calamity will not occur.[43]

In the Japanese context these accounts are not as startling as they sound to most Westerners; nevertheless, any general scientific standards of causality would classify as irrational such explanations of healing and natural disasters. Scientists would probably also balk at the story told to me by one Gakkai member about an acquaintance killed in an auto accident: owing to the man's condition of enlightenment, his body never decomposed but remained in a state of apparent peaceful sleep until the moment of cremation several days later.

Nevertheless, Gakkai members apparently do accord science some validity. In one recent poll, in response to a question on the possibility and means of accomplishing man's salvation, 78 per cent of the Gakkai members in the sample chose the answer "Both science and religion are necessary."[44] But the consistent protestations of the power of faith made by large numbers of Gakkai members lead one to suspect that members value simple explanations and solutions to the point of rejecting or ignoring secular criteria of truth and rationality.*

If, in studying self-alienation in Gakkai members, we find that the members' personality characteristics resemble the authoritarian personality described by T. W. Adorno and his colleagues, then we should also find a likeness to Kornhauser's "totalitarian man," who is

---

* Unfortunately there is no dependable data on this question. Possibly this similarity to the mass man model may be more cultural that specific to the Gakkai; one should recall the general nonrationality of Japanese religion noted above.

potentially more of a threat to the survival and stability of democratic political systems than is mass man.[45] One facet of the authoritarian personality as defined by Adorno is a strong social conventionalism;[46] thus a brief treatment of cultural and social conservatism in Gakkai members will be useful here. We are also interested, of course, in behavior conducive to the stability of democratic systems. There are other threats to democracy than those posed by a nonattached, alienated mass; one of them is a social and normative attachment to a past, such as Japan's, in which the culture was dominated by undemocratic norms and values.

Gakkai members appear to be fairly typical of the Japanese population with respect to their traditionalism or social conservatism. A national survey on the Japanese national character carried out in 1963 asked numerous questions dealing with such attitudes; of nine questions that clearly dealt with traditionalism, Gakkai members responded more conservatively than the overall sample to four questions, less conservatively to two questions, and similarly to three questions.[47] On the questions to which members responded more conservatively, controls for educational level, age, and sex revealed Gakkai members as relatively traditional in each category. In most cases, however, the difference from the national average was only a few percentage points; and since the sample of Gakkai members contained only ninety-four persons, one cannot conclude that Gakkai members are appreciably more conservative than the general populace.

In two additional surveys, whose data could not be subjected to controls, Gakkai members again appeared to differ only negligibly from the general population.[48] Since Gakkai members were concentrated in the social strata more likely to make such responses (the less educated, the lower in socioeconomic status, and so on), whether or not Gakkai members were in fact more conservative than others in their immediate socioeconomic context cannot be determined. In one of two local surveys run for the government in 1964,[49] on three of seven questions dealing with conservatism, Gakkai members were equally or less traditional than nonmembers on every educational level. They were less traditional than nonmembers on two more of the questions, and in their responses to the remaining two questions were equally or more traditional than nonmembers on every educational level. Considering the fact that Gakkai members come predominantly from the less educated strata, their apparent equivalence to the sample as a whole suggests that for their demographic group their social orientations may be quite advanced.

Gakkai activists do not appear to vary significantly from the general public in their degree of social conservatism. In the national character study cited above, the answers of activists roughly paralleled those of the less active (in terms of frequency of practice, i.e., prayer, attendance, and shakubuku) and, again, the only conclusion possible is that Gakkai activists cannot be described decisively as either more or less conservative than their fellow Japanese.[50]

A similar conclusion is all one can draw from a comparison of Gakkai members with the authoritarian personality studied by Adorno and his associates. According to Adorno, there is a "potential fascist" personality syndrome, characterized by:

(1) Conventionalism: an extreme emphasis on conventional norms and values.
(2) Authoritarian submission: a total and uncritical submission to authority.
(3) Authoritarian aggression: extreme antipathy toward those who violate conventional values.
(4) Anti-intraception: opposition to the subjective and imaginative.
(5) Superstitution and stereotypy.
(6) Power and "toughness": emphasis on the assertion of power and on dominance-submission relationships; identification with power figures.
(7) Destructiveness and cynicism: diffuse, general hostility toward the world.
(8) Projectivity: the perception of one's own emotional impulses realized in one's environment, especially those impulses that seem evil.
(9) Sex: an overconcern with supposed sexual goings-on in society.[51]

This list includes many of the specific characteristics of classic fascism.[52] It also notes several elements that seem to be facets of the Gakkai belief system—the unquestioning acceptance of authority, the aggressive tendencies visible in shakubuku, the superstition, and the hostility toward a heretical outside world.

Attempting to measure the presence of authoritarian personality characteristics in individuals, Adorno and his colleagues devised the California F[ascism]-Scale, a series of questions to be answered on a continuum ranging from "strongly disagree" (scored as −3) to "strongly agree" (scored as +3). Since agreement with any question should reveal an authoritarian tendency, high total and mean scores represent configurations tending toward the authoritarian personality type. Several empirical studies do "indicate that the scale makes reliable discriminations between clinically identified groups of adults and against the definition of 'anti-democratic trends' used by Adorno."[53] The F-scale has apparently been proven to be a valid tool for measuring authoritarian personality traits, but just what types, whether Communist, fascist, or whatever, is open to debate.[54] However, the exact nature of the authoritarianism revealed by the test is of less concern to this study than several doubts that recent research has cast on the usefulness of the F-scale.

Any effort to test the Japanese or, in particular, Gakkai members must take into account a phenomenon known as "positive response set" or "acquiescence set," i.e., the tendency to agree to any question regardless of its content. Certain social groups, when tested with both ordinary F-scales and reversed F-scales (so that agreement denotes *non*authoritarian tendencies), have shown an inherent inclination to agree with all questions, whatever the substance or wording.[55] This acquiescence set by respondents commonly varies inversely with their education. Its influence is strongest when the questions asked are ambiguous (as are many on the F-scale). Since it is a common observation that the Japanese prefer whenever possible to answer questions affirmatively, a cultural acquiescence set apparently exists that should make the Japanese appear artificially authoritarian in F-scale tests. The members of the Gakkai, furthermore, come from the less educated and less sophisticated strata; therefore, regardless of true authoritarian tendencies, their F-scale scores presumably should be higher than those of the general population. For this reason, unless F-scale scores of Gakkai members were to register notably higher than those of nonmember Japanese, one could not infer that the Gakkai is a collectivity of authoritarians.

The California F-Scale as adapted for use in Japan by Muramatsu Tsuneo has been utilized for several studies in that country. Groups of Japanese tested by Muramatsu averaged from 4.38* for a sample of urbanites to 4.72 in one village.[56] By contrast, a sample of Americans tested by Adorno scored a mean of 3.81 on the test. The difference is interesting—the Japanese scored from 15 to 24 per cent higher than the Americans—but comparisons without recognition of cultural differences are not particularly useful.

In late 1967, I administered the Muramatsu version of the California F-Scale to a total of 135 Gakkai members attending zadankai in various parts of Tokyo. This group was not representative of the Gakkai membership as a whole, since all were, by reason of their attendance, relatively active. Moreover, 93 per cent of them occupied some rank in the organization—and 85 per cent held two or more positions. It may be valid to consider the sample roughly representative of Gakkai activists in the Tokyo area. Gakkai officials may have

---

* A score of 4 is at the middle of the 7-point scale: −3 is scored as 1, +3 as 7.

directed me to certain zadankai because they felt that these zadankai would provide "proper" answers; thus it is probable that the sample included doctrinally dependable—i.e. activist—members.

The mean score of the Gakkai members was 4.63, higher than the mean scores of Muramatsu's urban samples (4.38 and 4.44) and roughly equivalent to those of his rural samples (4.53, 4.58, and 4.72).[57] Thus the difference between the Gakkia members' mean and that of the lowest-scoring group of nonmembers was only .25, less than 8 per cent. And one cannot impute a higher acquiescence set to this Gakkai sample than to urban Japanese as a whole; at least the distribution of the sample by educational level was exactly the same as that of the overall population of Tokyo as shown by a *Yomiuri Shimbun* poll of early 1967.[58]

Certain other demographic characteristics of the sample affect generalizations about the Gakkai. Men, young people (especially members in their twenties), and the better-educated were all overrepresented: the men scored relatively high, the young scored markedly lower, while in contrast to Muramatsu's findings, education made no apparent consistent difference in members' scores. In sum, one cannot discern any significant contrasts between the Gakkai sample and the general population, and one cannot extrapolate from the demographic composition of the sample to that of the Gakkai as a whole in order to generalize.

But a more significant finding may be possible. F-scale scores varied directly with age, length of membership, and degree of activism in terms of the number of offices held. The suspicion that higher scores are due to longer membership or to activism and the commitment it bespeaks is at least understandable; in both cases one might infer that something about the Gakkai's socialization process, either its technique or its content, leads to higher—i.e. more authoritarian—scores. In the case of length of membership, however, the correlation really seems to be between age and high score, since long-time believers, who score highest, are almost always in the older age group.

Furthermore, when one correlates scores with length of membership and then controls for degree of activism, the correlation vanishes. If, however, scores correlated with activism are controlled for either age or length of membership, the correlation remains; that is, in nearly all age and length-of-membership groupings activists score higher than nonactivists while hyperactivists (three or four offices) score highest of all. Moreover, the naturally higher scores that accrue to older age do not appear to be raising the scores of activists, since the older members of the sample do not tend to be among the relatively active.

Thus the data derived from the F-scale permit only two statements. First, Gakkai scores are not high enough, and comparison of the relative compositions of the Gakkai sample and the overall Gakkai membership does not provide one with guidelines clear enough, to justify a claim that members of the Society, either the rank and file or the officeholding activists, are significantly more authoritarian than the general Japanese public, at least insofar as authoritarianism can be measured by means of the California F-Scale. Second, although differences in score are not significant, considering the size of the sample, there does seem to be a positive correlation between activism and higher scores. Whether this represents the natural selection, after conversion, of preconversion personality characteristics, or the inculcation, as part of the socialization process, of certain attitudes that contribute to higher scores, is unclear. Whatever the reason, there is a tendency among activists in the Society to score higher than others on the F-scale test.

In an effort to shed light on the still murky issue of authoritarianism among Gakkai members, some additional data may be cited. In a survey run in the Tokyo area, 42 per cent of a sample of Gakkai members scored high in authoritarianism on a scale developed by Alan Roberts and Milton Rokeach.[59] This proportion was slightly greater than the 35 per cent of nonmember respondents who scored high on the scale, and almost exactly the same as the proportion of all believers in religion who scored high (41 per cent). However, since the Gakkai sample included only forty-five persons, the proportional difference is not statistically significant. The percentage of traditional Buddhist and Shintō followers who scored high was even greater—45 per cent—than the percentage of high scorers among the Gakkai. Several additional studies provide partially relevant data that dispute the possibility of authoritarianism among the Gakkai.[60] Thus, although the evidence presented in this section suggests that members of the Gakkai are relatively more self-alienated than are the Japanese as a whole, whether they fit perfectly the mass man model is questionable. Certainly, the average Gakkai member is no more authoritarian than the average Japanese. The possible link between activism and authoritarianism should be noted, but no absolute level of authoritarianism exists sufficient to permit broad generalizations about the Sōkagakkai elite.

HUMAN ALIENATION

Kornhauser lists "social alienation," i.e., a lack of trust in other people, as one of the primary aspects of alienation in mass man; other theorists emphasize this feature even more strongly.[61] Data concerning the faith Gakkai members feel in others are scarce. A study done by the Gakkai itself in a housing development in suburban Tokyo represents the Society's official social ideal. It indicates that Society members are deeply trusting of their fellow citizens and their relationships with their fellows—much more so than the development's residents as a whole.[62] A more objective survey conducted in Tokyo in 1965 by Dator indicates the opposite: 56 per cent of a subsample of Gakkai members scored "low" in "faith in people," as opposed to 40 per cent of the Dator sample professing belief in some religion and 39 per cent of those who denied adherence to any religion.[63] Gakkai members also scored lower in "faith in people" than any of the subsamples of believers from other religious groups distinguished in Dator's data.

Elsewhere in this study evidence was presented indicating that Gakkai members do have ties with secondary social groups, including groups not related to the Society; such data seem to contradict Dator's results. In addition, Dator's sample of forty-five Gakkai members is too small to permit generalization. Still, his data are all that are available dealing directly and specifically with the problem of interpersonal distrust, and therefore one must consider his findings before trying to draw any conclusions.

The reverse of mass man's interpersonal distrust is his extreme partisanship in the relationships that he successfully establishes. Kornhauser summarizes the nature of the relationship between mass movements and their members as submission to the organization and hostility toward the outside world.[64] Such hostility breaks down the patterns of behavior needed for the stable functioning of democratic systems. Though democracy entails partisanship, it must be within limits: opinions must be "expressible openly" or one of the elements of the "democratic formula" is lacking.[65]

Almond and Verba show that in five nations the intensity of interparty partisanship varied inversely with education.[66] Thus we might expect the Kōmeitō's supporters, regardless of their possible "massness," to be more partisan than the adherents of other Japanese political parties—and as Gakkai members, to be more partisan than the adherents of other Japanese religions.[67] However, whatever partisanship Gakkai members feel apparently does not lead to exclusive support for the Kōmeitō. In three surveys of Gakkai members, the proportions voicing support for the Kōmeitō or its predecessors were 72 per cent, 46 per cent, and 30 per cent.[68] A local survey of Gakkai activists indicated that this particular subgroup is more partisan: in response to a question regarding political parties specifically *not* to be supported, 18 per cent of the low-ranking Gakkai members answered "All except Kōmeitō," in contrast to 42 per cent of the higher-ranking activists who chose this answer.[69] But a nationwide poll in 1963 revealed no substantive difference between the propensity of activists and relatively apathetic believers to support the Kōseiren.[70]

Apparently the Society's ability to convert believers, i.e. religious partisans, into political partisans is limited. Intense political partisanship, though undoubtedly present in certain cases, does not appear to characterize the Gakkai membership. Available survey and interview data suggest also that moderate religious partisanship is the predominant pattern among the members. A study published in 1962 indicated that Gakkai members recognized the social necessity of cooperation with individuals and groups of other religious persuasions; it noted a "surprising" degree of tolerance and liberalism, considering the Gakkai's constant doctrinal attacks on heresy and heretics.[71]

A series of case studies of Gakkai members suggests that the Society's general ideal of harmonious social intercourse comes closer to representing the members' inclinations than any image of intensely exclusivist, highly partisan zealots.[72] Believers expressed great tolerance for other religions and their adherents and a marked reluctance either to criticize other faiths or to press shakubuku activity on unfamiliar or unfavorably disposed persons. The reasons for this tolerance may be largely cultural—the deviant intolerance of Nichiren Shōshū may be giving way to a traditional impulse toward moderation in religious partisanship. Whatever the reason, it seems clear from the data available that the members of the Gakkai are not absolutely intense in their partisanship, either religious or political. Relative to other Japanese they are probably more partisan,[73] but their moderate characteristics appear more significant.

From the millennium-seekers of the Middle Ages to the artisan followers of Pierre Poujade, the members of mass movements have exhibited intense envy of those in more favored circumstances. Envy of the rich is perhaps a permanent sentiment of the poor; mass man is quite likely to belong to the lower economic strata or to some other marginal or deprived group, and hence to feel antipathetic toward anyone who enjoys whatever he lacks, be it social, economic, or psychological. The lower-middle- and lower-class envy so notable in medieval millenarian mass movements contributed to the moral indignation of those who supported Hitler.[74] And the Poujadists, too, felt threatened and envious. Their use of the epithet *les gros*, "the fat ones," symbolized their disgust with all those who apparently prospered while the artisans and merchants were increasingly ignored. No solid data exist concerning feelings of social or economic envy among Gakkai members, but extensive interviewing exposed no signs of vindictive or hostile sentiment that could be described as envy.

The data relating to the possible human alienation of Gakkai members—to distrust of people, intense partisanship, and envy—do suggest a resemblance between the members of the Society and the mass man model. The resemblance is partial; impressionistic evidence concerning partisanship, and especially envy, introduces contradictions. It is also relative; Gakkai members seem only slightly more alienated than the average Japanese. Extensive nonpartisan relationships, especially political commitments, are maintained by believers. And widespread tolerance refutes the impression of a uniformly and highly exclusivist collectivity.

SYSTEMIC ALIENATION

In this examination of Gakkai members' alienation from social subsystems, we shall first consider instrumental alienation, a personal dissatisfaction with the outputs of the economic, social, and political systems. Next we shall consider general systemic alienation, antipathy toward the system—particularly the political system—regardless of the system's performance vis-à-vis the individual.

Many theorists have proposed that the mass elements in a society tend to harbor more frustrations and unfulfilled expectations about the performance of the social and economic systems than do the general populations of these societies. Empirical observers have noted that the members of mass movements generally have come from social strata most subject to social and economic deprivations and frustrations.[75] The Gakkai, whose membership is drawn mainly from such strata, has been called a "little man's movement": a meeting point for those left behind in Japan's postwar rise to affluence, who see the nation growing rich while they themselves are still scraping by, playing some sort of mental pachinko.[76]

An examination of attitudes among Gakkai members indicates that members are dissatisfied with economic conditions and their jobs both absolutely and relatively. Two-thirds of a small sample of Gakkai members in Tokyo articulated dissatisfaction with society in general; roughly half said that there was "suffering" in their daily lives.[77] In two surveys where comparisons are possible, Gakkai members and Kōmeitō supporters appeared much more liable to dissatisfaction with their livelihood than did others, although Kōmeitō supporters are not as alienated as are supporters of the Communist Party.[78] However, one nationwide and two local surveys provide contradictory data. In a national poll run by the *Mainichi Shimbun*, Kōmeitō supporters were more positive than the supporters of any other political party in their evaluation of the changes in their livelihood over the previous year.[79] One of the local surveys, done in Tokyo, suggests that the majority of Gakkai members are satisfied with their jobs; the other, from Fukuoka, implies that proportionately fewer Gakkai members are dissatisfied with their jobs than are nonmembers.[80]

A more social and less economic form of dissatisfaction may be indicated by data concerning status aspirations among Gakkai members. Azumi, in a study of Society members in Tokyo, noted a marked discrepancy between the relatively high educational level of activists and the generally low status of their jobs, and hypothesized that activists would be subject to status frustration.[81] Table 16 provides cor-

TABLE 16

Status Aspirations of Sōkagakkai Members and of Nonmembers

Class to Which Respondent Aspires	Class in Which Respondent Places Himself				
	Capitalist	Middle	Working	Other, Don't Know, No Answer	Total Persons
(Sōkagakkai Members; n = 23*)*					
Capitalist	—	4	6	—	10
Middle	—	2	6	1	9
Working	—	—	1	—	1
Other, don't know, no answer	—	—	—	3	3
Total	—	6	13	4	23
(Nonmembers; n = 209*)*					
Capitalist	5	22	29	2	58
Middle	—	35	76	—	111
Working	—	—	24	—	24
Other, don't know, no answer	—	—	—	16	16
Total	5	57	129	18	209

roborative evidence from another survey of Gakkai members in Tokyo; the sample, though quite small, may be distributed significantly.[82] Only 26 per cent of the Gakkai members were satisfied with their present status, compared to 31 per cent of the nonmembers, whereas 70 per cent of them voiced a desire for higher status, versus 61 per cent of the nonbelievers. With such unequal samples this difference might be meaningless; one should note, however, that not only do more Gakkai members than nonmembers seem dissatisfied with their status, but more also desire to reach a higher status. Whereas 46 per cent of the working-class believers wanted to be capitalists, only 23 per cent of the working-class nonmembers did.

The contrast of this possibly relatively intense status aspiration with the relatively low education of Gakkai members and the relatively low perception by Gakkai members of the possibility of job advancement is significant in several respects. It may indicate a lack of realism among working-class Gakkai members who dream of capitalist status. The confrontation of aspiration and reality (low education), leading to low perception of possible promotion, may have two results. First, compensatory fulfillment may be sought in a different, nonsocioeconomic sphere. The great frequency of noneconomic motives for entry into the Gakkai suggests that some members may be seeking spiritual satisfaction through a net of fulfilling human relationships, sublimating their status frustration to the intangible rewards of peer-group esteem.[83] Second, if the Society does not resolve frustrating contradictions between aspiration and reality or if, on the contrary, it exacerbates the frustration,* then alienation from an unjust and unfulfilling social system may be building in the membership.

Instrumental alienation from the political system has three aspects: alienation from incumbents, from policies, and from institutions. In a series of five national polls run in 1965 and 1966, Kōmeitō supporters indicated strong disapproval of the Satō cabinet; they were more negative than any political group except the Communist Party.[84] In addition, according to the three of these five surveys that were carried out by the *Mainichi Shimbun*, they were relatively pessimistic concerning the future performance of the political system—again, less pessimistic only than the Communists. A nationwide survey by the *Asahi Shimbun* revealed that 44 per cent of a sample of Kōmeitō sup-

---

* DeGrazia, pp. xv–xvi, and Hoffer, pp. 116–17, assert that mass movements do not alleviate feelings of frustration, anxiety, and fear, but in fact intensify them and their violent behavioral consequences.

porters thought the representatives in their local assemblies were doing an unsatisfactory job; the corresponding proportions of adherents to other parties were Communists 37 per cent, Socialists and Democratic Socialists 34 per cent, and Liberal Democrats 24 per cent.[85] It has been argued that political pessimism and cynicism among the lower social strata do not necessarily indicate authoritarianism, but may be eminently justified by the treatment that the less privileged classes receive at the hands of politicians.[86] Justifiable though such cynicism may be, however, what is more important for the purposes of this study is the fact of alienation. Such alienation may be ameliorated through political measures; nevertheless if it erupts into action the consequences for the stability of a democratic political life could be the same as if the cause were pathological authoritarianism.

Two national *Mainichi Shimbun* surveys suggests that the policy orientation of Gakkai members is negative, like their incumbent orientation. To the question on twelve domestic issues, "How has the Satō cabinet performed?", Kōmeitō supporters responded negatively on nine and positively on none; the Communist subsample was the only group consistently more negative.[87] A subsequent poll asked how respondents thought twelve domestic issues would be handled in the future; as usual, Communist Party supporters were most pessimistic about the possible success with which these issues would be met, and Kōmeitō supporters ranked next.[88]

The dissatisfaction of Gakkai members (or at least of the Kōmeitō supporters among the membership) with governmental structures parallels their sentiments regarding incumbents and policies.[89] In a poll by the *Asahi Shimbun* in November 1966, respondents were asked how they evaluated the overall performance of the political system. Twenty-six per cent of the national sample—and only 8 per cent of the sample of Kōmeitō supporters—thought the system was performing "well" (*umaku*), whereas 42 per cent—as opposed to 74 per cent of the Kōmeitō backers—thought it was not.[90] The Kōmeitō subsample was the most negative of any group of party supporters.

Members of the Gakkai voice considerable discontent with their positions in Japanese society and economy and with the performance of the political system. The socioeconomic data are contradictory, but taking them in combination with the strong potential for alienation suggested by status-aspiration and (among better-educated activists) education-status discrepancies, one can surmise that Gakkai members are in fact more alienated from the socioeconomic system than the average Japanese. Certainly politically, Gakkai members appear to hold relatively strong negative feelings, second only to those of the Communists. But one must qualify the conclusion that members of the Gakkai are as instrumentally alienated as mass man. It was impossible to control the data presented in this section for socioeconomic factors such as education, age, and social class; whether Sōkagakkai members are more alienated than others in similar circumstances is problematical. Furthermore, what appears to be economic alienation may simply be the coming to the fore of less easily soluble economic problems after autosuggestion and perceived divine benefit have alleviated the physical and psychological problems that originally induced a member to convert. A study by the Gakkai itself suggests that the problems bringing one into the faith are those that are later alleviated by divine benefit. Spiritual and health problems are primary motives in conversion, but economic and occupational problems become increasingly salient to members as time passes.[91]

Another reason to qualify any deductions made is that the persons described as Gakkai members in most of the data on political alienation were in fact Kōmeitō supporters. They were thus the relatively politicized and perhaps relatively more partisan element of the Gakkai membership; they may have been drawn to politics by their greater dissatisfaction with the present state of the political system. That this might be the case is suggested by the data from Dator's 1965 Tokyo survey of Gakkai members.[92] Using a scale measuring mistrust of public officials, Dator found that Gakkai members were no more mistrustful of officials than were any of those professing belief in a religion. Moreover, Gakkai members appeared to be less mistrustful than persons professing no faith in any religion. It is possible that among the membership of the Gakkai as a whole there is less alienation—especially political alienation—than exists in the politicized sector of the membership. Yet it seems fair to surmise that Gakkai believers are more instrumentally alienated from their social, economic, and political context than is the rest of the Japanese population.

In contrast to instrumental alienation from the political system, which no doubt every citizen feels at times, a general alienation from the system as such is more peculiarly a feature of the mass man syndrome. The followers of mass movements in the past were clearly highly alienated from the polities under which they lived.[93] Numerous studies have indicated a relatively high incidence of attitudes subversive to democratic systems among the social elements constituting the major part of the Society's believers: antiauthoritarian attitudes and social and political tolerance of minorities and deviants vary directly with educational level, both in Japan and elsewhere.[94] Destructive attitudes, as examined here, are general antipathy toward the political system per se and indirect subversion of democratic systems—such as opposition to the practical features of the "democratic formula."

The political structure I consider here in relation to general systemic alienation is the constitution, and in particular the provisions of the constitution dealing with the emperor and the military. Two national surveys of 1965 and 1967 indicate that Kōmeitō supporters roughly parallel the other opposition parties (and are thus stronger in this direction than the nation as a whole) regarding the need to protect the constitution and the suitability of the present constitution to Japan (only 10 per cent of the Kōmeitō's backers declared the constitution "unsuitable").[95] However, these two polls had small samples of Kōmeitō supporters; the government's 1965 constitution survey, with a much larger sample ($n = 349$), suggests that, relatively, Kōmeitō supporters are quite negative about the constitution.[96] Table 17 tabulates the responses to three relevant questions. In the first and third questions, the only ones where controls were possible, the negativity of Kōmeitō supporters holds up under controls for age, sex,

TABLE 17

Responses to Three Questions from the Japanese Government's
1965 Constitution Survey

Questions and Responses	National Sample	Kōmeitō Supporters
Question 5: Do you think the present constitution is suitable to Japan?		
Think so	33.0%	25.8%
Think not	25.0	35.3
Other, don't know, no answer	42.0	38.9
Question 29: All in all, do you think the present constitution is good or bad?		
Good	41.1	31.2
Bad	6.3	12.4
Can't say unconditionally	25.7	29.2
Other, don't know, no answer	26.8	27.2
Question 30: What should be done about the constitution?		
Should be revised	6.0	9.5
Should be thoroughly studied	42.0	43.5
Should be protected	13.0	9.5
Other, don't know, no answer	39.0	37.5

education, class, and political party support (Kōmeitō supporters being more negative than either Liberal Democrats, Socialists, or Democratic Socialists). The reasons for this negativity are not known. Possibly it represents a nationalistic rejection of an American-made constitution, but in the same survey Kōmeitō supporters responded in almost exactly the same way as the national sample to the question, "Do you think that the present constitution was forced upon Japan by the United States?" One therefore suspects that the source of their relative negativity lies elsewhere.

In their attitudes toward the emperor, three studies indicate that members of the Gakkai feel little different than other Japanese.[97] The only discernible difference is that, according to the 1965 government poll, the Kōmeitō supporters in favor of retaining the emperor system were more in favor of increasing the political powers of the currently symbolic role than the general public or the supporters of either the LDP or the Socialists were, even when responses were controlled for sex, age, and education. Kōmeitō supporters also paralleled the national sample in their responses to questions concerning the military provisions of the constitution. They were just as aware of and acquiescent to the war-renouncing Article IX and just as desirous of a Self-Defense Force, at its present force level or strengthened.[98]

The attitudes of Gakkai members on the powers of the emperor hint that a possible rightist orientation could be the source of their dissatisfaction with the constitution. This, however, is a most tenuous conjecture. One can only say that significant relative dissatisfaction with the fundamental structure of Japanese politics does exist in the politicized element of the Gakkai.

THE DEMOCRATIC FORMULA

The three elements of the democratic formula—commitment to the undefined ideal of democracy, support of the principle of majority rule, and support of the principle of minority rights—serve to distinguish those who pay lip service to constitutional norms from those who actually uphold a democratic system such as Japan's. This has been clearly demonstrated through surveys including questions about the respondent's preferred ideal social or political system. Gakkai members, although they voice slightly less support for democracy generally and the Japanese sociopolitical system in particular than the general public does, show no radical alienation. Gakkai members have a slight tendency to favor socialist ideologies and institutions to democratic ones, but their preference seems to lie more with a

TABLE 18

Responses to the Question "In the Future, Toward What Direction Should Japan Advance?"

Preferred Future State	Party Supported						
	Liberal Democrat	Socialist	Democratic Socialist	Kōmei	Communist	None	National Sample
Welfare state (reformed capitalism)	50.0%	36.0%	50.0%	46.0%	20.0%	48.0%	45.0%
Social democracy	16.0	48.0	40.0	27.0	15.0	16.0	24.0
Capitalism as it exists	19.0	4.0	3.0	7.0	—	10.0	11.0
Communism	.2	1.4	—	.4	54.7	.8	1.3
Don't know, no answer	15.0	10.0	7.0	18.0	9.0	26.0	18.0
Total (rounded)	100.2%	99.4%	100.0%	98.4%	98.7%	100.8%	99.3%

welfarist democracy than with any thoroughgoing Marxian socialist system.[99] One nationwide survey indicated that, relatively, Gakkai members had a slightly less positive orientation toward democracy as an undefined "ism" than did the general public. They were also markedly less positive regarding "capitalism" and, relatively, slightly more positive regarding both "socialism" and "liberalism" (*jiyū-shugi*).[100] Another national poll, offering a more explicit set of alternative systems, elicited the responses given in Table 18.[101]

The principle of thoroughgoing majority rule has never been fully supported by the Japanese people; "majority tyranny" by the ruling party in the Diet is a recurring cry of the opposition. One might expect the Kōmeitō, as part of this opposition, to have reservations concerning majority rule, and what data are available suggest that the Kōmeitō's supporters are roughly as committed to majority rule in the Diet as the Socialists, much more committed than the Communists, and much less committed than the Liberal Democrats. Compared with other members of the opposition, then, supporters of the Kōmeitō are not notably undemocratic. And since majority rule is not democratic when the interests of the minority are ignored, the position taken by the Kōmeitō and other opposition parties may even be beneficial to Japanese democracy. However, it is also quite possible that the entire opposition is undemocratically oriented; at any rate, about 30 per cent of Kōmeitō and Socialist supporters either excuse or advocate obstruction and resistance in the Diet to Tory efforts at self-assertion.[102]

In any case, the large and apparently growing element of charisma in the Gakkai runs counter to the idea of majority rule. It is hard to imagine a devout believer putting a majority ruling of any kind before a fiat of President Ikeda, and the degree of charismatic attraction visible even to the outside observer suggests that the norm of majority rule does not enjoy much support among the members of the Society.

In their observation of civil rights, Gakkai members generally convey an initial impression of considerable liberalism. In the 1965 constitutional attitudes survey, Kōmeitō supporters were 33 per cent more likely than members of the sample as a whole to assert that individual liberties and rights were being insufficiently respected. They were 50 per cent more likely to claim that such liberties and rights were sometimes unjustly restricted on the pretext of "national interest" or "the good of society."[103] This 1965 survey data corroborates findings from an earlier survey of 1963, in which Gakkai members (both activists and nonactivists) were found to be 33 per cent more likely than the general public to give priority to individual rights over the public interest. In a nation with an anti-individualistic tradition such as Japan's, such an orientation is beneficial for the maintenance of a democratic polity.[104] The relatively liberal indications of the surveys hold good, with rare and slight exceptions, when controls for age, education, and sex are applied.

However, contradictory evidence exists. The 1965 constitutional attitudes survey indicates that Kōmeitō supporters share the general population's sense of the proper relative weight of individual rights versus public interest; they appreciate the need to restrict liberties occasionally in the public interest. Only a minority took clearly individualistic positions.[105] This finding does not signify any qualitative difference between Gakkai members and other Japanese,* but it is noteworthy as a sidelight on the viability of democracy in Japan. Moreover, in the same 1965 poll Kōmeitō supporters were almost 20 per cent more likely than other persons to agree that individual liberty was sometimes overemphasized to the detriment of the public good; and the Kōmeitō backers agreeing were 50 per cent more likely than non-Kōmeitō supporters to say that incidents of such detrimen-

---

* Although it might be significant that of the 43 per cent of the Kōmeitō backers who gave public interest precedence, only one-third (14 per cent) thought more restrictions on individual liberties were necessary.

tal overemphasis were "very frequent."[106] This relatively collectivist orientation of the Kōmeitō supporters holds generally for each group of respondents categorized by sex, age, and education. Finally, Kōmeitō backers appeared more collectivity-oriented than the supporters of either the LDP or the Socialists.

On specific kinds of rights the attitudes of Gakkai members seem ambiguous. According to the 1965 constitutional attitudes survey, Kōmeitō supporters resembled the general public in upholding the individual's right to silence when faced with self-incrimination and in supporting restrictions on the right to strike and demonstrate.[107] As for restrictions on the freedom of political organizations, Kōmeitō supporters were relatively slightly conservative, tending not to sanction organizations that indulged in violence.[108] On the question of freedom of individual expression, however, Kōmeitō supporters were more likely than other respondents in practically every sex, age, and educational group to advocate complete liberty. Those among them who did advocate such freedom were more likely than were agreeing nonbelievers to go so far as to accept attacks on the parliamentary system. It is significant that the margin by which Kōmeitō supporters surpassed other respondents in their liberalism on this issue varies directly with age and inversely with education: those whom one might have expected to be least liberal—the old and the less educated— were most liberal relative to the general populace.

Respect for freedom of expression does not appear to be universal among Gakkai members, however. A small segment of the membership has a penchant for letters of protest—and sometimes of vitriolic attack—that they send to persons who write "misinformed" or "mistaken" articles or books concerning the Gakkai. Many of these letters are simple criticism, but some are intolerant in tone; one such letter stated, "When you slander good people, honest people, you must receive divine punishment."[109]

The size of this apparent minority is impossible to determine. In one survey, in opposition to 90 per cent of a sample of nonmembers who declared that one ought to consider possible annoyance to others in any proselyting effort, 50 per cent of a sample of Society members claimed that since propagation is for the good of the proselyte it is all right even if he is angered by the effort.[110] Table 19, which records the responses to a question on freedom of religion included in a poll of Gakkai members,[111] also indicates a conditional acceptance of individual rights among some of the membership.

Gakkai members seem to be sufficiently sympathetic to the three

TABLE 19

Sōkagakkai Members' Attitudes on Freedom of Religion

Views Concerning Religious Belief	General Gakkai Sample	Members by Degree of Activism (in terms of extent of participation)		
		Attend All Activities	Participate Occasionally	Participate Seldom
Religious belief is free, but this means freedom to choose the right thing, and Nichiren Shōshū is the only right thing	29.1%	50.0%	33.3%	14.3%
Religious belief is completely free	38.7	37.5	55.6	28.6
Don't know	32.2	12.5	11.1	57.1
Total	100.0%	100.0%	100.0%	100.0%

elements of the democratic formula to preclude any judgment that they are strongly (or perhaps even relatively) undemocratic. They are collectively somewhat less positive about "democracy" than is the populace in general; however, their apparent welfare-socialist tendency seems to be compatible with the processes of political democracy.

On the question of majority rule one can make no firm statement, although the norm of majority rule does not seem to enjoy great support among those making up the greater part of the Gakkai's membership. Data through which one could compare Gakkai members to the public at large are lacking, but, in light of the charismatic attractions of President Ikeda, one might suppose that commitment to formal majority rule is relatively low in the Society.

The data available regarding the attitudes of Gakkai members on minority rights are not definitive. Many members hold the view that individual rights are occasionally overemphasized to the detriment of the public good, and that, consequently, public interests should receive more emphasis. This stance is contradicted by a relatively strong sentiment in the Gakkai that rights are excessively restricted and insufficiently respected, and by a relatively liberal outlook on several types of individual rights. The inference of liberalism is limited by the surmised existence within the Gakkai's membership of a militantly intolerant minority. Demographic controls on responses to several questions on civil liberties suggest, though, that the greatest relative edge held by Gakkai members over the general public is in the groups—the more aged, the less well-educated, and the lower in socioeconomic status—that are generally least in touch with democratic norms.

Two possible overall orientations toward the democratic formula are suggested by the data: the "sophisticated-democratic" and the "cynical-collectivist." The first implies that Gakkai members, although they recognize the occasional damage done to public interests in excessive observation of individual rights, are willing to accept this damage because they also realize the great importance of these rights. Members thus simultaneously respect individual rights and perceive the injustice of their restrictions. The second position implies that the opinions of Gakkai members are accurately summed up in their negative views regarding the constitution, the collectivist implications of their perception of violated public good, and their intolerance of heretical expression. The members' lukewarm support for majority rule and their strong emphasis on individual rights reflect only the normal sensitivity to their position that Gakkai members, like the members of any other minority, feel.

It is most probable that the majority of the believers in Nichiren Shōshū are not overly sophisticated. But neither, in my view, are they necessarily relatively collectivist, nor are they more cynical than their fellow Japanese. Their views on "isms," though abstract and undefined, contribute to this conclusion, as does their relatively strong defense of freedom of expression. In addition, although Table 19 indicated that Gakkai members are relatively intolerant, only half of the most active subgroup chose the intolerant answer—religious freedom is the freedom to choose the right religion; the majority of the members did not subscribe to this view.

In sum, Sōkagakkai members seem to be more liable to systemic alienation than the Japanese people in general, and they also appear to be more alienated from themselves and from their fellow men. But in each case the degree of relative alienation is modest (insofar as one may make subjective attempts at measurement). Where comparison is possible, Gakkai members fall far short of Communist Party supporters in antipathy toward others and toward one's environment; a composite alienation scale used by Dator in his survey of Gakkai members in the Tokyo area suggests that Society members may be closer to the general public than they are to the Communists.[112] The proportion of Gakkai members scoring high on Dator's scale was 38 per cent—virtually the same as the 34 per cent of believers in the traditional religions, and only slightly greater than the 30 per cent of those professing no religious belief. In any case, to be more alienated than the national, societal mode is not necessarily to be an archetypical mass man; to be less alienated than the modal Communist is not necessarily to be a stable, responsible, satisfied citizen.

To leave the matter by saying that Gakkai members are relatively "mass-like," as the data on social nonattachment and alienation suggests, begs the question of the relevance of the mass man model for democratic systems. No doubt there are methods for determining relative individual degrees of undemocratic potential. Such distinctions, however, are of less interest to the politician in a democratic political system than is some kind of absolute judgment: is X subversive of democracy or is he not? If some threshold of applicability could be discerned either conceptually or preferably empirically, the theoretical mass model would be more useful. The qualities of mass man—nonattachment and alienation—already examined in the individual members of the Gakkai do not pinpoint such a threshold. The data indicate that the members of the Society are relatively close to a threshold—i.e., that the members are relatively available for behavioral mobilization by mass movements—but they do not reveal a neat resemblance to mass man.

Perhaps the behavioral aspect of the model is most important: do Gakkai members exhibit the pattern of action, particularly political action, that characterizes mass man? Although the potentialities suggested by the social and psychological analysis of the model (described here as "relative" or "potential massness") are of great importance to those with preventive or remedial goals, the behavioral aspect (conceived of here as revealing absolute presence or absence of massness) will be of most interest to the politician.[118] The discovery that behavior is crucial would also be of interest theoretically; if one aspect of the mass man model could be established as the most significant, then the research priorities of future studies could be set accordingly.

INSTABILITY

Availability for mobilization by mass movements is the first important factor in gauging the potential for mass political activity. We have already tentatively concluded that the modal Gakkai member exhibits a degree of social nonattachment and alienation that sets him apart from some imaginary average Japanese and renders him relatively available for mobilization. The second factor is mass man's unstable behavioral tendency, the periodic fluctuation from apathy to direct action in an effort to achieve remote goals. In investigating the behavioral tendencies of the members, we shall first try to estimate the potential for mass behavior and then examine the empirical record of action, which it is assumed will more or less reflect this potential.

Apathy can be reduced to its behavioral and cognitive aspects; it takes the form either of a lack of interest or a lack of awareness. According to a number of studies, both aspects tend to vary with demographic characteristics in several Western countries as well as in Japan: the less-educated, the old, women, and those with lower-status occupations are more likely than others to lean toward indifference and inaction.[114] All of these tendencies, with the exception of age, suggest that Gakkai members will be relatively apathetic. None of the data available do indicate, however, that the members should be classed as apathetic. Cognitively, Gakkai members are as well or better informed regarding the constitution and its various parts as any of the general public; this relative awareness holds when controlled for age, education, and socioeconomic status.[115] As in their responses to questions on rights, the older and less educated believers are the best-informed relative to their nonmember counterparts. Moreover, as we shall see, there are indications that Gakkai members' awareness on specific political policies, though peculiarly focused, is comparable to that of nonmembers.

Behaviorally, it has been suggested already that Gakkai members may be more active in terms of experience in public office than the general populace. They also appear as likely as anyone to work with others on local problems and to contact local and national political figures.[116] Gakkai members definitely do not evince any relative tendency not to vote.[117] In the purely verbal area of behavior, one *Yomiuri Shimbun* survey of Tokyoites provided the data in Table 20, which other polls corroborate.[118] Whether such data can be taken to represent actual behavior is unknown; still, the Kōmeitō supporters do appear more interested than either the general electorate or its supposedly politicized sector, the supporters of other political parties.[119]

For most individuals the predominant focus of interest and activity is immediate and personal. For example, in a 1954 study in the United States, where the participant citizen image is a norm, 80 per cent of the respondents indicated that they worried most about solely personal and familial matters.[120] If the available data are any indication,

TABLE 20
Responses to the Question "Do You Talk About the Coming April 1967
Gubernatorial Election at Home or at Work?"

Frequency of Discussion	Respondents by the Parties They Support					Total Sample
	Liberal Democratic	Socialist	Democratic Socialist	Communist	Kōmei	
Very often	13.6%	9.7%	11.1%	16.1%	23.6%	11.7%
Sometimes	30.0	42.0	45.8	32.3	36.4	34.2
Not often	36.6	31.9	31.9	41.9	25.5	34.3
Not at all	18.5	16.4	9.7	3.2	12.7	17.2
Don't know, no answer	1.3	—	1.4	6.5	1.8	2.7
Total (rounded)	100.0%	100.0%	99.9%	100.0%	100.0%	101.1%

the Japanese, including Gakkai members, are no different from Americans in this immediacy of focus.

The doctrines of Nichiren Shōshū are replete with utopian goals, but it is highly unlikely that the majority of the members feel a compulsion to attain these goals. When members talk of the benefits they have received through faith, the ultimate goals of the movement are scarcely ever mentioned; when they speak of their own aims, the context of their aspirations seems to be quite immediate. A few surveys clarify this observation. Out of one sample of only thirty-six Gakkai members, none mentioned remote objectives when questioned about his aims in life; eleven persons answered in purely immediate and material terms—"build my own home," "become economically secure," "own my own shop," and so on; and another eleven spoke more abstractly of family security, their children's growth, and family happiness.[121]

Although the Gakkai member's focus of attention cannot be described as remote, it is possibly a little broader and less personal than is that of the average citizen. One Gakkai spokesman surmised that, although immediate interests might be paramount to new members, in time the believer's horizon expands into social consciousness and altruism.[122] This could be so; one national and one local survey do suggest a relative breadth of focus among believers. To the question "What is the most important thing in the world?", the overwhelming majority of a sample of nonmembers answered "family," whereas of a sample of believers about one quarter responded "society" or "the world."[123] A question in the same survey on the proper mode of living for man elicited from Gakkai members the comparatively frequent response "one should live to eliminate the injustice in the world." The 1963 survey on national character hints at the same attitude: Gakkai members were slightly more likely than others to profess an inclination to live for society rather than for personal wealth, prestige, or comfort.[124]

Nevertheless, though Gakkai members may be relatively altruistic in an abstract fashion, they do seem to be more immediate in focus on specific political issues than is the general public. On domestic issues—e.g., the Tokyo gubernatorial election, or policies regarding political corruption, price stabilization, tax cuts, and housing problems—Kōmeitō supporters appear to be roughly as interested as supporters of other parties, and more interested than the overall electorate.[125] On foreign policy questions, however, Kōmeitō adherents are relatively apathetic, as indicated by the rather high frequency of "don't know" responses or of no response at all.[126]

What may in fact characterize the members of the Sōkagakkai is not a remoteness of behavioral focus but a fairly immediate focus (leaving aside for the moment the question of international affairs) combining ignorance, or parochialism, and activism. Gakkai members are definitely not apathetic; their inclinations to talk, vote, and participate in public office indicate this. Their approach to social and political matters is immediate, with a possible relative breadth of abstract social orientation. But they appear to be even more parochial than the general public on some specific political issues. A 1961 poll that compared the extent of political information and contact with the ward assembly in any form with the voting rates of Tokyoites shows a paradoxical pattern of activism and ignorance (see Table 21).[127]

A more recent survey of views on the 1965 Upper House election illustrates a parallel tendency: early closure of opinion concerning candidates; relative interest in and optimism about the prospective electoral performance of one's own party; and (relatively) great ignorance of and lack of interest in any other political party.[128] This possible ignorant-activist pattern does not imply remoteness of focus, but activism in the absence of knowledge is hardly responsible; and where such activity is frustrated, even greater alienation may result than might ordinarily be engendered by failure.

The Gakkai provides sufficient organization and continuity of effort and purpose to fulfill Kornhauser's definition of a movement. If its members were in fact mass men one might expect a collective proclivity for violence or other types of illegal or socially deviant behavior. Instances of such behavior are on record, although they have

TABLE 21

A Comparison of Political Awareness and Voting Rates Among Tokyoites

| High Score Areas | Respondents by the Parties They Support | | | | |
	Liberal Democratic	Socialist	Democratic Socialist	Communist	Kōmei
Extent of information	26.9%	25.2%	25.5%	19.0%	12.5%
Contact with ward assembly	48.4	41.4	47.9	33.3	53.2
Voting rate	70.3	69.1	73.4	61.9	84.4

been perpetrated by a small minority; "heretical" priests have been set upon and harangued mercilessly for hours, as have reluctant subjects of shakubuku. The record of criminal behavior in connection with certain political campaigns is equally clear, and so are instances of intimidation, invasion of privacy, and coercion. One must note, however, that such behavior has never been universally practiced, and almost no such incidents have occurred since the early 1960's. Today less than half of those once converted by the Gakkai profess membership; of those who do articulate their belief, approximately half cannot be called active in terms of participation in events, attendance at meetings, officeholding, reading of sacred texts, or proselyting. In conversation members evince considerable tolerance and reluctance to pursue such a socially deviant (though not necessarily undemocratic) act as aggressive shakubuku, or even to speak ill of other faiths. It is difficult to envision these people as members of a mass movement—they simply do not seem inclined toward the direct action necessary.

To be sure, impressions can be misleading. And then, too, there is almost certainly an element within the Gakkai membership that could be mobilized toward any goal whatsoever. In the words of one young girl activist, "If President Ikeda told us to demonstrate, I'd demonstrate in front of the Diet until I died." Fully 90 per cent of one sample of Gakkai activists replied in the affirmative when asked if they would participate in a Gakkai-sponsored street demonstration.[129] While the term "demonstration" includes such innocuous activities as the Kōmeitō's outdoor lecture meetings in Sasebo, one may assume that many members of this activist group would be willing to pursue more extreme actions. It is also probable that although the proportion of the Gakkai's entire membership with this degree of enthusiasm is small, it is in the neighborhood of 500,000 persons.

Thus in this aspect of the mass man model one again encounters a problem already mentioned: the discrepancy between elite and rank and file. The non-elites evidently do not tend toward illegal or deviant action, nor, apparently, would it be easy to mobilize them for such action. The elites, the activists, although they have not been involved in illegal action for the past several years, do appear sufficiently committed to the Gakkai to be open to mobilization toward whatever goals it specifies.

Despite the activists, in the total behavioral picture of the typical Gakkai member there is not enough potential for or empirical record of direct action to justify describing the modal believer as a mass man. The potential for mass behavior may well exist in the Gakkai; but for the present no threshold between possibility and practice has been crossed. Thus one surmises that the Gakkai member is closer to the average Japanese than to the average Japanese Communist or to the mass man model.

Kornhauser's model of mass man is useful in a study of the members of the Gakkai, for it provides a framework on which to hang all the data on members relevant to a democratic polity. Almost all the data necessary to fill out this framework are available, but in no single aspect are they authoritative. Nevertheless, I venture to conclude that the mass man model does not fit the Gakkai member; it does not seem justifiable to declare that either the modal Gakkai member (as he might appear from a number of attitude surveys) or practically any of the individual members I met in the course of this study has the characteristics of mass man, with all the accompanying political implications.

This conclusion, however tentative, suggests that there may be inconsistencies between reality and the political tendencies that Almond and Verba, Lipset, Kornhauser, McClosky, and others attribute to certain socioeconomic and demographic elements. Three reasons for such apparent inconsistencies are possible: either the correlation theorized by these social scientists is spurious; or the relationship is valid but accidentally culture-bound; or the fact of membership in the Sōkagakkai represents an intervening variable between demographic, socioeconomic, and psychological factors on the one hand, and political behavior and thus relevance for the political environment on the other.

CHAPTER 10

The Sōkagakkai as a Mass Movement

ACCORDING TO William Kornhauser, "mass movements are miniature mass societies; totalitarian movements are miniature totalitarian societies."[1] Carrying his reasoning a step further, we can assume that between mass men, movements, and societies there will be parallels in internal structure, psychology (or ideology), behavior, and the implications for democracy.

It has been cogently argued that mass movements—i.e., activist organizations of disaffected persons who attempt to better their conditions through methods not always compatible with established political processes—need not be undemocratic.[2] Social movements may seem to threaten stability without actually threatening the basic principles of a political system; they may even serve to invigorate a system that would otherwise ossify. However, such movements, operating within the existing social and political framework, do not come under the definition of a mass movement used in this study. "Direct, unmediated action" has been taken here to mean the sort of deviance that either militates against the entire system within which it exists, or else threatens the basic tacit norms of formal rules that regulate behavior within the system. Certain forms of "demonstration" do not, in their Japanese context, constitute deviance from the generally accepted "rules of the game"; accordingly, participation in peaceful demonstrations alone does not make an organization a mass movement. In this study, a mass movement is a movement that, because of a certain configuration of structural, ideological, and behavioral attributes, has destructive implications for democratic political systems.

Kornhauser's model of a mass movement may be viewed as a parallel to his model of mass man. The mass movement is unattached to the larger social environment just as mass man is isolated and un-attached. The movement's internal structure is characterized by weak, noninclusive intermediate groups, whose nature causes the organiza-tion's elites to be accessible to the direct influence of the members.

The ideology of the mass movement reflects the mentality of the mass man, mirroring his belief in the powerlessness of the individual. The resulting sense of life's futility outside the movement fosters self-alienation among the membership. Another facet of this mental-ity, simplism, is a stylistic characteristic of the mass movement doc-trine rather than part of its actual content. (Related to this charac-teristic are the properties of the authoritarian personality; to what extent are these reflected in the ideology of the movement and there-fore to what extent can it be classified as a totalitarian movement?) Yet another property, human alienation, is common to both the ideology of a mass movement and the outlook of a mass man; it is empirically visible as distrust of people generally and of "outsiders," i.e. nonbelievers, in particular, as extreme partisanship and lack of cooperativeness, and as envy of apparently more privileged socio-economic groups. And finally, systemic alienation, too, is a shared characteristic; most important, like mass man the ideology of the mass movement rejects the "democratic formula."

As for behavioral characteristics, those of the mass movement will resemble mass man's, since mass movements are made up of mass men. The movement, of course, attempts to mobilize behavior and thus will not wear mass man's apathetic aspect. It will, however, direct its activities toward remote, abstract, and extreme objects, and these activities will be unmediated, direct, and highly deviant or illegal.

Since according to Kornhauser mass movements are collectivities of mass men and their actions thus aggregations of mass behavior,[3] is there a need to study other than the members of such movements? Can the political implications of such movements be inferred ac-curately enough through sociological examination and no more? This chapter is based on the assumption that where there is commitment to an ideology, the content of the ideology, the degree to which it has been internalized by followers, and the selective process of internal-ization may all be worthy of study. Kornhauser has generally not at-tempted to relate the analysis of the mass man to the analysis of the mass movement. Having studied the micro level (mass man) in rela-tive isolation in Chapter 9, we shall now study the macro level (mass movement), and shall then explore their interaction.

The nature of most of the data used in this chapter—Gakkai written materials and interviews—precludes direct comparison with other organizations in Japan. In the absence of a yardstick to measure relative "massness" I have been forced to rely on subjective assessments of the absolute proximity of the data to the model. The impossibility of making comparisons within the immediate Japanese context is a weakness that I have tried to make up for by occasionally comparing the Gakkai with mass movements throughout history.

STRUCTURE

When we think of the Gakkai in its environment, it is necessary to think not only of the actual ties between the Society and other political, social, and religious systems but also of the ideal connections or the official attitudes of the Gakkai toward its environment. Does it see itself as part of its context? And in its socialization activities does it inculcate identity or separatism in its members? In what direction (toward social attachment or detachment) does the socialization process of the Society push the members?

Ideal connections. We find that the Society definitely considers itself part of Japanese society. It does not set itself off as an isolated colony of the elect: "It is a great mistake to think of the Sōkagakkai as a religious organization, a specific religious organization, or suchlike; the Sōkagakkai itself is the solidly unified manifestation of the true populace of Japan."[4] But the identification with Japanese society is absolute—the Gakkai does not connect itself with any social grouping smaller than the entire society. Real class consciousness of the Marxist persuasion is absent from Gakkai doctrines; what consciousness does appear seems to be a diffuse defensiveness directed toward the "better-off" and the more prestigious social strata.[5] Thus the social attachment of the Gakkai might be a meaningless attachment to some abstract Japanese society, and not, in fact, to any concrete social entity.

The intention of the Gakkai socialization process does not seem to be to produce persons with relatively few ties to their social environment. The social aspects of the Gakkai value system are consistent with those of Japanese culture in general: both include the importance of interpersonal relationships and interpersonal harmony.

Politically the Gakkai sees itself as connected to its environment, in particular (albeit informally and intermittently) to other political organizations. Although proclaiming itself an entirely new political phenomenon, the Kōmeitō seems to have internalized the practical norms of the parliamentary system, and certainly considers itself one of many actors in this system. It also recognizes that cooperative ties with other political actors are essential if its own activity is to bear fruit.

The political aspects of Gakkai socialization do not seem intended to lead toward detachment from the Japanese political context, either. Though hard data are lacking, there is strong impressionistic evidence that the Society serves to introduce many previously apathetic persons into the political system. In addition, the Gakkai explicitly tries to expand the political consciousness of its believers. Its efforts are directed toward creating actors within the existing political system; the Gakkai does not seem to be trying to create totalitarian cadres to overthrow the political system.

The Gakkai's ideal connections with its religious environment are for all practical purposes nonexistent. Exclusivity is the very essence of the teachings of Nichiren Shōshū regarding other faiths. Full socialization into the Society's ideal patterns of relationship to other religions would render the Gakkai member almost completely isolated from the larger Japanese religious environment.

Actual connections. Actual relationships between the Gakkai and the rest of Japanese society are few, though increasing. The Society contains within its own organization a full network of subsidiary social structures that largely obviate external ties with any group. Rather than tie in with the larger social nexus, the Gakkai restricts its social relationships to those with people who are already bound to the Society by belief.

Politically, the Gakkai has created an extensive set of relationships with its environment. On the micro level, the Citizens' Discussion Centers link the Kōmeitō to the lowest local and personal levels of political articulation. In assemblies the party has participated in numerous ad hoc alliances with other parties, being, perhaps, more prone to see such coalitions as an effective bargaining tool than other parties of the opposition. In line with its exclusion of other (i.e. heretical) religions, the Sōkagakkai has to date remained aloof from all other religious organizations. Recently the Gakkai did supposedly make overtures to an interdenominational religious group but was rebuffed.[6]

The socialization process of the Society in all its aspects—social, religious, and political—seems to lead to a decrease in actual attachment to the non-Gakkai environment. The data presented earlier concerning political mobilization and the cutting off of social and communication contacts with the secular society through time all suggest that the socializing experience within the Society tends to cut the individual member off from his non-Gakkai context. In the case of social and political connections this actual pattern, if it exists, contradicts the Gakkai's ideal pattern of environmental ties: the Gakkai constantly adjures the faithful to "Be good members of society!"; similarly, it ostensibly endeavors to create out of its membership a collectivity of aware, active, responsible political actors.

However, at the same time, the Gakkai tries to subsume every aspect of the individual member's social activity under its network of organizations. Similarly, the information the Gakkai member receives about the political system through such media as the *Kōmei Shimbun* is concerned only with the system as it affects and is affected by the Kōmeitō. Thus, at the same time that the Society advises each believer ideally to be a full member of society and polity, it may well be (perhaps unconsciously) drawing its members away from their social and political context. Whether or not this is happening must be determined through a more detailed examination of the interaction of the official Gakkai teachings and the attitudes and behavior of the members, a task we shall attempt in the next chapter. But up to this point, examination of the teachings of the Gakkai indicates that the ideal purposes of the socialization process and both the ideal and actual states of the Gakkai as an organizational entity do not constitute a condition of nonattachment to or isolation from society or polity.

The three fundamental features of mass collectivities are: the isolation of primary relationships; weak and noninclusive secondary (intermediate) relationships; and the centralization of tertiary relationships (i.e., relations with the national government in a mass society, or relations with the central elite in a mass movement).[7] On the basis of the last point the Gakkai is unquestionably a mass movement. Ideally, all relationships with the organization are centralized, the central authorities direct all collective behavior, and there is no competing locus of power in the organization. Whatever discrepancies may exist in this center-periphery relationship are the result of intruding real patterns of intermediate relationships and structures.

The significance of primary relationships in a mass movement is in their integration into secondary structures. The family is not isolated from the larger organization; it is a socializing agency of ever-increasing importance, and as such contradicts the premise that personal relationships in a mass are isolated from and irrelevant to the larger social context. But in Japan, secondary relationships as well as primary have a familistic character. Therefore, in examining intermediate structures one may fruitfully study primary relationships also.

| | INTERMEDIATE GROUPS | |
	Strong	Weak
Inclusive	Communal society	Totalitarian society
Non-Inclusive	Pluralist society	Mass society

INTERMEDIATE GROUPS

FIGURE 2

Kornhauser provides a typology of societies according to patterns of secondary relationships (see Figure 2).[8] Assuming that analogous patterns exist in social organizations on subsocietal levels, one can say that ideally intermediate groups within the Gakkai are quite weak, and the Gakkai can therefore be categorized as either totalitarian or mass. Despite the multiplicity of intermediate groups in the Gakkai's present structure, the idea of strong or autonomous secondary relationships (vis-à-vis the Gakkai as a whole) is anathema.[9]

In the Gakkai structure, tertiary relationships are quite ideally mass-like: direct and unmediated. Primary relationships, however, (in terms of one's relation to the Gakkai through one's family) are ideally integrated with the larger Gakkai context. As for whether or not there are any strong intermediate groups within the Society that may weaken the members' tertiary relationships, the data are not clear. We know, however, that the strongest motive for members joining the Society often seems to be to satisfy the needs for a warm, intimate, small group. This drive combined with strong intrafamilial relationships suggests a nonmass element in the Gakkai. Still, there is a need for further empirical studies before any final conclusions may be drawn.

The ideal pattern of secondary relationships within the Gakkai is one of multiple, noninclusive but mutually reinforcing, intermediate groups; the total effect, as one will recall from the discussion in Chapter 5, is one of almost complete inclusivity. Such a structural configuration, of weak and inclusive intermediate groups, is more typical of totalitarian than mass societies and movements. Multiple associational relationships, according to pluralist theorists of democracy, are beneficial to the maintenance of democracy when they are crosscutting, not when they are overlapping in such a manner that they add up to a monolithic unity.[10]

The Gakkai's system of secondary groups differs both from the inclusivity of Sigmund Neumann's "parties of total integration" (e.g., Communist and fascist parties) and from those movements that achieve inclusivity through extensive use of front groups.[11] In parties of total integration the party assumes total control over all aspects of the individual member's behavior; the Gakkai makes no such demands and plainly requires complete conformity only in the area of religious observance. The Gakkai does have its front groups in the sense that certain groups act as screens between the movement and society; through them the movement's teachings and goals appear more attractive, perhaps, and potential members can be more readily recruited. But Gakkai secondary groups are designed much more to socialize full members and give them opportunities for participation than they are to attract and propagandize prospective converts.

The overall influence of the Gakkai's structure on the members is toward great inclusivity. The pressure is more latent than manifest, since no overt demands are made. It may be unintentional; no Gakkai literature mentions any necessity to participate in Gakkai secondary groups (peer, neighborhood, or interest) to the exclusion of all others. But the effect is almost certainly the Gakkai's ideal—any member who is ideally committed to the beliefs of Nichiren Shōshū should naturally prefer to belong to the "right" group, be it a political party, an orchestra, a youth group, a local block association, or a labor union. There is a contradiction in Gakkai ideology that simply must be accepted—between the latent inclusive ideal and the manifest ideal of social attachment described on pages 217–19 above.

Like the Gakkai member's relational network, the ideal communication framework that surrounds him conduces to inclusivity. Believers are continually exhorted to read for a minimum of twenty minutes per day; occasionally readings outside of Gakkai sources are recommended, but such recommendations are perfunctory.[12] Furthermore, one should not read aimlessly and simply let one's ideals be formed by what the material states; one should read all books in light of the teachings of Nichiren Shōshū, evaluating and criticizing them from the Gakkai viewpoint.[13]

The actual inclusivity of secondary relationships in the Gakkai is certainly less than ideal, but until the interactions of macro ideal and micro actual are more thoroughly studied, one must rely on the ideals the Gakkai espouses to evaluate the Society's organizational nature. In the case of intermediate groups the Gakkai resembles not a mass movement but a totalitarian movement, with weak but inclusive secondary relationships.

Two conditions of mass society and, by Kornhauser's analogy, of mass movements, are the availability of non-elites and the accessibility of elites.[14] Non-elites are available for mobilization by mass movements by virtue of their nonattachment to and alienation from their social and political environment. In this chapter we are concerned only with structure; other aspects of availability and accessibility are discussed in Chapters 9 and 11.

		AVAILABILITY OF NON-ELITES	
		Low	High
ACCESSIBILITY OF ELITES	Low	Communal society	Totalitarian society
	High	Pluralist society	Mass society

FIGURE 3

Figure 3 illustrates the way Kornhauser types societies (and, by inference, social movements) with regard to elites and non-elites.[15] Kornhauser takes as the index of elite accessibility the degree to which non-elites participate in the selection of elites.[16] However, he also speaks of the "manipulation" and "mobilization" of elites by non-elites, made possible by the absence of mediating secondary groups between the two.[17] Kornhauser's first index of accessibility is the most easily operationalized of the three, but in the case of the Gakkai it is quite misleading. In the matter of personnel selection the Gakkai elite is almost absolutely inaccessible: in every case leaders are either co-opted or chosen by higher leaders on the basis of personal achievement in examinations and proselyting. And influence on the selection of leaders by institutionalized non-elite groups is as low as in any totalitarian regime. To speak of the Gakkai elite as totally inaccessible to non-elites, however, is to overlook one of the potentially most important factors in the Gakkai's growth and solidarity: i.e., the ability (either real or perceived) of non-elites to influence elites, and the perceived attentiveness of elites to non-elite interests.

Two contrasting views of the influence of non-elites on elites are those of Reverend Joseph Spae of the Oriens Institute and Nishihira Shigeki of the Institute for Statistical Mathematics, both of Tokyo. According to Spae, Gakkai elite decisions are carried out by a "machine-like" organization; the leaders can impose any policy or candidate on the members without the least fear of objection or loss of electoral support.[18] In Spae's opinion, the ease with which the elite exercises its control is due as much to the Japanese population's inherent receptivity to command as to the authoritarian methods of Gakkai leaders; still, the end product is elite inaccessibility. Nishihira's interpretation is that the Gakkai leaders are actually "the followers of the followers."[19] According to this view, the Gakkai elite (much like Kornhauser's mass society elite[20]) has no real internalized motives or goals but relies on rank-and-file opinion for its direction, responding rather than leading.

My own view is that both Spae and Nishihira offer only partially valid interpretations of the condition of the Gakkai elite; that it is, in fact, autonomous and accessible simultaneously. The extent of access is not consonant with the model of totalitarian movement, and the manner of access—mediated, indirect, and regularized—resembles the dominant pattern in pluralist societies and movements.[21] The idea of democratic-centralist organization is applicable: the Gakkai assiduously solicits opinions from the rank and file on general matters as well as on the specific tactics and policies determined at the top of the organization. Such opinions no doubt help the leaders to avoid decisions that might run the risk of being rejected by the members.

Once decisions have been made, however, they are implemented downward through the various branches of the Society in much the same way as in a democratic-centralist Communist party, apparently with immediate and unquestioning obedience. It is improbable that the elite could impose any decision on the membership, but at the same time, no case of resistance to any elite-determined measure has been documented to date. The sanctions that the Society can impose—collective approbation, excommunication, or denying the legitimacy of the individual's efforts at worship—are not sufficient to prevent large-scale defections. No instance of collective defection has been recorded, however, and the data on apostasy that do exist indicate that the fault lies more with general patterns of organization and activity (constant mobilization in particular) than with any elite despotism or inaccessibility.[22]

The high but mediated and regulated elite accessibility that exists in the Gakkai renders it unlike a mass movement. The centralist features of the organization give elites the autonomy necessary for effective operation, but its democratic aspects both increase commitment in the lower ranks of the Society and permit more efficient vertical communication.

In many of its formal, i.e. ideal, aspects the Gakkai's structure resembles that of a mass or, more ominously for Japan's democratic system, a totalitarian movement. In formal social attachments this is not so; the Gakkai has strong, extensive organizational ties, both ideal and actual, to society and politics. In addition, the Gakkai socialization process does not seem designed to detach members from secular society and the political system. But the structure of internal relationships in the Society gives a different impression.

Thus the Gakkai's structure presents a confusing picture, one that suggests some of the operational shortcomings of Kornhauser's model. There is, for instance, a direct contradiction between the attachment and elite-accessibility aspects of the Gakkai and its intermediate group structure. At this stage of analysis no conclusion can be reached about the Gakkai's similarity to a mass movement. Whether this enforced inconclusiveness reflects real internal contradictions in the Society or is due to the insufficiencies of the data or the model will be a subject of Chapter 11.

IDEOLOGY

Like mass man's orientation toward himself and his environment, mass movement ideology is characterized by alienation. The Gakkai claims that it deals expressly with the problem of alienation, that it seeks to restore man to himself and to a harmonious relationship with society and nature—and is thus diametrically opposed to the implications of mass ideology.[23] But if we examine the Society's ideological orientation toward such subjects as man's intrinsic worth and potency, the trustworthiness and virtue of people interacting in society, and the value of the concrete social and political systems within which the Gakkai operates, possibly we will find a contradiction. We will see that patterns of evaluation and expression indicate considerable alienation of the Society itself from its environment, and that actual socializing influences increase alienation in the membership.

Self-alienation. The term "self-alienation," as used here, does not mean alienation of the Gakkai from itself as an organization, but rather the implications of Gakkai teachings for self-alienation among the members. As we have seen, ideas of alienation typically begin with a sense of man's powerlessness and life's futility, a sense that finds relief in submitting to some exclusive source of potency.[24] Another attribute, paralleling the characteristics of mass man, is a stylistic simplism that denigrates rationalism, realism, and truth. In testing for these characteristics, we shall consider, in addition, whether the limiting case of programmatic authoritarianism exists in the Gakkai's ideology.

The idea of human impotence, common to some forms of Judaism and Christianity,[25] does not occur in the religious or political traditions of Japan. None of the traditional sects espouses a doctrine of original sin, which is perhaps a necessary cultural ingredient of philosophical self-alienation. Nor do any of the traditional faiths posit the basic evil of human nature, another source of self-alienation. The Gakkai also rejects any negative evaluation of human nature. In the words of President Ikeda, "For better or for worse, that which influences the social environment, which changes the environment, is none other than we ourselves.[26] History changes mankind, but men advance history. Human will cannot but cause the development of history."[27] But also present in the Gakkai's teachings is the alienating sense that humans are impotent when isolated from the single truth and the organization that possesses it. For example, all successes, large or small, are divine reward, the gift of the gohonzon, and all political measures that benefit the populace are ipso facto the result of the Kōmeitō's exertions.[28]

Moreover, simply concurring in such beliefs is not enough. The individual is not competent to worship on his own; organizational activity is essential to the realization of divine benefit. As Ikeda says, "In the world of faith one must not go alone. If one does not attend meetings and have contact with many people, the establishment of full, true, deep faith becomes impossible. *Man is weak. There is nothing so weak as one alone*" [italics mine].[29] The position expressed here is clear: without faith, or even with faith but without the Gakkai, man is nothing. He is impotent, insignificant, futile. In the words of one defector, "I became sceptical when I found that they were working to turn me against society. They told me I was socially scarred, a frustrated member of the proletariat and without hope except through the organization."[30] It seems apparent that the potency and power initially attributed to man in Gakkai doctrine are conditional upon belief in Nichiren Shōshū. Man is not encouraged to believe in his own intrinsic worth or capability but is repeatedly told that whatever positive qualities he may have are due to the grace of the transcendent gohonzon.

In its simplism, the Gakkai is further congruent ideologically with the model of the mass movement. Although the Society asserts that not its easy answers but the exalted nature of its philosophy is responsible for its success, the Gakkai's constant assertion of faith's omnipotence alone in the absence of—or even in the face of—complicating knowledge suggests the extent to which simplification is pursued. To the person who says "If I can understand, then I'll believe," the Gakkai responds, "The 'let's understand' attitude is of the world of academics. . . . The 'let's believe' attitude is life. . . . One must think of religion in terms of the latter attitude."[31] In other words, "You can receive divine favor according not to your knowledge of the philosophy but to your faith in the gohonzon. Knowledge without faith is nothing but the obstacle to your faith."[32]

In the Gakkai faith consistently takes precedence over knowledge and truth.* In other religions, too, faith that contravenes truth and common sense is no rarity; one is impressed with "the amazing credulity of a large section of our [American] population" as evidenced by their religious beliefs,[33] and the strained circumstances in which many of the adherents of these bizarre sects live suggest that they feel the intense desire for comprehensible order that characterizes mass man.

Faith also takes precedence over the usual secular criteria of causality—natural, political, and social. An earthquake in Niigata prefecture was attributed to the scores of heretics in the area; a train wreck in the Tsurumi area was caused by the existence of a heretical shrine nearby.[34] The dictates of simplicity produce political explanations that may contribute to the separation of Gakkai members from secular reality. Success in the 1965 House of Councillors elections was accounted for by the vigorous prayer of the faithful; and electoral successes in general are "nothing else but victories of faith."[35]

The simplism in this theory of causality is plain: the root of all

---

* The very trinity of values that the Gakkai postulates—beauty, gain, and good—does not mention truth. In the view of the Society, man's objective is happiness, to be attained through the creation of value. What is true is not necessarily either beautiful, profitable, or good, from the point of view of contributing to man's happiness; truth is thus not intrinsically valuable.

evil is heresy, the cause of all good is faith. Such unicausal explanations of social and natural phenomena are typical of mass and totalitarian ideologies[36] and of the rigid and intolerant persons who generally tend to be among those most fanatically attached to social movements.[37] The adherents of the American extreme right wing, with its cabalistic interpretation of social phenomena as based on a universal Communist conspiracy, are typical.[38]

In recent years tendencies toward a more complex interpretation of natural and social phenomena have appeared in the Sōkagakkai's teachings. Foremost among the signs is the Kōmeitō's thoroughgoing secularism, which has necessitated a two-sided view of the universe; Kōmeitō publications recognize that it is the electorate, not divine assistance, that decides elections.[39] The second indicator is the attenuation of some of the more extreme positions the Society has taken regarding the relative efficacy of faith and of medical science; recently the positive emphasis on medicine has increased. The third sign is the admonition that without hard work prosperity will not be forthcoming, regardless of the vigor of one's faith. Believers are warned, "Do not presume upon the gohonzon" (*Gohonzon ni amaeru na*); the power of the gohonzon is infinite, but without adding effort to prayer one will receive nothing.[40] Finally, one may note that in the most recent edition of the Gakkai's official introductory book in English, *The Nichiren Shōshū Sōkagakkai*, references to the *o-nikuge*, a supposedly still living tooth of St. Nichiren kept at the Taisekiji but never shown to nonbelievers, have been deleted.[41] However, these tendencies are only possibilities; even their designation as "tendencies" is speculation. One must acknowledge the overall simplism of the Gakkai.

A full evaluation of the Gakkai calls for a comparison of the Society ideologically with a totalitarian movement, i.e., with the features of the authoritarian personality expanded into the ideal doctrinal characteristics of an organization. The features of the authoritarian personality on which data are available for comparison with the Gakkai are those dealing with sex, superstition, destructiveness, submission, and aggression.[42]

The authoritarian mentality is puritanical, ultramoralist, and preoccupied with the imagined evils of present-day sexual conduct. The Gakkai, by contrast, takes a moderate, though perhaps slightly conservative, view of sexual behavior. Providing no strict commandments, it specifically recognizes that man would be unable to adhere to unrealistic restrictions on any aspect of his behavior, and ridicules any religion trying to impose excessively stringent commandments. But license is not sanctioned. President Ikeda, in his *Guidance Memo,* presents an image of woman that is esssentially in accord with prevailing Japanese standards of morality. The Gakkai's constant admonition, "Be a good member of society," seems to sum up the movement's orientation toward general behavior and matters of sex: basically conventional and moderate, with no odd or intense fixations.[43]

The fundamental tenet of Gakkai belief, the primacy of heretical religion as a causative agent, is in my opinion superstition pure and simple. In accord with this belief, heretics in general, corrupt politicians in particular, and indeed all natural and social phenomena are stereotyped for easy consumption and interpretation by the Gakkai membership. However, the cynical, destructive doctrinal analog of the authoritarian personality is not seen in the Gakkai.[44]

The Gakkai ideology includes a considerable element of hostility; however, one somehow suspects that over recent years this antipathy has taken an abstract and rhetorical turn. This is an extremely subjective evaluation—there are highly qualified students of the Society, such as Reverend Spae, who take a much less sympathetic view and can justify their position by literal interpretation of the Gakkai's statements. In addition, though there is nothing in Gakkai theology to compare with *Mein Kampf,* there is certainly more hostility in the *Shakubuku Handbook* or the *Risshō Ankoku Ron* than in the *Communist Manifesto,* Lenin's *State and Revolution,* or his *Imperialism, the Highest Stage of Capitalism.* But to whatever degree ideological authoritarianism may be inferred in the absence of behavioral authoritarianism, I would conclude that in Gakkai doctrines its manifestations fall short of the authoritarian extreme.

Authoritarian submission is an extreme form of a sense of powerlessness and futility; its religious side is epitomized in the teachings of Martin Luther and its political nature in the ideology of Nazism. Typically, it reflects the "idea of the unworthiness of the individual, his fundamental inability to rely on himself and his need to submit" to some leader (or force) who can compensate for his weakness.[45] The idea of totally submissive and non-self-reliant man has no place in Gakkai beliefs. The counterpart of authoritarian submission in the follower of a totalitarian movement is the nature of the movement's leadership. Whether the leader is collective, as in the case of a Leninist Communist elite, or individual, as in the case of a fascist *fuehrer,* the submission required of the rank and file is ideally total—as is the freedom of the elite. As was suggested in the treatment of Gakkai structure, the degree of access that the non-elite has to the elite removes the Society from the category of totalitarian movements in this respect.

Moreover, the Gakkai projects an explicit image of leadership that differs from either a Communist party or a fuehrer. In the words of Ikeda, "One must absolutely not become an authoritarian leader." "Authoritarianism and commandism must absolutely not exist in the Gakkai."[46] Vertical relationships within the Gakkai are epitomized by the term *shitei-funi*, literally, "teacher and pupil are indivisible." This term does not imply that self-alienated followers in their "escape from freedom" totally surrender their personalities to that of the leader. Rather it connotes a reciprocal and intimate relationship of mutual help, guidance, and diffuse emotional commitment.[47]

President Ikeda, in the *Guidance Memo*, presents an extensive list of the attributes a leader must have to sustain this sort of relationship. It becomes plain in talking to the president that he considers these norms of leadership applicable to himself as well. He reiterates that although he holds a position of organizational leadership he is really no better than any other believer. He is quite frank; to the question, what is it like being Sōkagakkai president? he once responded, "I am the ruler of Japan; its president, monarch of its spiritual world, leader of all its thought and culture, and holder of supreme authority."[48] This isolated remark has been widely cited as an example of megalomania; it conflicts sharply with the favorable personal impression he makes, which certainly has nothing of pomposity or hubris in it. It seems likely that his answer was meant as a realistic appraisal of his position as it is defined doctrinally and perceived by a great many of the faithful; wide reading of his speeches and essays and personal conversations lead me to believe that the following statement more accurately reflects Ikeda's temperament. On being told that some believers regard him as a divine figure, Ikeda answered,

I am very touched at their respect, but they go too far. It would be dreadful if such a misconception should spread among the members. . . .

Can a person such as I . . . be thought of as a living god or a Buddha-in-carnation? It is sheer nonsense! . . . If there should be a man who folds his hands to me in worship, my face will surely become deformed. I ask you not to do this. It is the gohonzon only that you should worship. . . .

If a man should over-respect the president . . . the Sōkagakkai would be degraded to the level of the heretical sects.[49]

In sum, Gakkai leaders do not appear either to inculcate or to expect authoritarian submission.

On occasion authoritarian aggression has been apparent in informal proselyting activities; quite possibly the belligerence of President Toda reflected a highly authoritarian degree of aggressiveness, but such belligerence has had no official sanction for several years. Nevertheless, the aggressive impulses apparently released in shakubuku are intense enough to suggest a pathological drive to dominate and defeat. Although no estimate of their numbers is possible, it is most probable that there are aggressively authoritarian persons in the Society.[50]

The concern of this chapter, however, is with formal organizational aggressiveness. That the Gakkai is aggressive is unquestionable; that it is at present more so than is any vigorously proselyting religious group is debatable. The Society speaks of relations between religious groups as "a matter of victory or defeat," and has created such organs as the "Tenrikyō–Risshō Kōsei Kai Liquidation Committee," which carries out programs directed expressly against two rival sects. But in recent years the Gakkai has taken a distinct approach of "hate the sin, not the sinner,"[51] and its aggression seems to be increasingly abstract and rhetorical. Except to the extent that vigorous propagation by any religious group is deviant behavior in Japan, the Gakkai does not appear notably more aggressive formally than any evangelical religion, and certainly not so much so as to merit the description "authoritarian."

Thus, with the exception of superstitiousness, none of the aspects of the authoritarian personality examined here appear to characterize the Gakkai. One final, additional note may be made of a measurement of "totalitarianism" proposed by Herbert McClosky on the basis of a proclivity to accept "unfairness or brutality," "cruelty and even ruthlessness," and the suffering of "a lot of innocent people" in the pursuit of "great purposes" or "great changes for the benefit of mankind."[52] The Society certainly acknowledges that kōsen-rufu and ōbutsu-myōgō are such great purposes; but it condemns other political movements for their cruelty, sacrifice, and aggression and rejects those methods in its own activities.[53] All enterprises that entail sacrificing one group or subjecting it to misfortune for the benefit of another are ipso facto bad, whether they are products of German Nazism, Russian Communism, or Japanese Imperialism.[54] In the achievement of kōsen-rufu, according to President Ikeda, "There must not be a single person sacrificed. Not one person must become a victim. . . . Even if there is [but] one victim, even if there is [but] one unhappy person, even if *kōsen-rufu* is attained by sacrificing these people, that is not the true will of Nichiren. Nichiren would not be happy."[55]

Self-alienation does appear, then, to be one characteristic of the

Gakkai's formal ideology. Typical of the Society are unicausal explanations and interpretations and a consistent simplism in prescription that often ignores the natural and social sciences and common sense as well. Reiteration of the impotence and insignificance of man outside the Gakkai can hardly be expected to increase the believer's sense of intrinsic individual worth. The Gakkai itself explicitly maintains that it reduces the alienation of its believers and returns them to themselves and to society as full individuals and useful members of the human collectivity. But on the basis of the view of man contained in Gakkai doctrines and the simplistic style of these doctrines, one must suggest that at least by the measure of self-alienation the Sōkagakkai as a formal organizational entity does resemble a mass movement. It does not, however, resemble a totalitarian movement, and it contradicts the criteria suggested by both Adorno and McClosky for such movements.

Human alienation. No specific data are available concerning generalized trust of people in general or of particular groups as the Gakkai may feel it. Content analysis of Gakkai media would probably give an accurate indication of official organizational perceptions of social groups. But I have relied on a nonquantitative study of the Gakkai's official relationships with other groups, both as Society media idealize them and as they are actually carried on, to detect the factors of human alienation (i.e., distrust of people in general, intense partisanship in social relationships, and a diffuse envy of all those social elements perceived to be better off in any way than the perceiver). Pluralist theories of democracy suggest that a balance of operational conflict and fundamental normative consensus, social cooperativeness, and limited partisanship constitute the most stable social basis for democratic systems.[56] The limited partisanship and cooperation are made possible by the consensus on broad rules of conduct in political and social action, among other things. But these theories also recognize the inevitability and value of conflict in democratic society.

It has been asserted that the Gakkai's concern for social harmony is not compatible with pluralist democracy, and even that groups such as the Gakkai "deny the permanence of human conflict, elevate the value of order over freedom, and work for a completely peaceful, happy, and orderly society by the elimination of people, ideas, or institutions which they think are the cause of human misery."[57] The Gakkai expressly denies this assessment. In his *Politics and Religion* President Ikeda asserts that schism, dissonance, inconsistency, and conflict are natural social behavior and that the idea of Buddhist

Democracy recognizes and encompasses them all; and in conversation high Gakkai officials have backed up this position.[58]

The Gakkai's relationships with other religious groups have usually been characterized by total conflict. "As for evil clerics," says Ikeda, "Buddha's command is 'Torment them thoroughly.' "[59] "Buddhism is a battle. In faith there is no compromise. Only after attacking slander, attacking and attacking thoroughly, and banishing it, will a peaceful world be realized where believers, and nonbelievers too, can live in peace of mind."[60] Other sects are attacked indiscriminately; all are in collusion with corrupt politicians, all are covetous, opportunist, and mercenary, and all (aside from their general malign influence) have evil designs on the Gakkai as the embodiment of true religion.

One should note, however, in reference to the behavioral aspect of the Gakkai, that even when Ikeda created the Tenrikyō–Risshō Kōsei Kai Liquidation Committee in the more extreme days of 1960, he specified that the means for wiping out the sects was individual shakubuku, "a one-to-one struggle on the lowest level," not organizational conflict.[61] This distinction is one that the Gakkai is careful to make, and one that has received increasing emphasis in recent years. According to an official Gakkai publication, those who call the Gakkai uncooperative, partisan, or exclusivist are confusing "strict pureness in the religion with cooperativeness within the society." Though believers assert that their faith is sublime and pure, they are good members of society and can interact harmoniously with other fellow-citizens regardless of their religious beliefs.[62]

And even this assertion of superiority in an absolute framework is now made in less extreme fashion than was once the case. In the early 1960's some observers began to discern a thaw in the Gakkai. The *Seikyō Shimbun* has become markedly less vitriolic since 1962 and 1963; the term *shōju* (moderate propagation) was introduced in 1964; and by 1967 Gakkai members could say, "If someone feels he is happy with the Nembutsu or Shingon sect, that's O.K."[63] Since 1962 a tolerance and a willingness to work with other groups on nonreligious matters has developed.[64]

This thaw is perhaps one facet of the process of maturation and moderation through which it has been suggested all religious movements must pass, and thus one might expect it to continue and extend to other aspects of the Gakkai.[65] But although it has already affected the Gakkai's view of adherents of other sects, the movement's basic ideological orientation toward other religious organizations is still intolerant, distrustful, uncooperative, and highly partisan. There is nothing whatever in the *Shakubuku Handbook* or Ikeda's *Lectures on the Risshō Ankoku Ron* suggesting that the existence of other religious organizations is tolerable, justifiable, or acceptable.[66]

Both the political and the nonpolitical aspects of the Gakkai's possible alienation from other types of actors in its environment can be examined. Politically, from the beginning the Gakkai has ideally been nonpartisan, pragmatic, cooperative (within limits), and nonexclusive, and has always maintained the formal freedom of members to express themselves. The Kōmeitō is certainly cooperative, if not entirely trusting, toward other parties. Several representatives of both the Kōmeitō and the Gakkai have insisted that the party is willing to cooperate with any parliamentary force to maximize the people's welfare—even with the representatives of other religious groups.[67] The numerous ad hoc alliances made during the 1967 session of the House of Representatives—on occasion even including the Communists—attest to the sincerity of the Kōmeitō's assertion. Such trust and cooperation apparently end on the steps of the Diet, however; the Kōmeitō prefers organizational integrity in its direct contacts with the people. Chairman Takeiri has stressed the need to collaborate in order to amass a sufficient intraparliamentary force, but "as for outside the Diet, it's completely unthinkable."[68] The January 1968 Sasebo lecture meetings of protest, held apart while other parts of the city were resounding with noisy and violent Zengakuren demonstrations, are a case in point.

There are, in addition, limits to the Kōmeitō's willingness to trust, compromise, and cooperate in parliament. The corrupt LDP is an unsuitable partner for a coalition government, according to President Ikeda, although if in the future the party's quality should change a possible coalition could not be ruled out.[69] But at present the only coalition possible would comprise the Socialists, the DSP, and the Kōmeitō, "excluding the Communist Party."[70] And there are bounds to the nonpartisan attitudes of the Kōmeitō; though non-Gakkai members are welcome as Kōmeitō members, it is doubtful that the party would nominate a nonbeliever for office—Kōmeitō candidates must first of all appeal to the Gakkai membership.[71]

In its relations with labor unions, the Gakkai appears to be drifting toward alienation; but here the cause is largely with the unions themselves. The Gakkai's history has been marked by a series of confrontations with labor unions: six times court cases have resulted from alleged union infringement of the rights of Gakkai-member unionists to political expression.[72] As was surmised above, the short-comings of the Japanese labor unions seem to have contributed significantly to the Gakkai's present size; it also seems likely that they were largely responsible for the Gakkai's decision in 1967 to establish its own labor union. The very decision denotes the crossing of some threshold into alienation from the present union system. Other influences at work were an appraisal of the present power of the laboring class; the Gakkai's desire to increase the scope of its control over the lives of its members; and the aim of achieving an organized electoral base in labor for the Kōmeitō similar to those of the Socialists and Democratic Socialists. The Gakkai claims that its union will be nonpartisan, open, and cooperative with other unions; however, it would not be wise to ignore the element of alienation involved in the decision.

In all, however, the Gakkai does not seem to be sufficiently uncooperative, exclusivist, and mistrustful of other actors in its environment to merit the description "alienated" in the sense of a doctrinally alienated mass movement. The specific ideological antipathy felt toward other religious actors is to be expected of any militant religious group; but since it does not carry over into political or social policy and practice, or even into all the phases of Gakkai interaction with other religious groups, one could not call the Gakkai's general alienation from social groups excessive. Furthermore, the only discernible present trend seems to be toward greater openness and intercourse with the social environment.

In Gakkai ideology there seems to be none of the diffuse envy of groups that appear relatively better off, an envy that often characterizes religious and social lower-class movements in general and mass movements in particular.[73] Gakkai leaders frequently remind their followers that together they possess the sole and most sublime truth and that they need not feel inferior to anyone; but such encouragement is never at the expense of any other social group. President Toda was more extreme—on one occasion he stated that the poor, the weak, and the suffering made the best believers, whereas managerial and professional people and those with secure lives were "no good."[74] President Ikeda, too, has mentioned a sort of retribution: of the achievement of kōsen-rufu and all its wonders he has told the faithful, "at that time, how greatly will those who ridicule or slander you now repent, and be envious. This is the absolutely accurate postulate of Buddhism."[75] These statements are among the most extreme that can be construed as "vindictive" or "envious." There is simply no figure in Gakkai dogma to compare with the plutocrats, *les gros,* the imperialistic monopoly capitalists, the rich and crafty Jews, or the blasphemous materialists, who have all served as social foci for frustration, anxiety, envy, and hate in past mass movements. Given the additional data presented on social distrust, uncooperativeness, and exclusivist partisanship, one can tentatively conclude that the formal doctrine and practiced ideology of Sōkagakkai do not demonstrate the human alienation typical of a mass movement.

Systemic alienation. The ideologies of historical mass movements have been characterized by antipathy both to the concrete social and political systems within which they exist and to the more abstract structures and ideals associated with democratic forms of government. The alienation from the immediate system is clear, whether it is Lenin speaking bluntly of destroying the Russian state; the anti-Semites of nineteenth-century Europe or their offspring, the Nazis, attacking the governments of Austria or Weimar Germany; or the Poujadists denouncing the Fourth Republic.[76] And the state against which Lenin aimed his attack in *State and Revolution* was the liberal, bourgeois-democratic state with all its meretricious constitutional and parliamentary accoutrements; the ideals rejected by both the Austrian anti-Semites and the National Socialists were those of parliamentarism and party politics, the rule of law, legal equality, and freedom of expression and behavior; what the Poujadists were rejecting was representative democracy.[77] The ideals of majority rule, minority rights, and democracy itself (in the non-Communist sense) have no place in the ideology of mass movements.

The ideology of the Sōkagakkai will be studied here as it applies to the concrete phenomena of the Japanese environment and to the three elements of the democratic formula previously discussed. It is assumed for the purposes of this study that neither the official Gakkai media nor the leaders personally interviewed are engaged in deceiving their audiences about the true orientations of the Society.

In contrast to many of the mass movements of history, the Gakkai does not formally contemplate any notable structural changes in the political or social system. Excepting a series of rather grandiose plans for urban redevelopment and redistribution of wealth, the Gakkai policy position is one of conserving existing institutions. As an opposition political party, the Kōmeitō is naturally antipathetic toward the present incumbents, and it misses no opportunity to criticize their policies; its antipathetic criticism, however, does not surpass that of the other opposition parties except that it is directed at the other opposition parties as well as at the LDP. In general, the Kōmeitō's negative attitude toward the actual workings of Japanese politics and economics is to be expected of an opposition party.

That the Gakkai's oppositionism does not carry over into alienation from the total political system suggests that it is the natural attitude of an opposition party. The Society does take a strong stand in favor of the existing system, both its constitutional basis and its parliamentary, liberal, pacifistic, and democratic manifestations.

When our country resuscitated herself as a democratic, peace-loving nation from the first defeat in her history and the rubble of war, we enacted the present Constitution, which we can be proud of before the world, with a clear-cut mention of sovereign power in the hands of the people, a declaration of intention to work in the cause of maintaining peace and of renunciation of war, and a guarantee of basic rights for the people.

This spirit of the Constitution is the kind of matter which should be proclaimed and propagated not only in Japan but in other nations of the world with a view to establishing a world of peace and prosperity. . . .

Kōmeitō hereby wishes to declare its firm resolve to crush . . . attempts to trample democracy and peace underfoot and suppress basic human rights through the malicious revision of the Constitution.[78]

The role of remonstrating with the authorities has a prominent place in Gakkai scripture and ideology; brushes with the law that are sometimes interpreted as remonstrations are thus sanctioned.[79] But such attitudes never approach wholesale condemnation of "the state" (in the relatively abstract Leninist sense) or of the immediate institutional framework within which the Gakkai and Kōmeitō operate.

As for the first element of the democratic formula, attachment to the abstract notion of democracy, the Gakkai is almost vehemently positive. One can see from the political platform of the Kōmeitō that democracy in the abstract occupies a very prominent place, as does respect for human dignity. A verbal commitment to democracy is certainly not incompatible with undemocratic ideology, nor with the aims of mass movements. But in the Gakkai's case one finds neither the specialized definitions that allowed such disparate figures as Mussolini and Mao Tse-tung to label their regimes democratic, nor the conditional acceptance that actually invalidates the supposed commitment.[80]

Naiveté, however, may be present. The Gakkai's idea of democratic society is unrealistically sophisticated: according to Ikeda, the social requisites for a democratic system are a general high level of education; "full and sound knowledge"; social morality; awareness, civic duty, patriotism, and tolerance; and the general willingness to stand up against unjust ideologies and politics.[81] The Society shows an unwarranted expectation regarding the inclination of the people— any people—to participate in or even take an interest in politics, as well as a historically unwarranted faith in the amenability of people in general to democratic behavioral norms. In fact, the Gakkai shows a refreshing, though occasionally immature, idealism in its advocacy of democracy.*

The Gakkai's ambivalent attitude toward the concrete factors of the democratic formula contrasts sharply with its wholehearted acceptance of abstract democracy. In the religious sphere, naturally, the Society does not accept the validity of majority rule, nor, as a religious organization, does the Gakkai feel that the charismatic and rather dictatorial administrative style of President Ikeda is improper. It is pointed out that Nikkō Shōnin, the founder of Nichiren Shōshū, was one of six disciples but was nevertheless the true successor; the believers of Nichiren Shōshū are a minority today, but this in no way keeps their faith from being the most exalted of all religions.[82] Nevertheless, though a religion's validity must be determined on an absolute plane, on the level of ordinary human existence, where political behavior takes place, majority rule is sufficient to determine right and wrong.[83]

In principle, various particular applications of majority rule are favored by the Gakkai. For example, the proper form of a democratic political system, according to President Ikeda, is a bicameral parliament that accurately represents the whole people.[84] To represent the people fairly and thus validate majority rule, the legislature must be constituted through fair election by an enlightened, politically aware populace.[85] The fact that the Gakkai does not consider either today's elections fair or today's electorate aware raises doubts about the Society's real present commitment to majority rule.

The second condition that justifies majority rule in the eyes of the Gakkai is full prior discussion and debate, with adequate respect for minority views.[86] Again, the Gakkai's opinion that such views are not at present sufficiently respected suggests the possibility that the Society may reject the validity of Diet decisions. The Kōmeitō has reiterated its support for majority rule in principle, but it also warns that if the Liberal Democrats attempt to force legislation through the Diet the party's attitude "will change."[87] The party declares itself committed only to democratic procedures; if the ruling party

* One should recall, however, that disillusioned idealism can be a source of the most intense cynicism.

tries to railroad bills through the Diet, then "even if the form is parliamentarist, the true nature is nothing but dictatorial, fascist, antiparliamentarist action," absolving the Kōmeitō of its obligation to comply.[88]

A final reference to majority rule that has gained considerable currency among observers of the Society is the following statement by President Ikeda:

Rather than having a great number of irresponsible men gather and noisily criticize, there are times when a single leader who thinks about the people from his heart, taking responsibility and acting decisively, saves the nation from danger and brings happiness to the people. Moreover, if the leader is trusted and supported by all the people, one may call this an excellent democracy.[89]

One might also call it Bonapartism, but according to Vice President Akiya Einosuke, no dictatorial principle was intended by the remark. Akiya drew an analogy with the decisive action that President Kennedy took on his own responsibility in the Cuban missile crisis, without waiting for Congressional approval.[90] In noncritical situations, though, Akiya emphatically insists that the Gakkai "absolutely protects parliamentary politics."

The conditions applied by the Gakkai to its acceptance of majority rule in political matters are not necessarily inconsistent with the criteria of "polyarchal democracy" set forth by Robert Dahl.[91] Whereas a preference for majority rule indicates support for democratic practices, a total acceptance of the principle, ignoring the possibility of majority tyranny, is neither responsible nor realistic. The stipulation that elections be fair is justifiable; and the recognition that at certain moments collective survival may require unilateral executive initiative is only realistic.

The inclinations of the Gakkai toward majority rule are thus limited, but it is for each observer to say whether or not they are undemocratically limited. I would assume honesty (albeit perhaps naive honesty) on the part of Gakkai leaders who explain the conditional acceptance of majority rule, but considering the literal proximity to the mass movement model that certain of these conditions imply, one also must reserve doubts about the genuine commitment of the Gakkai to majority-rule norms.

The problem of minority rights is one with which all religions that claim supreme validity for themselves must struggle. In the encyclical *Libertas Praestantissimum* Pope Leo XIII, the father of Christian Democracy, said, "any liberty, except that which consists in submission to God and in subjection to His will, is unintelligible," seemingly speaking out against freedom of religious belief and against freedom of expression, conscience, and education.[92] Even the more recent work of Jacques Maritain proposes an intuitively unworkable combination of religious absolutism and political freedom,[93] but in reality a modus vivendi has been reached in several countries suggesting that the Gakkai's similar doctrinal blend of religious absolutism and secular relativism is compatible with democratic politics.

In the opinion of Reverend Spae this suggestion is fatuous.[94] In contrast to the Catholic Church, which realizes the exigencies of political democracy and accordingly dilutes its religious absolutism to harmonize with religious freedom, the Gakkai, he asserts, does not recognize and would not accept the necessary discrepancy between ideal and actual religious purity. The Gakkai as a faith would reject the religious freedom of minorities and the Gakkai as an organization would reject the rights of the individual vis-à-vis the collectivity.

Certainly the ultimate goals of the Gakkai are collective;[95] its immediate goal, however, is individual human revolution, and its elaborate denunciations of any and all enterprises that entail involuntary sacrifice suggest that the Society at present places great emphasis on the individual in its beliefs. In any case, in its ideology it never calls for the total submersion of the individual to the collectivity that is the leitmotif of mass movements, the goal of anomic man, and an integral part of the authoritarian personality.[96] But in practice the individual is subordinated to the group. This is perhaps an unescapable phenomenon of Japanese society, and in this respect the Gakkai is probably no more undemocratic than any other Japanese organization—but the fact remains.

Considering particular rights such as freedom of expression and religious belief, one must entertain doubts about how the orientations propagated by the Gakkai may benefit democratic society. Articles and books considered unfair or mistaken are criticized in the official Gakkai media with a vehemence bordering on paranoia; and it is difficult to imagine the Society respecting the freedom of critical expression were the Kōmeitō to take power.

In past years many blatantly biased, inaccurate, and irresponsible articles concerning the Gakkai have appeared. The Gakkai has been likened to "Hitler and his hordes" and described as "a militant, antidemocratic... sect" whose "organization and methods are similar to those of Communism and Fascism. Like Chinese Communism's 'thought reform,' Sōka Gakkai has 'shakubuku.'... Like the early

Nazi movement, it looks like a crackpot outfit—but it's growing rapidly. Its ceremonies ... at the foot of sacred Mount Fuji last year [1964] had all the trappings of Hitler's Nurnberg conclaves."[97] However, in recent years coverage has become more balanced and objective, with the notable exception of the left-wing press. At the same time, though, the Gakkai has become increasingly strident in its denunciations of "erroneous" works. Criticism is variously labeled "irresponsible," "know-nothing," "antisocial," "unqualified," "criticism for the sake of criticsm."[98] It looks as if criticism is considered ipso facto irresponsible, and the Gakkai couples its attacks with reminders that rights and freedoms imply and require responsibility. In many cases the Society's statements clearly threaten freedom of speech:

Today's weekly-magazine journalism ... has reached the ultimate in vulgarity. Certainly, this must be called irresponsible, antisocial behavior; there is no true "freedom of speech" therein.[99]

Really, is it good that such things as irresponsible journalism be permitted in society? ... The time will certainly come when the masses themselves will hand down judgment.[100]

True "freedom of speech" should be permitted to the speech that teaches justice to the masses and is based on correct principles that guide toward a value[-creative] way of living; shouldn't evil speech and dishonest speech be eliminated from this world?[101]

Representatives of the Gakkai reject all allegations that the Society would in any way infringe on the valid exercise of any constitutional right.[102] Any response by the Gakkai is and would be limited to a "multilateral campaign of debate."[103] Nevertheless, it seems that the Gakkai media might be creating a hostile "they," a vague external enemy composed of all those who criticize. It is difficult to imagine a fully socialized and deeply committed member of the Gakkai with a genuine belief in the legitimacy of criticism that extended to the Society itself.

The authenticity of the Gakkai's acceptance of religious freedom is also in doubt. The writings of Nichiren are replete with admonitions to wipe out heresy;[104] dire promises of the divine punishment that accrues to resistance to proselyting sound immediate and violent;[105] and the statements of President Ikeda are occasionally open to unfavorable interpretation.

Freedom of religious belief. This is absolutely correct. Exactly so. However, freedom of religious belief must also be freedom of doctrinal debate and propagation. ...

However, is it the responsibility of the nation, or of the governors, that the people are taken in by vulgar teachings? Is it the responsibility of the people themselves? Is it the responsibility of the founders of heretical religions? Is it due to insufficient strength of those who spread the True Law?[106]

According to the interpretations of Gakkai leaders, the responsibility lies with the people and with the propagators of the True Law. The drive to eliminate heresy is not a matter of political relevance: "we protect freedom of belief to the utmost"; "freedom of religion is the fundamental principle of democracy"; "if the Kōmeitō becomes the ruling party, religion will be kept strictly free."[107] Belief and non-belief, it is suggested, dissemination, proselyting, rejection, and criticism, are all accepted and protected.[108] And to the suggestion that eliminating heresy implies eliminating heretics, Vice President Akiya replies that the Gakkai clearly recognizes the necessary division of ideal religious purity and practical tolerance that Reverend Spae has the movement rejecting.[109] At all times human beings are to be treated with respect and compassion; in the Kōmeitō such treatment takes precedence over doctrinal injunctions to militance.[110]

The role of minority rights in Gakkai ideology is unclear. Ambiguities, contradictions, and opportunities for sharply contrasting interpretation abound in the Gakkai's treatment of minority rights and majority rule. In fact, the only part of the democratic formula on which the Gakkai takes an unambiguous, and positive, stand is the abstract factor of democracy itself.

In the absence of empirical behavioral evidence, my subjective approach is to give the Gakkai the benefit of all doubtful points contained in its doctrine. Based on this personal interpretation of the Gakkai's protestations of support for personal liberties combined with the Society's unambiguous, positive orientation toward both democracy and the structures of the Japanese political system, I conclude that the Gakkai does not reflect the systemic alienation typifying mass movements and therefore may not be termed a threat to democracy on those grounds.

Although one can recognize close proximity to the model on several points and a moderate resemblance overall, the Gakkai does not seem to exhibit the general alienation characteristic of a mass movement either, at least as evidenced in its ideology. Preaching as it does the impotence of man outside the faith, and typified as it is by a simplism that overrides considerations of reason and science, Gakkai ideology does seem to contribute to any feelings of self-alienation that members might already harbor. But the Gakkai does not appear to be alienated from other social actors in its environment. Its religious exclusivism is reasonable; its social and political behavior is ideally characterized by pragmatism, cooperation, and openness.

BEHAVIOR

Like an individual, a group may be unattached to and alienated from its environment without being a mass movement in the fullest anti-democratic sense if, in its behavior, it adheres to the informal norms and legal rules regulating social (and especially political) behavior. One may gauge potential for mass behavior from unattachment and alienation: theoretically, this increases the possibility of predictions about the political system from the model; practically, this enables other social and political actors to focus on the causes of unattachment and alienation in such ways that they can counteract the social strains and whatever conduces to such unattachment and alienation.

There is one aspect of behavior that is itself partly potential; i.e., the objectives of behavior that may be seen ideally in doctrine. Ideally the Gakkai meets the criteria of a mass movement almost exactly. The combined idea of kōsen-rufu and ōbutsu-myōgō, though perhaps conceivable, hardly seems realistic. And even were this goal to be achieved, the naive idea that all human conflict would be submerged in harmony and the facile prediction that every individual's absolute happiness would blend with the prosperity of every human society sound utterly utopian. Finally, the notion that all heretical religions will naturally die out, thus removing the cause of all human misery and ushering in an era of euphoria, even has a threatening overtone, as the word "die" suggests.

The Gakkai has certainly aroused suspicion with their description of the means to be used in achieving their remote goals. Statements such as "In the near future the world will worship the Gohonzon, and the Japanese people must soon begin bringing this about"[111] and "Japan is the savior of the world and Sōkagakkai is the savior of our country"[112] are not reassuring to those who recall Japan's last major attempt to extend its influence to other shores.

In practice, the Gakkai has created an elaborate set of intermediate and immediate goals toward which it directs its activities pragmatically: short-term shakubuku drives and political campaigns aid the Gakkai, and prayer and participation bring divine benefit to the believer. Immediate goals also receive much more attention than remote ones in the Gakkai media; but rhetorical references to utopia are included almost everywhere.

The constant reference to unrealistic goals may well be turning into a form of lip service operating to legitimize other enterprises (especially political) that in fact may be developing into ends in themselves. Moreover, as was suggested in another chapter, utopian goals may neither receive much attention from nor create much allegiance in the average member. Nevertheless, we must acknowledge the Society's proximity to another feature of the mass movement model in the remoteness and utter fantasy of many of its goals.

Direct action contravening both social norms and legal rules is the behavioral characteristic of a mass movement, whether religious[113] or political.[114] Much evidence exists that gives the impression of violent ideological predilections in the Gakkai. Nichiren, in the *Risshō Ankoku Ron*, asserted that killing heretics did not constitute murder, and that government should "extirpate heresy with the sword";[115] "the persecution of the enemies of the Lotus Sutra is the highest divine blessing."[116]

And there is an indisputable empirical record of illegal actions on the part of Gakkai members. Japanese government records implicate believers in such incidents as beating a supposedly "lazy" member; beating one member and threatening several others who spoke of leaving the Society; attempting to murder a landlord who forbade his tenants to read their prayers loudly; invading numerous temples of other sects and burning a temple of Konkō-kyō, another new religion; several cases of shakubuku that ended in violence; destroying the paraphernalia of other religions in the homes of new converts on numerous occasions (a previously sanctioned practice known as *hōbō-barai* or "cleaning out of slanderous things"); and the firing of several employees by the president of their firm because they would not convert to Nichiren Shōshū.[117] In a number of instances, Gakkai-member schoolteachers took advantage of their relationships with pupils to gain access to parents for the purpose of shakubuku. In at least one case such a teacher told the parents that if they converted their child would be cured of his illness; if not, he would become "abnormal."[118]

One notable feature of these data is that nearly all the incidents occurred before 1957. Another is that nearly all of them appear to have been the spontaneous and officially unsanctioned work of individuals or small groups of believers. Thus, although these cases constitute strong evidence in support of the proposition that the Gakkai membership includes a contingent of mass men, they do not necessarily signify that the official organization is itself a mass movement.

In other, infrequent cases, however, the movement's official sanction (which would enable the government to dissolve the Gakkai in accord with the provisions of the Religious Juridical Persons Law)[119] seems to have been in effect: in 1952 a group of believers led by President Toda set upon an aged monk at the Taisekiji, tore off his vestments, and dragged him to Makiguchi's grave, where they forced him to write an apology for having advocated collaboration with the authorities during the war. No legal action was taken, but the incident shows that officially, too, the Gakkai has at least overstepped the bounds of legality.[120]

The Society also has a record of direct political action. In the 1950's election-law violations were numerous, particularly those involving ostensible shakubuku that was in fact illegal door-to-door canvassing.[121] Again, the connection between the formal organization and the perpetrators of these crimes is tenuous. One anti-Gakkai book claims that official directives ordered participation in canvassing activities;[122] in any case, the Gakkai did on occasion defend its members post facto, attacking the police for their "illegal persecution" of the Society.[123] And again, significantly, documented incidents of these violations date, almost without exception, from before the incumbency of President Ikeda.

The Gakkai officially, if obliquely, acknowledges the events that have contributed to its unfavorable public image. As one official pamphlet puts it, "There might be times when some too ardent members in earnest go overboard with their method of persuasion that might suggest their methods being compulsory."[124] President Ikeda is more explicit:

There may be some fanatic believers in our Society who misunderstand or misinterpret the teachings of Nichiren and the interpretations of the Sōkagakkai. Their individual words and deeds are liable to be interpreted as obedience to orders of the Society itself.

In the Sōkagakkai none of the presidents—neither Mr. Makiguchi, Mr. Toda, nor myself, or the chief leaders—have ever given orders to burn family altars, ancestral tablets, or to destroy tomb stones.[125]

As the quotation makes clear, the Gakkai today neither denies the past religious excesses of members nor condones them.

The present stand of the Gakkai on direct, illegal political action is also explicit, and it does not appear to be the position typical of a mass movement. Even a leftist critic of the Society admits that "all mass behavior that opposes authority has been skilfully excluded."[126] Where Japanese law or Gakkai directives have been violated, the official response is often excommunication. In past instances where believers were arrested for election-law violation, the Gakkai protested their innocence in these cases but did not condone such infractions per se. In fact, what the Gakkai is attempting to foster in regard to political action is just what it has asserted it wants: an increased tendency among the members to pursue political goals through institutionalized channels. "The awareness President Ikeda hoped for among the members was one that would eliminate the pessimistic, scornful view of politics as something with which clean people did not concern themselves, as something devilish wherein one had always to join hands with demons."[127]

The Gakkai's opposition to and avoidance of direct and illegal collective action are as marked as its proscriptions of individual illegality. The Society reserves the possibility of street demonstrations if certain crucial interests are involved; but it was careful in January 1968 to contrast its own form of "demonstration," the Sasebo lecture meetings, with the simultaneous bloody actions of Zengakuren and Communist party supporters. One student of the Gakkai suggests that the threats of demonstration are largely a strategic bluff: the more intense the opposing minority appears to be, the less likely the Liberal Democrats are to try to force through legislation.[128] Indeed, one suspects that the violence of the Gakkai has become increasingly rhetorical, and that the longer the Society participates in the sanctioned forms of political expression the less likely it is that reversion to earlier, more direct forms of action will occur.

The Sōkagakkai, as a formal organization, is not a mass movement as defined by Kornhauser. There is definitely potential; this is very clear. Structurally, the ideal pattern of intermediate relationships in the Gakkai—weak and inclusive—has parallels with totalitarian movements. Ideologically, the Society's formal position regarding the individual human being seems quite possibly to increase self-alienation; and the movement's views on majority rule and minority rights leave one with serious doubts about a real attachment to democratic principles. In the realm of behavior, Gakkai doctrine provides millenarian goals and scripture that clearly justify repressing heretics.

However, ideally the Gakkai does not seem to be intent upon detaching its members from their non-Gakkai social context; the Society's internal structure allows for mediated vertical communication and influence that are more suggestive of pluralist than of mass movements. Conceivably the Gakkai might be alienating man from himself; but it seems to offer an example of openness toward other actors in its social and political environment that contradicts an assumption, in accordance with the mass movement model, of exclusiveness, partisanship, uncooperativeness, and programmatic envy. Moreover, the Gakkai takes a strongly protective stand toward the constitution and toward democracy in the abstract that would seem to threaten neither the concrete system nor the abstract concept.

The Gakkai's behavioral record includes informal violence and crime. This record *is* informal, however, and—if one does not interpret the years of Ikeda's tenure as a temporary aberration of moderateness or as an eight-year exercise in duplicity—the movement has explicitly repudiated such actions in favor of an ideal stand supporting legal means and constitutional procedures, a stand that is reflected in the actual patterns of official Gakkai action.

CHAPTER 11

The Sōkagakkai and the Individual

THE SŌKAGAKKAI is organized to instill in its members ideal patterns of thought and behavior, but its individual members are concerned with fulfilling certain personal needs through their membership. These two objectives may be incompatible. Moreover, beyond the Society's conscious socializing aims, membership may produce latent socializing effects that do not necessarily either reinforce or conform to the official ideals. In this chapter we shall consider the nature of interaction between organization and member within the Gakkai.

ASSOCIATIONAL THEORY

A study by Almond and Verba of political attitudes in the United States, Great Britain, Italy, Germany, and Mexico indicated that citizens who were members of some voluntary association felt more politically competent than did those who were not, and that those who thought they belonged to a politically relevant association felt even more competent.[1] In three of the nations, such subjective competence correlated positively with pride in and emotional attachment to the political system; pluralist theorists conclude that membership in voluntary organizations is associated with increased allegiance to the political system.[2] A further pluralist inference is that the more associational memberships and subjective political competence in a society, the more stable and legitimate the political system.[3]

Whether or not the mere presence of associational memberships contributes to stable democratic or other political systems is questionable. A society with a great number of diverse, crosscutting voluntary groups may be a relatively favorable setting for a democratic polity, but such an associational network, though perhaps necessary for stable democracy, is not sufficient in itself. For example, in a nation characterized by a general cultural bias against democratic norms and practices, perhaps no number of voluntary associations could further the stable existence of democracy. One would have to say that, other things being equal, strong associational behavior is beneficial to democratic systems.

But, of course, other things are not always equal. Cultural influences may be crucial. In the other two nations studied, Germany and Italy, allegiance to the political system was not affected at all by feelings of subjective political competence, though such competence did increase with membership in organizations.[4] Qualitative variations in association must also be considered. From the pluralist premise that many associations are beneficial to democracy one cannot deduce that any particular association, in itself or simply as an addition, is beneficial. To assert that the appearance of a group like the Ku Klux Klan is beneficial to American democracy simply because it increases the number of voluntary associations is farcical. And trying to assess the significance of a single group like the Gakkai on the basis of the pluralist premise is pointless. One cannot infer quality of membership from the fact of membership but must consider it separately.

Viewed as a type of socialization, associational membership has three aspects: content, structure, and environment. Content means the specific ideology inculcated; structure means the methods and techniques by which the ideology is implanted. Structure may vary with content—different parts of the ideology may be communicated in different ways. Both structure and content have their manifest and latent and intended and unintended aspects: an organization may be neither aware that it is implanting certain ideas in its members nor intent on their inculcation; at the same time, the organization consciously wants and openly attempts to transmit certain ideas.

Socialization into a given group may influence the extent of an individual's social attachments, the degree of his alienation (i.e., his availability for mobilization), and even the form that mobilization itself could take. The very methods and techniques of socialization have their own effects. Does socialization result in increasingly satisfying, fulfilling, and moderating social relationships between the individual and society, or does it isolate him? Does it decrease alienation, by relieving frustration through new forms of self-fulfillment,[5] by dispelling anxiety and insecurity,[6] and by giving the member new faith in himself, his fellows, and his social and political environment? Or does it simply deflect, temporarily repress, or even intensify the aggressive tendencies springing from frustration?[7] Does it create external enemies, new threats, and new anxieties and insecurity? Does it inculcate disdain or hate for oneself, for others, and for society and the political system? Finally, can socialization of those who are already unattached and alienated be described as mobilization into the behavioral patterns of mass movements? It may be that socialization actually inhibits alienation and unattachment.

Almond and Verba's data reflect the significance of environment in the socialization process. According to their research, in Germany and Italy, both countries with experiences of profoundly antidemocratic and now-discredited political systems, subjective political competence had no effect on general attachment to the political system.[8] Almond and Verba inferred that for cultural, historical, and individual personal reasons, any political system in these nations would have a low degree of legitimacy. The parallel between these nations and Japan in culture and recent political history is interesting and might be kept in mind as one studies Japanese associations.

The theory and data available suggest first that mass movements tend to focus primarily on alienation and mobilization and operate to intensify alienation and its consequences, not to alleviate them;[9] and second that the alienation aspects of Kornhauser's mass models are more important than the nonattachment aspects.[10] Thus, now adding the previous assertions made concerning the significance of the behavioral aspects of the models, one can establish a hypothetical sequence of decreasing importance (both theoretical and practical): behavior, alienation, nonattachment.[11] The theoretical relevance of this progression lies in its attempt to assign relative weights to the various aspects of Kornhauser's model. Its practical relevance lies in the implication that those who would forestall, deflect, transform, or remedy mass conditions would most fruitfully observe behavioral tendencies and address themselves to reducing the causes of mass behavior—alienation in particular—rather than the manifestations.

PATTERNS OF INTERACTION

Nothing could be more basic in a study of the interaction of an organization and its members than the ideas of congruence and incongruence.

Congruence. A condition of congruence that does not entail any attitudinal or behavioral change in the members may occur either by selective entry (i.e., only those who agree with the formal ideology joining the organization) or by natural selection (i.e., only those who agree with organization's ideals remaining in the group) or by a combination of these processes. The ideal attributes of the organization and the actual attributes of the rank and file are nearly identical, since the members are trying to internalize the ideals and realize them in thought and behavior.[12]

Data indicate that entry into voluntary associations happens neither by chance nor by blind imitation, but is "in large part an expression of important emotional dispositions."[13] Owing to such dispositions, "people tend not to 'expose' themselves to communications which conflict with their own predispositions, but instead to seek support for their opinions and attitudes in favorable communications."[14] Persons who, it develops, have entered with incongruent aims or predispositions tend to drop out of the association, thus increasing the proportion of the total membership that agrees with the ideals and narrowing the gap between ideal and actual.[15] But despite selective entry and natural selection, "there is often a great gap between the top leaders' notions of the [ideal] purpose of the organization and those of the [actual] members at the bottom."[16] Such a divergence results from contradictions between the ideal, intended, and manifest patterns of socialization, ideology, and behavior and the actual, unintended, and latent patterns.[17]

The interaction between organization and membership can have various results. The organization may influence the members, or vice versa. Antagonistic patterns of thought and behavior may coexist through a sort of compartmentalization. Naturally, influence need not be one-way all the time. Nor is it strictly accurate to speak of the "results" of interaction; we are considering a constant process of influence and counterinfluence that affects an organization's general proximity to some model such as Kornhauser's model of the mass movement.

Incongruence: organizational influence on members. There is a body of data that leads one to suspect the Gakkai's proximity to the mass movement model is due mainly to the Society's organizational influence. The ability of groups to influence individual patterns of thought and action is well known:

Commitments to democratic procedures and ideals by the principal organizations to which low-status individuals belong may also influence these individuals' actual political behavior more than their underlying political values, no matter how authoritarian. . . .

Commitments to other values or institutions by individuals (cross-pressures) may also override the most established predispositions.

For this reason, "the specific propensity of given social strata to support either extremist or democratic political parties, then, cannot be predicted from a knowledge of their psychological predispositions or from attitudes inferred from survey data."[18] These statements bear out Kornhauser, who looks on a mass movement as mass man writ large, as well as the Gakkai, which officially claims the ability to instill Truth in its believers. The Gakkai is not selective with its converts, for any person can be made into a true believer.[19]

The Society unrealistically sees all believers as activists. Actually, most new converts are at best lukewarm in their faith and present the Society with the immediate problems of first keeping them in the Gakkai, then inducing action, and finally arousing zealous belief. In solving these problems the Society uses varied means (both incentives and deterrents) designed to hold, mobilize, and socialize members. These means may be physical, material, normative-symbolic, and ecological. Physical constraints are of little use in a voluntary association within a free society. But material incentives and deterrents, especially those founded on the ideas of divine benefit and its opposite, divine punishment, play a major role—as do such normative suasions as promotion and demotion. Ecological manipulation is crucial: by controlling or withholding favorable reactions and acceptance—group leaders can powerfully influence the member to adopt at least the outward forms of faith.

The Gakkai applies these incentives and deterrents through various printed media, large- and small-scale gatherings, and interpersonal groups of sufficient number and variety to permit members to exist almost entirely within the Gakkai social network. This combination of controls seems well fashioned to maximize organizational influence over the members. Such influence, at least over the members' verbal and physical behavior, is likely to be greater where members identify strongly with both peers and leaders and acceptance as one of the group is important to them; where the organization comes close to monopolizing the communications received by its members (through both impersonal media and, especially, direct social interaction); and where the organization is highly centralized.[20] The Gakkai actively promotes identification and centralization, and either consciously or unconsciously it attempts to control communications. The need for acceptance is an ideal condition that the Gakkai assumes is also actually felt by members. Thus the Gakkai's influence over its members should be relatively high, especially over longtime members and activists, who according to survey data identify strongly and limit their sources of information to Gakkai materials. Despite the further indications of survey data that the Gakkai does not entirely monopolize communications to its members, the other ecological and symbolic incentives and constraints used by the Gakkai imply a relatively high degree of organizational influence.

Another facet of influence by the organization is its attempts to guide the thoughts and actions of members. Presumably the organization will find it easiest to produce in members the verbal and physical behavior that, without being socially deviant, will lead to acceptance or promotion. Members' attitudes that are unrelated to the needs of belonging, identification, and belief will be more difficult to influence. Similarly, behavior that deviates markedly from society's norms will be more difficult to achieve. Thus one might expect the Gakkai's influence on its members to be greatest (in terms of the model) in the area of nonattachment: the extent to which a member must participate in Gakkai activities and rely on Gakkai communications to ensure acceptance may lead gradually to the attenuation of his non-Gakkai contacts.

Incongruence: members' divergent motives. Evidently, one cannot assume that the influence on members of the formal organization's ideals meets with no counterinfluences. As social and cultural patterns and popular attitudes may be more important to the functioning of a political system than are its formal structures, so perhaps the independent attitudes and informal behavior patterns of members count for at least as much as organizational influence in giving a movement its character and actual emphasis. Data reinforce an impression that the official goals and ideologies of organizations are often only tenuously connected with the individual's reasons for continued membership. "Men may become attached to a party, a community, [a religious group,?] or a nation by forces that have nothing to do with ideology or consensus."[21] Gerhard Lenski, in a study of religion in Detroit, found that the religious subcommunity, i.e., the social collectivity of believers, had a much stronger influence on believers' attitudes than the official side of their religious belief had, i.e., membership in a church.[22] A study of Gakkai members in Fukuoka City showed that fully half of the rank and file polled evinced no interest whatsoever in whether the Gakkai grew in members or not; and only 24 per cent claimed to have a "serious interest" in this important organizational goal.[23] For the members questioned in this survey the pursuit of official goals does not seem to be the primary reason behind continued membership—then what is?

Some of the possible motivations to entry and membership are entirely unrelated to Shōshū beliefs, e.g., primary interest in intraorganizational status or in political activity. But aside from sincere in-

terest in the beliefs of Nichiren Shōshū or interest in the specific benefits of belief, the most frequent motivation for entry and sustained
membership is the hope of satisfying personal psychological or social
needs.[24] Certain data suggest that the gratification of primary human
needs bears no relation to the official goals and norms of the organization, and that only the thoughts and actions in which conformity
is required in order to satisfy these needs come under the decided influence of organizational ideals.[25]

What sort of benefits do members motivated by these needs perceive? In a series of case studies of Gakkai members, the majority
made such statements as "I've changed," and "I've become self-con-
fident."[26] An exconvict with a record of extortion, theft, and narcotics
violations told the following story:[27] "My nickname used to be 'The
Bear.' I was constantly driven by an impulse to slice up anyone I saw.
I was ostracized by the gang. All the tough guys, hoods, and gangsters
would run from me." After his release from prison and before he had
joined the Gakkai, this man reported that neighbors shunned him
and he was fired from successive jobs. "It's for this very reason that I'm
so very, very grateful to the members of the Gakkai. They're the only
ones who treat me like a human and don't at all care about my past
record. I'm now a *chikubu-chō* [district chief]; where in this world
would I, an exconvict who used to be like a wild animal, be given such
a post of responsibility?" Whether or not such people as this man are
the ones who are uninterested in official ideals is not known; but testi-
monies like his point to the conclusion that the search for personal
and social gratification is the alternative focus of interest keeping organizational apathetics in the Gakkai.

Little change in attitudes is required for the gratification of primary needs within the Society. Considerable data indicate that many
Gakkai members do not feel inclined to attend activities, to read
Gakkai media or scriptural materials, or to perform specified rituals;
apparently in many cases organizational influence is too weak to
change even these relatively superficial patterns of behavior. In the
Society's efforts to induce deviant behavior such as shakubuku a
similar failing may be observed: no more than half of the membership
appears to take part.[28] Marked discrepancies between ideal and actual
are visible in matters on which the Gakkai's official position is clear,
on political issues in particular. The most striking example of this
concerns the constitution: the Gakkai firmly supports the present
constitution, but the membership in general is markedly negative
about it.[29]

The preliminary and as yet empirically deficient assumption I would make from the partial data is that Sōkagakkai believers are born, not made. The Gakkai attracts or at least retains those who are already basically in agreement with Gakkai precepts; it does not successfully resocialize converts into entirely new patterns of thought and action. It seems reasonable that if superficial behavior patterns cannot be changed, then neither can more deeply held social attitudes; many cases of unchanged behavior lead to the belief that congruence between basic social orientations and Gakkai ideals is due to initial similarities, not to successful indoctrination. It is conceivable that converts can be resocialized into organizationally ideal patterns without influencing their behavioral tendencies, and that the preliminary observation presented above represents this phenomenon. But this possibility is contradicted by evidence (again, partial) that many members share certain typical Japanese social attitudes that the Gakkai specifically rejects; among these are religious tolerance and the feeling that religious groups should not participate directly in the political process.[30] The adherence of many members to these culturally sanctioned beliefs suggests an unreconstructed, pre-Gakkai orientation that has resisted, and coexists with the effects of, socialization.

So far in our discussion of theory and patterns of interaction we have seen that the often contradictory influences of organizational ideals and the motivations of members have some bearing on the nature of the Gakkai as a possible mass movement. Once again turning to Kornhauser's model of the mass movement, we shall now ask such questions as: does the interaction result in more or less attachment of organization and member to the larger society; does it lead to more or less alienation of members from themselves and of members and organization from other people and from social and political contexts; and does it conduce to unstable, direct pursuit of remote or utopian goals? We shall focus also on the participants in this interaction: where, in terms of the model, is the influence of members' pre-Gakkai attitudes primary, and where is organizational socialization into ideal patterns successful? Finally, we shall focus on the various elements of democracy, as defined in Chapter 9. Social nonattachment is the least significant aspect of the mass model when investigating the Society's potential for either "massness" or undemocratic political implications; behavior is the most significant aspect. Thus as the following analysis moves from nonattachment to alienation to behavior, one may find this progression becoming increasingly significant to an evaluation of the political implications of the Gakkai.

EXCLUSIVITY AND INCLUSIVITY

To what extent members of the Gakkai are nonattached to their social environment, and to what extent organizational socialization is responsible for their nonattachment, can be estimated using two related concepts: the exclusivity and inclusivity of their relationships. Exclusivity means a state of social nonattachment except for one's relationship with a movement.* Inclusivity means the degree to which one's relationship with an organization like the Gakkai expands to encompass an ever greater proportion of one's life. The two terms are related, for the more inclusive a relationship is, the more exclusive it is likely to be.

In addition to the nonattachment of members to society, the ideal and actual internal structure and process of the organization will be referred to in terms of whether a man in the Gakkai is in a position analogous to that of a man in a mass society or a mass movement: i.e., are his secondary relationships weak and non-inclusive? And as a consequence of the presence or absence of secondary groups and of the strength or weakness of such groups, the extent and nature of the organizational elite's accessibility to influence by non-elites will again come under observation.

The Gakkai's ideal of social interaction, except for the members' religious behavior, is not exclusivity. But at the same time, data on individual members' social ties indicate an actual influence by the Society toward exclusivity. Believers have been accused of retreating from life's misfortunes, ignoring reality, and escaping into a world of internal (the daimoku, the gongyō) and external (shakubuku, organizational participation) activity that reduces contacts and affinity with society.[31] Certain opinion surveys do suggest that Gakkai members screen out information unrelated to their organizational interests.[32] The Gakkai, too, by consistently explaining and simplifying everything in religious terms, may be isolating its believers from the secular world.[33]

This exclusivist tendency may even work explicitly against Gakkai ideals; such a phenomenon has been noted in other movements.

* This one relationship must be postulated since, in contrast to the ideal mass man, the member of a mass movement has ipso facto at least one social attachment.

There is ... evidence to suggest that the communist party's demand for dedication often produces consequences which are quite in conflict with the other doctrinal and practical demand that the party maintain close contact with the masses. A process of isolation from the outside world appears to take place as individuals move into the inner core of the movement.[34]

In spite of exclusivist tendencies in the organization and its members, however, there is reason to believe that the largest part of the membership is closer to the Gakkai's socially interactive ideal than to the unattached mass man. Even if shakubuku does not necessarily constitute a fulfilling, harmonious social relationship, it does serve to tie the individual to his social environment; the total process of socialization into the Gakkai is an opportunity to learn about society and polity in a way that can make entry into the complex, ultramodern world of urban Japan easier for the less educated and lower-class persons comprising the majority of the faithful.[35]

Survey data also indicate that the faithful do not as a whole succumb to the socially isolating influences of socialization; i.e., they are not an unattached, free-floating human mass, conceivably available for mobilization by any movement with any goals. The more committed and more active members, however, apparently *can* be influenced by the socialization process and do constitute a source of potential mass behavior.

The Gakkai has no explicit ideal concerning the inclusivity of its relationship with its members, but looking at the Society's manifest efforts to create a network of groups that could encompass every facet of behavior, both religious and secular, we can assume that the ideal, though latent, is one of total inclusivity. The actual degree of inclusivity of the relationship is highly conjectural: The "activists" who read only the *Seikyō Shimbun* and *Dai Byaku Renge* may spend their social life with acquaintances who have no associations with the Gakkai whatsoever, whereas those who attend the meetings of the Student Division, their kumi and block, the Fuji Symphony Orchestra, and the Kayō Club may never look at any scriptural or organizational media. The need to make such distinctions is doubtful, however. Only those who satisfy their needs through the zadankai and individual worship seem likely to maintain the non-Gakkai nature of most if not all of the secular sphere of their lives; such members even seem reluctant to immerse themselves in any more of the Gakkai's doctrine and activities than is necessary to meet their needs.

It appears, though, that the influences toward exclusivity implicit in the Gakkai's socialization process are paralleled by influences toward inclusivity. As the activist strengthens his Gakkai-related social and communications ties, they replace the non-Gakkai ties that once occupied the same parts of his life. Where organizational commitment is deep (for whatever reason), one can expect that believers will be motivated to place increasing areas of their lives under the ever-expanding Gakkai umbrella. The social patterns of the membership are at least consistent: the activists tend to be exclusively and inclusively tied to the Society, whereas the rank and file do not. But the Gakkai's ideals are inconsistent; it is unreasonable to suppose that the members should fully participate in society and simultaneously be involved in Gakkai-related groups at all points of their experience. It is perhaps since this ideal is latent that the Gakkai is able to persist in the inconsistency.

The concepts of inclusivity and exclusivity also bear on internal structure and process in the Society. And neither the ideal nor the actual pattern of structures within the Gakkai indicates that the Gakkai is a mass movement. Ideal and actual, however, vary from the model in different directions. Ideally, secondary structures in the Gakkai are weak vis-à-vis the central leadership and inclusive vis-à-vis the membership; and an organization with weak and inclusive intermediate groups approximates a totalitarian, not a mass, movement. But in reality Gakkai intermediate groups, especially the lower-level groups of the vertical line, may well have an intrinsic strength and autonomy quite at odds with the Gakkai ideal. The possibility that kumi and han have some autonomy is suggested by the fact that the periodic meetings of these units are not scheduled from above as are the meetings of all larger groups. Also, membership records are kept at these lower levels; even the central leadership of the Gakkai does not know precisely the total active membership of the Society.

But such strength in the Gakkai's secondary groups does not mean that they have any significant power in relation to the central organization. To have that sort of power the secondary groups would have to be organized, as they are not. Yet they do constitute a set of structures that could, if not ably managed, obstruct the organization's major programs and turn out a membership indifferent to certain ideals, goals, and activities of the Gakkai. The intermediate group structure, though weak, is not as weak as the Gakkai's ideal stipulates; one might even rank it moderately close to the strong intermediate structure of the pluralist model.

Moreover, despite the ideal inclusivity attempted through the creation of a wide variety of secondary groups, the non-inclusive nature of rank-and-file membership suggests that the Society has developed the mass or pluralist type of non-inclusive intermediate group structure, rather than the totalitarian inclusive type. In combination, the intermediate structure appears to be one of either strong and non-inclusive (i.e. pluralist) or weak and non-inclusive (i.e. mass) secondary relationships. Whichever is the case, the actual structure of the Gakkai is not clearly mass, and certainly not totalitarian. It is incongruent with both the Gakkai's structural ideal (signifying the primacy in this area of influences from the membership) and the model of the mass movement.

There is no contradiction in the internal process of the Gakkai. The Gakkai's ideal is high elite accessibility—though regularized and mediated—much like the accessibility that typifies pluralist systems. Impediments to this access are noticed and countered; as President Ikeda has observed, with organizational growth and the proliferation of elite duties Gakkai leaders have become increasingly busy, and "personal contact among members has been weakened. This is indicative of the fact that relations among members have become less intimate. Personal contact is very important in maintaining one's faith; otherwise faith will be lost."[36] But actually, as well as ideally, non-elite access to the elite is still extremely high. Leaders are in constant view at meetings on the lower levels of the organization; President Ikeda meets frequently with groups of members around the country. And the many cases handled by the Citizens' Discussion Centers— several hundred thousand per year—suggest the extent to which Gakkai members take seriously the ideal opportunities open to them of indirect access to the elite.

ALIENATION

Self-alienation. Insofar as a mass movement is composed of persons alienated from themselves, the Sōkagakkai as a social collectivity approximates a mass movement; this approximation is probably strengthened by self-estranging influences exerted on believers in the course of socialization. The Gakkai's official ideal is familiarity with complex doctrine, not oversimplification. But this ideal receives only lip service; the Gakkai has actually reduced its teachings to a bare minimum of unicausal explanations and personal goal-seeking. Knowledge is not really necessary—faith is all that really counts. The membership of the Gakkai is, if anything, more simplistic in its outlook than is the organization, and it is quite possible that here the membership is influencing the organization. For example, fairly sophisticated official interpretations of the relative worth of medical science and faith (especially with regard to neurotic and psychosomatic disorders) are carried in the *Seikyō Shimbun* along with testimonials attributing omnipotence to religious belief in all matters from sore feet to cancer. In certain ways the organization must come down to the level of its members—the addition of pronunciation aids in the written media of the Gakkai is one such instance, and oversimple explanations of complex disorders may be another. Converts appear to bring a simplistic orientation to the Gakkai, which responds by addressing itself to this simplism and not to either the real and complicated secular world or the elaborate doctrinal corpus that is the official ideal.

The Society's ideal with respect to the inherent capability of man sees man as the only possible agent of world revolution but is equally explicit on the absolute necessity of not only faith in Nichiren Shōshū but active participation in the Gakkai: "By oneself, faith cannot last, nor is it possible to live a life overflowing with divine benefits."[37] Gakkai members are similarly ambivalent, but there is reason to believe that their sense of self-alienation is relatively strong. The deprecation of self discernible in Gakkai ideology conceivably contributes to this condition. We have already remarked on the contrasting sense of political potency.

The zadankai certainly serves as a structure of self-expression within which the individual can act as a positive being and be recognized as such by others. The whole process of advancement operates on the basis of personal effort and achievement.[38] But if such experiences and opportunities create greater acceptance of the self as a legitimate actor, this is not discernible in the data available. Although the Gakkai proclaims in abstract terms its doctrinal efficacy against all forms of alienation, its socialization process has brought no significant alleviation of self-alienation. Either the social and economic spheres of the average member's life exert more influence on his outlook than the Gakkai allows for, or the alienating elements in Gakkai teachings are more salient to the member than its integrative elements. In either case the resulting condition is the kind of collective self-alienation that is more or less typical of mass man.

Totalitarian or authoritarian man, however, is not approximated, either by members' attitudes or by official doctrine, nor does the actual experience of life in the Gakkai context seem calculated to instill authoritarian norms. Only two features of the Society are relevant to possible authoritarianism. One is the relatively authoritarian tendency inferred from the higher F-scale scores of activists. The other, and perhaps an explanation of the first, is the ambiguity of the Gakkai's ideal stand on several elements of the authoritarian syndrome, an ambiguity that creates a place in the organization for persons with authoritarian tendencies. The Society is conventional, though moderately so, in its social mores. Anyone seeking a power figure has both the gohonzon and President Ikeda; anyone with aggressive impulses, or a generally hostile and destructive outlook, has the practice of shakubuku. The Gakkai's injunctions to believe, and only then to try to know, are anti-intellectual; and personal faults may be projected outward onto the heretical and degenerate world. Finally, with regard to stereotypy the Gakkai is explicitly congruent with the model.

Yet neither the official ideal nor the attitudinal configuration of the Gakkai's general membership is truly "authoritarian." Given the members' educational level, the F-scale scores obtained were, if anything, lower than anticipated. By contrast, the less extreme form of self-alienation characteristic of mass man does seem to be empirically approximated by the Gakkai's membership, and its socialization process seems to contribute to whatever self-alienation the new convert may feel.

Human alienation. Relative to other members of Japanese society, the members of the Sōkagakkai appear to be somewhat less trusting of people in general and somewhat more partisan in their associational commitments. In both these respects their attitudes contradict both the Gakkai's official ideal of interpersonal relationships and the actual trend of its activities, and suggest an affinity to alienated mass man. This slight suggestion, however, is effectively contradicted by the ideal and actuality of official norms. The whole thrust of the Gakkai's socialization effort is toward creating "good members of society." Leaders and rank and file alike are specifically admonished to trust one another and to extend mutual help and encouragement,[39] and the unrestrained self-revelation indulged in at zadankai suggests that trust is considerable. Conceivably none of this trust extends to non-Gakkai society; yet what trust obviously exists, combined with the Gakkai's overt efforts to increase trust, is more persuasive than the opposite findings based on sketchy survey data.

Although the Gakkai's membership is on the whole partisan, its partisanship is not in general extreme, nor is it congruent with the more highly partisan features of the official ideal. The Gakkai ideal prescribes intense partisanship only toward other religious actors, and even in this area concessions are made to smooth social intercourse. The members in effect ignore the ideal. They maintain extra-Gakkai social contacts and friendships, vote for parties other than the Kōmeitō, and perform their propagation duties with a laxity that contrasts with the extreme partisanship of mass man.

The orientation of the Gakkai toward other spheres of social life seems to contradict the model of a mass movement. There is no discernible envy, either ideological or attitudinal or operational.[40] Distrust and partisanship exist among the members, but they are neither decisively shown nor seemingly very intense. Alongside their ideal and actual cooperativeness in social and political action, their religious partisanship appears increasingly rhetorical. To be sure, Gakkai activists—as one might suspect—are more likely than the rank and file to vote for the Kōmeitō, to decrease their ties to non-Gakkai society, and to engage in shakubuku and other partisan practices; yet nothing suggests that they feel any more alienated from their fellowmen than other Gakkai members. Indeed, insofar as official organizational activity has any influence, it is in the opposite direction.

Systemic alienation. The Sōkagakkai's manifest ideal is the promotion of closer affective ties in all areas of life. The Gakkai claims to create good neighbors, hard workers, and responsible citizens, and to do so by attacking the sources, not merely the manifestations, of estrangement and dissatisfaction. According to the Society, faith gives a man the confidence necessary for successful action in his social, economic, and political surroundings.[41]

As for instrumental alienation, that is, personal antipathy toward one's environment, the perceived enjoyment of tangible divine benefits might be expected to bring some degree of relief. Several surveys indicate that most Gakkai members do in fact perceive themselves as enjoying divine benefits (goriyaku or kudoku), and that this perception increases with length of membership and activism. Whether the increase is due to natural selection or to the self-delusion of those deeply committed to the Gakkai for other reasons, or both, is not clear, but the prevalence of the feeling is indisputable. In five samples of the general Gakkai membership those reporting positive kudoku varied between 50 and 75 per cent[42] (with a sample of new converts reporting the lowest incidence of benefit), whereas in three samples of activists the convinced recipients of divine mercy varied roughly from 80 to 90 per cent.[43] In addition, one might suspect that the prospect of gaining status by dint of individual effort and of achieving academic rank without formal education would make the under-educated and relatively deprived feel relatively less alienated.

However, a comparison between Gakkai members' perceptions of divine blessings received and their sense of alienation from society seems to belie the Gakkai's claim that it attacks alienation at the roots. Gakkai members evince relatively great dissatisfaction with the social and economic system, and by no means all of this dissatisfaction predates their entry into the Society. One small survey showed that whereas perceived kudoku varied positively with length of member-ship, satisfaction with one's job varied inversely, and dissatisfaction with society was uninfluenced.[44] Another local survey of Society members shows the same inconclusive picture: activists perceived much more kudoku but were scarcely more satisfied with their jobs than nonactivists.[45]

The explanation offered by many[46] is intuitively acceptable, namely that the Gakkai's denunciation of the secular world and its insistence that kudoku comes from faith alone combine to alienate the believer from the secular social and economic system and cause him to deny all connection between occupational effort and divine reward: "In other words, they believe they can survive in this world only because their idol Buddha is their savior. . . . Because of his blessing, they believe, they can earn money and support their families. The mem-bers don't think that the wages they receive from their employers are the rewards of their labor."[47] The testimony of defectors corroborates this inference. Several lower-level leaders who left the Gakkai re-ported that believers, regardless of their problem, were inevitably told, "Just pray harder."[48] The possible secular causes of misfortune were irrelevant; the solution to every problem lay strictly in prayer and Gakkai activity.

Also, the Gakkai's constant attacks on the Japanese political system, its incumbents, and the policies they espouse can hardly make its members happier with the system's instrumental aspects. No doubt these attacks represent in part a concession to the membership, and in part a calculated appeal to other elements in the electorate. But they are also the inescapable conclusion of Gakkai beliefs about the secular state, and it would be a mistake to interpret them wholly as a capitula-tion or an inducement. To be sure, certain of the Society's political activities—notably the Citizens' Discussion Centers and the Kōmeitō itself—might well serve to decrease instrumental alienation from the political system. Nevertheless, the overall effect of the Gakkai's politi-cal pronouncements seems to be the other way. There are no firm data indicating that socialization into the Gakkai increases instrumental alienation—either social, economic, or political—but neither can one assert that the socialization process appears to diminish the considerable instrumental alienation that Gakkai members apparently feel.

Despite its incessant criticism of the political system in action, the Gakkai takes a stand of absolute and unflinching protection toward the system per se as embodied in the constitution. However, members of the Gakkai, though informed as well as or better than the average Japanese about the contents of the constitution, are notably more negative than the general populace about the charter and more open to the idea of revision. This relative negativity held up under demographic controls in a nationwide survey conducted in 1965 in which professed Kōmeitō supporters served as the Gakkai sample.[49] That the contradiction between rank-and-file attitudes and organizational ideals was striking in this committed group makes the finding even more significant.

There are two possible explanations for this contradiction. First, individuals entering the Gakkai may bring considerable systemic alienation with them and either resist the ideal orientations fostered by the Society or else find in the socialization process some latent negative orientation toward the system that confirms their previous attitudes. Second, the persons who enter the Gakkai may not be relatively more alienated than their fellow Japanese but may experience such powerful latent influences in the socialization process that by the time they have been politicized into support of the Kōmeitō they have developed a marked antipathy toward the political system.

I prefer the first explanation. Most Sōkagakkai members come from the socioeconomic strata most likely to be frustrated, discontented and dissatisfied. The Gakkai experience does seem broadening; Gakkai members are surprisingly aware socially and politically;[50] if the Gakkai socialization process exercises no influence toward diminishing whatever instrumental alienation exists, then this broadening of experience may simply lead to general systemic alienation where none had existed before. In addition, as opposed to the ideal socialization that the Gakkai claims to perform and that creates responsible, loyal political actors, the actual socialization process does appear to include a large measure of highly negative orientations toward the system. Proclaiming that the entire polity is rife with heresy, graft, self-seeking, and evil would surely have some negative effects. The result seems to be a bifurcation between the Gakkai's ideal lack of alienation from the political context and the actual systemic alienation of the rank and file, which could lend itself to mass political behavior.

The possible latent alienation in the Gakkai's actual stance toward the overall Japanese political structure may be offset by the Society's position on the various elements of the "democratic formula." The Gakkai is as unremitting in its support of abstract democracy as it is in its defense of the constitution. And here the actual orientations of members appear to be in general agreement with Gakkai ideals. The members view democracy slightly less positively than does the general populace and much less effusively than does the organization, but they do appear to lean toward a somewhat socialist, revisionist capitalist system that is compatible with democracy.

Both the Gakkai and its members take an ambivalent, inconclusive position on majority rule. The Society takes an ideal stand supporting majority rule in political and other secular affairs (though only where full consideration is given to minority viewpoints), but in actual operation both democratic and undemocratic elements enter the decision-making procedures. In the *Rules of the Sōkagakkai* the Society's formal structure appears clearly and completely authoritarian: the president is in full and formally unlimited command. Ikeda's view is that "Examination, debate, and administration ought to be carried on democratically, through the knowledge of many. But as for leadership and objectives, I give them."[51] As Ikeda notes, below the level of supreme command democratic procedures are to be followed—but these procedures are not stated so as to explicitly include majority rule.[52]

Observation of the Society's actual workings reveals that vertical communication, by which the rank and file find that the members' views are taken into account by their leaders, contains the germ of a majoritarian orientation—something missing in many Japanese organizations of whatever type. But the congruence of actual Gakkai processes with democratic norms is still doubtful. Though Ikeda explicitly denies it,[53] the charismatic quality of his authority may completely overshadow whatever introduction to majority rule the Society provides. Moreover, the rather sophisticated distinction drawn between the absolutist religious plane and the relativist secular plane may be beyond the typical member's powers of comprehension, and along with it the justification for majority rule in politics.

The Gakkai's ideal and actual stands on minority rights are also at odds. The Society fully supports all of the rights and freedoms specified in the constitution, and in particular goes to great lengths denying any intent to infringe upon freedom of religion. Its tirades against criticism, however, hint at a disregard for freedom of expression, and the volume of such tirades may instill in the faithful this attitude to some degree. Ideally, within the Gakkai all are equal; membership appears to be a continuing lesson to disregard educational, social, and economic status differences. But whether members carry over this view to general society is another matter. The rank and file's general orientation toward minority rights is positive, but among the more active members the attitudes toward freedom of expression and religious faith parallel those of the official Gakkai media.

The Sōkagakkai's formal approval of the elements of the democratic formula does not offset the actual state of systemic alienation discernible in the Society. Informal rank-and-file attitudes and actual, though often latent, socialization influences reinforce each other to produce a general alienation in the Gakkai that is similar to the overall alienation characterizing the mass movement model. Where ideal and actual socialization both contradict members' alienation—as in the case of human alienation—rank-and-file alienation does not seem to offset organizational characteristics. But where latent influences seem to coincide with pre-Gakkai attitudes, explicit ideals are not influential enough to alleviate the feelings of alienation and the consequent potential for mass political behavior.

BEHAVIOR

Characteristic of the behavior of mass movements is the direct pursuit of remote goals; mass man typically vacillates between this pursuit and apathy. At the present the behavior of the Gakkai and its members does not fit the model. Neither Gakkai ideals, nor rank and file behavioral patterns, nor the actual behavioral example of the Gakkai's official activities exhibits apathy or unstable behavior. The Society neatly divides each year into periods of expansion through shakubuku, guided consolidation, and study; activity is constant, at times even hectic, but it is stable and patterned. Though Gakkai media make constant references to rather remote ideal goals, the average member is apparently little concerned with them.[54]

As for actual behavioral patterns, we can only try to infer potential for behavioral mobilization; by inferring resemblance to the model we can analyze aspects of social reality and make predictions beyond the obvious behavioral phenomena. Behavioral phenomena are useful to analysis both in their presence and, in significant cases, in their absence. In the Gakkai, for instance, where a degree of social non-attachment and a significant degree of alienation exist, the absence for the past several years of either ideal or actual mass political behavior raises the question of what possible factors may be limiting the availability of members for mobilization or accounting for the nonmobilization of an available membership.

The members' immediacy of focus may be strengthened by the actual operations of the Society. Since the early 1960's the Gakkai's actual behavior has included the pragmatic and increasingly moderate pursuit of realistic goals. These intermediate-range goals serve to keep hopes high when ultimate goals seem unattainable; and members may even see in these shorter-range goals something analogous to their own private goals. This immediacy of focus could explain the absence of mass behavior on the part of Gakkai members despite their relative unattachment and alienation—i.e., their relative availability. Although socialization into the Society may not diminish one's alienation from society and the political system, it may diminish the aggressive behavioral consequences by providing the compensations of the zadankai. Thus, because of the immediacy of focus of members, alienation from the secular world may coexist with a disinclination toward mass or other forms of deviant behavior, and may in fact increase the organization's difficulties in influencing the members toward any form of collective behavior.

Nevertheless, mobilization is not impossible, and remote objectives are not absolutely necessary for mobilizing large numbers of people. If the rewards promised are immediate and tangible and the behavior required is not too deviant, as in the case of the present form of shakubuku, personal motivation may produce a proselyting force of several million persons. Even this figure, however, represents no more than half of the professed membership of the Sōkagakkai.[55] Members who make statements such as "I only talk about religion with other members of the Gakkai,"[56] "Yes, I do *shakubuku*. But I don't press it so unreasonably as people say.... I don't do it at work. Matters of religion shouldn't be taken into the company,"[57] and "I'm not particularly pressured to proselyte. It's completely up to the individual, since increasing the number of members isn't the objective of this Society,"[58] are not fully available for mobilization into the forms of behavior that characterize mass politics.

Indeed, members' actual patterns of thought and activity conflict so with Gakkai ideals that one wonders how far the majority are available for *any* collective action. The ideal of permanent mobilization—behavioral and psychological, religious and political[59]—is seldom approximated in actuality.[60] There are enough meetings of various types to keep a real activist busy almost every night[61] but, as with shakubuku, it appears that only about half of the members even claim to participate regularly. Table 22 shows the distribution of attenders and non-attenders according to one survey.[62] The Gakkai itself is even less optimistic about attendance rates, suggesting that respondents in surveys are painting themselves in more active colors than is actually the case.[63] One han chief estimated that perhaps 20 per cent of the members of his unit were "of firm faith" and "enthusiastically active."[64] Compared to the followers of other Japanese religions Gakkai members are quite active;[65] but in general the evaluation of another Gakkai leader seems to be borne out: "The only ones who really believe are a number of leaders."[66]

The Gakkai is not spectacularly successful in mobilizing its followers to political action, even to such nondeviant behavior as voting for Gakkai candidates;[67] however, members who have been politically mobilized appear to be quite disciplined. Two national surveys carried out in early 1965 found professed Kōmeitō supporters to be more disciplined than any other party's supporters, 90 per cent in one poll and 100 per cent in the other voicing the intention to vote for Kōmeitō candidates.[68] Similar discipline appeared in three surveys of expected voting behavior in the Tokyo gubernatorial election of 1967.[69] Other data suggest contradictory tendencies: although in a 1965 national survey, the party affiliation of candidates appeared to be much more important to Kōmeitō supporters than to supporters of the other major parties,[70] two other national polls showed Kōmeitō

TABLE 22

Attendance at Zadankai

	HAN ZADANKAI			
KUMI ZADANKAI	Always or Almost Always Attend	Usually Attend	Seldom or Scarcely Ever Attend	Total
Always or almost always attend	*30.59%*	*2.99%*	1.87%	35.45%
Usually attend	*1.12*	*11.94*	2.61	15.67
Seldom or scarcely ever attend	.37	1.12	47.38	48.87
Total	32.08%	16.05%	51.86%	99.99%

NOTE: Figures in italics suggest the proportion of hard-core activists.

backers little different from supporters of other parties in the relative weight they assigned to party or individual in their selection of candidates.[71]

In addition to physical mobilization, many of the "faithful" are unavailable for mental mobilization along the ideal lines of Gakkai doctrine or Kōmeitō policy. The Society's ideal is ideological uniformity and internal consistency. But such consistency does not exist, either manifestly or latently, in the minds of most members: analysis of the attitudes of a sample of Gakkai members by Tanaka Kunio in 1963 revealed belief systems so scattered, inconsistent, and at odds with Gakkai doctrine that no body of beliefs describable as "ideology" of any sort (much less officially sanctioned Gakkai ideology) could be discerned.[72] As for manifest acceptance of ideology, only 37 per cent of one sample of rank-and-file members stated that they would follow a Gakkai instruction if it conflicted with personal viewpoint; in contrast, 73 per cent of the leaders polled would follow such instructions.[73]

On specific points of religious and political policy the same discrepancy between organization ideal and rank-and-file reality is found. Many religious ideas are successfully inculcated in the membership—notably the general idea of unicausality and the relationships between worship and reward, laxity and misfortune. Nevertheless, it is not possible to influence members totally on religious matters.[74] It is even less possible to successfully inculcate political beliefs. In a September 1962 local survey 56 per cent of a sample of believers said they had never even heard of the Kōseiren; another 28 per cent had heard of the party but knew nothing at all of its policies.[75] Among members who are aware that the Gakkai is involved in politics, not all agree that such involvement is a good thing. One observer in the early 1960's recorded conflicting views on the wisdom of religious participation in the political system,[76] and as late as 1964, twenty-two of the thirty-six respondents in a poll of believers in Tokyo said that religious groups should not go into politics.[77] Certainly, thirty-six is hardly a reliable sample; interestingly, however, in every subgroup those opposing Gakkai political participation had been members for a longer time and were more active than proponents of participation.

There are indications that Gakkai members are mentally susceptible to influence on specific policies only in ways one would expect of them even before conversion. When asked in a 1967 poll in Tokyo, "What do you want the new governor to focus on first of all?" Kōmeitō backers were 80 per cent more likely than either the supporters of any other party or the total sample to choose "housing problem" and over twice as likely as either other type of group to choose "welfare."[78] On issues on which one would assume incongruity between individual pre-Gakkai attitudes and official ideals—such as religious intolerance, social attachments, or political participation by religious groups—that incongruence is still discernible among established members.

Whether believers come to the Society or are created by it, the significant point is that there are many members—perhaps half a million—who are available for mobilization. The professions of absolute devotion and undying obedience that one hears from a few zealots sound sincere and give the impression that those making them are amenable to any type of behavior the Gakkai elite may choose to prescribe. It is likely that members who show the greatest degree of social and political alienation are concentrated in this most deeply committed half million. But these members, one might also assume, are most deeply motivated to adhere to the formal, ideal teachings of the Gakkai and especially to the pronouncements of President Ikeda. And since the behavioral ideal and operational actuality of the Gakkai during the 1960's, outlined by President Ikeda, have been moderation, increased cooperativeness and openness, decreased partisanship, and explicit proscription of all forms of deviant or illegal behavior, these loyal adherents have not been called on to circumvent the social norms or legal rules of the Japanese society and polity.

Thus the situation with regard to behavior seems to be one of mutual interaction of collective tendencies and organizational ideals. The great majority of members are neither sufficiently unattached, sufficiently alienated, nor sufficiently devoted to a remote ideal to make extreme methods of mobilization toward utopian goals possible. In another portion of the membership, however, past record and present zeal indicate that availability for mobilization does exist; nothing more than the present official choice of short-range ideals and tactics may be keeping the activist hard core out of the streets. The scriptural justification of violence and the existence of ultimate and utopian goals, if invoked with more than the present rhetorical effort, could activate several hundred thousand of the more ideologically committed believers to practically any form of behavior.

The detailed application to the Sōkagakkai of the models of mass movement and mass man shed some light on both the utility of the models and some of my earlier assumptions. The assumption that

Kornhauser's models of man and movement were an oversimplification was borne out. Not only is there ample room for interaction, both harmonious and conflicting, between the collective and the individual levels of a social movement, but there are further distinctions that must be drawn between varying degrees of activism in members and between ideal and actual, latent and manifest patterns of thought and behavior. It was assumed that the most significant aspects of the mass models, in descending order, were behavior, alienation, and unattachment. Behavior still seems to be most important, especially in light of the existing alienation among the membership. This alienation, which exists despite considerable attachment,[79] appears with or without nonattachment to be sufficient to make mass behavior a possibility among the most active element, thus further suggesting how crucial are behavioral tendencies and restraints.

It was also assumed that the nondeviant behavior and attitudes on which relevant Gakkai views were clearest would be the most susceptible to organizational influence. It appears that the only real organizational influence exerted on most members depends on the attitudes, needs, and motivations that members may have brought into the Gakkai with them; a penchant for simplistic thinking, a receptivity to the idea of divine benefit, and a political interest in welfare, housing, and other matters of immediate concern can be assumed in the majority of converts. That distinct changes could not be wrought in the faithful is partly because social and communications ties to secular society are maintained by most members and because, although identification with the Gakkai is no doubt of great psychic importance to most members, the "Gakkai" on which many members focus their loyalty may not be the entire Gakkai organization but its intimate tako-tsubo aspect.

Where deep commitment to ideology, leadership, and organization exists one may surmise greater changes in members' attitudes: increasing detachment from the secular world, decreased faith in oneself except as a member of the Gakkai, and alienation from society and polity. But even nondeviant behavior such as attendance at meetings is successfully instilled in no more than half of the membership. And on matters not directly related to the needs and desires of the majority of members, even clear statements of the Gakkai position do not suffice to alter members' views or even to stimulate their interest; Kōmeitō supporters' views on several planks of the party's foreign policy platform indicate this conflict.

A final assumption was that determining the degree of congruence between the Sōkagakkai and the mass movement model would permit some generalizations about the relevance of the Gakkai for democratic political systems in general and the Japanese system in particular. Although the Gakkai does not completely fit the model (and therefore one might be tempted to assume that it is not incompatible with a democratic system), several factors, such as members' alienation from specific Japanese political structures, their ambivalence toward certain abstract democratic norms, and the organization's latent influences toward alienation and detachment, suggest there could be friction between the organization and its general democratic or specific Japanese environment. At what point such friction becomes actual rather than potential is the question to which we now turn.

CHAPTER 12

The Sōkagakkai and Its Japanese Environment

THE SŌKAGAKKAI'S relations with its Japanese environment have often been characterized by friction. When the Society first appeared outsiders were put off by its intolerance and the practice of shaku-buku; then as observers began to look more closely at the organization and its teachings they discovered, in addition to the blatantly materialistic principle of divine benefit and the rather farfetched interpretations of reality, a disturbing element of nationalism and quasimilitarism.

The opprobrium with which the Gakkai has been regarded is part of that directed against all of the new religions. Their unsophisticated teachings and oversimplification have repelled the highly articulate Japanese intelligentsia, who have ridiculed or warned against their faith cures, bizarre tenets, and hopes for world regeneration. Rival clerics deride the new religions as "perversions of true religion perpetrated by greedy impostors."[1] But the Gakkai is looked upon with even more disfavor. One index of this disfavor is a survey run in 1964: 42 per cent of the respondents chose the adjective "fanatical" to describe the Kōseiren and 46 per cent termed the Gakkai "extremely repulsive," "frightening," or "heretical."[2] A recent clinical study by psychologist Yamaguchi Akira provides more specific attitudinal data. Nonmembers held a generally negative view of the Gakkai (those who had been subjected to shakubuku were most negative); they saw it as unobjective, unscientific, autocratic, arbitrary, destructive, negative, and selfish.[3]

An evaluation of the Gakkai's image and the organization's efforts to change that image should also consider, in passing, the Gakkai's critics. The Japanese intelligentsia's ridicule and condemnation of the new religions is typical of their elitist, intellectually arrogant orientation toward the more unsophisticated and less "progressive" masses.[4] Many critics of the Gakkai have had religious and political axes to grind,[5] and many have based their estimates on scant knowledge of Nichiren Shōshū.[6] Furthermore, they seem not to recognize that attacking irrationalism, doctrinal distortions, philosophical shallowness, and materialism in the Gakkai little affects the Society (which, after all, owes much of its growth to these features) and does nothing to explain the movement's origins, present role, and social and political significance. Adverse criticism does, however, constitute one aspect of the Gakkai's relationship with its environment.

PRESENT RELATIONS WITH THE ENVIRONMENT

In 1938 Emil Lederer warned, "Japan is faced with what seem to be insurmountable difficulties. . . . She appears to be struggling through a period that shatters the foundations of the Japanese spirit without giving in exchange anything more than technological guidance."[7] His observation is also a telling description of the immediate postwar situation, and it has some validity even today. The Gakkai—along with the other new religions—is perhaps most beneficial to its social and cultural environment in coping with this dilemma of Japanese life, as we have seen. For the majority of Gakkai members belief means attachment to society, even though their social ties and communication are in many cases moderated by the Gakkai channels and structures through which ties are established. As numerous testimonials assert, belief means new volition in work, new devotion to family, a new pattern and order in life, and a new sense of responsibility toward society. It means that life need not be an interminable pachinko game. The Gakkai structures that conceivably benefit the social environment are the kumi and han, the basic vertical line groups, and their zadankai, which serve to make the individual feel he has a place within the established social and political framework; this may be interpreted critically as simple conservative support of the status quo, but for better or for worse it does conduce to social stability in simultaneously decreasing social apathy and the potential for deviant social behavior.

The Society and the other new religions are stressing as never before the relevance of religion to daily personal and social life. In the Gakkai's case this emphasis often produces friction; however, one cannot say just on that basis that the relationship of the Gakkai to society is bad for either side. The Gakkai in fact plays the role of gadfly to the Japanese social and religious systems, which have felt and reacted to its sting. The success of the Gakkai Student Division has prompted reflection and new effort among other political and religious student organizations. A similar defensive reaction has resulted in new cooperation between the old and the new religions; although the initial primary goal of groups such as the All-Japan Buddhist Association (*Zen Nihon Bukkyō-kai*)[8] and the Union of New Japanese Religious Groups (*Shin Nihon Shūkyō Dantai Rengō-kai*)[9] was the negative one of countering the growth and influence of the Gakkai, this very intention led to a thorough examination of religion's role in Japanese society and of the lethargic condition of most organized religions in Japan. Japan's religious world is now in ferment, and "perhaps one result of this ferment will be to establish a new outlook on religion which will make it a truly positive and creative social force in Japan."[10]

Latent harm to the social environment can be found in the Gakkai socialization process insofar as socialization leads to social detachment among more active believers. Additional latent, socially harmful effects of Gakkai membership can be seen in the Gakkai manner of treating the individual human self, and more obviously in the effects membership has on human alienation and systemic alienation. (For example, the attacks on the environment that the Gakkai permits itself are scarcely calculated to integrate the faithful into Japanese society.) Moreover, Gakkai activities appear in some ways (especially in their frequency) to increase rather than decrease the sum total of alienation, hostility, and conflict in Japanese society. Children who have been practically deserted by activist parents have fallen into delinquency;[11] the inactive or nonmember husbands of activist wives have been subjected to intense domestic strain;[12] a number of defectors cite as their reasons for disillusionment an almost total lack of spare time with consequent familial discord and disintegration.[13] The Gakkai is aware of such problems and recommends moderate practice if family or community opposition is severe;[14] but the implications of active belief are clear.

At present the Society does not display any marked tendency toward deviant social behavior, either ideally or actually. But along with the past record of violence and illegality come infrequent suggestions that deviant behavior is still sanctioned. President Ikeda in his biography of Toda Jōsei justifies the visits of Gakkai-member teachers to their pupils' homes for the purpose of converting the parents. In one incident related by Ikeda a teachers' union official who objected to this practice later died, insane; in another an official became ill and had to cease working.[15] And the widely publicized attempts of the Kōmeitō in late 1969 to suppress Fujiwara Hirotatsu's critical work, *Sōkagakkai wo Kiru,* are disturbing to any follower of the course of Japanese democracy.

FUTURE RELATIONS WITH THE ENVIRONMENT

Future relations between the Gakkai and its social and cultural context can best be predicted—if they can be predicted at all—by extrapolating present relationships. The alienation that socialization may cause, for example, could result in availability for mass behavior. One inevitable future internal development that may affect the relationship of the Gakkai with its environment is the gradual appearance of a social community of Gakkai believers. The present penchant for marriage within the Gakkai has already been mentioned[16] as has the inclination (which varies, apparently, with activism and length of membership) to see the Gakkai as a social reference group.[17] And though the growing role of the family as an agent of general Gakkai socialization and the possible function of the Sōka Schools and Sōka University are difficult to estimate, it is most probable that all these agencies will lead to greater social, kinship, and geographic ties among members. Gerhard Lenski's *The Religious Factor,* a study of religion in Detroit,[18] suggests the import of such a developing social community. Lenski found that religious affiliation had two aspects: the associational, by which he meant membership in a goal-oriented, formally organized church; and the communal, by which he meant faith as a subculture, a community of religiously like-minded persons based on kinship and social ties.[19] Lenski found that previous explanations of the connection between religious zeal and intolerance and political extremism did not adequately describe the implications of religious affiliation; some evidence suggested that high associational involvement contributes to increased tolerance, but that "the religious subcommunities *foster and encourage a provincial and authoritarian view of the world.*"[20] One cannot assume that the increased integration of members' families into the Gakkai will increase friction with the larger social environment, but this, or at least greater social nonattachment, could well be the result.

In speaking of the Gakkai's future social development, critics are generally concerned with whether any real development can be expected to take place. Is the Gakkai simply one of several passing manifestations of the postwar period of strain or is it a firmly rooted actor in the Japanese religious system, one that will survive? Many of the new religions have been transitory phenomena, and as the particular strains that gave rise to new sects by the hundreds in the immediate postwar period fade away, one can expect that many of the more specialized faiths will fade with them. Other new sects drawing on the most traditional social elements, the politically ignorant, the diseased, and the abjectly poor will also decline, whereas still others will grow to become, like the century-old innovation Tenrikyō, established actors in the Japanese religious world. But to which group does the Gakkai belong?

The Gakkai has a firm foothold on the edges of Japanese society, but it has yet to show that it will be accepted by the core of society, i.e., by organized labor, the peasantry, the relatively stable and secure urban middle class, and the intelligentsia. Unless the Society can devise some new appeal or these social elements develop a new susceptibility to its original appeal, the Gakkai must remain a fringe religion, limited to the deprived and the uneducated.

Some do see the Gakkai as essentially a transitory phenomenon, "characteristic of Japan at this stage of its economic and social development. . . . Doctrinally, it is for the credulous, but the credulous are declining in numbers, not increasing, as educational levels rise. . . . It posits a crisis philosophy, and fewer Japanese feel a sense of crisis." In other words, "the sudden expansion of Soka Gakkai should probably be regarded as a temporary phenomenon of a society in rapid change."[21] Undoubtedly the Gakkai is in part the result of forces released during a process of change; however, the conclusion that it is "temporary" may be wrong: perhaps because of differences in causative factors, doctrine, organization, and leadership, the Gakkai has grown just at the time when a decrease in credulity and the sense of crisis may be behind the decline of other new sects.

And if the growth of the Gakkai itself has reached its peak—in mid-1969 the proponents of the "limit theory" seemed nearly justified—Kōmeitō power is still far from its zenith. As noted above, there is a time lag between conversion and politicization; in many localities the Kōmeitō may be building as yet untapped reserves of votes whose effect will be felt in future elections.

To write off either the Kōmeitō or the Gakkai as temporary is to disregard three factors. First, no matter how affluent Japan becomes, relative differences in status, income, power, health, and security will continue to exist,[22] and the deprived sector will continue to turn to such panaceas as splinter sects. Second, environmental changes—a major depression, a war, or perhaps some extreme international crisis —could extend the size of the social strata now attracted to the Gakkai. And third, environmental changes or new doctrinal appeals could enable the Gakkai to attract more levels of society: increased maturity, moderation, and sophistication may make the Society more acceptable to the better educated urban sector.

Japanese society contains four relatively deprived groups: the urbanites, the socially mobile, the small businessmen, and the peasantry. The urbanites, especially rootless new urbanites from the rural areas, will increase during the coming decade at least; the labor shortage in some sectors of urban industry should lead to pay increases that will become more and more of an incentive for living in the cities.[23] The new urbanites often constitute a "psychologically drifting mass";[24] as such they have already proved susceptible to the Gakkai's appeal. Whether they turn to religion or politics for solutions to practical problems is unknown; political solutions will probably be the future trend, but the Gakkai is not as likely to suffer from the process of cultural secularization as are many other new sects. As urban concentration continues, many Japanese will see that their vital needs— more social security and welfare, better public transit, water supply and sewage, and housing—are the subjects of Kōmeitō policies.[25]

The socially mobile, experiencing vertical changes in status either upward or downward, undergo a psychic stress the consequences of which are as yet unclear. In a society characterized by a high degree of social mobility, however, we might expect to find a permanent place for at least a few splinter religious groups. According to a study published in 1959, Japan has, absolutely, a high degree of vertical mobility and a moderately high degree of downward mobility. The mobility patterns of more developed nations suggest that both the overall mobility and particularly the downward mobility will persist and perhaps even increase.[26]

As for the small businessmen and entrepreneurs, squeezed between efficient big industry and highly organized labor unions, they can be expected to remain and to continue to be deprived, at least for the foreseeable future. The proportion of the total Japanese economy in the hands of small enterprises is still large, and no extrapolation of present trends indicates its disappearance. The percentage of the Japanese work force employed in factories of five to ninety-nine workers shifted from 41.8 per cent in 1921 to 41.4 per cent in 1935, 49.1 per cent in 1951 and 47 per cent in 1959.[27] In 1959 enterprises with less than 100 employees also represented 98 per cent of all Japanese manufacturing establishments, 56 per cent of all manufacturing employees, and 34 per cent of all manufacturing output.[28] This phenomenon is not limited to Japan; in several nations the role of small business in the economy has shown "surprising stability" since World War I:

Evidence appears to refute the belief that, in a given country, the relative role of small manufacturing establishments must continue to fall indefinitely. ... Rather, empirical evidence strongly suggests that in a given country, once a critical minimum level of modern industry is established, the role of small factories does not decline with time but holds an equal position in the future development and expansion of the manufacturing economy.[29]

But though the small business sector seems likely to remain, what will its condition be? The experiences of developing economies suggest that until the small-scale sector modernizes sufficiently to balance the sooner modernized, large-scale sector it will experience overall economic inefficiency and strain.[30] The economic insecurity of a fair part of this sector is likely to continue for at least the next several years. Hence the Gakkai may have a relatively stable source of converts in this social group.

The peasantry is the only one of the four relatively deprived groups in which the Gakkai has to date made no striking advances. "Relatively prosperous and unalienated,"[31] looked after by the ruling party in Tokyo, and still relatively strongly tied to the traditional religions (and thus antipathetic toward the new ones), the farmers have so far displayed little receptivity to either the Gakkai or the Kōmeitō, although the party vote is growing slowly in absolute size in nearly all prefectures.

Income, industrialization, and "modernization" vary markedly from one region of Japan to another, and the disparities seem to be increasing.[32] Although the rural areas are not hotbeds of dissatisfaction, a minority do feel deprived,[33] and as the mass media continue to publicize the affluent life enjoyed by some urbanites that minority may increase. At present the key factor keeping the Gakkai from tapping rural discontent is religion; if the Kōmeitō could divorce itself from the Gakkai in the eyes of the electorate it could probably extend its power much further into the countryside.

This is only conjectural, for to date religious and community ties in the rural areas have made groups like the Gakkai superfluous, and have even led to active resistance to such groups. Similarly, the educational level, sophistication, and economic stability of the urban middle class and intelligentsia and the economic security and organization of the unionized working class have seriously hindered, though not entirely rendered useless, the Society's efforts among these groups.[34] Clearly Gakkai numbers could increase if the social strata normally attracted by the Gakkai sharply increased as a proportion of the Japanese population or if the Gakkai approach for some reason began to be relevant to widespread, acute social problems.

JAPANESE NATIONALISM

Nationalism in postwar Japan has been more cultural than political, and so has the Gakkai's handling of this facet of its relationship to its environment. It is doubtful that any social movement could grow to the size of the Gakkai if it totally rejected the historical values and symbols of the society in which it arose. The "new" Japanese religions that have grown most—Tenrikyō, Risshō Kōsei Kai, and Seichō no Ie—all show links with traditional culture. Does the Gakkai show similar links?

Insofar as nationalism means a sort of national consciousness, the Japanese are and have long been an intensely nationalistic people, but nationalism has many manifestations and the more striking are not the most important today. In the words of Maruyama Masao, "It would not be quite right to say that the old nationalism had either died out or qualitatively changed. It would be more precise to say that it had vanished from the political surface only to be inlaid at the social base in an atomized form."[35] It is clear that this "social nationalism" is politically relevant, although to Maruyama it does not appear to be an autonomous force:

Even if there is a systematic effort to recentralize the dispersed and amorphous national sentiments of today, it does not seem likely that sufficient strength can be mobilized for the resultant nationalism to be an independent political force. In all likelihood the new creation from old fabric will be joined to a higher political force, perhaps to an international power. It will then be permitted to exist only in so far as it serves to further the latter's set political goals.[36]

Some of the Kōmeitō's statements suggest that if nationalist sentiments came to a head the Kōmeitō might take on the role of the "higher political force." Sociologist Nagai Michio has described the Gakkai as one aspect of a culturally nationalist reaction to the West.

The flourishing of the Nichirenite new religions in general—Sōka-gakkai, Risshō Kōsei Kai, Reiyūkai, and others—has been described as "a reflection of the rising surge of national self-respect, the national image or purpose that the Japanese appear to be searching for."[37] The Gakkai claims traditional sanction from the 700-year history of Nichiren Shōshū and declares that Nichiren is the original, eternal, omnipotent Buddha of the Lotus Sutra; since the disestablishment of State Shintō, therefore, the Gakkai has been the only major Japanese religion with an indigenous deity. Given the universalist goals of the Gakkai, this means also that the proper object of worship for all mankind is a Japanese.[38] This congruence with the cultural and historical elements of the environment may make the Gakkai a credible religious alternative and an appealing channel for the articulation of nationalistic political attitudes.

But repeated mention in both Kōmeitō and Gakkai media of the "mission of the Japanese people,"[39] the use of banners, armbands, martial songs, and military terminology, and the often-cited horseback "troop review" held by President Toda before 13,000 members of the Youth Division in 1954[40] have all contributed to the image of the Gakkai as a "fascist" organization.* Still, the superficially militaristic characteristics of the Gakkai organization are certainly no more pronounced than are those of the Salvation Army. Furthermore, to counteract the "fascist" image the Gakkai now plays up the persecution of the early 1940's as a glorious example of resistance to the militarist regime,[41] and in its teachings and political policies it is totally antiwar.[42] The nationalist position that the Gakkai and Kōmeitō take is political only in its rejection of what is considered Japan's servile adherence to American political interests. The nationalism that the Gakkai advances means taking justified pride in Japanese accomplishments, in Japanese national development, and in Japanese upbringing. The Society urges the Japanese people to avoid fawning attitudes toward foreigners and to feel confidence, integrity, and resolve as Japanese.[43]

Gakkai members apparently are at present neither ultranationalist nor militarist. In a nationwide survey of 1963 that included the question, "Which are superior, Japanese or foreigners?"[44] the responses showed that Gakkai members were more "nationalist" than nonmembers in every age, sex, and educational grouping (see Table 23). But

* "Fascism" is used by the Gakkai's critics as a general pejorative term to denote an evil non-Communist political system or movement with totalitarian, militaristic, and chauvinistic features.

TABLE 23
"Nationalist" Attitudes in Japan, 1963

Respondents	Japanese Seen as Superior to Foreigners	Japanese Seen as Inferior to Foreigners	Japanese and Foreigners Seen as Equals	Unable to Generalize	Other, Don't Know, No Answer	Total
Total sample	33%	14%	16%	27%	10%	100%
Sōkagakkai members	42	15	15	22	6	100

a 1966 survey showed that this national sentiment was not militaristic (see Table 24). Asked whether Japan needed a Self-Defense Force, a majority of Kōmeitō supporters said yes; however, when asked why they thought the Self-Defense Force was necessary, 35.4 per cent of the Kōmeitō supporters replied that it was needed for disaster relief and similar catastrophes, 20.4 per cent said that it was necessary for internal national security, and only 5.8 per cent thought the force was necessary to withstand foreign invasion.[45] The same indifferent orientation toward militarism is suggested in a 1966 survey by the *Yomiuri Shimbun* (see Table 25) in which the question, "What would you do if Japan were invaded?" was asked.[46] Compared to other groups of politicized Japanese the Kōmeitō supporters took the most optimistic view, were least likely to fight, and were most likely to flee an invader. This may be another indication of alienation from the political system; it may be a sign of alienation from the nation; but it is certainly not the sort of response one would expect from a militaristic group.

TABLE 24
Perceived Necessity of a Japanese Self-Defense Force, 1966 Survey

Attitudes	Respondents by Political Party Affiliation					
	Communist	Socialist	Kōmei	Democratic Socialist	Liberal Democratic	None
Self-defense Force considered necessary	21.4%	58.4%	66.8%	77.1%	84.6%	66.7%
Self-defense Force considered unnecessary	68.7	26.5	20.8	14.1	4.6	11.2
Other, don't know, no answer	9.9	15.1	12.4	8.8	10.8	22.1
Total	100.0%	100.0%	100.0%	100.0%	100.0%	100.0%

TABLE 25
Reactions to an Invasion of Japan

Responses	Respondents by Political Party Affiliation					
	Commu- nist	Social- ist	Kōmei	Demo- cratic Socialist	Liberal Demo- cratic	National Sample
I would fight	37.9%	34.0%	22.9%	44.7%	40.2%	34.5%
I would remain quiet and not fight	6.9	18.1	15.7	17.5	16.5	16.5
I would flee (to the mountains or overseas)	3.5	4.8	12.9	3.9	5.4	5.3
I do not believe such an event will occur	24.1	25.3	28.6	24.3	24.0	24.5
No answer, don't know	27.6	17.8	20.0	9.7	14.0	19.1
Total	100.0%	100.0%	100.1%	100.1%	100.1%	99.9%

If the Japanese political system were to undergo serious prolonged crisis or to break down completely popular political sentiment easily might swing to the right.[47] In such a situation the Gakkai might assume a central role. Apart from Gakkai scriptures and structure, which most critics stress, one can posit that the leaders' responsiveness to and claimed personification of public opinion might result in an unprincipled effort to lead opinion further along the direction of current trends. The Gakkai's connection with Nichiren would make its nationalistic appeal quite credible, and the available activist element in the Gakkai could make the appeal's impact quite possible. The Gakkai's statements and actions when the first ten-year period of the United States–Japan Mutual Security Treaty came to an end in 1970 provide an example of the movement's behavior during times of aroused nationalist sentiment and of its ability to resist extremist pressures and temptations.

The implications of the Gakkai for its sociocultural environment are mixed. It is viewed in a largely unfavorable light by the rest of society, although it works assiduously to improve its image and may be succeeding—at least with respect to the popular conception of the Kōmeitō. The functions that the Gakkai performs in its social context are often beneficial—the lessening of strains of discontent among deprived groups, for example. Given the apparent absence of institutional alternatives to the Gakkai, these functions may be performed by similar religious groups in the future. However, the Society's interaction with its environment is not always smooth. It serves as a gadfly, as we have said, thus paining certain groups, and it is unfavorably received in many circles. Furthermore, some of the Gakkai's influences on its environment are not beneficial. It has the potential for creating an alienated group whose presence could conceivably disrupt the stability of society. Whether or not the Gakkai could become a threat to stability depends very much on its leadership. It is quite possible that the Society, through its ties with Nichiren and through its advocacy of antimilitarist feelings of national confidence, pride, and integrity, not only could encourage a healthy sense of national identity but could influence nationalist sentiment along nonextremist channels. But Nichiren Shōshū scripture does contain all of the necessary ingredients for expansionist, xenophobic chauvinism; and the harmony between the Gakkai and the cultural and political nationalism of its environment suggests that in an atmosphere of strong nationalist sentiment the Gakkai leaders could, if they chose, generate collective and even mass action on a scale much greater than the mobilizing of the activist minority alone would involve.

JAPANESE POLITICS

In its relationship with its political environment the Gakkai is working for greater harmony and increased acceptance. The approach it found successful in the immediate postwar years was no longer valid in the relatively stable and affluent 1960's. Moreover, the Gakkai over the years had reached a size and strength that permitted a less defensive, more confident outlook;[48] politicization hastened this change as Gakkai leaders learned that exclusivism and extreme attacks on other religions worked against them in the political arena.[49] Accordingly both tactics and policies were altered. The Gakkai elaborated its platform and adopted more concrete proposals affecting local politics. In parliament, pragmatic cooperation became the rule. There are indications that this thaw has had good results.[50] The Japanese electorate, which generally considers politicians dishonest, apparently accepts the Kōmeitō politicians' descriptions of themselves as honest men. Kōmeitō policies frequently address problems of almost universal concern, and generally reflect majority opinion. The Kōmeitō vote is gradually increasing nationwide, especially in areas where the vote exceeds the claimed Gakkai membership,[51] indicating a growing political congruence with the environment.

Nevertheless, the activities of the Kōmeitō produce friction as well, for with the expansion of the Gakkai into the suburban sector of society has come a change in the nature of its opposition. What was once largely a vying with other religious sects for the adherence of the urban lower class has become in part a competition with other political parties for the votes of the new urban and suburban middle class.[52] Kōmeitō inroads have aroused the Communist Party in particular; the Japan Communist Party magazine *Vanguard* (*Zen'ei*) has scathingly attacked the Gakkai and the Kōmeitō.[53] The political activities of Gakkai-member unionists have also created friction. Court cases where the right of free political expression has been upheld, for example, have caused political conflicts with labor unions, conflicts that will almost certainly be exacerbated by the Gakkai's creation of its own union and subsequent competition for members. In parliament, too, inharmony has occurred. Kōmeitō representatives, claiming inexperience, have disregarded certain precedents and points of etiquette that smooth the relations between legislators,[54] and the party's increasing opposition will certainly produce more acrimonious debates in parliament. As the Kōmeitō increases its power throughout the nation, more chances for the disruption of the parliamentary process will occur.

In one respect, however, policy-oriented opposition by the Kōmeitō will decrease friction, for the Kōmeitō's behavior will become more predictable and its position more identifiable. At present, observers seem obsessed with a desire to pin the Kōmeitō somewhere on a right-left political spectrum; they are distrustful of any political group that cannot be categorized in this way. This feeling of distrust is often felt much more by intellectuals and so-called political commentators than by the political actors who must deal directly with the Kōmeitō in and out of parliament.

Present relations. According to Harry Eckstein, "A government will tend to be stable if its authority pattern [i.e., its attitudes toward and practices and applications of authority] is congruent with the other authority patterns of the society of which it is a part."[55] In other words, democratic authority patterns in nongovernmental organizations, for example, add to the stability of a democratic political system. With some reservations it can be said that the actual organizational experience of members of the Gakkai is in many ways more democratic than the experience gained by members of most other Japanese organizations. The access (even though mediated) to attentive and responsive elites, the opportunity for two-way communication and for self-expression, and the application of authority at least in part as the response to majority opinion are not striking features of most Japanese organizations. Moreover, the Gakkai offers these socializing experiences to the social elements least likely to encounter them elsewhere.

Gakkai membership, then, is a way for the otherwise voiceless elements of the Japanese electorate to have political roles. Clearly political activism is not necessarily always beneficial for a democracy, nor is apathy always bad.[56] But, "in the infinitely complex series of events which cause a society to move toward even mildly authoritarian patterns, the failure of these groups to exercise political power may be more dangerous than any political success they might have."[57] If one accepts that excluding a large number of persons from the political process may threaten a democratic polity, then the Gakkai's politicizing function is beneficial for the Japanese political system. In this light particularly, the Kōmeitō's vociferous upholding of the constitution and democratic values is also clearly salutary to the system. And democracy in Japan needs such public promotion. In surveys taken since the end of the war the proportion of respondents who positively support either the constitution or the unconditional guarantee of civil liberties has seldom approached a majority.[58] When "the Socialist party readily repudiates parliamentary process and retaliatory violence bursts out among ultranationalists, the general public stands apathetically by. One suspects that the average citizen has only a fleeting concept of his responsibility to the democratic state."[59]

The gadfly role of the Gakkai has specific political and religious-political aspects. The almost twenty-year reign of the Liberal Democrats in Japan has been marred by numerous scandals; although it is hard to say what effect the Kōmeitō's constant investigations, accusations, and revelations of wrongdoing have had on the conduct of Japanese politicians, there is a widespread feeling that this muckraking has in fact made the LDP more careful, and an appreciation of the Kōmeitō's efforts to keep politicians honest. The success and scope of the Citizens' Discussion Centers have spurred similar endeavors by the other parties.

The Gakkai also seems to have stimulated otherwise moribund religious groups to participate in society and politics. Political interest by religious organizations is nothing new in Japan,[60] but a broad program of political education or even of social concern was largely lacking in religious groups until the Gakkai began to seem a distinct political threat.[61] None of these groups has attempted to organize its own political party; rather, they generally restrict themselves to recommending candidates and to efforts at mobilizing their adherents to vote for these candidates.[62]

The new relevance of these religious groups is not an unalloyed benefit for the Japanese political system. There are signs that the established parties are choosing candidates with religious bloc votes in mind, courting politicized religious groups, and even assisting in the creation of such groups.[63] The possibility that religious organizations might become mere appendages of the parties bodes ill for the stability of Japanese democracy. Nevertheless, any process that renders Japanese religion more relevant to the postwar era must be considered, in a time when Japan is still "in search of her soul," to be of benefit to the nation;[64] and if, in the words of one Buddhist cleric, it is possible to "break the shell of the established religions and take a step out into society,"[65] the Gakkai will have been an important causative agent in this process. But the Gakkai must also be held largely responsible if the new politicization of Japanese religion results in a religious reinforcement of political cleavages.

Future relations. Whatever threat the Society poses to its political environment is still potential. Gakkai scripture contains a set of utopian goals and justifies using extreme means to attain them, and a number of Gakkai members are available for extreme efforts. Were the Gakkai leaders to stress the more remote ideals founded in scripture, the result could be several hundred thousand Japanese in pursuit of the millennium. In addition, if the Gakkai's ideal orientations with respect to systemic alienation, social nonattachment, and some aspects of the "democratic formula" became more manifestly and intentionally similar to certain latent actual orientations, many more persons could be made available for mobilization to mass behavior.

The primary elements of Gakkai undemocratic potential are thus activist availability and leaders' choices. The moderate political course pursued by the Kōmeitō for the last several years has not been so explicitly in line with certain characteristics of Gakkai ideology and activity that one can have firm expectations about the future; one may have reservations about the firmness of principle among the Gakkai's leaders in certain situations. Nevertheless, in light of the recent behavior of leaders and the impressions I received from extended contacts with them, I would assume that their decisions will be responsible.

The present road along which the movement seems to be traveling appears to be in the direction of deliberate harmonization. This route might ultimately lead to non-Gakkai Kōmeitō members and candidates, to considerable electoral support from nonmembers, and to Kōmeitō participation in a coalition cabinet. The candidacy of Abe Ken'ichi in the 1967 Tokyo gubernatorial election and the campaign strategy in the 1969 general election[66] may be considered important steps in this process: the Gakkai has explicitly begun entering contests it knows it cannot win.

But the incongruence of religious purity and political expedience represents a larger problem facing the Gakkai now and in the future: the need to reconcile internal integration with adaptation to the external environment. To adapt may necessitate such a compromise of doctrinal principle that the internal cohesion of the Society may be dangerously weakened. Considerations of internal unity may limit the extent to which adaptation can be pursued and thus affect the Gakkai's significance to its environment.

Possibilities and Problems

IN THIS BOOK we have studied the Gakkai by using two different approaches. In Part I we were concerned with describing the Society thoroughly: its background, ideology, membership, recruitment and indoctrination practices, organization, goals, and political involvement. Part II was an attempt to apply a sociological theory to the movement; there we explored whether or not the typical Gakkai member could be described as a mass man and similarly whether the collectivity itself could accurately be called a mass movement. In this concluding chapter we speculate about the future. By inference and by identification of possible trends and problems we will talk about the Society's adaptation to its Japanese context, its methods of socialization, its efforts to attain goals, and its internal integration.

POSSIBILITIES: ADAPTATION AND SOCIALIZATION

During the 1960's the Gakkai may have almost fully exploited the social elements most likely to follow an exclusivist and doctrinaire approach. Its continued expansion, then, appears to depend on stressing adaptation and on broadening the Society's appeal. The elements of the Japanese population most attracted by the Gakkai approach may or may not expand; the Kōmeitō may or may not increase its range of voters; and the Society may or may not alter or modify its approach in order to bring its ideals more into line with those of other social, religious, and political organizations. Whatever the case, the Society's success in adapting to its environment will be associated with such factors.

One channel for broadening the Gakkai's appeal is politics. Although replacing the religious focus with a political one would change greatly the nature and appeal of the Gakkai,[1] the coexistence of political and religious elements is one of the basic reasons for the relative success of the Gakkai among the Japanese new religions. Secularization and moderation in style and attitude, and nationalism and welfarism in ideology are features well calculated to give the movement breadth, and they are explicit goals of the Kōmeitō.

One of the greatest obstacles blocking the Kōmeitō's efforts to capitalize on the inherent appeal of its platform, however, is the party's connection in the popular mind with the Gakkai (a connection apparently unaffected by Kōmeitō leaders' withdrawal from Gakkai posts in early 1970). To overcome this obstacle either the Gakkai must become fully acceptable to the Japanese public, which means that the internal integration of the Gakkai would suffer, or the Kōmeitō must separate itself more thoroughly from the Gakkai. Such a separation could be effected either in terms of ideology or in terms of practical policy. Since Kōmeitō media are already almost exclusively secular, an ideological separation is relatively unimportant. Separation in practice, however, could have serious effects on the Gakkai's internal condition, for the organization's unique blend of religion and politics has been a factor in attracting converts. And if the Kōmeitō disavowed certain Gakkai tenets or cooperated with other political forces so closely as to obscure the essential unity of party and Gakkai, its utility as an arm of the Gakkai obviously would be seriously impaired.

Kōmeitō cooperation with other parties might include the joint backing of candidates. It was rumored that the Gakkai's backing of the conservative candidate Azuma Ryūtarō in the 1963 Tokyo gubernatorial election aroused considerable opposition among the younger and more leftist leadership;[2] whether or not this is true, some of the reasons given by the Kōmeitō for Abe Ken'ichi's independent candidacy in the 1967 election do suggest that considerations of internal unity were a factor in the Kōmeitō's rejection of all the other parties' candidates.* Selection of a non-Gakkai member as a Kōmeitō candidate would be a similar move, but an unlikely one at present. The flexibility shown by the Gakkai in repudiating its original stand against politicization and then against any move into the Lower House attests to the Gakkai's ability to adapt for practical reasons. But whether the votes gained by a non-Gakkai candidate would offset

---

* Nevertheless, interparty cooperation appears to be a growing trend, as witness the joint Liberal Democratic–Democratic Socialist–Kōmei backing of Shibata Mamoru in the April 1970 Kyoto gubernatorial election.

the detrimental effect of such a merging with the political environment is doubtful.

The present trend toward adaptation discernible in the Gakkai suggests that in the future the socialization process will be less centralized, perhaps making the dissemination of ideal patterns of thought and behavior easier. As the Gakkai grows older, the function of socialization will pass into member-families. Ideals instilled in childhood increase the chances that at least nominal faith will be maintained throughout adult life; at the same time, though, more of the cultural tolerance typical of the Japanese may come into play when families produce young believers than when the organization recruits them. As a result socialization may become a more stable but less enthusiastic and less exclusivist process, which might turn the Gakkai into a denominational form of religious organization.[3] At the same time, despite Gakkai denials of such a possibility, Gakkai ideals may enter the formal educational process of those attending the Sōka schools. Socializing influences here might well lead to the creation of a highly indoctrinated elite. The effect of both of these developments will be the increased significance of what Lenski calls the "communal" aspect of religion, i.e., the congregation as a social collectivity. Although it is not possible to generalize from the American to the Japanese context, we do know that such religious *gemeinschaften* tend to be characterized by parochialism and rigidity.[4]

The Gakkai, then, will probably be able to cut back its formal socialization effort once familial socialization becomes more developed. However, if this less militant, less exclusivist brand of socialization should lead to a more lackadaisical and tolerant outlook than the Gakkai leadership finds tolerable, a doctrinaire reaction might ensue that could cause a large proportion of the membership to defect. As it is, the defection rate in the Gakkai is 50 per cent or more. The present socialization process seems more alienating than the Gakkai realizes or intends, and the actual zadankai does not seem to be the comprehensive socialization structure envisioned by the Society. Perhaps the quality of socialization in terms of stable membership will improve as the family assumes the function; it will almost certainly become more relaxed.

There are other elements in the Gakkai that bear on the organization's adaptation. The tolerance and openness of members seem to exceed that of the organization; this characteristic may not contribute to the recruitment of new members, but the example of a socially nondeviant membership should, in time, make an impression on the general public that will prepare the way for realizing other Gakkai goals more easily.

PROBLEMS: GOAL ATTAINMENT AND INTEGRATION

An organization can attain its goals only to the extent that it can mobilize its members to belief and action, and here the Gakkai has major difficulties. The faithful have not been aroused to universal propagation, universal support for the Kōmeitō, or even universal attendance at Gakkai functions and acceptance of Gakkai communications media. And if the Gakkai tried today to mobilize its members to a course of mass political action few would respond. If the current moderating trend continues, goals might become easier to achieve, since less deviant action would be required. As indoctrination becomes more a part of childhood socialization, generalized commitment should become more stable—although mobilization for activist or mass behavior may become more difficult.

At the top of the Society, too, there are problems. One of these involves the quality of leadership. The one-man rule of President Ikeda is in some ways inefficient, but Ikeda's competence and stature in the movement probably stifle criticism, making change difficult. The delegation of authority has invited such blunders as the Tokyo ward elections of 1967; Ikeda as much as admitted that his lieutenants left much to be desired when after these elections he announced that henceforth he would himself choose candidates.[5]

Problems of attaining goals also relate to the question of integration: how is the degree of internal unity necessary for efficient operation to be maintained as the organization seeks to grow? And how is the need for integration to be reconciled with the present tendency to reach goals through greater politicization, with all of its concomitant compromises? Without a doubt, the Gakkai is the largest and best-integrated organization to appear in all of Japanese history. A cultural predilection for factionalism, fed by the preference for small group contexts over bureaucratized relationships, apparently often contributes to internal division in large social collectivities of all types in Japan. Against this setting the continued high level of integration in the Gakkai seems incredible. Observers generally expect internal divisions to appear; I would agree that although the Gakkai's integrating subsystem seems to be functioning well enough at present, in the Japanese cultural context any temporary breakdown could lead to irreparable schism.

Factionalism, then, is a problem. But individual malintegration is an even greater one. Many members defect, or at least cease attending and professing commitment. Many, no doubt, joined hoping to remedy a specific problem; long and fruitless effort or else success may remove the motivation and lead to apostasy. Among leaders the typical cause of defection is the Society's unrelenting drive to achieve goals and mobilize followers: the leaders operate under intense pressure, and since they receive no pay and must take jobs aside from their Gakkai duties, nearly all of their spare time is taken up by Gakkai responsibilities.[6] The Society recognizes the problems of malintegration and defection to the extent that official media now refer frequently to *taiten* (defection, apostasy),[7] and President Ikeda has found it necessary to speak on the subject:

There are former leaders of the Sōkagakkai who have forsaken their faith and have brought forth harsh and unjust criticisms against this religious organization. This is a horrible thing.[8]

You [High School Division members] will surely grow up to be leaders of Japan and of the world but, at that time, you must not forget the *Gohonzon* and the Sōkagakkai. The sin of those who once believe Nichiren's Buddhism and then begin to criticize it is the deepest of all.[9]

As the Gakkai grows, activities proliferate, and the social strata most susceptible to shakubuku are thoroughly proselyted, both leaders and rank and file will feel an increasing tension. It may be that only constant mobilization has kept the Gakkai growing, and relaxation might result in backsliders outnumbering converts; but to continue constant mobilization could produce even more malintegration. The key to this problem may be the family; if the rate of recruitment and socialization in the family should reach the point where it matches the rate of defection, then the pressure to proselyte and teach could be relaxed. The type of believer produced by recruitment and socialization within the family might not be militant enough to persuade the leadership that shakubuku could safely be reduced; nevertheless, present organizational trends suggest that the future will see more familial socialization, subsequently more moderation, and less defection of members due to pressure or dissatisfaction with the faith.

Another hindrance to integration is members who are opportunist, dishonest, or otherwise insincere — whom the Gakkai refers to as "worms in the bowels of a lion."[10] Such members try to use the Gakkai organization to further their own ends (e.g., they consider the membership as a potential business clientele or a bloc of votes), attempt to achieve high rank simply to satisfy their greed for status, or worship solely with the idea of narrow personal benefit.[11] The organization specifically singles out for attack the member who plays on Gakkai ties in order to borrow money. This problem is so often mentioned it apparently is a persistent one;[12] at present all loans of money between Gakkai members are absolutely banned. The penalties for violation include excommunication, and preventive measures are largely symbolic, such as the explicit promise of dire divine punishment.[13] The relatively infrequent mention of these penalties in Gakkai media suggests that numerically this problem is a minor one. Members' misbehavior is much more important to the Gakkai's public image, especially where a member's activity is criminal, but the Gakkai seems to be quite successful in forestalling such activity.

Various observers have asserted that there are in the Society groups — "factions" is definitely putting it too strongly — oriented rather markedly toward presidents Makiguchi, Toda, and Ikeda. A tacit distribution of posts among the various membership groups according to age, interest, or education is quite possible; such a distribution may even be an important element in preventing factionalism. But this type of division seems to present relatively little threat for the future: with organizational growth there will certainly be no dearth of posts with which to keep all at least relatively satisfied, and with each year the followers of President Ikeda will become relatively more numerous as the older leaders die out. However, the Gakkai does take specific steps to prevent dissensions based on personal allegiance. Ikeda's attitude toward himself is a case in point. He considers himself and all members of the Gakkai to be mere mortals; personal revelation and personalized divinity have absolutely no doctrinal sanction. Japanese religions have shown themselves to be particularly prone to break up over such issues; that some members invest Ikeda with quasi-divine properties suggests one cannot entirely eliminate the Japanese tendency to blur the line separating human religious leaders from their divine sources of legitimacy. But the application of such properties to other individuals in the organization has been successfully circumvented, and probably will continue to be in the future.

The likelihood of schism along educational lines is greater. The Gakkai tries assiduously to attract students and intellectuals; it is reasonable to expect that insofar as they succeed, these elements will gravitate by the Gakkai's merit system to the top posts. If this should happen the probable consequence will be increased distance between the intelligentsia and the mass members, resulting in problems of communication, responsiveness, mobility, and cohesion. It is possible that this sort of division is already appearing. The younger leaders of the Gakkai and the Kōmeitō are better educated than their elders,[14] and Ikeda's suggestions that future leaders come from the Student Division are increasingly explicit. Indeed, one former leader, criticizing internal Gakkai procedures, complained that persons with a poor educational record had little chance of being appointed to high office.[15]

The proper balance between principle and pragmatism, between purity and flexibility, is difficult to strike. For the short run the Gakkai appears to have opted for adaptation. If present Gakkai trends and prevalent Japanese social and economic conditions hold, the Gakkai will drift gradually toward the moderate nonmilitant stance of the Japanese religious establishment. There is the possibility that some element of the membership, if not the president himself, will try to reverse this trend by revitalizing the Society. Barring unforeseen economic and political unheaval, however, the course of moderation without revitalization seems most probable. All of the potential for mass behavior, for elite irresponsibility, and for radical changes in size and orientation induced by economic or political crisis may be taken into account, but to the extent prediction is possible, present trends suggest the Gakkai's gradual transformation from a sect into a church.[16]

Clearly, the compromise-cohesion problem could also arise in the relations between the Gakkai and the Kōmeitō. The Gakkai insists that the Kōmeitō cannot exist apart from the Society; but as Gakkai politicization continues it becomes increasingly likely that dissension will develop between those who may wish to compromise for political reasons and those who may wish to remain religiously pure.[17] The possibility of division is increased by the appearance of functionally specialized personnel. One can distinguish among the twenty top Gakkai leaders such primarily political figures as Takeiri Yoshikatsu, Tashiro Fujio, Suzuki Kazuhiro, and Ninomiya Bunzō and such primarily religious figures as Kodaira Yoshihei, Morita Kazuya, Nakanishi Haruo, Seiryū Tsutomu, and Harada Tatsuru.[18] Most of the leaders hold both kinds of roles, but as time passes one can expect further specialization (such as the January 1970 organizational reform) that could reinforce ideological differences.

Actually, the integration-adaptation dilemma might develop within the Kōmeitō rather than between the Gakkai and Kōmeitō. Secular and religious factions could appear and divide the party. But the more likely sources of party schism are disagreements between right and left and nonideological tactical differences. Some observers have surmised a right-left split personified by Takeiri Yoshikatsu on the right and Yano Junya on the left;[19] any such split, though, would probably arise not independently but in combination with nonideological disagreements over tactics. So far the Kōmeitō's success has encouraged unity; failure at the polls when tactical debate had taken place before unity was established could have the opposite effect. The Kōmeitō's support of Azuma in the 1964 Tokyo gubernatorial election is rumored to have aroused internal opposition, which reappeared in 1967 as the force demanding an independent Kōmeitō candidate. Also, the tactical blunders accompanying the Tokyo ward elections of 1967 may have irritated the feelings of some party members, and rancor may still persist.[20]

Adjusting the tension between adaptation and integration seems to me to be the primary potential problem facing the Society. This process is the "routinization" we spoke of in our examination of the Gakkai's development: the quest for harmony with the environment, but not at the cost of organizational and doctrinal identity and integrity; the development of functionally specific groups; the changes of strategy and tactics necessitated by efforts to broaden appeals and to bring in increasing numbers of converts and votes; and the coping with difficulties in integration created by the desire to maintain constant mobilization. The adaptation-integration question is epitomized by the differences between the Gakkai and the Kōmeitō, differences reinforced by personal functional specialization. For this reason a Gakkai split along religious and political lines is most easily imaginable.

Failure to cohere might take a less spectacular form than open rift. Excessive adaptation might reduce the identity and integrity of the Gakkai to such a point that the Society simply disappears as an independent body. More likely is the possibility that familial socialization will prevent such a disintegration, though it will not suffice to maintain large-scale numerical growth. Present internal trends point to increasing institutionalization and moderation. Whether or not that process will keep step with the development and secularization of the Kōmeitō sufficiently to prevent a schism one cannot foresee.

APPENDIXES

A Note on Data and Methodology

The data on the Sōkagakkai used in this study were collected primarily during two year-long visits to Japan, in 1962–63 and in 1967. They consist of secondary and primary materials—books, periodicals, and newspapers, a large number of opinion surveys; interviews with Gakkai members at various levels of the organization; and statistics from various elections during the period 1955–68. In each part of this study the relevant sources of information are cited; at this point a brief description of the uses made of the various types of data is in order.

Secondary sources were used in all phases of the study, in creating and comparatively applying an analytic framework as well as for information on the history, organization, membership, and official ideology of the Gakkai. The theoretical works in English of greatest utility are those by Kornhauser and Lipset; the Prothro and Grigg article is equally important in elaborating one aspect of the model. Material on the Gakkai in English can be found in works by Offner and van Straelen, Thomsen, Schecter, MacFarland, Hesselgrave, Ramseyer, Brannen, and Dator, and in my own previous writings; Hesselgrave's and Dator's are the only primarily empirical studies. Material on the Gakkai in Japanese can be found in books by Saki and Oguchi, Kasahara, Takase, Togawa, Murakami, Ishida Ikuo, Nakaba, and Tsurumi et al. Some of these authors, especially Saki and Oguchi and Murakami, reveal a Marxist bias; nevertheless, both the facts and the interpretations in these works were of great help. Of special relevance are Takase's biography of Ikeda Daisaku and Nakaba's chapter 4, with biographical material on the leaders of the Society.

The Society's multilingual publishing activities provide abundant primary sources. Most useful in this study were the daily newspaper *Seikyō Shimbun*, the daily *Kōmei Shimbun* (the official newspaper of the Kōmeitō or Clean Government Party, the Gakkai's political arm), and the monthly theoretical journal *Dai Byaku Renge (Great White Lotus)*. A number of "classics," such as the *Shakubuku Kyōten (Propagation Handbook), Nichiren Shōshū-Sōkagakkai,* and Kodaira's *Sōkagakkai,* provided the foundation for the descriptive sections of my study. Finally, the writings of President Ikeda Daisaku are an invaluable source of information on the official stand taken by the Gakkai on practically every issue it considers worthy of note. The most complete presentation of Ikeda's religious and political thought to date appears in his *Risshō Ankoku Ron Kōgi (Lectures on the "Treatise on the Pacification of the Nation Through the Establishment of Righteousness"* of Nichiren).* Much of the same material is presented in a popularized form in *Ningen Kakumei (Human Revolution)*, Ikeda's fictionalized biography of his predecessor, President Toda Jōsei; and some of it is reiterated in his *Seiji to Shūkyō (Politics and Religion)* and *Kagaku to Shūkyō (Science and Religion)*.†

All of these works, with the exception of *Risshō Ankoku Ron Kōgi*, are now available in English translation; in addition, a number of primary sources originating in English are available. The *Seikyō News* and its successor, the *World Tribune* (now a thrice-weekly newspaper), a pamphlet series entitled *This is the Sōkagakkai*, and the comprehensive, official English work *The Nichiren Shōshū Sōkagakkai* provided much of the data on which my analysis of the official ideals of the Gakkai is based; in addition, the many testimonials and letters to the editor carried in Gakkai newspapers give a vivid picture of the individual needs and interests that are fulfilled through Gakkai membership.

Politically relevant primary sources include the *Kōmei Shimbun*, Ikeda's *Seiji to Shūkyō*, and a host of press releases from the Kōmeitō, supplemented at election time by formal policy pamphlets. For an exhaustive presentation of such policies and the ideas behind them the Kōmeitō has published the four-volume *Fukushi Keizai e no Michi (The Road to Welfare Economy)* and the two-volume *Taishū Fukushi wo Mezashite (Toward Mass Welfare)*.

A number of top-echelon representatives of the Gakkai interviewed by the author offered explanations of ideals presented in Gakkai media. How these ideals are interpreted on lower levels of the organization came out in visits to local cell discussion meetings and conversations there with both leaders and rank-and-file members. The

---

* The Gakkai prefers "True Religion" to "Righteousness" as the translation of *sho*.

† Volume I of *Ikeda Kaichō Zenshū (Complete Works of President Ikeda)*, containing these two essays, has already appeared. Ikeda's *Shidō Memo (Guidance Memo)* and *Shidō Shū (Collected Quotations on Guidance)* express the Gakkai ideals concerning leadership in faith and action.

interviews with top leaders provided little new information; these men have thoroughly internalized official ideology, and in most cases a thorough advance reading of Gakkai publications enables one to predict their responses to certain questions. For this reason I depended on the high-level interviews primarily for explication of fine points of policy and doctrine and for gaining impressions of these leaders. In contrast, interviews on lower levels provided candid personal interpretations of Gakkai goals, tactics, and characteristics that often conflicted with official positions.

Approximately two dozen opinion surveys of varying magnitude and focus were used in this study, mostly for determining the attitudes of the Gakkai rank and file (a list of the surveys used appears in Note 7 of Chapter 9). Although in most cases these surveys were performed by agencies of high integrity and competence—journalistic, academic, governmental, and professional polling groups—there are several conditions affecting their use and interpretation. First, owing to financial considerations, the only original survey run for this study was an F-scale test administered to a small number of Gakkai members. In all other cases it was necessary to work with the results of samples and questions often composed for other purposes than mine. Thus it was necessary to select from the surveys the questions that seemed most amenable to interpretation through the theoretical framework used here.

Second, in every case the sample size (n) of Gakkai members involved was far too small to enable the drawing of firm conclusions from the data. The proportion of members contained in national surveys rarely exceeded 4 per cent; that is, perhaps one hundred persons in a survey with a total sample of 2,500. Local samples of Gakkai members were commonly in the range of $n = 25$–75. To attempt, on the basis of an n of 100, to form hypotheses about the modal attributes of members of an organization of several million persons is precarious; to draw conclusions is folly. Several indicators of "massness" were used, and wherever possible surveys with independently constructed samples were cited.* Where contradictions between surveys appear these too are cited.

Third, and partially offsetting the first two difficulties, is the nature of the samples of Gakkai members obtained. In many cases the sample turned out to be one of Kōmeitō supporters, identified through their responses to questions on political affiliation, not religious inclination. Assuming that politicized Gakkai members† are relatively

---

* This is a standard method of compensating for measurement error. See Blalock, p. 158.

† Almost all vocal Kōmeitō supporters are Sōkagakkai members; in two recent and representative surveys the proportions of Kōmeitō supporters claiming Gakkai membership were 87.5 per cent and 100 per cent. See Verba; Okabe, p. 49.

highly committed to the Society and are therefore more ideologically orthodox and more active than the average member, the answers of this group to questions concerning doctrinal orthodoxy and organizational commitment and activism have been treated as a standard.

Fourth, in every case where a subsample of Gakkai members or Kōmeitō supporters was drawn from a larger sample, the distribution of responses of the total sample includes the responses of the Gakkai subsample; thus deemphasizing any difference there may actually have been between the total sample exclusive of Gakkai members and the Gakkai members themselves. Unfortunately, comparisons between Gakkai members and nonmembers are not always possible because many of the surveys directly concerned with the Gakkai or Kōmeitō used no control groups. This did not hinder intramembership comparisons between, for example, activists and nonactivists, but it did render extremely difficult any comparison of Gakkai members with other Japanese. Where Gakkai subsamples were drawn from larger samples, this was no problem.

Taking all of these conditions into consideration, the surveys that proved most helpful were those by Suzuki Hiroshi, Dator, and Verba and his associates; the Japanese newspapers *Mainichi* and *Yomiuri* also provided helpful material. The Japanese national character studies by the Institute of Statistical Mathematics (see the bibliographical entries of Hayashi, Suzuki Tatsuzō, Suetsuna, and Tōkei Sūri Kenkyū-jo) are illuminating on general cultural trends. And the Japanese government's annual survey of popular attitudes concerning the constitution (see in Bibliography Naikaku Sōri Daijin Kanbō Kōhō-shitsu), with an n of 349, provided the most reliable data on the political attitudes of Kōmeitō supporters available anywhere.

Finally, the election statistics of greatest utility in this study (presented in Appendix D, Fig. D.1, Tables D.1–D.4 below) were those from the House of Councillors elections of the last thirteen years, showing the steady growth of Sōkagakkai electoral power. The increase of Gakkai intraparliamentary political strength in terms of legislative assembly seats held by Kōmeitō representatives on all levels of government is shown in Appendix D, Tables D.5–D.11.

Sōkagakkai Membership Figures

TABLE B.1

Rate of Increase of Sōkagakkai Membership

Year	Absolute Size (In Families)	Absolute Increase (In Families)	Rate of Increase
1953	.07 million		
1954	.16	.09 million	130%
1955	.30	.14	87
1956	.38	.08	38
1957	.55	.17	45
1958	.80	.25	45
1959	1.05	.25	31
1960	1.42	.37	35
1961	1.90	.48	34
1962	2.37	.47	25
1963	3.05	.68 (.58)	29 (24)
1964	3.90	.85 (.75)	28 (25)
1965	5.07	1.07 (.97)	27 (25)
1966	5.44	.37 (.67)	7 (13)
1967	6.13	.69	13
1968	6.48	.35	6
1969	7.00	.52	8

NOTE: Figures in parentheses represent an attempt to prorate the Society's downward revision of membership figures (by 500,000 families) in 1966 by subtracting 100,000 families from each of the preceding three years and adding 300,000 to the period 1965–66.

SOURCES: *Up to 1955*: Saki and Oguchi, p. 211; "Sōka Gakkai and the Nichiren Shō Sect," *Contemporary Religions in Japan*, Mar. 1960, p. 62; Takagi, *Shinkō Shūkyō*, p. 71; Takase, *Dai San Bummei*, p. 171; Thomsen, p. 85.

1955–63: Kasahara, *Seiji to Shūkyō*, pp. 187, 193, 206; Saki and Oguchi, p. 211; *Seikyō News*, Sept. 15, 1962, Dec. 3, 1963; Takase, *Dai San Bummei*, p. 181; Thomsen.

1963–69: *Japan Times*, Jan. 15, 1967; Kasahara, *Seijito Shūkyō*, p. 273; Kōmeitō Press Release, Feb. 13, 1968; Nakaba, "Shichinen," p. 122; *Seikyō News*, May 19, Oct. 6, Nov. 3, Dec. 2, 1964; *Seikyō Shimbun*, May 4, Aug. 1, 1967; *Seikyō Times*, Vol. 4, No. 6, June 1969, p. 11; *World Tribune*, May 15, 1965, March 8, July 7, Sept. 13, 1966.

TABLE B.2

Growth of the Sōkagakkai Student Division

Year	Membership	Year	Membership
1957	500	1963	20,319
1958	1,200	1964	51,000
1959	2,000	1965	100,000
1960	2,850	1966	150,000
1961	6,000	1967 (May)	180,000
1962	12,000		

SOURCE: *Seikyō Shimbun*, June 30, 1967.

Administrative Structure of the Sōkagakkai and the Kōmeitō

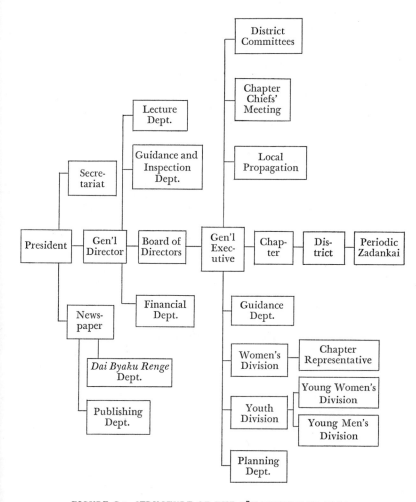

FIGURE C.1. STRUCTURE OF THE SŌKAGAKKAI IN 1951

SOURCE: Kasahara, *Seiji to Shūkyō*, p. 43.

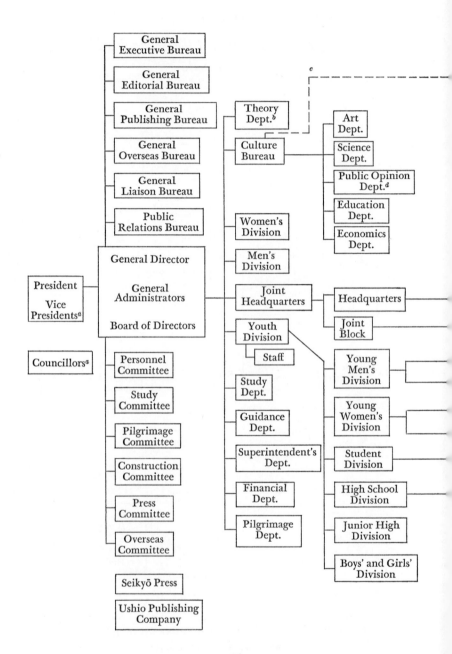

```
                    ┌─ General
                    │  Executive Bureau
                    │
                    ├─ General
                    │  Editorial Bureau
                    │
                    ├─ General          ┌─ Theory                    ┌─ Art
                    │  Publishing Bureau │  Dept.ᵇ                   │  Dept.
                    │                   │                           │
                    ├─ General          ├─ Culture ─────────────────┼─ Science
                    │  Overseas Bureau  │  Bureau                   │  Dept.
                    │                   │                           │
                    ├─ General          │                          ├─ Public Opinion
                    │  Liaison Bureau   │                          │  Dept.ᵈ
                    │                   │                           │
                    ├─ Public           ├─ Women's                  ├─ Education
                    │  Relations Bureau │  Division                │  Dept.
                    │                   │                           │
                    │  General Director ├─ Men's                    └─ Economics
                    │                   │  Division                    Dept.
   ┌─ President      │  General         │
   │  Vice ──────────┤  Administrators ─┼─ Joint ──────────────────── Headquarters
   │  Presidentsᵃ    │                  │  Headquarters
   │                 │  Board of        │                           ┌─ Joint
   │                 │  Directors       ├─ Youth                    │  Block
   │                                    │  Division
   │                                    │     └─ Staff              ┌─ Young
   │  Councillorsᵃ   ┌─ Personnel       │                          │  Men's
   │                 │  Committee       ├─ Study                    │  Division
   │                 │                  │  Dept.
   │                 ├─ Study           │                          ┌─ Young
   │                 │  Committee       ├─ Guidance                │  Women's
   │                 │                  │  Dept.                   │  Division
   │                 ├─ Pilgrimage      │
   │                 │  Committee       ├─ Superintendent's        ┌─ Student
   │                 │                  │  Dept.                   │  Division
   │                 ├─ Construction    │
   │                 │  Committee       ├─ Financial               ┌─ High School
   │                 │                  │  Dept.                   │  Division
   │                 ├─ Press           │
   │                 │  Committee       └─ Pilgrimage              ┌─ Junior High
   │                 │                     Dept.                   │  Division
   │                 └─ Overseas
   │                    Committee                                  └─ Boys' and Girls'
   │                                                                  Division
      Seikyō Press

      Ushio Publishing
      Company
```

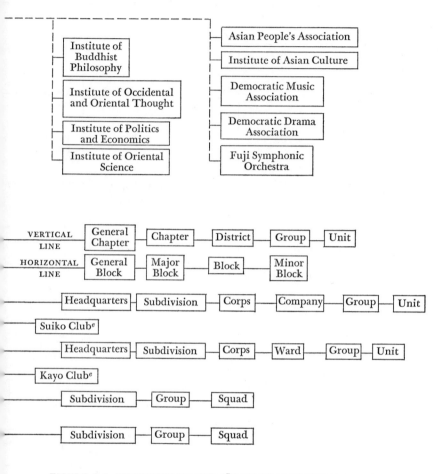

FIGURE C.2. STRUCTURE OF THE SŌKAGAKKAI IN JANUARY 1970

SOURCE: Adapted from *World Tribune*, Oct. 3, 1967.
 [a] Positions of Vice President and Councillor created January 1970. "Sōkagakkai no Soshiki," mimeo., Tokyo, 1970.
 [b] *Seikyō Shimbun*, April 30, 1967.   [c] Sōkagakkai Overseas Bureau, No. 3, pp. 7–8.
 [d] Takase, *Kōmeitō*, p. 315.   [e] *World Tribune*, Aug. 14, 1965.

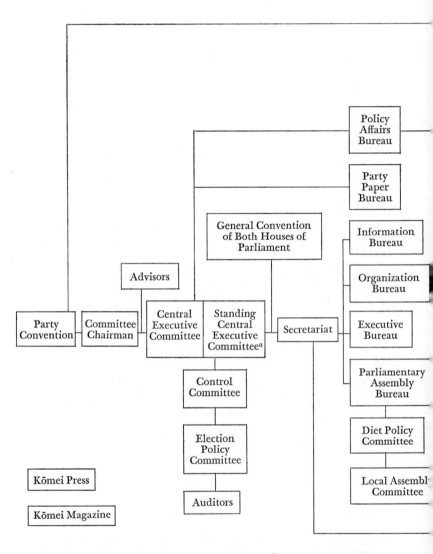

FIGURE C.3. STRUCTURE OF THE KŌMEITŌ IN JANUARY 1970

SOURCES: Adapted from *Kōmeitō—Clean Government Party*; Takase, *Kōmeitō*, pp. 316–17.
  a Standing Central Executive Committee created January 1970. Communication from Akiyama Tomiya to author, April 11, 1970.

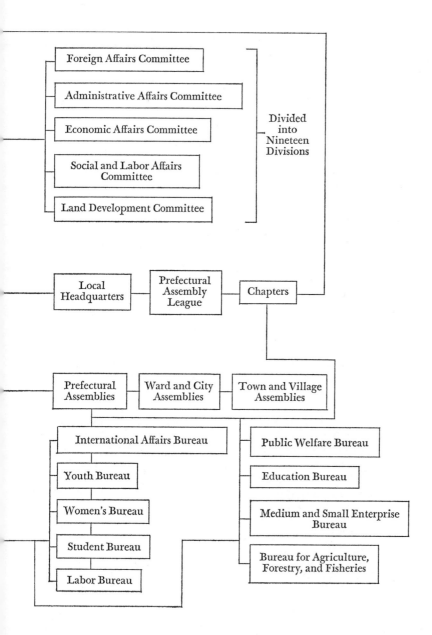

Foreign Affairs Committee	
Administrative Affairs Committee	
Economic Affairs Committee	Divided into Nineteen Divisions
Social and Labor Affairs Committee	
Land Development Committee	

| Local Headquarters | Prefectural Assembly League | Chapters |

| Prefectural Assemblies | Ward and City Assemblies | Town and Village Assemblies |

International Affairs Bureau	Public Welfare Bureau
Youth Bureau	Education Bureau
Women's Bureau	Medium and Small Enterprise Bureau
Student Bureau	Bureau for Agriculture, Forestry, and Fisheries
Labor Bureau	

Support, Strength, and Electoral Performance
of the Sōkagakkai and the Kōmeitō

The 250 members of Japan's House of Councillors are elected by two methods: 150 of them come from local election districts, and the rest are chosen in a national election. Every voter casts two votes. The term of office is six years, and every three years approximately seventy-five locally filled seats and fifty nationally filled seats are contested. The parties and organizations that put up more than one national candidate for the Upper House national election need to manage their potential votes carefully. The party must estimate its possible nationwide total vote and its geographic distribution; calculate the minimum vote required for a candidate to be among the fifty winners; and tell its supporters how to vote so as to win the largest number of seats. Votes may be wasted if all of a party's voters vote for one man out of several party contenders, or if some voters support a candidate whose election is already assured.

The Gakkai follows such a strategy: it divides the country into zones for each national Kōmeitō candidate by estimating the necessary minimum vote and the number of Kōmeitō voters in each zone; it then instructs Gakkai members in each zone to vote for the specified candidate. The success of this strategy is seen in the results of the Upper House election of 1965, in which all nine of the Kōmeitō candidates were successful.

Candidate	Total Votes Received	Percentage from	Zone
Harada Tatsuru	490,000	93%	1
Yamada Tetsuichi	550,000	87	2
Nakao Tatsuyoshi	432,000	94	3
Yaoi Hidehiko	550,000	93	4
Kodaira Yoshihei	562,000	95	5
Kuroyanagi Akira	461,000	95	6
Kashiwabara Yasu	607,000	86	7
Tada Shōgo	578,000	91	8
Miyazaki Masayoshi	479,000	96	9

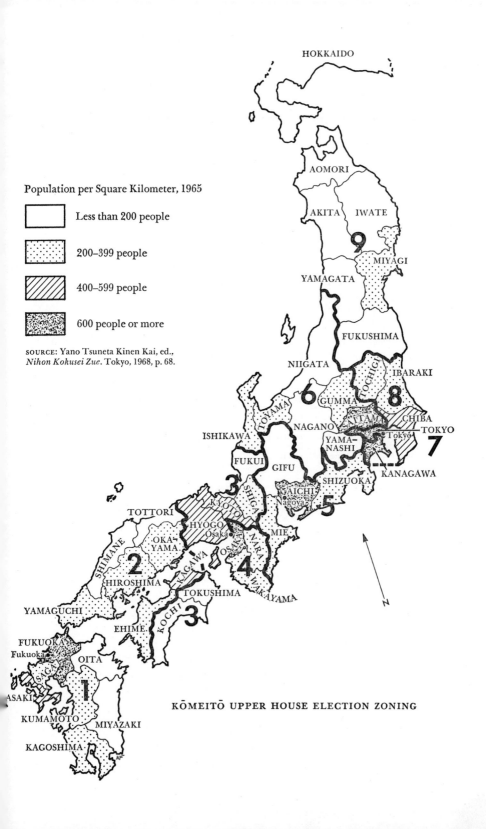

Population per Square Kilometer, 1965

Less than 200 people

200–399 people

400–599 people

600 people or more

SOURCE: Yano Tsuneta Kinen Kai, ed.,
Nihon Kokusei Zue. Tokyo, 1968, p. 68.

HOKKAIDO

AOMORI

AKITA   IWATE

9

MIYAGI

YAMAGATA

FUKUSHIMA

NIIGATA

TOCHIGI   IBARAKI

6   GUMMA   8

TOYAMA

NAGANO   SAITAMA   CHIBA

ISHIKAWA   YAMA-   TOKYO
NASHI   Tōkyō

FUKUI   7

GIFU   KANAGAWA

3   SHIZUOKA

TOTTORI   KYOTO   SHIGA   AICHI
Nagoya

HYOGO   5

OKA-   Osaka   MIE
YAMA   2   NARA   OSAKA

SHIMANE   KAGAWA   4

HIROSHIMA   WAKAYAMA

YAMAGUCHI   TOKUSHIMA

EHIME   KOCHI   3

FUKUOKA
Fukuoka   OITA

SAGA

ASAKI   1   KŌMEITŌ UPPER HOUSE ELECTION ZONING

KUMAMOTO   MIYAZAKI

KAGOSHIMA

N

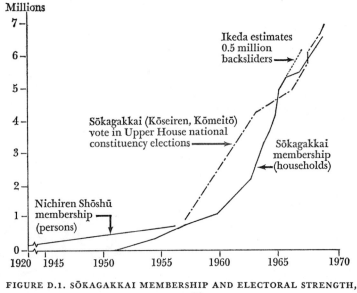

Millions

FIGURE D.1. SŌKAGAKKAI MEMBERSHIP AND ELECTORAL STRENGTH,
1920–68

NOTE: 1956 Upper House election: vote-to-membership ratio—2.44:1.
    1959 Upper House election: ratio—2.32:1.
    1962 Upper House election: ratio—1.52:1.
    1965 Upper House election: ratio—.96:1.
    1968 Upper House election: ratio—1:1.
SOURCES: See Appendix B; Sangi-in Jimukyoku; *Mainichi Shimbun*, July 9, 1968; *Seikyō Times*,
Vol. IV, No. 6, June 1969, p. 11.

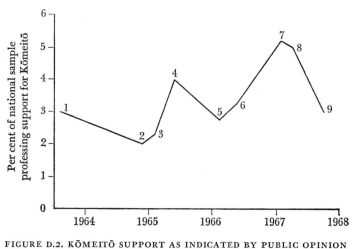

FIGURE D.2. KŌMEITŌ SUPPORT AS INDICATED BY PUBLIC OPINION
SURVEYS, 1963-67

SOURCES: (1) Sept. 1963: *Mainichi Shimbun.* (2) Nov. 1964: *Mainichi Shimbun.* (3) Feb.
1965: Naikaku Sōri Daijin Kanbō Kōhō-shitsu, *Kenpō,* p. 140. (4) June 1965: *Mainichi Shimbun.* (5) Mar. 1966: *Yomiuri Shimbun.* (6) May 1966: *Mainichi Shimbun.* (7) Mar. 1967:
Yomiuri Shimbun. (8) April 1967: *Asahi Shimbun.* (9) Sept. 1967: Verba *et. al.*

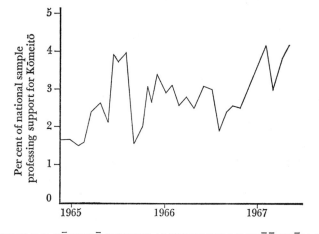

FIGURE D.3. KŌMEITŌ SUPPORT AS INDICATED BY CHŪŌ CHŌSA SHA
PUBLIC OPINION SURVEYS, 1964-67

SOURCE: *Chūō Chōsa Sha* (Central Research Service), Tokyo.

TABLE D.1

Upper House Elections, National Constituency: Sōkagakkai
Absolute Vote by Prefecture

Prefecture	1956 Vote	1959 Vote	1959 Pct. change	1962 Vote	1962 Pct. change	1965 Vote	1965 Pct. change	1968 Vote	1968 Pct. change
Hokkaidō	50,471	71,822	+ 43%	141,859	+ 97%	197,250	+39%	261,161	+32%
Aomori	11,835	28,373	+140	39,835	+ 40	51,271	+29	66,942	+31
Iwate	6,729	19,790	+190	39,022	+102	35,460	− 9	49,382	+39
Miyagi	31,944	42,448	+ 33	60,647	+ 43	60,465	—	93,626	+55
Akita	20,910	35,084	+ 68	50,416	+ 44	35,443	+ 6	58,130	+ 9
Yamagata	13,531	35,472	+162	50,513	+ 42	54,451	+ 8	63,305	+16
Fukushima	31,558	56,979	+ 81	68,251	+ 20	93,117	+36	117,783	+27
Ibaraki	26,542	57,372	+116	103,109	+ 80	123,848	+20	136,247	+10
Tochigi	23,400	40,935	+ 75	67,072	+ 39	85,764	+28	100,420	+17
Gumma	35,992	55,888	+ 55	79,646	+ 43	87,477	+10	116,718	+33
Saitama	56,347	72,755	+ 29	128,241	+ 76	161,497	+26	229,229	+42
Chiba	31,740	53,508	+ 67	125,558	+136	156,092	+24	221,823	+42
Tōkyō	142,553	256,734	+ 79	493,251	+ 92	647,378	+27	741,343	+15
Kanagawa	69,996	133,339	+ 90	225,228	+ 68	260,798	+16	375,992	+44
Niigata	20,819	49,532	+138	80,862	+ 63	80,999	—	128,269	+58
Toyama	5,112	14,725	+188	25,349	+ 72	26,255	+ 4	41,089	+56
Ishikawa	3,057	11,249	+268	21,363	+ 90	27,924	+31	47,703	+69
Fukui	3,445	10,809	+213	25,188	+133	24,656	− 2	36,653	+49
Yamanashi	9,945	18,882	+ 91	31,151	+ 64	37,987	+22	52,219	+37
Nagano	26,265	49,441	+ 88	85,261	+ 72	93,329	+ 9	129,233	+39
Gifu	6,452	28,936	+349	68,361	+136	106,901	+56	134,970	+26
Shizuoka	51,600	81,132	+ 57	142,412	+ 76	182,013	+28	226,291	+24

Aichi	24,050	103,130	+328%	179,021	+ 74%	229,230	+28%	257,546	+12%
Mie	4,418	32,470	+658	70,855	+142	93,308	+32	115,155	+23
Shiga	2,392	13,691	+473	20,099	+ 47	31,269	+56	39,976	+28
Kyōto	19,262	56,466	+193	87,751	+ 85	116,133	+32	141,858	+22
Osaka	69,954	205,406	+194	266,319	+ 30	449,324	+69	563,402	+25
Hyōgo	28,968	118,013	+310	212,405	+ 78	213,164	—	347,883	+63
Nara	5,399	27,434	+407	34,285	+ 25	61,288	+79	66,953	+ 9
Wakayama	10,665	38,987	+264	55,129	+ 41	72,396	+31	95,182	+32
Tottori	6,386	19,972	+213	28,070	+ 40	39,101	+39	46,187	+18
Shimane	1,630	12,281	+657	29,958	+144	39,309	+31	50,325	+28
Okayama	25,333	71,434	+182	101,658	+ 42	127,010	+25	150,281	+18
Hiroshima	9,581	55,847	+484	109,538	+ 96	134,016	+22	180,564	+35
Yamaguchi	2,403	46,708	+185	80,574	+ 73	88,546	+10	107,271	+21
Tokushima	1,756	19,249	+994	47,927	+144	49,862	+ 4	70,863	+42
Kagawa	5,702	22,121	+288	60,738	+174	56,603	− 7	78,394	+39
Ehime	4,898	37,124	+658	74,932	+102	98,494	+32	132,460	+35
Kōchi	11,002	32,398	+194	51,372	+ 59	50,215	− 2	75,630	+51
Fukuoka	46,590	123,140	+164	185,457	+ 51	176,233	− 5	257,032	+46
Saga	3,620	24,727	+583	28,246	+ 14	28,780	+ 2	47,601	+65
Nagasaki	6,112	47,231	+672	60,887	+ 29	58,534	− 4	80,494	+38
Kumamoto	10,113	54,418	+438	63,028	+ 16	69,882	+11	94,259	+35
Oita	2,441	20,256	+730	37,679	+ 86	45,733	+22	69,028	+51
Miyazaki	4,572	31,107	+580	40,739	+ 31	49,130	+21	65,178	+33
Kagoshima	3,914	47,986	+113	56,545	+ 18	71,755	+27	94,450	+32
Totals	991,540	2,486,801	+143	4,124,269	+ 35	5,097,682	+19	6,656,500	+13

NOTE: Figures for 1968 are unofficial.
SOURCES: Sangi-in Jimukyoku, *Mainichi Shimbun*, July 9, 1968.

315

TABLE D.2

Distribution of Sōkagakkai Vote in Upper House National Constituency Elections, by Prefecture (Percentage)

Prefecture	1956	1959	1962	1965	1968
Hokkaidō	5.1%	2.9%	3.4%	3.9%	3.9%
Aomori	1.2	1.1	1.0	1.0	1.0
Iwate	.7	.8	1.0	.7	.7
Miyagi	3.2	1.7	1.5	1.2	1.4
Akita	2.1	1.4	1.2	1.0	.9
Yamagata	1.4	1.4	1.2	1.1	1.0
Fukushima	3.2	2.3	1.7	1.8	1.8
Ibaraki	2.7	2.3	2.5	2.4	2.0
Tochigi	2.4	1.7	1.5	1.7	1.5
Gumma	3.6	2.3	1.9	1.7	1.8
Saitama	5.6	2.9	3.1	3.2	3.4
Chiba	3.2	2.1	3.0	3.1	3.3
Tōkyō	14.4	10.3	11.9	12.7	11.1
Kanagawa	7.1	5.4	5.5	5.1	5.6
Niigata	2.1	2.0	2.0	1.6	1.9
Toyama	.5	.7	.6	.5	.6
Ishikawa	.3	.5	.5	.5	.7
Fukui	.3	.4	.6	.5	.6
Yamanashi	1.0	.8	.8	.7	.8
Nagano	2.7	2.0	2.1	1.8	1.9
Gifu	.7	1.2	1.6	2.1	2.0
Shizuoka	5.2	3.3	3.4	3.6	3.4
Aichi	2.4	4.1	4.3	4.5	3.9
Mie	.4	1.3	1.7	1.8	1.7
Shiga	.2	.6	.5	.6	.6
Kyōto	1.9	1.9	2.1	2.3	2.1
Osaka	7.1	8.3	6.4	8.8	8.5
Hyōgo	2.9	4.8	5.2	4.2	5.2
Nara	.5	1.1	.8	1.2	1.0
Wakayama	1.1	1.6	1.3	1.4	1.4
Tottori	.6	.8	.7	.8	.7
Shimane	.2	.5	.7	.8	.8
Okayama	2.6	2.9	2.5	2.5	2.3
Hiroshima	1.0	2.3	2.7	2.6	2.7
Yamaguchi	.2	1.9	1.9	1.7	1.6
Tokushima	.2	.8	1.2	1.0	1.1
Kagawa	.6	.9	1.5	1.1	1.2
Ehime	.5	1.5	1.8	1.9	2.0
Kōchi	1.1	1.3	1.2	1.0	1.1
Fukuoka	4.7	4.9	4.5	3.5	3.9
Saga	.4	1.0	.7	.6	.7
Nagasaki	.6	1.9	1.5	1.1	1.2
Kumamoto	1.0	2.2	1.5	1.4	1.4
Oita	.2	.8	.9	.9	1.0
Miyazaki	.5	1.2	1.0	1.0	1.0
Kagoshima	.4	1.9	1.4	1.4	1.4
Total Sōkagakkai Vote:	100.0%	100.0%	100.0%	100.0%	100.0%

NOTE: Figures for 1968 are unofficial.
SOURCES: Sangi-in Jimukyoku; *Mainichi Shimbun*, July 9, 1968.

TABLE D.3

Sōkagakkai Vote in Upper House National Constituency Elections
As Percentage of Total Vote, by Prefecture

Prefecture	1956	1959	1962	1965	1968
Hokkaidō	3.5%	5.1%	7.6%	10.8%	12.8%
Aomori	3.3	7.2	8.5	10.1	12.9
Iwate	1.5	4.2	6.7	5.7	8.5
Miyagi	5.9	7.5	8.7	8.7	13.1
Akita	4.4	7.4	8.5	8.9	10.8
Yamagata	2.4	6.4	7.8	8.6	10.6
Fukushima	4.1	7.6	7.5	10.4	12.9
Ibaraki	4.5	8.5	13.3	15.8	17.7
Tochigi	4.7	8.0	11.1	13.4	15.1
Gumma	6.0	8.5	11.5	12.3	15.3
Saitama	7.8	9.7	13.1	14.8	18.6
Chiba	5.2	7.3	14.0	16.3	19.6
Tōkyō	6.8	10.0	13.4	15.9	15.5
Kanagawa	8.6	13.6	15.8	16.3	18.8
Niigata	2.6	5.6	8.0	7.5	11.5
Toyama	1.3	3.8	5.6	5.6	8.1
Ishikawa	.8	2.5	5.1	6.4	9.5
Fukui	1.1	3.4	6.5	6.4	9.9
Yamanashi	3.4	5.8	8.8	10.4	14.9
Nagano	.3	6.0	8.7	9.9	13.8
Gifu	1.2	5.1	9.5	13.9	15.2
Shizuoka	5.5	7.7	11.0	14.4	15.9
Aichi	2.1	8.1	10.6	12.5	13.4
Mie	.8	6.1	10.8	14.0	16.7
Shiga	.8	4.5	5.5	8.5	10.1
Kyōto	3.6	7.6	11.6	14.0	15.5
Osaka	5.5	14.3	12.6	18.7	19.9
Hyōgo	2.6	10.1	14.1	12.7	18.6
Nara	2.1	9.7	9.8	17.5	17.3
Wakayama	3.0	10.6	12.4	16.3	20.4
Tottori	2.6	7.5	9.6	13.2	15.9
Shimane	.4	3.2	6.6	9.0	11.9
Okayama	4.1	10.6	13.7	17.4	19.0
Hiroshima	1.3	6.7	11.5	13.6	17.6
Yamaguchi	.4	7.6	11.8	13.3	15.6
Tokushima	.8	6.5	13.8	14.1	20.5
Kagawa	1.6	5.7	13.9	13.5	20.1
Ehime	1.0	6.3	11.7	14.8	20.5
Kōchi	3.7	8.3	12.3	12.4	20.2
Fukuoka	4.1	9.2	12.0	11.4	15.0
Saga	1.0	6.5	7.4	7.6	12.0
Nagasaki	1.2	8.3	9.8	9.8	12.9
Kumamoto	1.6	7.7	8.7	9.7	12.9
Oita	.5	3.9	7.1	8.7	12.9
Miyazaki	1.1	7.2	9.1	10.6	13.9
Kagoshima	.6	6.2	7.1	9.0	11.9
Sōkagakkai Percentage of Total Vote	3.5%	8.5%	11.5%	13.7%	15.5%

NOTE: Figures for 1968 are unofficial.
SOURCES: Sangi-in Jimukyoku; *Mainichi Shimbun,* July 9, 1968.

TABLE D.4

*Concentration of Sōkagakkai Vote in 12 Urban Prefectures
in Upper House National Constituency Elections*

	Percentage of Total Sōkagakkai Vote from Each Prefecture				
Prefecture	1956	1959	1962	1965	1968
Saitama	5.6%	2.9%	3.1%	3.2%	3.4%
Chiba	3.2	2.1	3.0	3.1	3.3
Tōkyō	14.4	10.3	11.9	12.7	11.1
Kanagawa	7.1	5.4	5.5	5.1	5.6
Shizuoka	5.2	3.3	3.4	3.6	3.4
Aichi	2.4	4.1	4.3	4.5	3.9
Kyōto	1.9	1.9	2.1	2.3	2.1
Osaka	7.1	8.3	6.4	8.8	8.5
Hyōgo	2.9	4.8	5.2	4.2	5.2
Okayama	4.1	2.9	2.5	2.5	2.3
Hiroshima	1.3	2.3	2.7	2.6	2.7
Fukuoka	4.1	4.9	4.5	3.5	3.9
Total	59.3%	53.2%	54.6%	56.1%	55.4%
Percentage of total national electorate in these prefectures	45.2	46.4	48.6	50.7	[no data]
Percentage of total national vote from these prefectures	40.7	42.8	45.8	47.6	50.3

NOTE: Figures for 1968 are unofficial.
SOURCES: Sangi-in Jimukyoku; *Mainichi Shimbun*, July 9, 1968.

TABLE D.5

Sōkagakkai Performance in Upper House Elections

	Election Year				
Performance Category	1956	1959	1962	1965	1968
Seats contested	c. 125	c. 125	c. 125	c. 125	c. 125
Sōkagakkai candidates[a]	6	6	9	14	14
Candidates elected	3	6	9	11	13
Percentage of candidates elected	50%	100%	100%	79%	93%
Seats held by Sōkagakkai	3	9	15	20	24
Percentage of total seats held by Sōkagakkai[b]	1.2%	3.5%	6%	8%	9.6%

SOURCES: Sangi-in Jimukyoku; *Mainichi Shimbun*, July 9, 1968.
[a] "Sōkagakkai" comprehends Kōseiren and Kōmeitō.
[b] Total of 250 seats in Upper House, half contested every 3 years.

TABLE D.6

Sōkagakkai Performance in Lower House Elections of 1967 and 1969

Performance Category	1967	1969
Seats contested	486	486
Kōmeitō candidates	32	76
Candidates elected	25	47
Percentage of candidates elected	78%	62%
Seats held by Kōmeitō	25	47
Percentage of total seats held by Kōmeitō	5.1%	9.7%
Total vote	45,996,561	46,989,884
Kōmeitō vote[a]	2,472,371	5,124,666
Kōmeitō share of total vote[a]	5.4%	10.9%

SOURCES: 1967: *Asahi Shimbun*, Jan. 31, 1967. 1969: *Mainichi Shimbun*, Dec. 29, 1969.
[a] Unofficial figures.

TABLE D.7

Total Sōkagakkai Strength in Local Legislatures

| Performance Category | Election Year | | | |
	1955	1959	1963	1967
Seats contested[a]	56,524	45,735	45,867	42,963
Sōkagakkai candidates	54	304	842	1,249
Candidates elected	53	272	824	1,108
Percentage of candidates elected	98%	89%	98%	89%
Seats held by Sōkagakkai	53	272	824[b]	1,108[c]
Percentage of contested seats won by Sōkagakkai	.1%	.6%	1.8%	2.6%[c]

NOTE: Elections for nearly all local administrative units are held in the same month.
SOURCES: 1955; Takase, *Kōmeitō*, pp. 320–21; Jichichō Senkyo-kyoku. 1959: Jichishō Senkyo-kyoku. 1963: Takase *Kōmeitō*, pp. 320–21. 1967: Jiji Tsūshinsha, *Jiji Nenkan*, 1968 ed. (Tokyo), pp. 267–69. Interim totals in notes b and c below: Nakaba, *Chōryū*, pp. 308–9. Nakaba's statistics include Gakkai members running as independents; government (Jichichō and Jichishō) and Jiji Tsūshinsha figures do not.
[a] Decreases in seats contested due to amalgamation of local administrative units.
[b] 1,087 after by-election of April 1963.
[c] Number of seats held and percentage of contested seats won calculated from official government (not interim) figures.

TABLE D.8

Sōkagakkai Performance in Prefectural Assembly Elections

Performance Category	Election Year		
	1959	1963	1967
Seats contested	2,537	2,568	2,605
Sōkagakkai candidates	4	40	94
Candidates elected	3	39	84
Percentage of candidates elected	75%	97%	89%
Seats held by Sōkagakkai	3	39	84
Percentage of total seats held by Sōkagakkai	.1%	1.5%	3.2%
Total vote	35,939,447	36,050,710	35,000,000[a]
Sōkagakkai vote	60,467[b]	615,118	1,210,905
Sōkagakkai share of total vote	.2%	1.7%	3.5%

NOTE: Tokyo excluded.
SOURCES: 1959: *Asahi Shimbun*, April 17, 1959; Takase, *Kōmeitō*, pp. 320–21; Jichishō Senkyo-kyoku. 1963: Takase, *Kōmeitō*, pp. 320–21; Jichishō Senkyo-kyoku. 1967: *Asahi Shimbun*, Feb. 10, April 15, 17, 1967.
[a] Unofficial figure.
[b] Memo from Akiyama Tomiya to the author, May 20, 1968.

TABLE D.9

Sōkagakkai Performance in Tokyo Metropolitan Assembly Elections

Performance Category	Election Year				
	1955	1959	1963	1965	1969
Seats contested	120	120	120	120	126
Sōkagakkai candidates	1	11	17	23	25
Candidates elected	1	3	17	23	25
Percentage of candidates elected	100%	27%	100%	100%	100%
Seats held by Sōkagakkai	1	3	17	23	25
Percentage of total seats held by Sōkagakkai	.8%	2.5%	14.2%	19.2%	19.8%
Total vote	2,669,321	3,415,950	3,944,040	3,900,000	4,527,996
Sōkagakkai vote	19,312[a]	144,251[a]	143,826	506,706	784,090
Sōkagakkai share of total vote	.7%	4.2%	10.5%	13.3%	17.3%

SOURCES: 1955: Jichichō Senkyo-kyoku; Takase, *Kōmeitō*, pp. 320–21. 1959: Takase, *Kōmeitō*, pp. 320–21; *Asahi Shimbun*, April 25, 1959; Jichishō Senkyo-kyoku. 1963: Jichishō Senkyo-kyoku; Takase, *Kōmeitō*, pp. 320–21. 1965: Kasahara, *Seiji to Shūkyō*, pp. 279–80. 1969: *Mainichi Shimbun*, July 13, 14, 1969.
[a] Memo from Akiyama Tomiya to the author, May 20, 1968.

TABLE D.10

Sōkagakkai Performance in City Assembly Elections

Performance Category	Election Year			
	1955	1959	1963	1967
Seats contested	9,034	10,507	12,090	12,020
Sōkagakkai candidates	21	215	640	953
Candidates elected	20	192	623	900
Percentage of candidates elected	95%	89%	97%	94%
Seats held by Sōkagakkai	20	192	623(716)[a]	900(1,186)[a]
Percentage of contested seats won by Sōkagakkai	.2%	1.8%	5.2%	7.1%
Total vote	14,725,487	18,347,034	20,587,248	25,974,960
Sōkagakkai vote	39,000[b]	378,127[b]	1,325,134	2,301,963[b]
Sōkagakkai share of total vote	.3%	2.1%	6.4%	8.9%

NOTE: Includes the five largest cities.
SOURCES: 1955: Jichichō Senkyo-kyoku; Takase, *Kōmeitō*, pp. 320–21. 1959: Takase, *Kōmeitō*, pp. 320–21; Jichishō Senkyo-kokyu; *Asahi Shimbun*, April 30, 1959. 1963: Takase, *Kōmeitō*, pp. 320–21. 1967: *Asahi Shimbun*, Feb. 13, April 17, 28, 1967; *Japan Times*, May 2, 1967; Jichishō Senkyo-kyoku, *Senkyo Nenkan*, 1969, pp. 164–65. Interim totals in note *a* below: Nakaba, *Chōryū*, pp. 308–9.
[a] Figures in parentheses are interim totals (of April 1963 and November 1967) produced by by-elections.
[b] Memo from Akiyama Tomiya to the author, May 20, 1968.

TABLE D.11

Sōkagakkai Performance in Tokyo Ward Assembly Elections

Performance Category	Election Year			
	1955	1959	1963	1967
Seats contested	938	970	1,021	1,039
Sōkagakkai candidates	32	74	136	202
Candidates elected	32	74	136	124
Percentage of candidates elected	100%	100%	100%	61%
Seats held by Sōkagakkai	32	74	136	124(131)[a]
Percentage of contested seats won by Sōkagakkai	3.3%	8%	13%	12%
Total vote	2,287,602	2,752,468	2,844,385	3,897,773
Sōkagakkai vote	59,422[b]	170,118[b]	335,385	463,987
Sōkagakkai share of total vote	2.6%	6.2%	11.8%	11.9%

SOURCES: 1955: Takase, *Kōmeitō*, pp. 320–21; Jichichō Senkyo-kyoku. 1959: Takase, *Kōmeitō*, pp. 320–21; Jichishō Senkyo-kyoku; *Asahi Shimbun*, April 30, 1959. 1963: Takase, *Kōmeitō*, pp. 320–21. 1967: *Asahi Shimbun*, April 14, 18, 1967; *Kōmei Shimbun*, May 3, 1967; Jichishō Senkyo-kyoku, *Senkyo Nenkan*, 1969, pp. 164–65. Interim total in note *a* below: Nakaba, *Chōryū*, pp. 308–9.
[a] Figure in parentheses is interim total (in November 1967) produced by by-elections.
[b] Memo from Akiyama Tomiya to the author, May 20, 1968.

Notes

(For complete authors' names, titles, and publication data for items cited in short form in the Notes, see the Bibliography, pp. 355–69.)

The following abbreviations are used in the Notes:

AJ	Asahi Jānaru	NYW-T&S	New York World-
AS	Asahi Shimbun		Telegram & Sun
CSM	Christian Science	NKS	Nihon Keizai Shimbun
	Monitor	SN	Seikyō News
CN	Chūgai Nippō	SS	Seikyō Shimbun
DBR	Dai Byaku Renge	SSS	Shin Shūkyō Shimbun
JT	Japan Times	SJ	Shūmo Jihō
KS	Kōmei Shimbun	TP	Tōkyō Pōsuto
LT	London Times	WT	World Tribune
MS	Mainichi Shimbun	YS	Yomiuri Shimbun

INTRODUCTION

1. Functionalist terms are used here as in Levy: *structure*: "a pattern, i.e., an observable uniformity, of action or operation" (p. 57); *function*: "a condition, or state of affairs, resultant from the operation ... of a structure through time" (p. 56); *eufunction*: "a condition, or state of affairs, that (1) results from the operation ... of a structure of a given unit through time, and that (2) increases or maintains adaptation or adjustment of the unit *to the unit's setting*, thus making for the persistence of the unit" (p. 77); *dysfunction*: "a condition, or state of affairs, that (1) results from the operation ... of a structure of a given unit through time, and that (2) lessens the adaptation or adjustment of the unit *to the unit's setting*, thus making for a lack of persistence (i.e., a change in or dissolution) of the unit" (p. 77).

Lipset, p. 27, defines democracy as "a political system which supplies regular constitutional opportunities for changing the governing officials, and a social mechanism which permits the largest possible part of the population to influence major decisions by choosing among contenders for political office.... This definition ... implies a number of specific conditions: (1) a 'political formula' or body of beliefs specifying which institutions . . . are legitimate (accepted as proper by all); (2) one set of political leaders in office; and (3) one or more sets of recognized leaders attempting to gain office."

The "political formula" of democratic politics is defined by Prothro and Grigg, pp. 276 *et seq.*, as acceptance of democracy in the abstract and acceptance of the principles of majority rule and minority rights.

2. Lipset, ch. 4.

3. Bell, "Theory of Mass Society," p. 75.

4. Tōkyō Daigaku Shakaigakka *et al.*, p. 29; Mannheim, *Man and Society*, pp. 60–61; Gerson, pp. 145–49; Tinder, pp. 7 *et seq.*; Apter, *Ideology*, pp. 33 *et seq.*

5. For a description of such a society see Bell, "Theory of Mass Society," p. 76.

6. Kornhauser, p. 14.

7. *Ibid.*, pp. 59–61, 107 *et seq.*, 237.

8. *Ibid.*, p. 14; for a similar definition see Selznick, pp. 281 *et seq.*

9. Kornhauser, p. 39.

10. *Ibid.*, pp. 43–48; see also Selznick, pp. 292–97.

11. Kornhauser, p. 227.

12. *Ibid.*, pp. 43–48.

13. Bell, "Theory of Mass Society," p. 76.

14. Kornhauser, p. 227.

15. Ike, "Experiment," pp. 22–27.

16. Sorokin; Fromm, p. 19; Kornhauser, p. 125; Durkheim, pp. 211 *et seq.*

17. Fromm, p. viii.

18. Kornhauser, p. 64.

19. Lederer, *State*, pp. 10, 140–50; Riesman, *Crowd*, pp. xl–xli; Almond and Verba, ch. 10; Eckstein, pp. 281–83; Lipset, p. 77; Mannheim, *Man and Society*, pp. 96 *et seq.*; Kornhauser, ch. 3.

20. Almond and Verba, pp. 264–65; Kornhauser, pp. 67–72.

21. Durkheim, p. 380.

22. Nakane, pp. 48 *et seq.* Miss Nakane's presentation is rather extreme. Cross-national data collected by Verba *et al.* indicate that a higher proportion of Japanese than Americans are members of some secondary group; the fact that in Japan neighborhood associations, the PTA, and labor unions are often more compulsory than voluntary in large part explains this situation, but the fact of multiple memberships must be borne in mind when reading the Nakane material.

23. Langdon, pp. 72–90, 198, 281–83; Ike, "Experiment," pp. 10–12; Suzuki Eitarō, *Genri*, p. 218.

24. Lipset, pp. 114–16; Kornhauser, pp. 212 *et seq.*; Philip Converse in Apter, *Ideology*, p. 213; Almond and Verba, pp. 315–16; McClosky, p. 379.

25. Schaar, p. 173.

26. Kahler, chs. 2, 3; Fromm, pp. 125 *et seq.*; Mannheim, *Man and Society*, p. 59.

27. Almond and Verba, p. 153, ch. 8.

28. *Ibid.*, pp. 113 *et seq.*; Almond, p. 63.

29. Wylie; Banfield.

30. Lane, *Ideology*, p. 162; Almond and Verba, pp. 18–22.

31. Lane, *Ideology*, p. 98; Lipset, p. 27.

32. Lipset, ch. 4; Philip Converse in Apter, *Ideology*, pp. 228–30; Mc-Closky, p. 378; Mannheim, *Man and Society*, p. 63; Adorno, *et al.*; Muramatsu Tsuneo, pp. 101–139.

33. Lipset, pp. 95–96.

34. Hobsbawm, ch. 7.

35. Lipset, pp. 150–51.

36. *Ibid.*, ch. 4; Almond and Verba, pp. 315–16.

37. Almond and Verba, pp. 211 *et seq.*, 315–16.

38. *Ibid.*, pp. 63 *et seq.*, 161–62, 168.

39. Schaar, pp. 194–95; Adorno, *et al.*, p. 220; Lenski, pp. 20 *et seq.*, 73–74.

40. Hofstadter, p. 73.

41. Lipset, pp. 97–100.

42. Kornhauser, pp. 43 *et seq.*

43. Bell, *End of Ideology*, ch. 1.

44. Lederer, *State*, pp. 38–39.

45. Fromm, p. 134.

46. Kornhauser, p. 47.

47. *Ibid.*, pp. 52–54, 59.

48. *Ibid.*, p. 84.

49. Cohn, *Pursuit*; Kasahara, *Tenkanki no Shūkyō* and *Kakumei no Shūkyō*; Aberle.

50. Talmon, *Origins and Messianism*; Hobsbawm.

51. Smelser; Braden, *Spirits* and *These Also*; Pope; Hoffmann; Hofstadter.

On Japanese new religions see Offner and van Straelen; McFarland, *Rush Hour*; Thomsen; Takagi, *Shinkō Shūkyō*; and the journal *Contemporary Religions in Japan*.

52. Wallace, p. 264; Lanternari.

53. Almond; Nolte; Stouffer; Cantril, *Politics*; Gerth; Lerner; Lasswell and Lerner; Bullock; Loomis and Beegle, p. 724; Hitler; Moore.

54. Parsons, *Structure*.

CHAPTER 1

1. English-language surveys: McFarland, *Rush Hour*; Offner and van Straelen; Thomsen. Japanese-language survey: Takagi, *Shinkō Shūkyō*.

2. Mombushō, *Shūkyō Nenkan* (Tokyo, 1965), pp. 131–57.

3. McFarland, "Religions," p. 57.

4. Smelser, pp. 15–20.

5. *Ibid.*, pp. 15–20.

6. Cf. *ibid.*, p. 345.

7. *Ibid.*, p. 310.

8. *Ibid.*, pp. 319–38.

9. McFarland, *Rush Hour*, pp. 11–12.

10. E.g., "Seinen no Shūkyōshin," pp. 270–72.

11. Oguchi, p. 206.

12. Dore, pp. 344–45.

13. *Ibid.*

14. *Ibid.*, p. 362.

15. Ikado, "Josetsu," p. 131; "Seinen no Shūkyōshin," pp. 270–72.

16. Kamishima, p. 42.

17. Dore, pp. 381 *et seq.*; Suzuki Eitarō, "Kindai-ka," pp. 17–18, and *Genri*.

18. Suzuki Eitarō, "Kindai-ka," pp. 17–18.

19. Dore, p. 246; Nakane, pp. 48 *et seq.*

20. Dore, p. 246.

21. *Ibid.*; Nakane, pp. 48 *et seq.*

22. Staley and Morse, pp. 17–20.

23. Takagi, *Shinkō Shūkyō*, pp. 97–98.

24. Shinohara, "Gimon," pp. 34–36.

25. Clark, p. 16.
26. Takagi, *Shinkō Shūkyō*, p. 15; Murakami, "Seinen," p. 43.
27. Naikaku Kanbō, *Shinkō Shūkyō*, pp. 83 *et seq.*
28. Offner and van Straelen, pp. 266–70; Hajime Nakamura, p. 400; Tatsuzō Suzuki, pp. 19–20; Fujimaki, p. 40; Dore, p. 66.
29. Hajime Nakamura, p. 409.
30. *Ibid.*, pp. 510–11.
31. For a discussion of this concept, see Maruyama Masao, *Nihon*, Part III.
32. Cohn, *Pursuit*, pp. 310–11.   33. *Ibid.*, p. 313.
34. Smelser, pp. 338–47.   35. Dore, p. 188.
36. *Ibid.*, p. 378.   37. Lifton.
38. Takagi, *Shinkō Shūkyō*, p. 89.
39. Kasahara, *Tenkanki no Shūkyō*, pp. 28–32.
40. Tōkyō Daigaku Shakaigakka *et al.*, pp. 39 *et seq.*
41. Maraini, p. 65. Maraini's observation, made in the 1950's, still applies.
42. *Nihon Hyakka Daijiten* (Tokyo, 1964), Vol. XI, p. 220. To assess the waning of the pachinko boom, compare these figures with Maraini's.
43. Maraini, pp. 65–66.
44. *Ibid.*, pp. 66–67.
45. Compare this environment with that of the French Poujadist movement, as opposed to that of the Nazi movement. Lederer, *State*, p. 65, Togawa, *Kōmeitō*, pp. 157 *et seq.*; Hoffmann, pp. 11–22.

CHAPTER 2

1. After Smelser, p. 8.
2. White, *Militant Religion in Japan*, pp. 19–26; McFarland, *Rush Hour*, pp. 71 *et seq.*; Nielson, pp. 7–9; Offner and van Straelen, pp. 121 *et seq.*, 143–44; Thomsen, p. 22; Watanabe, "Religions," pp. 159–61; Takagi, *Shinkō Shūkyō*, p. 7.
3. This section is adapted from the following Gakkai sources: Makiguchi; Sōkagakkai Kyōgaku-bu; Ikeda, *Kōgi*; Tōkyō Daigaku Hokekyō Kenkyū-kai; Kodaira, *Sōkagakkai*. In English, *Sōka Gakkai* and *Nichiren Shōshū Sōkagakkai*. Secondary English sources are White, *Militant Religion in Japan*; Ramseyer, "Sōka Gakkai"; Thomsen; McFarland, *Rush Hour*; Brannen, all bibliographic entries.
4. "Shūkyō Hōjin 'Sōkagakkai' Kisoku," 1966.
5. Nitta, p. 66.
6. For a complete study of Nichiren and his teachings, see Renondeau, *Doctrine* and *Bouddhisme*; Anesaki, *Nichiren*; Eliot. White, *Militant Religion in Japan*, and Ramseyer, "Sōka Gakkai," contain briefer treatments.
7. Quoted in Eliot, p. 279.
8. Brown; Morris, *Nationalism*.
9. Dator, "Interpretation," pp. 219 *et seq.*
10. *Ibid.*
11. Dator, "Interpretation," pp. 219 *et seq.*; Yamaguchi, pp. 41 *et seq.*
12. Interview with Akiya Einosuke, Vice President, Sōkagakkai.

CHAPTER 3

1. Cohn, *Pursuit*, pp. 312–13.   2. Smelser, pp. 352–55.
3. Cohn, *Pursuit*, p. 30.   4. Lederer, *State*, p. 65; Bullock.

5. See the Religious Juridical Persons Law as discussed by Woodard.
6. Nakaba, *Chōryū*, pp. 313–14.
7. For a more complete account of the early history of the Gakkai see Saki and Oguchi; Takase, *Dai San Bummei*; White, *Militant Religion in Japan*; Ramseyer, "Sōka Gakkai"; Sōkagakkai, *Nichiren Shōshū Sōkagakkai*.
8. This period is described vividly, though subjectively, by Ikeda in *Ningen Kakumei*.
9. Saki and Oguchi, p. 137.
10. This period is covered in greater detail in Takase, *Kōmeitō, Ningen Kakumei*, and *Ningen Fukkō*; Ishida Ikuo, *Sōkagakkai*; Murakami, *Sōkagakkai*. The available English sources—White, *Militant Religion in Japan*, Ramseyer, "Sōka Gakkai"—are somewhat dated now.
11. Smelser, pp. 355–64.
12. Lederer, *State*, pp. 230 *et. seq.*
13. Dore, p. 347.
14. Watanabe, "Religions," p. 162.
15. Saki and Oguchi, pp. 57 *et seq.*
16. Nakaba, "Shichinen," June 15, p. 120.
17. Saki and Oguchi, pp. 152 *et seq.*; Takagi, *Shinkō Shūkyō*, p. 71.
18. Takagi, *Shinkō Shūkyō*, pp. 72–73; Takase, *Dai San Bummei*, p. 148.
19. Tsurumi *et al.*, pp. 118 *et seq.*; Takase, *Dai San Bummei*, p. 151; Oguchi, p. 56.
20. For a biography of Ikeda, see Takase, *Ningen Kakumei*. English sources are White, *Militant Religion in Japan*; and Ramseyer, "Sōka Gakkai."
21. Flagler, p. 183.
22. Saki and Oguchi, p. 150.
23. Takase, *Ikeda Daisaku*, p. 22.
24. See, for example, the contradictory predictions made in Sōkagakkai, *Sōka Gakkai*, pp. 98–99; *SN*, 22.vii.63; *WT*, 7.viii.65; 3,5,10.v.66; and Sōkagakkai, *Nichiren Shōshū Sōkagakkai*, p. 156.
25. *WT*, 10.v.66.
26. For the 1967 goals, see *JT*, 15.i.67.
27. These features are discussed in greater detail in White, *Militant Religion in Japan*, and McFarland, *Rush Hour*.
28. Takase, *Dai San Bummei*, pp. 134–35; Sōkagakkai Overseas Bureau, No. 6, pp. 11–12; Ikeda, *Seiji to Shūkyō*, p. 242.
29. Ikeda, *Seiji to Shūkyō*, pp. 123–24; Takase, *Ningen Kakumei*, pp. 79 *et. seq.*
30. Takase, *Dai San Bummei*, p. 150.
31. Murakami, *Sōkagakkai*, p. 39.
32. Saki and Oguchi, pp. 143 *et seq.*
33. *Ibid.*, p. 13; Takase, *Dai San Bummei*, p. 174, *Kōmeitō*, pp. 120 *et seq.*
34. *WT*, 4.vi.66.
35. *SS*, 3.vi.66.
36. *SN* and *WT*, all issues, especially in 1967; *SS*, 1,4.v.67.
37. Takase, *Ningen Kakumei*, p. 241.
38. Troeltsch; Pope; Bryan R. Wilson, p. 3; Johnson, p. 88.
39. Takase, *Dai San Bummei*, pp. 121–22.

40. "Shūkyō Hōjin 'Sōkagakkai' Kisoku"; interview with Akiya Einosuke, Vice President, Sōkagakkai.
41. Troeltsch; Pope; Bryan R. Wilson; Johnson.
42. Takase, *Dai San Bummei*, p. 147; Murakami, *Sōkagakkai*, p. 108.
43. Murakami, *Sōkagakkai*, p. 112.
44. Takase, *Dai San Bummei*, p. 124.
45. Takase, *Ningen Kakumei*, p. 207.
46. Ikeda, *Shidō Memo*.
47. Takami, p. 291.
48. *DBR*, No. 194, July 1967, pp. 12–13.

CHAPTER 4

1. Mombushō, *Shūkyō Nenkan*, (Tokyo, 1965), pp. 148–49.
2. Nihonjin no Kokuminsei.
3. Verba *et al.*
4. Asahi Shimbunsha, *Asahi Nenkan* (Tokyo, 1967), p. 272, pp. 1, 5 of addenda after p. 272.
5. Togawa, *Kōmeitō*, p. 212.
6. *SS*, 1.ix.67; Yamaguchi, p. 225.
7. Murakami, *Sōkagakkai*, pp. 189 *et seq.*
8. *AS*, 17.vii.68.
9. Verba *et al.*; Nihonjin no Kokuminsei.
10. *WT*, 8.iii.66.
11. Nihonjin no Kokuminsei.
12. *SS*, 30.vi.67; 24.viii.67.
13. Nihonjin no Kokuminsei; Ishida Ikuo, "Shakubuku," pp. 85–86; Murakami, *Sōkagakkai*, pp. 28–29; Verba *et al.*
14. *SS*, 15.vi.67.
15. Suzuki Hiroshi, pp. 88–90.
16. *CSM*, 29.iv.66; Takase, *Kōmeitō*, p. 35; *Asahi Jānaru* Henshūbu, "Dai San Seiryoku," p. 19; Aruga, p. 62.
17. Saki and Oguchi, p. 166; Nihonjin no Kokuminsei; Dator, "Demographic Data."
18. Nihonjin no Kokuminsei; *MS*, surveys of Sept. 1963, Nov. 1964, June 1965, May 1966, Sept. 1966; Naikaku Sōri, unpub. data; *YS*, surveys of March 1966 and Jan. 1967.
19. Azumi "Functions," p. 6; White, California F-Scale data; Verba *et al.*
20. Dator, "Demographic Data."
21. *MS*, surveys of Sept. 1963, Nov. 1964, June 1965, May 1966, Sept. 1966; Naikaku Sōri, unpub. data; *YS*, surveys of March 1966 and Jan. 1967; *AJ*, 5.iii.67, p. 14.
22. Ibid.; Nihonjin no Kokuminsei; Verba *et al.*
23. Azumi, "Functions," p. 6; White, California F-Scale data.
24. Kornhauser, pp. 69–72; Arendt, pp. 336–37; Lipset, chs. 4, 5.
25. Lipset, ch. 5.
26. Maruyama Masao, *Thought and Behaviour*, pp. 57 *et seq.*
27. Almond, pp. 186–92.
28. Nihonjin no Kokuminsei; *MS*, surveys of Sept. 1963, Nov. 1964, June 1965, May 1966, Sept. 1966; Naikaku Sōri, unpub. data; *YS*, surveys of March 1966 and Jan. 1967; *AJ*, 5.iii.67, p. 14.

29. Dator, "Demographic Data"; *YS*, survey of March 1967; Tōkyō Daigaku Shakaigakka *et al.*, p. 108; Suzuki Hiroshi, p. 89; Tanaka Kunio, p. 125.

30. Ishida Ikuo, *Sōkagakkai*, p. 44; Kōmeitō press releases, undated.

31. White, California F-scale data; Azumi, "Functions," pp. 7–8.

32. Nihonjin no Kokuminsei; *YS*, surveys of March 1966 and Jan. 1967.

33. *MS*, surveys of Sept. 1963, Nov. 1964, June 1965, May 1966, Sept. 1966; *YS*, survey of March 1966.

34. *AS*, 27.i.67; 17.iv.67.

35. Watanuki, " 'Chudo Seiji,' " p. 17.

36. *YS*, survey of March 1967; *AS*, 27.i.67.

37. *AS*, 6.ii.67; Kiefer.

38. Nihonjin no Kokuminsei; *MS*, surveys of Nov. 1964, June 1965, May 1966, Sept. 1966; Naikaku Sōri, unpub. data; *AJ*, 5.iii.67, p. 14; *YS*, surveys of March 1966 and Jan. 1967.

39. Naikaku Sōri, unpub. data.

40. Dator, "Demographic Data"; Suzuki Hiroshi, p. 89; Tanaka Kunio, p. 125; Tōkyō Daigaku Shakaigakka *et al.*, pp. 103–4; *YS*, survey of March 1967.

41. Tōkyō Daigaku Shakaigakka *et al.*, p. 103.

42. This surmise is empirically based: see Takase, "Ikeda," p. 192.

43. Naikaku Sōri, unpub. data; these data are corroborated in Shinohara, "Gimon," pp. 70–71 and *AS*, 13.iv.67.

44. Suzuki Hiroshi, pp. 94–95.

45. *Ibid.*, pp. 93–94.

46. Takahashi Naoko.

47. Azumi, "Functions," p. 8.

48. Dator, "Sōka Gakkai in Politics," p. 237, Table 6.

49. Takase, "Ikeda," p. 192; Kasahara, *Kakumei no Shūkyō*, p. 278.

50. Naikaku Sōri, unpub. data; *JT*, 28.vi.67; Asahi Jānaru Henshūbu, "Kōmeitō," p. 14.

51. Suzuki Hiroshi, p. 95; Takahashi Naoko; Dator, "Demographic Data"; Ishida Ikuo, *Sōkagakkai*, p. 160; Tōkyō Daigaku Shakaigakka *et al.*, pp. 105–6.

52. Interview with Ikado Fujio, Religious Affairs Branch, Ministry of Education.

53. Azumi "Functions," p. 10.   54. White, California F-Scale data.

55. Azumi, "Social Basis," p. 12.   56. Nihonjin no Kokuminsei.

57. *Asahi Jānaru* Henshūbu, "Kōmeitō," p. 14.

58. Azumi, "Social Basis," pp. 12–13, and "Functions," p. 16; for a similar pattern, see *YS*, survey of March 1967.

59. *AJ*, 5.iii.67, p. 14.

60. Kornhauser, pp. 124–25; Arendt, p. 311; Lipset, pp. 138, 148 *et seq.*; Philip Converse in Apter, *Ideology*, p. 253; Loomis and Beegle, p. 730.

61. All *MS* surveys.

62. Sangi-in Jimukyoku; *MS*, 9.vii.67.

63. All *MS* surveys; Takase, "Ikeda," p. 192.

64. Lipset, pp. 144–45; Loomis and Beegle, pp. 725–27; Heberle, pp. 222 *et seq.*

65. Hoffmann, p. 12 and *passim*.

66. Braden, _Spirits_ and _These Also._
67. Pulzer, pp. 27, 279 _et seq._
68. Cantril, _Psychology_, p. 265; E. Y. Hartshorne in Parsons, _Essays_, p. 136, Note 3.
69. Gerth, p. 104.
70. Maruyama Masao, _Thought and Behaviour_, pp. 57–58.
71. Moore, p. 305.
72. Rogger and Weber, p. 14; E. Y. Hartshorne in Parsons, _Essays_, p. 136, Note 3.
73. Hoffmann, p. 115.
74. _Ibid._, pp. 198–201.
75. Hofstadter, pp. 69 _et seq._
76. Raymond Wolfinger _et al._ in Apter, _Ideology_, p. 267.
77. Lerner, pp. v-vii, 3, 5 _et seq._
78. Lasswell and Lerner, pp. 458 _et seq._
79. Almond, pp. 186–92.   80. Lasswell and Lerner.
81. Almond, pp. 186–92.   82. _Ibid._, pp. 194 _et seq._
83. Raymond Wolfinger _et al._ in Apter, _Ideology_, p. 267.

CHAPTER 5

1. Yanaihara, p. 17.
2. _SS_, 17.v.67.
3. _SS_, 25.vi.67.
4. Sōkagakkai, _Sōka Gakkai_, p. 131.
5. Bloom, p. 65.
6. Ikeda, _Seiji to Shūkyō_, p. 238, and _Kōgi_, pp. 220–21.
7. "Stamping in Nichiren's Footsteps," p. 1250.
8. Saki and Oguchi, pp. 203–04.
9. "Characteristics of the Upper House Election," p. 57.
10. Ikeda, _Kōgi_, p. 721.
11. _SS_, 19.x.67.
12. Sōkagakkai Overseas Bureau, No. 8, p. 3.
13. _SN_, 28.iv.64.   14. Hesselgrave, p. 25.
15. _SS_, 2.vi.67.   16. _SS_, 1.vi,viii,ix.67.
17. _SSS_, all issues in autumn 1967, "Kokuhaku" column.
18. Suzuki Hiroshi, p. 63; _SS_, 23.viii.67; Tōkyō Daigaku Shakaigakka _et al._, p. 72; Takahashi Naoko; Murakami, _Sōkagakkai_, pp. 27–28.
19. _SS_, 23.viii.67; Murakami, _Sōkagakkai_, pp. 27–28.
20. Vogel.
21. Suzuki Hiroshi, pp. 62–63; Tōkyō Daigaku Shakaigakka _et al._, pp. 111–12; Murakami, _Sōkagakkai_, pp. 13–14; _SS_, 23.viii.67.
22. Takase, _Dai San Bummei_, p. 133.
23. Suzuki Hiroshi, pp. 62–63.
24. _SS_, 29.viii.67; _SS_, 11.vii.67; _SS_, 15.vi.67.
25. Naikaku Kanbō, _Shinkō Shūkyō_, p. 8; Aochi, pp. 112 _et seq._; Azumi, p. 12.
26. Takase, "Daigaku," p. 26.
27. Takami, p. 293.
28. Naikaku Kanbō, _Shinkō Shūkyō_, p. 8; Azumi, p. 12; Murakami, _Sōkagakkai_, pp. 13–14; _SS_, 23.viii.67.

29. Tōkyō Daigaku Shakaigakka *et al.*, p. 72.
30. Suzuki Hiroshi, pp. 62–63.
31. Takami, p. 294.
32. Naikaku Kanbō, *Shinkō Shūkyō*, p. 86.
33. Sōkagakkai, *Nichiren Shōshū Sōkagakkai*, p. 39.
34. Tōkyō Daigaku Shakaigakka *et al.*, p. 72.
35. *SS*, 9.vi.67.
36. Compare with the Nazi and Communist systems of fronts and parallel groups: Ebenstein, p. 59; Selznick, p. 27. For further comparison with indoctrination practices in Nazi and Communist organizations, see Heberle, pp. 350–52, and Selznick, pp. 11, 27.
37. Dator, "Interpretation," p. 208.
38. *SS*, 1.ix.67.
39. *SS*, 1.vi,viii,ix.67.
40. Ike, *Politics*, pp. 26–28.
41. For evidence of the pressure under which lower-level leaders operate, see *SS*, 24.v.67;9.vi.67; *SSS*, all issues in autumn 1967, "Kokuhaku" column.

42. *WT*, 2.iv.65.
43. Yanaihara, p. 16.
44. Nishio, p. 14.
45. *SS*, 15.viii.67.
46. *SN*, 15.ix.62.
47. *WT*, 26.vi.65.
48. *Ibid.*, 8.iii.66.
49. Tōkyō Daigaku Shakaigakka *et al.*, p. 68.
50. *SS*, 5.v.67;6,11.vii.67.
51. Interview with Sasaki Toshiyuki, Sōkagakkai Public Relations Bureau; *WT*, 14.viii.65.

52. *SS*, 3.viii.67.
53. *Ibid.*, 4.viii.67.
54. *Ibid.*, 25.viii.67.
55. *Ibid.*, 12.v.67; 25.viii.67.
56. Murakami, *Sōkagakkai*, pp. 29–30.
57. Takase, "Daigaku," p. 25; *Asahi Jānaru* Henshūbu, "Kōmeitō," p. 15.
58. *SS*, 7.viii.67.
59. "Seinen no Shūkyōshin," p. 274; *SS*, 30.vi.67.
60. *SS*, 7.viii.67.
61. Kiefer; Vogel, pp. 113, 211–16, 227 *et seq.*
62. Vogel, pp. 113, 211–16.
63. Ikeda, *Ningen Kakumei*, pp. 168 *et seq.*
64. *SS*, 11,14.viii.67.
65. Kasahara, *Seiji to Shūkyō*, p. 104; see also *SS*, 9.vi.67.
66. *SS*, 31.v.67; 3,4,11,16,18,20,24,29,30.vi.67; 6.vii.67.
67. Saki and Oguchi, p. 193; *SS*, 30.vi.67.
68. *SS*, 28.iv.67; 19,31.v.67; 3,4,11,16,18,20,24,29,30.vi.67; 6.vii.67.
69. *SN*, 1.viii.62; Sōkagakkai Overseas Bureau, No. 3, pp. 7–8; *SS*, 5.v.67.
70. *SS*, 30.iv.67.
71. Morris, "Sōka Gakkai," p. 38.
72. Interview with Oguchi Iichi; interviews with several American Sōkagakkai members; *SN*, 14.iv.64.
73. *SN*, 14.iv.64; interview with Sasaki Toshiyuki, Sōkagakkai Public Relations Bureau.
74. Suggested by Almond, pp. 65 *et seq.*, with addition of the "intermediate" category.
75. Hesselgrave, pp. 185 *et seq.*

76. *Ibid.*
77. Sōkagakkai Kyōgaku-bu, pp. 358 *et seq.*
78. Hesselgrave, pp. 185 *et seq.*
79. "Shinsetsu Eisai-kō 'Sōka Gakuen' no Mae-hyōban," p. 36.
80. Interview with Hōjō Hiroshi, Vice President, Sōkagakkai.
81. "Shinsetsu Eisai-kō 'Sōka Gakuen' no Mae-hyōban," p. 36.
82. Interview with Hōjō Hiroshi, Vice President, Sōkagakkai.
83. "Shinsetsu Eisai-kō 'Sōka Gakuen' no Mae-hyōban," p. 36.
84. Interview with Hōjō Hiroshi, Vice President, Sōkagakkai.
85. The term is McLuhan's.
86. *SS*, 16.x.67.

CHAPTER 6

1. Almond and Powell, chs. 4–7.   2. Takase, *Kōmeitō*, p. 148.
3. *Ibid.*   4. *Ibid.*
5. The horizontal line closely parallels Communist and Nazi organizational structure; see United States Congress, p. 18; Ebenstein, p. 59.
6. "Stamping in Nichiren's Footsteps," p. 1255.
7. *SN*, 21.iv.64.
8. Takase, *Dai San Bummei*, p. 110.
9. Murakami, "Kōmeitō," p. 162.
10. Pope, p. 137.
11. *JT International Edition*, 20.iii.65.
12. *Ibid.*, 2.x.65; *WT*, 4.vi.66.
13. Sōkagakkai, *Nichiren Shōshū Sōkagakkai*, p. 28; Sōkagakkai Overseas Bureau, No. 3, pp. 7–8. Compare with the camouflaged front groups utilized by Communist parties: United States Congress, Senate Judiciary Committee, p. 90; Selznick, pp. 114 *et seq.*
14. Yamaguchi, p. 142; Nakaba, "Shichinen," June 1, p. 124.
15. Ikeda, *Seiji to Shūkyō*, p. 263.
16. Takase, *Dai San Bummei*, pp. 117–18.
17. Interview with Akiyama Tomiya, Chief, Sōkagakkai Overseas Bureau.
18. "Shūkyō Hōjin 'Sōkagakkai' Kisoku," 1957, 1962, 1966.
19. *SS*, 1.v.67. The General Affairs Committee had, in turn, grown to an unwieldy 57 members by January 1970, when the office of vice-president was created, a position immediately under the president. Hōjō Hiroshi, Akiya Einosuke, and Morita Kazuya were named to the post, the functions of which are as yet unclear—it is intended apparently to increase administrative efficiency. See *AS*, 5.i.70; *JT Weekly*, 10.i.70.
20. Murakami "Tenkanki," p. 54–55. However, in line with more recent efforts to depoliticize the Gakkai's public image, the Kōmeitō announced on January 5, 1970, that Takeiri and all other Kōmeitō legislators would resign their official Sōkagakkai posts. See *AS*, 5,6.i.70.
21. See *WT*, 5.iii.66, for a list of general administrators. Biographical information comes from Nakaba, *Chōryū*, pp. 172 *et seq.* The personal comments are from those whom the author has met.
22. Nakaba, *Chōryū*, pp. 172 *et seq.*
23. Olson, p. 14.
24. *AS*, 22.iii.67.

25. *SS*, 1.x.67.
26. *Ibid.*; communication from Akiyama Tomiya, April 11, 1970.
27. *SS*, 12.vi.67; 24.viii.67.   28. *Ikeda, Shidō Memo*, p. 19.
29. Takase, *Kōmeitō*, p. 158.   30. Nishio, p. 7.
31. Tōkyō Daigaku Shakaigakka *et al.*, p. 57.
32. Interview with Sasaki Toshiyuki, Sōkagakkai Public Relations Bureau.
33. Takase, *Kōmeitō*, pp. 96–97.
34. "Shūkyō Hōjin 'Sōkagakkai' Kisoku," 1966.
35. *WT*, 1.xi.66.
36. Braden, *These Also*, pp. 77, 126, 283.
37. Cohn, *Pursuit.*
38. Ramseyer, "Sōka Gakkai," p. 165, cites Saki and Oguchi, p. 137.
39. Takase, Kōmeitō, p. 124.
40. Nakaba, "Shichinen," May 15, 1967, p. 117.
41. *SN*, 28.iv.64.
42. Katz and Lazarsfeld, pp. xv, xix.
43. Cartwright, pp. 19–22.
44. Boulding, p. 161.
45. Gouldner.
46. Tōkyō Daigaku Shakaigakka *et al.*, p. 58.
47. Takase, *Kōmeitō*, pp. 156–57.
48. Suzuki Hiroshi, pp. 70, 72; Nakaba, "Shichinen," Oct. 15, pp. 154–55.

CHAPTER 7

1. Ikeda in *KS*, 1.i.67.
2. Ikeda, *Seiji to Shūkyō*, p. 112.
3. *Ibid.*, pp. 90–91, 160–61, 241–42; Takase, *Kōmeitō*, pp. 183–86.
4. For a discussion of the importance of such competence to democratic systems, see Almond and Verba, ch. 6.
5. Ikeda, *Seiji to Shūkyō*, pp. 160–61; Takase, *Kōmeitō*, pp. 183–86.
6. Ikeda, *Seiji to Shūkyō*, pp. 5–8, "Shūkyō to Seiji Rinen," pp. 307–8.
7. Ikeda, "Shūkyō to Seiji Rinen," pp. 305–8.
8. The problem of congruence or incongruence of certain nonpolitical attitudes and orientations with democratic political systems is discussed in Almond and Verba, ch. 8.
9. Ikeda, *Seiji to Shūkyō*, p. 140.
10. Interview with Ikeda Daisaku, President, Sōkagakkai. At least a few Gakkai leaders take a strong anti-Communist stand: Hōjō Hiroshi emphasized the anti-Communist role of the Kōmeitō in the 1965 Tokyo Municipal Assembly election, saying that "If it were not for the Kōmeitō ... the Communists would have gained even more [seats than they did]." *CSM*, 2.v.66. In an election campaign in Kita-Kyūshū City in 1965 the party used such slogans as "Communists: the enemies of the people." Murakami, "Kōmeitō," p. 170.
11. Ikeda, *Seiji to Shūkyō*, p. 140; Ikeda in *KS*, 1.i.67.
12. Ikeda in *KS*, 1.i.67; "Soko ga Shiritai Kōmeitō Seiken Kakutoku Kōsō," p. 19.
13. Ikeda, *Seiji to Shūkyō*, p. 140; Takase, *Kōmeitō*, pp. 302–4.
14. Ikeda, "Gimon ni Kotaeru," p. 70.

15. *Ibid.*
16. *SN*, 15.vii.62.
17. Ikeda, *Seiji to Shūkyō*, pp. 259 *et seq.*
18. *SN*, 15.viii.62.
19. "Sōkagakkai no Seiji Mokuhyō," p. 8; Maruyama Kunio, pp. 72–73.
20. Ikeda, *Seiji to Shūkyō*, Preface, p. 1; speech by Yano Jun'ya, Kōmeitō Secretary-General, at International House of Japan, Tokyo, May 23, 1967.
21. *SS*, 2.ii.67.
22. Ikeda, *Seiji to Shūkyō*, pp. 2–3.
23. Interview with Tada Shōgo, General Administrator, Sōkagakkai. In January 1970, when the Central Executive Committee had grown to forty members, the Kōmeitō announced the creation of a permanent executive council (*jōnin chūō kanbu-kai*) standing above the CEC, composed of Takeiri, Secretary-General Yano Jun'ya, representative Watanabe Ichirō, councillors Suzuki Kazuhiro, Tada Shōgo, and Kuroyanagi Akira, and Secretariat Director Nagata Takeshi. Hōjō, it was rumored, would resign his party post to assume the vice-presidency of the Gakkai. As part of a planned general separation of functions, it is probable that most or all of the CEC members will soon relinquish either their Kōmeitō or their Gakkai posts. See *AS*, 5,6.i.70; *JT Weekly*, 10.i.70.
24. Ikeda, *Seiji to Shūkyō*, pp. 137–38.
25. *SS*, 21.x.67.
26. For elaboration of the concept of "political culture" see chapters by Lucian Pye and Sidney Verba in Pye and Verba, pp. 3 and 512, respectively; Almond and Verba, ch. 1.
27. Ikeda, *Seiji to Shūkyō*, pp. 146–47.
28. Ikeda, *Kōgi*, p. 1002.
29. Takase, *Kōmeitō*, p. 201.
30. Ikeda, *Ningen Kakumei*, Vol. 3, p. 279.
31. Ikeda, *Seiji to Shūkyō*, p. 130.
32. Sōkagakkai Overseas Bureau, No. 6, p. 17. For a discussion of "interest aggregation" see Almond and Verba, ch. 5.
33. *SN*, 15.vii.62; Ikeda, *Seiji to Shūkyō*, p. 158.
34. Ikeda, "Gimon ni Kotaeru," p. 81.
35. Saki, "Seinen Shōkō," p. 131.
36. Ikeda, *Seiji to Shūkyō*, p. 246. 37. Tsuji Takehisa, p. 54.
38. Ikeda in *KS*, 8.i.67. 39. Takase, *Kōmeitō*, p. 216.
40. Ikeda in *KS*, 8.i.67. 41. Takase, *Kōmeitō*, pp. 198–201.
42. *SN*, 1.vii.62. The identity is now being reduced, at least superficially. In January 1970 Kōmeitō Chairman Takeiri announced that all Kōmeitō leaders would resign their Gakkai posts, retaining the status of "advisors" to the Society. See *AS*, 5,6.i.70.
43. Takase, *Kōmeitō*, pp. 192 *et seq.*, 203–4.
44. Although Ikeda imputes political inclinations to him as early as 1948. Ikeda, *Ningen Kakumei*, Vol. 3, pp. 156–57.
45. *Ibid.*, p. 271.
46. Murakami, "Kōmeitō," p. 161; Takase, *Kōmeitō*, pp. 306 *et seq.*
47. White, *Militant Religion in Japan*, pp. 174–75.
48. Ikeda, "Shūkyō to Seiji Rinen," p. 303.

49. *Ibid.*, p. 304.
50. *SN*, 15.vi.62.
51. *Ibid.*
52. White, *Militant Religion in Japan*, pp. 168 *et seq.*
53. One can see the voluminous results of their studies in Kōmeitō Seisaku-kyoku, *Fukushi Keizai* and *Taishū Fukushi.*
54. *SN*, 1.viii.62.
55. *MS*, 19.iv.63.
56. Quoted in Takase, *Kōmeitō*, p. 155.
57. Ikeda, *Seiji to Shūkyō*, pp. 258–59.
58. Quoted in Takase, *Kōmeitō*, p. 155.
59. Ikeda, *Seiji to Shūkyō*, pp. 127, 128, 130–34.
60. *Ibid.*, p. 230.
61. Fukatsu, p. 37.
62. "Soko ga Shiritai Kōmeitō Seiken Kakutoku Kōsō," p. 21.
63. Sōkagakkai Overseas Bureau, No. 6, pp. 4–5; interview with Sasaki Toshiyuki, Sōkagakkai Public Relations Bureau.
64. Takase, *Kōmeitō*, p. 270.
65. Ikeda, *Kōgi*, pp. 859, 861.
66. Kōmeitō Soshiki-kyoku.
67. Ikeda in *KS*, 8.i.67; "Soko ga Shiritai Kōmeitō Seiken Kakutoku Kōsō," p. 21.
68. Takase, *Kōmeitō*, pp. 270–71.
69. "Voting Characteristics Revealed in Pre-Election Opinion Poll—House of Councillor Elections, July 1965," pp. 5–6.
70. *AS*, 4.vii.67; *LT*, 18.xi.64.
71. *AS*, 13.ii.67.
72. *AS*, 4.vii.67; *JT International Edition*, 28.xi.64.
73. Kōmeitō Shoshiki-kyoku. This personnel overlap will be eliminated during the early 1970's.
74. "Kōmeitō: Iinchō Kōtaigeki to kore kara no Dekata," p. 12; *Asahi Jānaru* Henshūbu, "Kōmeitō," p. 11.
75. "Kōmeitō: Iinchō Kōtaigeki to kore kara no Dekata," p. 12.
76. Tsuji Takehisa, p. 55.
77. Takeiri, p. 19.
78. *TP*, 8.i.67.
79. "Kōmeitō Daigishi: 'Byōku Hinkon-reki' no Meisai," p. 32; a generally undependable magazine that appears to be reliable with respect to this particular case. See also Oya, p. 24.
80. "Kōmeitō Daigishi: 'Byōku Hinkon-reki' no Meisai," p. 32.
81. *KS*, 28.iv.67.
82. Takase, *Kōmeitō*, p. 21.
83. Ike, *Politics*, pp. 192–202; Watanuki, "Patterns," p. 464, note 28.
84. One should note especially in the 1968 Upper House election the 20 per cent of the vote garnered by the Kōmeitō in Shikoku (a rural area not noted for large numbers of believers) and the 2.6 million votes won in five urban prefectures containing only 1.3 million Gakkai members. *MS*, 9.vii.67; *AS*, 17.vii.68.
85. *AS*, 1.iii.67.

86. *SS*, 20.xi.67.
87. *JT*, 21.xi.67.
88. Kōmeitō press releases, 20.xi.67; 1.xii.67.
89. *JT*, 10.xii.67.
90. For expositions of Sōkagakkai policies before 1963 see White, *Militant Religion in Japan*, pp. 167 *et seq*.; Saki, "Shūkyō Seitō," p. 39; "Sōkagakkai no Seiji Mokuhyō," p. 7; Ramseyer, "Sōka Gakkai," p. 293.
91. For expositions of recent Kōmeitō policies, see Kōmeitō press release, 15.xi.66; Ikeda in *KS*, 8.i.67, *AS*, 18.iii.67, *JT*, 18.xi.67. Exhaustive treatment is found in Kōmeitō Seisaku-kyoku, *Fukushi Keizai* and *Taishū Fukushi*.
92. Arendt, p. 324.
93. *CN*, 25.iv.63.
94. Dator, "Interpretation," p. 232.
95. Kōmeitō Kikanshi-kyoku, *Tosei*, back cover.
96. *Ibid., passim*. The full coverage is much more specific and detailed than the summary given here.
97. Interview with Suzuki Kazuhiro, Chief, Kōmeitō Policy Bureau.
98. Kōmeitō Kikanshi-kyoku, *Jūten Seisaku*.
99. *JT International Edition*, 19.vi.65.
100. *JT International Edition*, 10.iv.65; Takase, *Kōmeitō*, pp. 231–32.
101. The earlier of these positions is presented in *SN*, 15.ix.62; the later is quoted from Miyamori, p. 175.
102. Tsuji Takehisa, p. 52.
103. *KS*, 25.viii.67.
104. Interview with Kuroyanagi Akira, Kōmeitō Member of Parliament.
105. *KS*, 25.viii.67.
106. *AS*, 17.x.67.
107. Takase, *Kōmeitō*, pp. 227–29.
108. Maruyama Kunio, pp. 74–75; Article IX of the Japanese constitution; "Sōkagakkai no Seiji Mokuhyō," p. 7.
109. *Ibid.*; Takase, *Kōmeitō*, p. 132.
110. Quoted in Saki, "Hihan," p. 207; Tsuji Takehisa, p. 53.
111. *SN*, 1.vii.62; "Sōkagakkai no Seiji Mokuhyō," p. 7; Takase, *Dai San Bummei*, pp. 284–85; Tsuji Takehisa, pp. 52–53.
112. "Sōkagakkai no Seiji Mokuhyō," p. 7; Tsuji Takehisa, pp. 52–53.
113. *SN*, 15.viii.62; Kōmeitō Kikanshi-kyoku, *Jūten Seisaku*; Ikeda, *Ningen Kakumei*, Vol. 3, pp. 216–69.
114. Takase, *Kōmeitō*, pp. 250–51.
115. Tsuji Takehisa, p. 53; Flagler, p. 186.
116. Flagler, p. 186.   117. Takase, *Kōmeitō*, p. 249.
118. *Ibid.*, p. 248.   119. *Ibid.*, pp. 257–58.
120. Saki, "Hihan," p. 209; Tsuji Takehisa, pp. 53–54.
121. Saki and Oguchi, p. 20.
122. *Kōmeitō—Clean Government Party*.
123. Takase, *Kōmeitō*, pp. 224 *et seq*.
124. *Ibid.*
125. *Ibid.*
126. *Kōmeitō—Clean Government Party*.

127. For an explanation of the present system, see Ward, pp. 53–54. For a general discussion of the relationship between party system and electoral system see Harry Eckstein's article in Eckstein and Apter, pp. 247 *et seq.*; and Duverger, Book II, ch. 1, esp. pp. 216 *et seq.*

128. *KS*, 25.vi.67. 129. *KS*, 18.x.67.
130. Tokoro, "Nichiren," p. 10. 131. Takase, *Kōmeitō*, p. 258.
132. *CSM*, 2.v.66. 133. Tokoro, "Kōmeitō," p. 112.

CHAPTER 8

1. Shōmoto, pp. 32–33.
2. *AS*, 6.ii.67.
3. Ikeda, "Gimon ni Kotaeru," pp. 81, 82.
4. Murakami, *Sōkagakkai*, pp. 143 *et seq.*
5. Takase, *Kōmeitō*, p. 62.
6. Dator, "Sōka Gakkai in Politics," p. 223.
7. *AS*, 3.ii.67; *JT International Edition*, 2.iii.68.
8. "Comprehensive Survey: Kōmeitō."
9. *AS*, 17.vii.68. 10. *JT*, 26.i.67.
11. *AS*, 21,22.ii.67; *JT*, 9,21.iv.67. 12. *JT*, 16.iv.67.
13. *AS*, 9.iii.67.
14. Azumi, "Functions," p. 17; Verba *et al.*
15. *KS*, 9.viii.67.
16. *AS*, 23,25.iii.67; *JT*, 26.iii.67; *SS*, 25.vii.67; *KS*, 30.i.68.
17. *KS*, 9.viii.67.
18. Murakami, "Kōmeitō," p. 167.
19. *JT*, 11.v.67; *AS*, 26.iv.67; *SS*, 11.v.67; *KS*, 12.v.67.
20. *JT*, 11.v.67.
21. Kōmeitō Kikanshi-kyoku, *Shiawase.*
22. Togawa, *Kōmeitō*, pp. 183 *et seq.*
23. *KS*, 7,30.vi.67; 23.vii.67. 24. *KS*, 17.viii.67.
25. Takase, *Kōmeitō*, pp. 44–45. 26. *KS*, 17.viii.67.
27. Takase, *Kōmeitō*, pp. 44–45. 28. *SS*, 2.ix.67.
29. *Ibid.*
30. Togawa, *Kōmeitō*, pp. 193–95; Kōmeitō Kikanshi-kyoku, *Shiawase.*
31. *KS*, 25.vii.67.
32. For an account of the direct-action tradition as manifested in the 1930's see Byas. For earlier manifestations see Marius Jansen, *Sakamoto Ryōma and the Meiji Restoration* (Princeton, 1961), Part III.
33. Takase, *Kōmeitō*, p. 268.
34. Interview with Hōjō Hiroshi, Vice President, Sōkagakkai; Sugahara.
35. *KS*, 19,20,23,27.i.68; Kōmeitō press release, 26.i.68.
36. Ishida Ikuo, *Sōkagakkai*, p. 140.
37. *JT*, 22.i.67.
38. Saki and Oguchi, p. 211.
39. White, *Militant Religion in Japan*, p. 178.
40. *Ibid.* 41. *Ibid.*, pp. 178–79.
42. Hesselgrave, p. 266. 43. Ikeda, *Kōgi*, pp. 70–71.
44. *KS*, all issues in Jan., March, April 1967.

45. *AS*, 1.v.63; *NKS*, 1.v.63.
46. White, *Militant Religion in Japan*, pp. 188–89.
47. Jichichō (-shō) Senkyo-kyoku, 1955, 1959, 1963; Ramseyer, "Sōka Gakkai," p. 300.
48. Jichishō Senkyo-kyoku, 1963.
49. Togawa, *Kōmeitō*, p. 188.
50. Murakami, "Toda Jōsei," p. 436; *JT*, 26.i.67.
51. *AS*, 31.i.67; *Asahi Jānaru* Henshūbu, "Dai San Seiryoku," p. 16.
52. *AS*, 31.i.67.
53. *Ibid.*
54. Ishida Takeshi, in *Annals of the Institute of Social Science*, No. 9, 1968, p. 39.
55. Shinohara, "Kiban," p. 31. This trend continued in the 1969 general election (see the tabulation below), in which the opposition parties won more of the total vote than they had in 1967 (47 per cent as opposed to 45.7 per cent) but shared it more equally among themselves. See *MS*, 29.xii.69.

Party	Votes Received	Percentage of Total Vote	Seats Won
Liberal Democrats	22,381,566	47.6%	288
Socialists	10,074,099	21.4	190
Democratic Socialists	3,636,591	7.7	31
Kōmei	5,124,666	10.9	47
Communists	3,199,030	6.8	14
Other	81,373	.2	0
Independent candidates	2,492,559	5.3	16
Total	46,989,884	99.9%	486

56. Tsuji Takehisa, p. 15; *AS*, 31.i.67.
57. Ide, p. 17.
58. *AS*, 6.ii.67.
59. *Ibid.*
60. Nishihira, "Senkyo," p. 51.
61. *Asahi Jānaru* Henshūbu, "Dai San Seiryoku," p. 20.
62. Nishihira, "Senkyo," p. 53.
63. *Asahi Jānaru* Henshūbu, "Dai San Seiryoku," p. 18. A comparison of the proportions of the vote won in each ward, city, and county of Tokyo is of little help in determining who are the Kōmeitō's primary competitors. Ranking the wards, cities, and counties according to their percentages of the Kōmeitō vote shows a slight positive correlation (.20) with a similar ordering of the LDP vote, and also with the Socialist vote (.24); there are marked negative correlations with the proportions of the vote won by the Democratic Socialists (−.49) and the Communists (−.51). This suggests that the Kōmeitō is more successful in competition with the established parties than with the minor parties, but the presence of many parties in each district precludes definite conclusions about just who is competing successfully against whom, where.
64. *AS*, 17.iv.67.
65. *AS*, 6.iv.67.
66. *AS*, 18.iv.67.
67. *KS* editorial, 16.iv.67.
68. *CN*, 8.v.63.

69. Interview with Sasaki Toshiyuki, Sōkagakkai Public Relations Bureau.
70. *AS*, 6.ii.67.
71. "Soko ga Shiritai Kōmeitō Seiken Kakutoku Kōsō," p. 20.
72. *AS*, 20,21,29.iii.67; 11,13.iv.67.
73. *AS*, 17.iv.67.
74. *KS*, 27,30.iv.67.
75. Jiji Tsūshinsha, *Jiji Nenkan* (Tokyo, 1968), p. 269; *JT*, 2.v.67. As Scott Flanagan notes, it is quite possible that both sets of figures are correct; the Gakkai's figures because the Gakkai knows which candidates are believers, and the official figures because local (especially village) assembly candidates usually run officially as independents.
76. *AS*, 30.iv.67.
77. Interview with Sasaki Toshiyuki, Sōkagakkai Public Relations Bureau.
78. *AS*, 30.iv.67.
79. Interview with Sasaki Toshiyuki, Sōkagakkai Public Relations Bureau. Similar reasoning seems to have been behind the Kōmeitō's decision to run 75 candidates in the next general election, though it expected only 40 to win. See *JT International Edition*, 7.ix.68.
80. *SS*, 4.i.68.
81. Murakami, "Tenkanki," pp. 55–57.
82. Jichishō Senkyo-kyoku, 1963.   83. Nishihira, "Senkyo," p. 52.
84. *KS*, 11.vi.67.   85. Nishihira, "Senkyo," p. 52.
86. *Asahi Jānaru* Henshūbu, "Dai San Seiryoku," p. 22; Ishida Takeshi, in *Annals of the Institute of Social Science*, No. 9, 1968, pp. 19 *et seq.*
87. Nishihira, "Senkyo," p. 59.
88. Kōmeitō press release, 3.vii.67.
89. *SS*, 4.v.67; *AS*, 3.ii.67; *JT International Edition*, 10.viii.68.
90. *SS*, 4.v.67.
91. *CSM*, 3.v.66.

CHAPTER 9

1. Kornhauser, chs. 6–8 on discontinuities, chs. 10–12 on susceptible social groups; DeGrazia, pp. xv–xvi; Sorokin, ch. 2.
2. Adorno *et al.*
3. Kornhauser, p. 111.
4. Prothro and Grigg, pp. 276 *et seq.*
5. Lipset, p. 27.
6. Prothro and Grigg, pp. 276 *et seq.*
7. The national surveys used in this study include the *MS* surveys of Sept. 1963 (N [of entire survey] = 2,836 persons, Nsg [N of Sōkagakkai-member or Kōmeitō-supporter subsample] = 86), Nov. 1964 (N = 2,954, Nsg = 59), June 1965 (N = 2,832, Nsg = 114), May 1966 (N = 2,902, Nsg = 94), and Sept. 1966 (N = 4,844, Nsg = 139); the *YS* surveys of March 1966 (N = 2,565, Nsg = 70) and Jan. 1967 (N = 1,765, Nsg = 55); the third National Character Survey conducted by the Tōkei Sūri Kenkyū-jo in 1963 (N = 2,698, Nsg = 94), covered in Hayashi, *Zusetsu*, Tōkei Sūri Kenkyū-jo, and Tatsuzō Suzuki; the February 1965 Japanese government survey of popular attitudes regarding the constitution (N = 15,863, Nsg = 349), also covered in Naikaku Sōri, *Kenpō*; various surveys by the Asahi Shimbunsha published

in *AS* and *AJ*, esp. *AJ*, 5.iii.67, pp. 10 *et seq*. (N and Nsg unknown); a survey by the Chūō Chōsa Sha (N = 1,678, Nsg = ?) covered in "Voting Characteristics Revealed in Pre-Election Opinion Poll—House of Councillors Elections, July 1965"; a survey on attitudes toward the constitution (N = *c*. 5,000, Nsg = *c*. 135) covered by Kobayashi, p. 134; a 1966 survey by Verba *et al*. (N = 2,657, Nsg = 108); and a survey by the Japan Broadcasting Association (N = 3,632, Nsg = 120) covered in NHK Hōsō Seron Chōsa-sho.

Local surveys used include those by Dator (N = 978, Nsg = 45), covered in that author's works cited in the bibliography; Azumi (Nsg = 386), covered in that author's works cited in the bibliography; Suzuki Hiroshi (Nsg = 268), covered in that author's work cited in the bibliography; Miss Takahashi Naoko (Nsg = 36), a student at Rikkyō University, Tokyo; the sociology departments of Tokyo University and Tokyo Women's University (N = 209, Nsg = 23), covered in Tōkyō Daigaku Shakaigakka *et al*.; and the *YS* survey of March 1967 (N = 1,038, Nsg = 65).

On F-scale usage in Japan, Muramatsu Tsuneo provided data from several localities; a survey was also made by this author (Nsg = 135). Comparisons were facilitated by Adorno *et al*.; the works of Coladarci cited in the bibliography; and the critical essays in Christie and Jahoda.

8. Yamaguchi; Naikaku Kanbō, *Shinkō Shūkyō*.

9. Tōkei Sūri Kenkyū-jo.

10. Suetsuna, p. 183.

11. Kornhauser, pp. 14, 237.

12. Lane, *Life*, pp. 167–68; Almond and Verba, pp. 252 *et seq*.; Stouffer, p. 127.

13. Kornhauser, Part III on marginal social elements, esp. pp. 180–214.

14. Cantril, *Psychology*, p. 168.

15. Raymond Wolfinger *et al*. in Apter, *Ideology*, pp. 275–76; see Selznick, p. 297, for an equivalent example of attached leftist extremism.

16. Almond and Verba, p. 248.

17. Data from survey by Verba *et al*. One should note that not all secondary groups are voluntary, however. The figure is inflated by the frequently quasi-compulsory nature of such organizations as neighborhood associations, labor unions, and the PTA, which are often cited.

18. Tōkyō Daigaku Shakaigakka *et al*., pp. 61–62.

19. Naikaku Sōri, *Kenpō*.

20. Tōkyō Daigaku Shakaigakka *et al*., pp. 61–62.

21. Takahashi Naoko.

22. Tōkyō Daigaku Shakaigakka *et al*., pp. 63–64; Dator, "Demographic Data"; Suzuki Hiroshi, pp. 83–84.

23. Arendt, p. 353.

24. Takahashi Naoko.

25. *MS* survey of June 1965.

26. Suzuki Hiroshi, pp. 74–75.

27. *Ibid*., p. 75.

28. *Ibid*., p .73.

29. *Ibid*., pp. 74–75, 82 *et seq*.

30. Lederer, *State*, p. 30; Kornhauser, p. 14.

31. Tōkyō Daigaku Shakaigakka *et al*., p. 122; Kobayashi, p. 134.

32. Suzuki Hiroshi, p. 69; Takahashi Naoko.

33. Lane, *Life*, pp. 167–68.

34. Kornhauser, p. 108.

35. Lane, *Life*, pp. 149–55; Almond and Verba, pp. 159 *et seq.*
36. Nitta, pp. 46–48.
37. Togawa, *Kōmeitō.* Unfortunately, no controls were applied to these data.
38. Tōkyō Daigaku Shakaigakka *et al.*, p. 110.
39. Yamaguchi, pp. 116–19.
40. *Asahi Jānaru* Henshūbu, "Kōmeitō," p. 16; Verba *et al.*
41. Arendt, p. 315.
42. *SS*, 22.vi.66; 2,3.vii.67.
43. *SS*, 10.ix.67; 17,18.vii.67.
44. Tōkyō Daigaku Shakaigakka *et al.*, p. 84.
45. Adorno *et al.*; Kornhauser, p. 11.
46. Adorno *et al.*, p. 228.
47. Nihonjin no Kokuminsei.
48. Naikaku Sōri, unpub. data.
49. Naikaku Kanbō, *Shinkō Shūkyō*, pp. 43–49.
50. Nihonjin no Kokuminsei.
51. Adorno *et al.*, pp. 1, 228.
52. E.g., Nazism. See Hitler.
53. Coladarci, "Measurement," p. 138.
54. Eysenck, p. 149; Richard Christie, in Christie and Jahoda, pp. 129–33; Rogin, p. 240.
55. Landsberger and Saavedra, p. 216; Agger *et al.*, p. 505.
56. Muramatsu Tsuneo, pp. 127–28.
57. *Ibid.*, pp. 127–28.
58. *YS* survey of March 1967.
59. Dator, "Demographic Data."
60. Summarized in White, *Mass Movement, Militant Religion*, pp. 464–66; Nihonjin no Kokuminsei; Suzuki Hiroshi, p. 86; Yamaguchi, pp. 116–19.
61. Kornhauser, p. 108; Toch, p. 69; Lane, *Life*, pp. 163 *et seq.*; Almond and Verba, pp. 227–31.
62. *SS*, 24.ix.67.
63. Dator, "Demographic Data."
64. Kornhauser, p. 112.
65. Almond and Verba, ch. 4.
66. *Ibid.*, p. 94.
67. There are clinical suggestions that this is so: see Yamaguchi, pp. 116–19.
68. Nihonjin no Kokuminsei; Takahashi Naoko; Tōkyō Daigaku Shakaigakka *et al.*, p. 99.
69. Azumi, "Functions."
70. Nihonjin no Kokuminsei.
71. Tsurumi *et al.*, pp. 88, 94–95.
72. Naikaku Kanbō, *Shinkō Shūkyō*, pp. 83 *et seq.*
73. See Dator, "Demographic Data."
74. Cohn, *Pursuit*, pp. 90, 99 *et seq.*; Fromm, pp. 95–96; Lipset, p. 131; Lasswell, p. 374.
75. Parsons, *Essays*, pp. 135–36; Lederer, *State*, pp. 51–52; Fromm, pp. 208 *et seq.*; Hoffman, p. xxiii; Lipset, pp. 171–73.
76. *JT*, 19.v.63.
77. Takahashi Naoko.

78. *YS* survey of March 1966; Tōkyō Daigaku Shakaigakka *et al.*, p. 98.
79. *MS* survey of June 1965.
80. Takahashi Naoko; Suzuki Hiroshi, p. 86.
81. Azumi, "Functions," p. 9.
82. Tōkyō Daigaku Shakaigakka *et al.*, p. 111.
83. *Ibid.*
84. *MS* surveys of June 1965, May 1966, Sept. 1966; *YS* survey of March 1966; Asahi Jānaru Henshūbu, "Kōmeitō," p. 16.
85. *AS*, 9.iv.67.   86. Agger *et al.*, p. 483.
87. *MS* survey of May 1966.   88. *MS* survey of Sept. 1966.
89. *MS* survey of June 1965 and *YS* survey of March 1967.
90. Asahi Jānaru Henshūbu, "Kōmeitō," p. 16; *AS*, 1.i.67.
91. Cited in Ikado, "Josetsu," p. 206.
92. Dator, "Demographic Data."
93. Cantril, *Psychology*, pp. 225 *et seq.*; Bullock; Hoffmann, p. xiv.
94. Stouffer, pp. 89–90; Prothro and Grigg; Lipset, p. 94.
95. Lipset, p. 142; *MS* survey of June 1965.
96. Naikaku Sōri, unpub. data.
97. *Ibid.*; *MS* survey of June 1965; Takahashi Naoko; Takase, "Daigaku," p. 28.
98. Naikaku Sōri, unpub. data.
99. Takahashi Naoko.
100. Nihonjin no Kokuminsei; a similar pattern is visible in NHK Hōsō Seron Chōsa-sho, pp. 40–41.
101. Kobayashi, p. 143.   102. *Ibid.*, p. 144.
103. Naikaku Sōri, unpub. data.   104. Nihonjin no Kokuminsei.
105. Naikaku Sōri, unpub. data.   106. *Ibid.*
107. *Ibid.*   108. Kobayashi, p. 137.
109. Murakami, *Sōkagakkai*, p. 224; Shinohara, "Gimon," p. 68.
110. Tōkyō Daigaku Shakaigakka *et al.*, p. 81.
111. Naikaku Kanbō, *Shinkō Shūkyō*, pp. 61–62.
112. Dator, "Demographic Data."
113. Selznick, p. 291.
114. Almond and Verba, pp. 52, 134–35; Lane, *Life*, p. 168; Ishigami, pp. 166–70; Yokogoshi, p. 33; *AS*, 3.iv.67; Naikaku Kanbō, *Mukanshin*, and *Mukanshin no Jittai*, pp. 65 *et seq.*; Verba *et al.*
115. Naikaku Sōri, unpub. data.
116. *Ibid.*; Verba *et al.*
117. Nihonjin no Kokuminsei; Verba *et al.*
118. *YS* survey of March 1967; Verba *et al.*
119. They appear more interested than other religious groups, too: see Dator, "Demographic Data."
120. Stouffer, p. 59.
121. Takahashi Naoko.
122. Interview with Sasaki Toshiyuki, Sōkagakkai Public Relations Bureau.
123. Tōkyō Daigaku Shakaigakka *et al.*, p. 122.
124. Nihonjin no Kokuminsei.
125. *YS* survey of March 1967 and *MS* survey of June 1965.

126. *YS* survey of March 1966.
127. Matsushita, p. 41.
128. "Voting Characteristics Revealed in Pre-Election Opinion Poll—House of Councillors Elections, July 1965," pp. 8–9.
129. Azumi, "Functions," p. 3.

CHAPTER 10

1. Kornhauser, p. 47.   2. Rogin, pp. 268, 282; Toch, p. 5.
3. Kornhauser, p. 47.   4. Ikeda, *Seiji to Shūkyō*, p. 199.
5. Ikeda, *Ningen Kakumei*, Vol. 1, p. 14.
6. Murakami, "Tenkanki," p. 54.
7. Kornhauser, ch. 3.
8. *Ibid.*, p. 84.
9. Although there is no structural ideal to match the Nazi concept of *Gleichschaltung*. See Franz Neumann, pp. 51 *et seq.*, 400 *et seq.*
10. Kornhauser, pp. 76 *et seq.*
11. Arendt, p. 367; Sigmund Neumann, pp. 404–5.
12. *SS*, 17.ix.67; *WT*, 21.iv.66.   13. *SS*, 29.ix.67.
14. Kornhauser, ch. 2.   15. *Ibid.*, p. 40.
16. *Ibid.*   17. *Ibid.*, p. 41.
18. Interview with Joseph Spae, Oriens Institute, Tokyo; for similar views see McFarland, *Rush Hour*, pp. 84–87; and Takase, "To-chiji Sen," p. 12.
19. Interview with Nishihira Shigeki, Tōkei Sūri Kenkyū-jo, Tokyo.
20. Kornhauser, p. 60.
21. *Ibid.*, p. 59.
22. Yui; *SSS*, all issues in Aug. 1967.
23. *DBR*, No. 194, July 1967, pp. 26 *et seq.*
24. Fromm, p. 171.
25. Especially to Lutheranism and Calvinism. It is also characteristic of many more ambiguously religio-ethical movements, e.g. Moral Rearmament. (See Cantril, *Psychology*, p. 168; Braden, *Spirits* and *These Also*; Fromm, p. 91.) Politically, the notion that one was damned if he strayed from adherence to a single objective truth was one of the primary tenets of the "totalitarian democracy" and "political messianism" of the eighteenth and nineteenth centuries (Talmon, *Messianism*, p. 164, and *Origins*), and culminated in the Bolshevist and fascist ideologies of the twentieth century.
26. Ikeda, *Kōgi*, p. 230.
27. *Ibid.*, pp. 114–15.
28. On individual goals see any issue of the *Seikyō Shimbun*; on political goals see Kōmeitō Kikanshi-kyoku, *Shiawase*.
29. *SS*, 27.vi.67.
30. "Stamping in Nichiren's Footsteps," p. 1255.
31. Sōkagakkai Kyōgaku-bu, 1961 ed., p. 347; 1967 ed., p. 334.
32. *WT*, 11.xii.65.   33. Clark, p. 15.
34. Sakamoto, "Shūkyō," p. 63.   35. *SS*, 17.i.67.
36. See, for example, Bullock, pp. 33 *et seq.*
37. Cantril, *Psychology*, pp. 39–40.
38. Hofstadter.
39. Ikeda in *KS*, 8.i.67.

40. *SS*, 12.ix.67. For the special significance of the term *amaeru* see Lifton and Doi.
41. Sōkagakkai, *Nichiren Shōshū Sōkagakkai.*
42. Adorno *et al.*, p. 228.
43. Ikeda, *Shidō Memo*, section on *Josei-zō.*
44. For the ideological epitome see Hitler; Muramatsu Takeshi, p. 62.
45. Fromm, pp. 38–39, 89, 111.
46. Ikeda, *Shidō Memo*, pp. 26, 72.
47. *Ibid.*, ch. 1; Ikeda, *Kōgi*, pp. 376–79; *WT*, 12.iii.66; *SN*, 13.x.64.
48. Takase, "Daihyō," pp. 54–55.
49. *WT*, 2.ix.65.
50. The same surmise is made by Dator in his "Interpretation," p. 225.
51. Interview with Akiya Einosuke, Vice President, Sōkagakkai.
52. McClosky, p. 365.
53. Togawa, *Kōmeitō*, p. 156.
54. Ikeda, *Kōgi*, pp. 171, 185–93, 492–93.
55. *WT*, 12.v.66; see also Ikeda, *Kōgi*, p. 758.
56. Lipset, pp. 1–2; Miyata, pp. 149–50; Almond and Verba, pp. 85–86, 237–38; Dator, "Interpretations," p. 240.
57. Dator, "Interpretations," p. 239.
58. Ikeda, *Seiji to Shūkyō*, pp. 153, 162; interviews with Hōjō Hiroshi and Akiya Einosuke, Vice Presidents, Sōkagakkai.
59. Ikeda, *Kōgi*, p. 905.
60. *Ibid.*, pp. 516–18, 891; *SS*, 3.x.67.
61. Kasahara, *Kakumei no Shūkyō*, pp. 259–63.
62. Sōkagakkai Overseas Bureau, No. 8, p. 9.
63. Babbie, pp. 101 *et seq.*; *CN*, 26.iii.63.
64. *CN*, 26.iii.63; Murakami, p. 54.
65. Lenski, p. 341.
66. Sōkagakkai Kyōgaku-bu; Ikeda, *Kōgi*; Brannen, "False Religions," p. 250.
67. Interview with Sasaki Toshiyuki, Sōkagakkai Public Relations Bureau; *AS*, 18.ii.67.
68. Takeiri, p. 19.
69. *AS*, 3.ii.67.
70. *Ibid.*
71. Interview with Sasaki Toshiyuki, Sōkagakkai Public Relations Bureau.
72. *JT International Edition*, 1.vi.68; Tsurumi *et al.*, p. 226.
73. Clark, p. 17; Cantril, *Psychology*, p. 248; Hoffmann, pp. 10, 162 *et seq.*
74. Oguchi, p. 37.
75. *WT*, 7.v.66.
76. Arendt, p. 307; Pulzer, pp. 32–33. The term "the state as the state" is Engels', quoted and explained in Lenin, pp. 15–20.
77. Pulzer, pp. 32–33; Bullock, p. 41; Hoffmann, pp. 213, 381; Lenin, pp. 15–20.
78. Kōmeitō press release, 11.iv.68.
79. *SS*, 2.vii.67.
80. Mao Tse-tung, "Mao-tun" and "Chuan-cheng"; Nolte, p. 7.
81. Ikeda, *Seiji to Shūkyō*, pp. 148–49.

82. *Ibid.*, pp. 97–98; Ikeda, *Shidō Memo*, p. 232.
83. Interview with Tada Shōgo, General Administrator, Sōkagakkai.
84. Ikeda, *Seiji to Shūkyō*, pp. 101–2.
85. *KS*, 1.i.67.
86. Ikeda, *Seiji to Shūkyō*, pp. 101–2.
87. *AS*, 14.ii.67.
88. *SS*, 12.viii.67.
89. Quoted in Takase, *Kōmeitō*, p. 218.
90. Interview with Akiya Einosuke, Vice President, Sōkagakkai.
91. Dahl, ch. 3, esp. p. 84.
92. Gilson, ed., pp. 70 *et seq.*
93. Maritain, chs. 4, 5, 6.
94. Interview with Joseph Spae, Oriens Institute, Tokyo.
95. Quoted in Saki and Oguchi, p. 60.
96. DeGrazia, pp. 171 *et seq.*; Fromm, ch. 5, Parts 1, 3; Adorno *et al.*, p. 228.
97. Saki, "Hihan," p. 199; "A New Face Called Sōka Gakkai Raises Old Problems in Modern Japan," p. 18; *NYW-T & S*, 30.i.65.
98. *SS*, 29.iv.67; 18.vi.67; 3.vii.67.   99. *Ibid.*, 8.vii.67.
100. *Ibid.*, 29.iv.67.   101. Miyata, p. 158.
102. Interview with Akiya Einosuke, Vice President, Sōkagakkai.
103. *SS*, 3.vii.67.
104. Quoted in Eliot, p. 425. For full text see Hori Nichiryō, p. 17; French translation by Renondeau, "Traité," p. 123.
105. Tanaka Jigohei, pp. 30–31.
106. Ikeda, *Ningen Kakumei*, Vol. 2, p. 194.
107. Ikeda in *KS*, 8.i.67.
108. Tsuji Takehisa, p. 55.
109. Interview with Akiya Einosuke, Vice President, Sōkagakkai; for a full presentation of the logic that absolutism leads to elimination see Dator, "Interpretation."
110. Interviews with Akiya Einosuke, Vice President, and Tada Shōgo, General Administrator, Sōkagakkai.
111. Sōkagakkai, *Sōka Gakkai*, p. 72.
112. "Religion in Japan in 1961," p. 35.
113. Cohn, *Pursuit*, pp. 188, 262 *et seq.*; Lanternari, ch. 6.
114. Bullock, p. 71; Nolte, p. 70; Hoffmann, pp. 134–35.
115. Quoted in Eliot, p. 277. Full text in Hori Nichiryō, p. 17; French translation by Renondeau, "Traité," p. 123.
116. Takase, *Dai San Bummei*, p. 170.
117. Mombushō, "Soshiki Ichiran-hyō," pp. 47–56.
118. One incident recorded in *YS*, 6.vii.56; Mombushō, "Sōkagakkai ni tsuite." Others from classified sources.
119. Woodard.
120. Nitta, pp. 26 *et seq.* A more recent incident suggests that the now-independent Kōmeitō is equally capable of violating the spirit, if not the letter, of the law. In late 1969 author Fujiwara Hirotatsu and his publisher came under Kōmeitō and Gakkai pressure to prevent the publication of Fujiwara's *Sōkagakkai wo Kiru*, a book sharply critical of the Gakkai. In

the opinion of Murata Kiyoaki, a longtime student of the Gakkai, the book is not an "academic analysis" but a sensationalistic polemic based on past events such as the one cited here; Murata considers the Gakkai response understandable if not justifiable. But the fact remains, despite Kōmeitō apologies and the resignation of one party figure, that the party made an official and extralegal attempt to repress free expression. See *AS*, 6.i.70; *JT Weekly*, 7.ii.70; Hirotatsu Fujiwara, "Sōkagakkai Unmasked," *Far Eastern Economic Review*, 12.ii.70, p. 19.

121. Takase, *Kōmeitō*, p. 110; Mombushō, "Ihan Jirei"; "Japan's New Church Militant," p. 418; Saki and Oguchi, p. 217.

122. Yui, p. 31.

123. Saki and Oguchi, p. 218.

124. Sōkagakkai Overseas Bureau, No. 5, p. 13.

125. *WT*, 2.ix.65.

126. Saki, "Honshitsu," p. 38.

127. Takase, *Kōmeitō*, p. 139.

128. Interview with Ikado Fujio, Religious Affairs Department, Ministry of Education.

CHAPTER 11

1. Almond and Verba, pp. 252–54.

2. *Ibid.*, pp. 204–5, 211.

3. *Ibid.*, p. 262.

4. *Ibid.*

5. Dollard *et al.*, pp. 8–9.

6. Parsons, *Essays*, p. 300.

7. Dollard *et al.*, pp. 8–9.

8. Almond and Verba, ch. 8, esp. pp. 197 *et seq.*

9. Hoffer, Part III; DeGrazia, pp. xv-xvi; Hoffmann, p. 401; Tanaka Tadao, p. 92.

10. For examples of alienated attachment see Raymond Wolfinger *et al.* in Apter, *Ideology*; Selznick, pp. 297 *et seq.* For a similar suggestion see Lane, *Life*, p. 27.

11. For examples of alienation without mass behavior see Prothro and Grigg, p. 276; McClosky, p. 361. Other writers go further, implying that unattachment is in fact not significant as either a causative or an explanatory factor in political behavior, particularly in mass political behavior. Cornelius and Tilly assert persuasively that persons with no social attachments will remain politically apathetic and inert in the face of attempts to mobilize them. These authors imply that mass movements (i.e., organizations of alienated persons bent upon or receptive to contravention of political and social rules and mores) are possible, but political behavior by mass men of the Kornhauser ideal type is not. If one accepts this argument one will pay special attention to the material on alienation and behavior presented in this book, and also to that on organizational influences. For if the argument is valid, organizations themselves (as patterns of social attachments) are an integral and absolutely essential part of mass political behavior per se. See Cornelius, Tilly, and Nie *et al.*

12. For a discussion of "ideal" and "actual" conditions and attributes see Levy, *Modernization*, pp. 26–30.

13. Adorno *et al.*, pp. 206–7.

14. Katz and Lazarsfeld, p. 96.

15. Lipset, pp. 91–92.

16. Dator, "Interpretation," pp. 208–9.
17. Levy, *Modernization*, p. 70.
18. Katz and Lazarsfeld, p. 48; Riesman, *Crowd*, pp. xxii–xxiii; Christie and Jahoda, p. 181. The quotation is from Lipset, pp. 91–92.
19. Compare this with Communist recruiting practices; see Almond, p. 167.
20. Katz and Lazarsfeld, pp. 31–32, 50–51, 69.
21. McClosky, p. 378; see also Almond, p. 103; Toch, p. 161.
22. Lenski, pp .181–82.
23. Suzuki Hiroshi, pp. 83–84.
24. For an example of such microcosmically focused loyalty in the German Wehrmacht see Shils and Janowitz, p. 368.
25. *Ibid.*; Naikaku Kanbō, *Shinkō Shūkyō*, p. 8.
26. Naikaku Kanbō, *Shinkō Shūkyō*, pp. 83 *et seq.*
27. Takase, *Ningen Fukkō*, pp. 116 *et seq.*
28. Nihonjin no Kokuminsei; Suzuki Hiroshi, pp. 73 *et seq.*
29. Naikaku Sōri, unpub. data.
30. Takahashi Naoko.
31. Mochizuki, p. 38.
32. "Voting Characteristics Revealed in Pre-Election Opinion Poll—House of Councillors Elections, July 1965," p. 10.
33. Sugita, p. 61.
34. Almond, pp. 169–70.
35. Suzuki Hiroshi, pp. 54–55; Takase, "Daigaku," p. 27.
36. *WT*, 11.i.66.
37. *SS*, 1.viii.67.
38. Ikado, "Josetsu," pp. 193–96; Miyata, p. 159; Ide, p. 17.
39. *SS*, 2.vii.67.
40. In fact, Ikeda has spoken out explicitly against envy of other persons. See *WT*, 28.vi.66.
41. *SS*, 29.iv.67.
42. Suzuki Hiroshi, p. 68; Takahashi Naoko; Shiobara, p. 49; Tsurumi *et al.*, p. 201; Naikaku Kanbō, *Shinkō Shūkyō*, pp. 56–57.
43. Shiobara, p. 49; Azumi, "Functions," p. 14; Naikaku Kanbō, *Shinkō Shūkyō*, pp. 56–57.
44. Takahashi Naoko.
45. Suzuki Hiroshi, p. 86.
46. Yanaihara, p. 17; *SSS*, all issues in Aug. 1967; Suzuki Hiroshi, p. 55; Shiobara, p. 49.
47. *JT International Edition*, 20.xi.65.
48. *SSS*, all issues in Aug. 1967.
49. Naikaku Sōri, unpub. data.
50. *Ibid.*
51. Takase, *Ningen Kakumei*, pp. 61–62.
52. For examples of "elections" see *SN*, 12.v.64 and *SS*, 1.v.67. However, an interview with Akiya Einosuke, Vice President, Sōkagakkai, showed that Gakkai leaders regard the Rules largely as "legalistic jargon" composed to satisfy the requirements of law. As a large organization and especially as a religious group, the Gakkai seems more democratic than the Rules would suggest.

53. Ikeda, "Gimon ni Kotaeru," p. 72.

54. See, for example, data in Azumi, "Social Basis."

55. Tatsuzō Suzuki, p. 22; Takahashi Naoko; Tsurumi *et al.*, p. 200; Ishida Ikuo, "Shakubuku," pp. 85–86; Murakami, *Sōkagakkai*, pp. 28–29.

56. Naikaku Kanbō, *Shinkō Shūkyō*, p. 90.

57. *Ibid.*, pp. 99–100.

58. *Ibid.*, p. 111.

59. Ikeda, *Ningen Kakumei*, Vol. 2, p. 302.

60. Ozawa, p. 169; Naikaku Kanbō, *Shinkō Shūkyō*, p. 8. Data collected by Verba *et al.* shows the same pattern: only 30 per cent of the Gakkai members had ever held office, assisted at meetings, or otherwise been positively active.

61. Ozawa, p. 169.

62. Suzuki Hiroshi, p. 73.

63. *SS*, 17,31.vii.67; Azumi, "Functions," p. 5, Note 1.

64. Ishida Ikuo, "Shakubuku," p. 86.

65. Hayashi, *Zusetsu*, p. 146; Dator, "Demographic Data."

66. Ishida Ikuo, *Sōkagakkai*, pp. 25–26. The Sōkagakkai is not alone in this problem: see Howe and Coser, pp. 529, 534.

67. See above, chapter 10, and Nihonjin no Kokuminsei. The proportion of believers who support the Kōmeitō, as indicated by Verba *et al.*, is 67.6 per cent. It is assumed that more complete politicization of the Gakkai membership rather than sampling differences accounts for the increase.

68. *MS* survey of June 1965; "Voting Characteristics Revealed in Pre-Election Opinion Poll—House of Councillors Elections, July 1965," pp. 1–2, 4.

69. *YS* survey of March 1967; Nishihira, "Minobe no Shiji-sō," pp. 87–88.

70. "Voting Characteristics Revealed in Pre-Election Opinion Poll—House of Councillors Elections, July 1965," pp. 6–7.

71. *YS* survey of March 1967; *MS* survey of June 1965.

72. Tanaka Kunio, Part III, esp. chs. 5, 6.

73. Suzuki Hiroshi, pp. 83–84.

74. Nihonjin no Kokuminsei; see esp. question on Premier's pilgrimage to Ise.

75. Suzuki Hiroshi, p. 76.

76. Tsurumi *et al.*, pp. 79–81, 89, 96.

77. Takahashi Naoko.

78. *YS* survey of March 1967.

79. A condition consistent with the observations of Raymond Wolfinger *et al.* in Apter, *Ideology*, and of Selznick, pp. 297 *et seq.*

CHAPTER 12

1. McFarland, "Religions," p. 62.   2. Muramatsu Takeshi, p. 48.

3. Yamaguchi, pp. 130–31.   4. Takase, *Kōmeitō*, p. 159.

5. Saki, "Honshitsu," p. 36, and "Hihan," p. 199; Miyamori, p. 170.

6. Takase, *Kōmeitō*, pp. 159–61.   7. Lederer, *Japan*, p. xi.

8. *MS*, 9.iii.63.   9. Murakami, "Seinen," p. 48.

10. Bloom, p. 63.   11. Takase, *Ningen Fukkō*, p. 142.

12. Ishida Ikuo, *Sōkagakkai*, p. 142.   13. Yui, p. 2.

14. *SS*, 28.iv.67.

15. Ikeda, *Ningen Kakumei*, Vol. 3, pp. 123 *et seq.*

16. Dator, "Demographic Data."
17. Ikeda, *Ningen Kakumei*, Vol. 3, pp. 123 *et seq.*; see also ch. 9 above.
18. Lenski. 19. *Ibid.*, pp. 20 *et seq.*
20. *Ibid.*, p. 328. 21. Olson, pp. 19, 23.
22. Aberle, pp. 210–13. 23. Ike, "Experiment," p. 17.
24. "Kōmeitō: Iinchō Kōtaigeki to kore kara no Dekata," p. 17.
25. Ike, "Experiment," p. 17.
26. The study showed that the vertically mobile proportion of the non-farm population in six industrially advanced nations in the mid-1950's was: United States, 30 per cent; West Germany, 31 per cent; Sweden, 29 per cent; Japan, 27 per cent; France, 27 per cent; Switzerland, 23 per cent. The proportion of upward-mobile persons (sons who did not follow in their fathers' footsteps as manual laborers) in the nonfarming populations of nine industrial nations varied between 26 and 44 per cent, and the proportion of downward-mobile persons (sons who became manual laborers where their fathers had not been such) varied from 13 to 38 per cent. The proportions for Japan were 33 per cent and 21 per cent respectively. Lipset and Bendix, pp. 17, 21, 25.
27. Staley and Morse, pp. 18–20.
28. *Ibid.*, p. 17.
29. *Ibid.*, pp. 18–21.
30. *Ibid.*, p. 22; Tsuji Takehisa, p. 53.
31. Olson, p. 13.
32. NHK Sōgō Hōsō Bunka Kenkyū-jo, pp. 5–7; Watanuki, "Change," pp. 4–5.
33. NHK Sōgō Hōsō Bunka Kenkyū-jo, p. 30.
34. These groups are not immune to the Kōmeitō's political appeal. One might note the seizure in all four prefectures in rural Shikoku of 20 per cent of the vote in the 1968 Upper House election. In addition, from five urban prefectures with a claimed Sōkagakkai membership of 1.3 million the Kōmeitō vote in the 1968 Upper House election was 2.6 million. What urban elements provided the difference is unknown, but the indication is that the Kōmeitō is successfully broadening and secularizing its appeal. See *AS*, 17.vii.68.
35. Maruyama Masao, *Thought and Behaviour*, p. 151.
36. *Ibid.*, p. 153.
37. Interview with Nagai Michio, Tokyo Institute of Technology; Bloom, p. 70.
38. Ishida Ikuo, *Sōkagakkai*, pp. 168–69.
39. *SS*, 20.xi.67; *KS*, 1.i.67.
40. Saki and Oguchi, pp. 142–43.
41. Sōkagakkai Overseas Bureau, No. 5, p. 12.
42. Ikeda, *Kōgi*, p. 152, *Ningen Kakumei*, Vol. 1, p. 3.
43. *SS*, 8.vii.67; Ikeda, *Shidō Memo*, pp. 214–15.
44. Nihonjin no Kokuminsei.
45. Kobayashi, p. 140.
46. *YS* survey of March 1966; a parallel pattern is visible in NHK Hōsō Seron Chōsa-sho, pp. 54–55.
47. Morris, *Nationalism*, p. 414; Kornhauser, pp. 124 *et seq.*
48. Kasahara, *Seiji to Shūkyō*, pp. 219–20; *CN*, 26.iii.63.

49. *CN*, 26.iii.63; interview with Joseph Spae, Oriens Institute, Tokyo.

50. In two Tokyo polls by the *Asahi Shimbun* in April 1967 and March 1968 the percentage of respondents professing dislike for the Kōmeitō fell from 33.9 to 18.6 per cent (see esp. Okabe, p. 49). The similar percentage in a national survey of late 1966 was already down to 14.1 per cent (Verba *et al.*).

51. *AS*, 17.vii.68.

52. Takase, "Ikeda," pp. 195–96.

53. Miyamori, p. 170; Saki, "Hihan," p. 199.

54. "Kōmeitō 'Shirōto' Giindan Genkōroku," pp. 16–17.

55. Eckstein.

56. Lane, *Life*, p. 343.

57. *Ibid.*

58. Ike, "Experiment," p. 24; Naikaku Sōri, unpub. data.

59. William Lockwood, in Ward and Rustow, p. 144.

60. Murakami Shigeyoshi, in Takahashi Kazumi, p. 80; Morris, *Nationalism*, pp. 141–42.

61. Bloom, p. 64; "Kōmeitō ni Idomu to Iu Nishi Honganji no Ito," pp. 16–17, 21; *JT International Edition*, 13.xi.65; *SJ*, No. 14, Jan. 1967, p. 12.

62. *AS*, 5.vii.67.

63. *AS*, 24,25.ii.67; "Kōmeitō ni Idomu to Iu Nishi Honganji no Ito," p. 21.

64. Spae, *Japan in Search of Her Soul*.

65. "Kōmeitō ni Idomu to Iu Nishi Honganji no Ito," p. 17.

66. *JT International Edition*, 7.ix.68.

POSSIBILITIES AND PROBLEMS

1. Olson, p. 22.

2. Interview with Ikado Fujio, Religious Affairs Department, Ministry of Education.

3. Niebuhr; Johnson, p. 88; Pfautz, p. 121; Bryan R. Wilson, p. 3.

4. Lenski, p. 328.

5. Nakaba, "Shichinen," p. 117.

6. Yui; *SSS*, all issues in autumn 1967, "Kokuhaku" column.

7. *SS*, 4.viii.67.   8. *WT*, 8.v.65.

9. *WT*, 21.v.66.   10. Ikeda, *Shidō Memo*, p. 132.

11. Kasahara, *Seiji to Shūkyō*, pp. 178–79, 181 *et seq.*

12. *Ibid.*, pp. 181 *et seq.*; *SS*, 31.vii.67; Saki and Oguchi, p. 122.

13. *WT*, 25.xii.65; 12.ii.66.

14. Saki, "Seinen Shōkō," pp. 124–25.

15. *SSS*, 20.ix.67.

16. Niebuhr; Pfautz, p. 121; Johnson, p. 88; Bryan R. Wilson, p. 3.

17. Togawa, *Kōmeitō*, p. 244; Sōkagakkai Kyōgaku-bu, 1967 ed., pp. 352, 357; Shiobara, p. 57.

18. Nakaba, "Shichinen," 1,15.x.67; 1.xi.67.

19. Hori Yoshio, p. 51; "To-Fuku-chiji Hiketsugeki no Butai-ura," p. 9.

20. *CN*, 9.v.63; interview with Ikado Fujio, Religious Affairs Department, Ministry of Education; conversation with John K. C. Oh, Marquette University.

Glossary

Chiku. District. Third level on the vertical line; made up of anywhere from five to ten han, or twenty-five to a hundred kumi.

-chō. -leader, -chief.

Chūdō seiji. Middle-of-the-road politics.

Daimoku. Sacred formula of Nichiren Shōshū that brings divine blessings when chanted.

Danchi. High-rise housing development.

Genkaisetsu. Limit argument; the assertion that Sōkagakkai growth has already peaked.

Genze riyaku. Divine benefit obtained in this life.

Gohonzon. Object of worship in Nichiren Shōshū; mandala symbolizing the eternal Buddha.

Gongyō. Worship service; prayer before the gohonzon.

Goriyaku. Divine benefit, blessing.

Han. Group. Second level on the vertical line; made up of anywhere from five to ten kumi.

Honbu. Headquarters. Sixth level on the vertical line; made up of several sō-shibu.

Ichinen-sanzen. "Three thousand worlds in a single moment": the mutual immanence of every thing and of every point in time.

Jōbutsu. Enlightenment.

Kachiron. Makiguchi Tsunesaburō's Theory of Value; also the title of a book by Makiguchi.

Kaidan. High sanctuary, symbol of kōsen-rufu of Japan.

Kōfuku (-ron). (Theory of) happiness.

Kōsen-rufu. Conversion of the world to Nichiren Shōshū.

Kudoku (-ron). (Theory of) divine reward.

Kumi. Unit. First level on the vertical line; may consist of up to ten families (about twenty adults).

Mappō. Latter Day of the Law; i.e., the present, degenerate era.

Ningen kakumei. Human revolution, enlightenment; also the title of a book by Ikeda Daisaku.

Obutsu-myōgō. Fusion of Buddhism and politics.

Pachinko. A Japanese form of pinball.

Riyaku. Benefit, gain.

Sensei. Literally, teacher. A form of respectful address.

Shae no san'oku. "The Three Hundred Million People of Shae." The criterion for declaring that kōsen-rufu of an area has been achieved—i.e., that one-third of its inhabitants have been converted.

Shakubuku. Literally, "to break and flatten"; propagation of Nichiren Shōshū.

Shibu. Chapter. Fourth level on the vertical line; made up of anywhere from five to ten chiku, or 125 to 1,000 kumi.

Shōhondō. Grand Main Hall at the Taisekiji.

Shōju. Mild-mannered propagation.

Sōgō-honbu. Joint headquarters. Seventh level on the vertical line; made up of several honbu.

Sō-shibu. General chapter. Fifth level on the vertical line; made up of several shibu.

Taisekiji. Head temple of Nichiren Shōshū.

Tako-tsubo (konjō). Octopus-pot (mentality); an emotionally fulfilling small group (and the need for one).

Zadankai. Irregularly held discussion meeting on the kumi, han, or chiku level of the vertical line.

BIBLIOGRAPHY

Bibliography

Aberle, David. "A Note on Relative Deprivation Theory as Applied to Millenarian and Other Cult Movements," *Comparative Studies in Society and History*, Supplement 2 (1962), p. 209.

Adorno, T. W., *et al.* The Authoritarian Personality. New York, 1950.

Agger, Robert, *et al.* "Political Cynicism: Measurement and Meaning," *The Journal of Politics*, XXIII (1961), 477.

Akiyama Tomiya. (Chief, Sōkagakkai Overseas Bureau.) Memos to author. May 20, 1968; April 11, 1970.

Almond, Gabriel. The Appeals of Communism. Paperback ed. Princeton, N.J., 1965.

——, and G. Bingham Powell. Comparative Politics: A Developmental Approach. Boston, 1966.

——, and Sidney Verba. The Civic Culture. Boston, 1965.

Anesaki, Masaharu. History of Japanese Religion. London, 1930.

——. Nichiren the Buddhist Prophet. Cambridge, Mass., 1916.

——. Religious Life of the Japanese People. Tokyo, 1961.

Aochi Shin. "Tōdai Sōkagakkai-in no Ishiki," *Gendai no Me*, Apr. 1967, p. 110.

Apter, David. Ideology and Discontent. Glencoe, Ill., 1964.

——. The Politics of Modernization. Chicago, 1965.

Arendt, Hannah. The Origins of Totalitarianism. New York, 1951.

Aruga Hiroshi. "Kōmeitō no Ronri to Kinō," *Sekai*, No. 257 (Apr. 1967), p. 58.

Asahi Jānaru Henshūbu. "Dai San Seiryoku Shinshutsu no Imi," *Asahi Jānaru*, Feb. 12, 1967, p. 16.

——. "Kōmeitō no Taishitsu to Kinō," *Asahi Jānaru*, Mar. 5, 1967, p. 10.

Ashizu Uzuhiko. "Shūkyō to Seiji," *Shūkyō Kōron*, Sept. 1962, p. 11.

Azumi, Koya. "Functions of Sōka Gakkai Membership." Unpub. paper, Columbia University, 1967.

——. "Social Basis of a New Religious Party: The Kōmeitō of Japan." Unpub. paper delivered at meeting of American Sociological Association, August 1967.

Babbie, Earl. "The Third Civilization: An Examination of Sōka Gakkai," *Review of Religious Research*, Winter 1966, p. 101.

Banfield, Edward. The Moral Basis of a Backward Society. Glencoe, Ill., 1958.

Basabe, Fernando M. Japanese Youth Confronts Religion. Tokyo, 1967.

Bell, Daniel. The End of Ideology. Glencoe, Ill., 1960.

———. "The Theory of Mass Society, a Critique," *Commentary*, XXII (1956), 75.

Bellah, Robert. "Religious Aspects of Modernization in Turkey and Japan," *The American Journal of Sociology*, LXIV (1958), 1.

———. "The Sociological Study of Religion." Unpub. paper. N.d.

———. Tokugawa Religion. Glencoe, Ill., 1957.

———, ed. Religion and Progress in Modern Asia. New York, 1965.

Blalock, Hubert M., Jr. Causal Inferences in Nonexperimental Research. Chapel Hill, N.C., 1964.

Bloom, Alfred. "Observations in the Study of Contemporary Nichiren Buddhism," *Contemporary Religions in Japan*, VI (1965), 58.

Boulding, Kenneth. Conflict and Defense. New York, 1962.

Braden, Charles S. Spirits in Rebellion. Dallas, Tex., 1963.

———. These Also Believe. New York, 1949.

Brannen, Noah. "False Religions, Forced Conversions, Iconoclasm," *Contemporary Religions in Japan*, V (1964), 232.

———. "Sōka Gakkai's Theory of Value," *ibid.*, p. 143.

———. "The Teaching of Sōka Gakkai," *ibid.*, III (1962), 247.

———. "A Visit to the Sōka Gakkai Headquarters," *ibid.*, Mar. 1961, p. 55.

———. "A Visit to Taisekiji, Head Temple of Sōka Gakkai," *ibid.*, June 1961, p. 13.

Brown, Delmer. Nationalism in Japan. Berkeley, Calif., 1955.

Bullock, Alan. Hitler, A Study in Tyranny. New York, 1964.

Bunce, William K. Religions in Japan. Rutland, Vt., 1955.

Byas, Hugh. Government by Assassination. New York, 1942.

Cantril, Hadley. The Politics of Despair. New York, 1958.

———. The Psychology of Social Movements. New York, 1941.

Cartwright, Dorwin. "Influence, Leadership, Control," in James March, ed., *Handbook of Organizations* (Chicago, 1965).

"Characteristics of the Upper House Election," *Japan Socialist Review*, July 15, 1962, p. 6.

Christie, Richard, and Marie Jahoda. Studies in the Scope and Method of *The Authoritarian Personality*. Glencoe, Ill., 1954.

Clark, Elmer T. The Small Sects in America. New York, 1949.

Cohn, Norman. "Medieval Millenarism: Its Bearing on the Comparative Study of Millenarian Movements," *Comparative Studies in Society and History*, Supplement 2 (1962), p. 31.

———. The Pursuit of the Millennium. Fairlawn, N.J., 1957.

Coladarci, Arthur. "The Measurement of Authoritarianism in Japanese Education," *California Journal of Educational Research*, X (1959), 137.

———. "The Professional Attitudes of Japanese Teachers," *Journal of Educational Research*, LII (1959), 323.

"Comprehensive Survey: Kōmeitō," *Shōri*, March 1968. Tr. Universal Information Service, Tokyo, Apr. 6, 1968.

Cornelius, Wayne. "The Political Sociology of Cityward Migration in Latin America: Toward Empirical Theory," in Francine Rabinovitz and Felicity Trueblood, eds., *Latin American Urban Annual*, Vol. I (Beverly Hills, Calif., forthcoming).

Dahl, Robert. A Preface to Democratic Theory. Chicago, 1963.

Dahrendorf, Ralf. Class and Class Conflict in Industrial Society. Stanford, 1959.

Dator, James. "Demographic and Attitudinal Data on Sōkagakkai Members." Unpub. paper prepared for presentation at annual convention of Association for Asian Studies, March 1968.

———. "The 'Protestant Ethic' in Japan," *The Journal of Developing Areas*, No. 1 (Oct. 1966), p. 23.

———. "The Sōka Gakkai: A Socio-Political Interpretation," *Contemporary Religions in Japan*, VI (1965), 205.

———. Sōka Gakkai, Builders of the Third Civilization. Seattle, Wash., 1968.

———. "The Sōka Gakkai in Japanese Politics," *A Journal of Church and State*, IX (1967), 211.

———. "Sōkagakkai no Seiji Undō," *Shisō no Kagaku*, No. 42 (Sept. 1965), p. 73.

DeGrazia, Sebastian. The Political Community. Chicago, 1948.

Doi, L. Takeo. "'Amae': A Key Concept for Understanding Japanese Personality Structure," in Robert Smith and Richard Beardsley, eds., *Japanese Culture* (Chicago, 1962).

Dollard, John, *et al.* Frustration and Aggression. New Haven, Conn., 1939.

Dore, Ronald P. City Life in Japan. Berkeley, Calif., 1958.

Durkheim, Emile. Suicide. Glencoe, Ill., 1951.

Duverger, Maurice. Political Parties. Tr. Barbara and Robert North. New York, 1963.

Easton, David. A Framework for Political Analysis. Englewood Cliffs, N.J., 1965.

Ebenstein, William. The Nazi State. New York, 1943.

Eckstein, Harry. Division and Cohesion in Democracy. Princeton, N.J., 1966.

———, and David Apter. Comparative Politics: A Reader. New York, 1963.

Eliot, Charles. Japanese Buddhism. New York, 1959.

Etzioni, Amitai. Modern Organizations. Englewood Cliffs, N.J., 1964.

———. "Organizational Control Structure," in James March, ed., *Handbook of Organizations* (Chicago, 1965).

Eysenck, Hans. The Psychology of Politics. London, 1954.

Flagler, J. F. "A Chanting in Japan," *The New Yorker*, Nov. 26, 1966, p. 137.

Fromm, Erich. Escape from Freedom. New York, 1961.

Fujimaki Hajime. "Sōkagakkai wa doko made Nobiru ka—Marukusushugi to Nichirenshugi," *Shūkyō Kōron*, May 1963, p. 37.

Fukatsu Eiichi. "Kōmeitō," *Asahi Jānaru*, May 1965, p. 35.

Gerson, Walter. "Alienation in Mass Society: Some Causes and Responses," *Sociology and Social Research*, XLIX (1965), 143.

Gerth, Hans. "The Nazi Party: Its Leadership and Composition," in Robert Merton *et al.*, eds., *Reader in Bureaucracy* (Glencoe, Ill., 1952).

Gilson, Etienne, ed. The Church Speaks to the Modern World. New York, 1954.

Gouldner, Alvin W. "Reciprocity and Autonomy in Functional Theory," in Llewellyn Gross, ed., *Symposium on Sociological Theory* (New York, 1959).

Gresser, Julian. "Kōmeitō: An Assessment of Its Political Orientation and Future Course." Unpub. paper, Harvard University, 1966.

Hamada Hon'yu. "Sōkagakkai ni yoru Taisekiji Kyōdan (Nichiren Shōshū) no Bokkō," *Shūkyō Kōron*, Sept. 1962, p. 18.

Hayashi Chikio. Nihon no Howaito Karā. Tokyo, 1964.

———. Zusetsu: Nihonjin no Kokuminsei. Tokyo, 1965.

Heberle, Rudolf. Social Movements. New York, 1951.

Hesselgrave, David J. A Propagation Profile of the Sōka Gakkai. Unpub. Ph.D. dissertation, University of Minnesota, 1965.

Hitler, Adolf. Mein Kampf. Ed. John Chamberlain. New York, 1939.

Hobsbawm, E. J. Primitive Rebels. New York, 1965.

Hoffer, Eric. The True Believer. New York, 1966.

Hoffmann, Stanley. Le Mouvement Poujade. Paris, 1956.

Hofstadter, Richard. The Paranoid Style in American Politics. New York, 1966.

Hori Nichiryō, ed. Nichiren Daishōnin Gosho Zenshū. 5th ed. Tokyo, 1961.

Hori Yoshio. "Kōmeitō no kore kara," *Ekonomisuto*, Mar. 7, 1967, p. 50.

Horkheimer, Max. Eclipse of Reason. New York, 1947.

Howe, Irving, and Lewis Coser. The American Communist Party. Boston, 1957.

Hyman, Herbert. Political Socialization. Glencoe, Ill., 1959.

Ichikawa Hakugen. "Nihon no Seijiteki Shūkyō," *Jiyū*, May 1963, p. 10.

Ide Yoshinori. "Seiji to Shūkyō no Issen ni Mondai," *Asahi Jānaru*, Mar. 5, 1967, p. 17.

Ienaga, Saburō. "The Japanese and Religion," *Contemporary Religions in Japan*, Dec. 1960, p. 1.

Iisaka Yoshiaki. "Shinkō Shūkyō no Seijiteki Yashin wo Megutte," *Nippon*, May 1966, p. 54.

Ikado Fujio. "Kindai Shakai ni okeru Kirisutosha no Taido," *Kirisutokyō Shigaku*, No. 10 (Sept. 1960), p. 29.

———. "Kyōdan Soshiki Ron Josetsu," *Tōyō Bunka Kenkyū-jo Kiyō*, XXXIV (1964), 109.

———. "Shinkō Shūkyō no Dōkō to Kadai," *Jiyū*, July 1964, p. 128.

Ike, Nobutaka. "An Experiment in Political Forecasting: Japan, 1965–75." Unpub. paper, Stanford University, 1966.

———. "Japan, Twenty Years After Surrender," *Asian Survey*, VI (1966), 18.

———. Japanese Politics. New York, 1957.

Ikeda Daisaku. Ikeda Kaichō Zenshū. Vol. I. Tokyo, 1967.
——. "Kōmeitō e no Gimon ni Kotaeru," *Jiyū*, No. 90 (May 1967), p. 68.
——. Ningen Kakumei. Vols. I–III. Tokyo, 1965–67.
——. Risshō Ankoku Ron Kōgi. Tokyo, 1966.
——. Seiji to Shūkyō. Tokyo, 1965.
——. Shidō Memo. Tokyo, 1966.
——. "Shūkyō to Seiji Rinen," *Chūō Kōron*, May 1963, p. 302.
Imazumi Isamu. "Sōkagakkai no Seijiteki Shinshutsu wo Kō Omou," *Shūkyō Kōron*, Sept.. 1962, p. 71.
Inoue Hayashi. "Shūkyō to Seiji," *Shūkyō Kōron*, Sept. 1962, p. 80.
Ishida Ikuo. "Shakubuku no Uchimaku," *Gendai no Me*, Sept. 1964, p. 85.
——. Sōkagakkai. Tokyo, 1965.
Ishida Takeshi. "Heiwa Kanjō no Shōrai," *Sekai*, No. 261 (Aug. 1967), p. 266.
——. "Yoron to Gaikō Seisaku," *Sekai*, No. 260 (July 1967), p. 36.
Ishigami Ryōhei. "Senkyo ni Arawareru Shimin no Seiji Ishiki," *Toshi Mondai*, Oct. 1953, p. 163.
Ishikawa Akihiro. " 'Kindaika' Ideorogii to Chūshō Kigyōsha no Ishiki," *Jimbun Gakuhō*, No. 54 (Mar. 1966), p. 87.
Isomura Eiichi. "Dai-toshi ni okeru Shimin to Senkyo," *Toshi Mondai*, Mar. 1955, p. 15.
——. "Toshi no Shakai Shūdan," *Toshi Mondai*, Oct. 1953, p. 35.

Jacob, Philip E., and James V. Toscano. The Integration of Political Communities. Philadelphia, 1964.
"Japan's New Church Militant," *Japan Quarterly*, Oct. 12, 1957, p. 418.
Jichishō (-chō) Senkyo-kyoku. Chihō Senkyo Kekka Shirabe. Tokyo, 1955, 1959, 1963.
Johnson, Benton. "A Critical Appraisal of the Church-Sect Typology," *American Sociological Review*, XXII (1957), 88.

Kahler, Erich. The Tower and the Abyss. New York, 1957.
Kamishima Jirō. Kindai Nihon no Seishin Kōzō. Tokyo, 1961.
Kasahara Kazuo. Kakumei no Shūkyō: Ikkō Ikki to Sōkagakkai. Tokyo, 1964.
——. Seiji to Shūkyō: Kiro ni tatsu Sōkagakkai. Tokyo, 1965.
——. Tenkanki no Shūkyō. Tokyo, 1966.
Katsube Gen. "Roku-jū Nendai no Shin-Fashizumu," *Gendai no Me*, Sept. 1964, p. 54.
Katsumata Seiichi. "Sōkagakkai no Seijiteki Shinshutsu," *Shūkyō Kōron*, Sept. 1962, p. 66.
Katz, Elihu, and Paul Lazarsfeld. Personal Influence. Glencoe, Ill., 1955.
Kiefer, Christie W. "Social Change and Personality in a White Collar Danchi." Unpub. paper prepared for the Center for Japanese and Korean Studies, University of California, Berkeley, November 15, 1967.
King, C. Wendell. Social Movements in the United States. New York, 1956.
Kishimoto, Hideo. Japanese Religion in the Meiji Era. Tr. John F. Howes. Tokyo, 1956.
——. "The Problem of Religion and Modernization in Japan," *Contemporary Religions in Japan*, Sept. 1960, p. 1.
Kitagawa, Joseph M. Religion in Japanese History. New York, 1966.

Kobayashi Naoki. "Seitō Shiji-sō ni miru Kenpō Ishiki," *Gendai no Me*, Oct. 1967, p. 134.
Kodaira Yoshihei. Sōkagakkai. Tokyo, 1963.
——. "Sōkagakkai Seikai Shinshutsu no Mokuteki," *Shūkyō Kōron*, Sept. 1962, p. 16.
Koestler, Arthur. Darkness at Noon. Tr. Daphne Hardy. New York, 1946.
Kōmeitō—Clean Government Party. Tokyo, n.d.
"Kōmeitō Daigishi: 'Byōku Hinkon-reki' no Meisai," *Asahi Geinō*, Feb. 28, 1967, p. 32.
"Kōmeitō: Iinchō Kōtaigeki to kore kara no Dekata," *Shūkan Yomiuri*, Feb. 17, 1967, p. 12.
Kōmeitō Kikanshi-kyoku. Kōmeitō no Jūten Seisaku. Tokyo, Oct. 15, 1966.
——. Shiawase Kizuku Kōmeitō. Tokyo, Oct. 1966.
——. Tosei no Kihon Seisaku. Tokyo, 1966.
"Kōmeitō ni Idomu to Iu Nishi Honganji no Ito," *Shūkan Gendai*, June 1, 1967, p. 16.
Kōmeitō Seisaku-kyoku. Fukushi Keizai e no Michi. 4 vols. Tokyo, 1965–67.
——. Taishū Fukushi wo Mezashite. 2 vols. Tokyo, 1966.
"Kōmeitō 'Shirōto' Giindan Genkōroku," *Shūkan Yomiuri*, Apr. 14, 1967, p. 16.
Kōmeitō Soshiki-kyoku. "Kōmeitō Kanbu Yakuin Ichiran." Mimeo. Tokyo, July 1967.
Kornhauser, William. The Politics of Mass Society. Glencoe, Ill., 1959.
Kudo, Takaya. "The Faith of Sōka Gakkai," *Contemporary Religions in Japan*, June 1961, p. 1.
Kuzutani Kazumasa. "Daigakusei no Shūkyōteki Taido to sono Haikeiteki Yōin ni tsuite," *Kumamoto Daigaku Kyōikugaku-bu Kiyō*, No. 13 (1965), p. 81.
——. "Shūkyō to Henken to no Kankei ni tsuite," *Kumamoto Daigaku Kyōikugaku-bu Kiyō*, No. 12 (1964), p. 70.

Landsberger, Henry A., and Antonio Saavedra. "Response Set in Developing Countries," *Public Opinion Quarterly*, XXXI (1967), 214.
Lane, Robert. Political Ideology. Glencoe, Ill., 1962.
——. Political Life. Glencoe, Ill., 1959.
Langdon, Frank. Politics in Japan. Boston, 1967.
Lanternari, Vittorio. The Religions of the Oppressed. Tr. Lisa Sergio. New York, 1963.
Lasswell, Harold. "The Psychology of Hitlerism," *Political Quarterly*, IV (1933), 373.
——, and Daniel Lerner. World Revolutionary Elites. Cambridge, Mass., 1965.
Lederer, Emil. Japan in Transition. New Haven, Conn., 1938.
——. State of the Masses. New York, 1940.
Lenin, V. I. State and Revolution. New York, 1932.
Lenski, Gerhard. The Religious Factor. Garden City, N.Y., 1963.
Lerner, Daniel. The Nazi Elite. Stanford, 1951.
Levy, Marion. Modernization and the Structure of Societies. 2 vols. Princeton, N.J., 1966.

——. The Structure of Society. Princeton, N.J., 1952.

Lifton, Robert Jay. "Youth and History," in *Studies on Modernization of Japan by Western Scholars* (Tokyo, 1962). Asian Cultural Studies: 3.

Lipset, Seymour Martin. Political Man. Garden City, N.Y., 1963.

——, and Reinhard Bendix. Social Mobility in Industrial Society. Berkeley, Calif., 1959.

Loomis, Charles, and J. Allan Beegle. "The Spread of German Nazism in Rural Areas," *American Sociological Review*, XI, (1946), 724.

Mainichi Shimbun. Unpub. data from surveys made by Opinion Research Department of *Mainichi Shimbun* in Sept. 1963, Nov. 1964, June 1965, May 1966, Sept. 1966.

Makiguchi Tsunesaburō. Kachiron. Tokyo, 1961.

Mannheim, Karl. Ideology and Utopia. New York, 1963.

——. Man and Society in an Age of Reconstruction. New York, 1940.

Mao Tse-tung. "Kuan-yü Cheng-ch'üeh Ch'u-li Jen-min Nei-pu Mao-tun ti Wen-t'i," *Jen min jih pao*, June 19, 1957.

——. "Lun Jen-min Min-chu Chuan-cheng," *Jen-min Jih-pao*, July 1, 1949.

Maraini, Fosco. Meeting with Japan. London, 1959.

Maranell, Gary M. "An Examination of Some Religious and Political Attitudinal Correlates of Bigotry," *Social Forces*, XLV (1967), 356.

Maritain, Jacques. Man and the State. Chicago, 1963.

Maruyama Kunio. "Ikeda Kaichō e no Muttsu no Shitsumon," *Gendai no Me*, Sept. 1964, p. 72.

Maruyama Masao. Nihon no Shisō. Tokyo, 1963.

——. Thought and Behaviour in Modern Japanese Politics. New York, 1963.

Masujima Hiroshi. "Seiji Shinshutsu no Imi to Haikei," *Gendai no Me*, Sept. 1964, p. 42.

Matossian, Mary. "Ideologies of Delayed Industrialization: Some Tensions and Ambiguities," *Economic Development and Cultural Change*, VI (1958), 217.

Matsushita Keiichi. "Kōzō Hendō to Sengo Minshushugi," *Sekai*, No. 257 (Apr. 1967), p. 33.

McClosky, Herbert. "Consensus and Ideology in American Politics," *American Political Science Review*, June 1964, p. 361.

McFarland, H. Neill. "Japan's New Religions," *Contemporary Religions in Japan*, June 1960, p. 35; Sept. 1960, p. 30; Dec. 1960, p. 24.

——. Rush Hour of the Gods. New York, 1967.

McGovern, William. From Luther to Hitler. Boston, 1941.

McLuhan, Marshall, and Quentin Fiore. The Medium Is the Massage. New York, 1967.

Mendel, Douglas. "The Japanese Voter and Political Action," *Western Political Quarterly*, X (1957), 849.

Merton, Robert K. Social Theory and Social Structure. Glencoe, Ill., 1957.

Mishima Yukio and Hōjō Hiroshi. "Warera Fushigi na Dōkyūsei," *Nippon*, Feb. 1965, p. 52.

Miyamori Shigeru. "Sangi-in Senkyo to Kaku Tō Hihan," *Zen'ei*, No. 238 (July 1965), p. 170.

Miyata Mitsuo. "Shūkyō Seitō to Minshushugi," *Sekai*, No. 233 (May 1965), p. 147.
Mochizuki Issei. "Kyōdan to Shūkyōteki Ningen Keisei," *Shūkyō Kōron*, Jan. 1963, p. 37.
Mombushō. "Sōkagakkai ni tsuite." Unpub. mimeo. Tokyo, n.d.
———. "Sōkagakkai no Zenkoku Ku Rikkōhosha ni kansuru Senkyo Ihan Jirei." Unpub. mimeo. Tokyo, 1956.
———. "Sōkagakkai: Soshiki Ichiran-hyō, Bōryoku Jiken Shū, Kōshoku Senkyo Hō Ihan Jiken Ichiran-hyō." Unpub. mimeo. Tokyo, 1957.
Moore, Barrington. Social Origins of Dictatorship and Democracy. Boston, 1966.
Morris, Ivan. Nationalism and the Right Wing in Japan. New York, 1960.
———. "Sōka Gakkai Brings 'Absolute Happiness,'" *New York Times Magazine*, July 18, 1965, p. 8.
Munakata Iwao. "Sōkagakkai Hatten no Haikei ni aru Mono," *Sophia*, Autumn 1964, p. 69.
Murakami Shigeyoshi. "Gendai Seinen to Sōkagakkai," *Shūkyō Kōron*, Sept. 1962, p. 43.
———. "Kōmeitō no Seiji Kōdō," *Sekai*, No. 233 (May 1965), p. 161.
———. "Seiji Shinshutsu no Haikei to Nihonteki Jōkyō," *Gendai no Me*, Apr. 1965, p. 40.
———. Sōkagakkai to Kōmeitō. Tokyo, 1964.
———. "Tenkanki wo Mukaeta Kōmeitō," *Sekai*, No. 257 (Apr. 1967), p. 47.
———. "Toda Jōsei to Shakubuku Daikōshin," *Chūō Kōron*, Apr. 1965, p. 436.
Muramatsu Takeshi. "Nihon no Kindaika to Nichirenshū," *Chūō Kōron*, Mar. 1965, p. 48.
Muramatsu Tsuneo. Nihonjin. Nagoya, 1962.

Naikaku Kanbō Naikaku Chōsa-shitsu. Nihon no Seijiteki Mukanshin. Shakai Fūchō Chōsa Shiryō No. 2. Tokyo, June 1961.
———. Seijiteki Mukanshin no Jittai to Keikō. Shakai Fūchō Chōsa Shiryō No. 24. Tokyo, Apr. 1964.
———. Shinkō Shūkyō ni kansuru Shakai-shinrigakuteki Kenkyū. Tokyo, [1965?].
Naikaku Sōri Daijin Kanbō Kōhōshitsu. Kenpō ni kansuru Seron Chōsa (1–10). Tokyo, Aug. 1966.
———. Unpub. data from survey of popular attitudes concerning the Japanese constitution made in February 1965 by Prime Minister's Office, Tokyo.
Nakaba Tadakuni. Nihon no Chōryū: Sōkagakkai Hatten no Ayumi. Tokyo, 1968.
———. "Sōkagakkai Gekidō no Shichinen," *Zaikai*, May 15, 1967, *et seq.*
Nakamura, Hajime. Ways of Thinking of Eastern Peoples. Honolulu, 1964.
Nakamura Katsunori. "Sōkagakkai no Seiji Puroguramu," *Jiyū*, Aug. 1963, p. 30.
Nakane Chie. "Nihonteki Shakai Kōzō no Hakken," *Chūō Kōron*, May 1963, p. 48.
Nakatani Hiromitsu. "Nihonjin no Shūkyō Ishiki," *Ryūkoku Daigaku Bukkyō Bunka Kenkyū-jo Kiyō*, No. 5 (1966), p. 45.
Neumann, Franz. Behemoth. New York, 1942.

Neumann, Sigmund, ed. Modern Political Parties. Chicago, 1956.
"A New Face Called Sōka Gakkai Raises Old Problems in Modern Japan," *Look*, Sept. 10, 1963, p. 18.
NHK Hōsō Seron Chōsa-sho. Kokumin Seron Chōsa "Nihon no Mirai-zo": Kekka no Gaiyō. Tokyo, Mar. 1966.
NHK Sōgō Hōsō Bunka Kenkyū-jo. Rokaritei Kenkyū: Sono Riron to Chōsa. Tokyo, 1967.
Nie, Norman, G. Bingham Powell, and Kenneth Prewitt. "Social Structure and Political Participation: Developmental Relationships," *American Political Science Review*, LXII: 2, 3 (June, Sept. 1969).
Niebuhr, H. Richard. The Social Sources of Denominationalism. Cleveland, 1957.
Nielson, Niels J. "Religion and Philosophy in Contemporary Japan," *The Rice Institute Pamphlet*, Jan. 1957.
Nihonjin no Kokuminsei. Unpub. data from Third National Character Survey made in late 1963 by Tōkei Sūri Kenkyū-jo, Tokyo.
Nishihira Shigeki. "Minobe Nihyaku-nijūman no Shiji-sō," *Jiyū*, No. 91 (June 1967), p. 82.
———. "Senkyo kara Mita Kaku Tō no Genjō to Shōrai," *Tembō*, Apr. 1967, p. 50.
Nishio, Harry K. "Comparative Analysis of the Risshō Kōseikai and the Sōka Gakkai," *Asian Survey*, VII (1967), 776.
Nitta Rinzō. Sōkagakkai, Kōmeitō no Shinsō. Tokyo, 1965.
Niwano Nikkyō. "Sōkagakkai ni taisuru Warera no Taido," *Shūkyō Kōron*, Sept. 1962, p. 22.
Niyeda, Rokusaburō. "New Religion in Japan," *Religions in Japan at Present*, 1958, p. 23.
Nolte, Ernst. Three Faces of Fascism. Tr. Leila Vennewitz. New York, 1966.

Offner, Clark B., and Henry van Straelen. Modern Japanese Religions. Tokyo, 1963.
Oguchi Iichi. Shin Shinrigaku Kōza IV: Shūkyō to Shinkō no Shinrigaku. Tokyo, 1956.
Okabe Keizō. "Seron-mushi no Jimin-tō ga Naze Tsuyoi?," *Asahi Jānaru*, June 23, 1968.
Okamoto Kōji. "Sōkagakkai ni okeru Sengo," *Sangyō Keizai Ronsō*, No. 1 (June 1966), p. 320.
Okui Fukutarō. "Kinrin Shakai no Soshiki-ka," *Toshi Mondai*, Oct. 1953, p. 23.
Okuma Ryōichi. "Seiji to Shūkyō," *Shūkyō Kōron*, Sept. 1962, p. 77.
Olson, Lawrence. The Value Creation Society. American Universities Field Staff, East Asia Series (Tokyo), XI: 6 (1964).
Oya Sōichi. "Sō-senkyo wo Kōsatsu suru," *Sandei Mainichi*, Feb. 12, 1967, p. 22.
Ozawa Nobuo. "Sōkagakkai: Kono Rinjin-tachi," *Tembō*, No. 78 (June 1965), p. 164.

Parsons, Talcott. Essays in Sociological Theory. Glencoe, Ill., 1958.
———. Structure and Process in Modern Societies. Glencoe, Ill., 1963.

Passin, Herbert, ed. The United States and Japan. Englewood Cliffs, N.J., 1966.

Pfautz, Harold. "The Sociology of Secularization: Religious Groups," *The American Journal of Sociology*, LXI (Sept. 1955), p. 121.

Pius XI. Forty Years After. Washington, D.C., 1931.

Pope, Liston. Millhands and Preachers. Paperback ed. New Haven, Conn., 1965.

Prothro, James, and C. W. Grigg. "Fundamental Principles of Democracy: Bases of Agreement and Disagreement," *The Journal of Politics*, XXII (1960), 276.

Pulzer, P. G. J. The Rise of Political Anti-Semitism in Germany and Austria. New York, 1964.

Pye, Lucian, and Sidney Verba. Political Culture and Political Development. Princeton, N.J., 1965.

Ramseyer, Robert. "The Sōka Gakkai," in *Studies in Japanese Culture: I* (Ann Arbor, 1965). Center for Japanese Studies, Occasional Papers No. 9.

——. "The Sōka Gakkai and the Japanese Elections of 1960 [sic]," *Contemporary Religions in Japan*, IV (1963), 287.

"Religion in Japan in 1961," *Contemporary Religions in Japan*, III (1962), 18.

Renondeau, Gaston. Le Bouddhisme japonais. Paris, 1965.

——. La Doctrine de Nichiren. Paris, 1953.

——. "Le 'Traité sur l'Etat' de Nichiren," *T'oung Pao*, XL (1951), 123.

Riesman, David. Individuality Reconsidered. Glencoe, Ill., 1954.

——. The Lonely Crowd. New Haven, Conn., 1961.

——, and Nathan Glazer. "Political Apathy: Its Social Sources and Subjective Meaning," in Bernard Rosenberg et al., *Mass Society in Crisis* (New York, 1964).

Rogger, Hans, and Eugen Weber. The European Right. Berkeley, Calif., 1965.

Rogin, Michael Paul. The Intellectuals and McCarthy: The Radical Specter. Cambridge, Mass., 1967.

Sakamoto Mamoru. "Kōmeitō, Sōka Teikoku e no Shuppatsu," *Jiyū*, Apr. 1966, p. 80.

——. "Shūkyō, Fashizumu, Minshushugi," *Gendai no Me*, Apr. 1965, p. 58.

——. "Sōkagakkai to 'Kōmeitō,'" *Jiyū*, Oct. 1964, p. 74.

Saki Akio. "Kōmeitō no Seisaku to Honshitsu," *Ekonomisuto*, July 27, 1965, p. 36.

——. "Kōmeitō no Seisaku wo Hihan suru," *Zen'ei*, No. 238 (July 1965), p. 199.

——. "Sōkagakkai no Shūkyō Seitō Kōsu," *Shūkyō Kōron*, Sept. 1962, p. 38.

——. "Sōkagakkai Seinen Shōkō no Shōgen," *Gendai no Me*, Feb. 1967, p. 124.

——. "Sōkagakkai to no Taiwa Shimatsu-ki," *Tembō*, No. 97 (Jan. 1967), p. 140.

——, and Oguchi Iichi. Sōkagakkai. Tokyo, 1960.

Sangi-in Jimukyoku. Sangi-in Giin Senkyo Ichiran. Nos. 4–7. Tokyo, 1957, 1960, 1963, 1966.
Sansom, George. A History of Japan 1334–1615. Stanford, 1961.
———. A History of Japan 1615–1867. Stanford, 1963.
———. Japan: A Short Cultural History. New York, 1943.
Schaar, John. Escape from Authority: The Perspectives of Erich Fromm. New York, 1961.
Schecter, Jerrold. The New Face of Buddha. New York, 1967.
Seiji Mondai Chōsa-kai. "Kōmeitō Shinshutsu no Hyōsō to Shinsō," *Nihon oyobi Nihonjin*, No. 1432 (Jan. 1966), p. 76.
"Seinen no Shūkyōshin," *Toki*, June 1966, p. 264.
Seki Jun'ya. "Shūkyō Hihan no Kagakuteki Taido," *Shisō no Kagaku*, No. 40 (July 1965), p. 89.
Selznick, Philip. The Organizational Weapon. New York, 1952.
Shils, Edward. "Ideology and Civility: On the Politics of the Intellectual," *Sewanee Review*, XLVI (1958), 450.
———, and Morris Janowitz. "Cohesion and Disintegration in the Wehrmacht," in Daniel Lerner, ed., *Propaganda in War and Crisis* (New York, 1951).
Shinohara Hajime. "Kōmeitō e no Gimon," *Sekai*, No. 257 (Apr. 1967), p. 67.
———. "Ryūdōka-suru Seitō no Kiban," *Ekonomisuto*, Feb. 14, 1967, p. 30.
"Shinsetsu Eisai-kō 'Sōka Gakuen' no Mae-hyōban," *Shūkan Gendai*, July 27, 1967, p. 34.
Shiobara Tsutomu. "Sōkagakkai Ideorogii," *Tembō*, No. 78 (June 1965), p. 34.
Shōmoto Mitsumasa. "Sōkagakkai no Seijiteki Shinshutsu,"*Shūkyō Kōron*, Sept. 1962, p. 32.
"Shūgi-in Shinshutsu no Kyōi," *Shūkan Shinchō*, May 20, 1963, p. 24.
"Shūkyō Hōjin 'Sōkagakkai' Kisoku." Tokyo, Feb. 10, 1957, June 1962, May 1, 1966.
Smelser, Neil Joseph. Theory of Collective Behavior. New York, 1963.
Sōkagakkai. The Nichiren Shōshū Sōkagakkai. Tokyo, 1966.
———. The Sōka Gakkai. Tokyo, 1960.
———, Kyōgaku-bu. Shakubuku Kyōten. Tokyo, 1961 and 1967.
———, Overseas Bureau. "This Is the Sōkagakkai" series. No. 2, No Boundary in True Religion. No. 3, Sōkagakkai and Culture Movement. No. 4, Practices of Believers. No. 5, Head Temple Taisekiji. No. 6, Sōkagakkai and Kōmeitō. No. 7, The Buddhist Democracy. No. 8, What Is Shakubuku? Tokyo, n.d. (most 1965?).
"Sōka Gakkai and the Nichiren Shō Sect," *Contemporary Religions in Japan*, Mar. 1960, p. 55.
"Sōkagakkai e no Soboku na Nijugo no Shitsumon," *Bungei Shunjū*, July 1963, p. 108.
"Sōkagakkai ga Hokoru Moto-Kazoku Risuto," *Shūkan Shinchō*, Sept. 23, 1967, p. 108.
"Sōkagakkai Kaigai de no Igai na Jitsuryoku Hyōka," *Shūkan Gendai*, Nov. 2, 1967, p. 20.
"Sōkagakkai no Seiji Mokuhyō," *Asahi Jānaru*, July 15, 1962, p. 6.

"Sōkagakkai Shinshutsu no Imi suru Mono," *Sekai*, No. 201 (Sept. 1962), p. 20.

"Sōka Gakkai Study." Unpub. manuscript, United States Information Service, Tokyo, 1960.

"Soko ga Shiritai Kōmeitō Seiken Kakutoku Kōsō," *Shūkan Gendai*, Feb. 28, 1967, p. 16.

Soothill, W. E. The Lotus of the Wonderful Law. Oxford, 1930.

Sorokin, Pitirim. Man and Society in Calamity. New York, 1942.

Spae, Joseph. Japan in Search of Her Soul. Tokyo, 1967.

Staley, Eugene, and Richard Morse. Modern Small Industry for Developing Countries. New York, 1965.

"Stamping in Nichiren's Footsteps," *The Economist*, Mar. 20, 1965, p. 1250.

Stanton, Alfred, and Stewart Perry. Personality and Political Crisis. Glencoe, Ill., 1951.

Stedman, Murray S. Religion and Politics in America. New York, 1964.

Stouffer, Samuel. Communism, Conformity, and Civil Liberties. New York, 1955.

Suetsuna Joichi. Nihonjin no Kokuminsei. Tokyo, 1961.

Sugahara Yoshinaga. "Kōmeitō no Ronri to Kōdō," *Gekkan Rōdō Mondai*, No. 91 (Dec. 1965), p. 58.

Sugita Masao. "Kōmeitō no Jirenma,' *Nippon*, Feb. 1965, p. 60.

Suzuki Eitarō. "Kindai-ka to Shimin Soshiki," *Toshi Mondai*, Oct. 1953, p. 13.

———. Toshi Shakaigaku Genri. Tokyo, 1957.

Suzuki Hiroshi. "Toshi Kasō no Shūkyō Shūdan," *Shakaigaku Kenkyū*, No. 22 (1963), p. 81; No. 24 (1964), p. 50.

Suzuki, Tatsuzō. "A Study of the Japanese National Character, Part III: The Third Nationwide Survey," *Annals of the Institute of Statistical Mathematics*, Supplement 4 (1966), p. 15. Tr. Nishiyama Sen.

Taguchi Fukuji. "Rinen to Seisaku no Mujun," *Gendai no Me*, Apr. 1965, p. 50.

Takagi Hiroo. Nihon no Shinkō Shūkyō. Tokyo, 1961.

———. "Shūkyō Seinen no Jittai to sono Yakuwari wa?," *Shūkyō Kōron*, Jan. 1963, p. 11.

———. "Sōka Gakkai Makes Advance into Political World," *Japan Socialist Review*, June 16, 1962, p. 53.

Takahashi Kazumi. "Shinkō no Seiji Rikigaku," *Gendai no Me*, Apr. 1967, p. 72.

Takahashi Naoko. Unpub. attitudinal survey by Miss Takahashi, Rikkyō Daigaku student, of Sōkagakkai members in Tokyo, 1963.

Takami Jun. "Sōkagakkai ni Tou," *Chūō Kōron*, Aug. 1962, p. 290.

Takase Hiroi. "Daigaku ni Ibuku Sōkagakkai," *Shūkan Gendai*, May 23, 1963, p. 24.

———. Dai San Bummei no Shūkyō. Tokyo, 1962.

———. "Ikeda Daisaku Shū-in Rikkōho no Haikei," *Gendai no Me*, Nov. 1967, p. 192.

———. Kōmeitō. Tokyo, 1964.

———. "Kōmeitō no Seisaku to Shūsaku," *Gendai no Me*, Mar. 1967, p. 95.

———. "1966-nen Yasei-ha Daihyō: Ikeda Daisaku," *Nippon*, Jan. 1966, p. 54.

———. Ningen Fukkō: Sōkagakkai ni Ikiru. Tokyo, 1964.

———. Ningen Kakumei wo Mezasu Ikeda Daisaku. Tokyo, 1965.

———. "To-chiji Sen Gojūman no Kagi wo nigiru Sōkagakkai," Shūkan Yomiuri, Feb. 17, 1963, p. 12.

Takeiri Yoshikatsu. "Seisaku wa Tetteiteki-ni Rongi," Asahi Jānaru, Mar. 5, 1967, p. 10.

Takeyama Michio. "Sōkagakkai wa Fassho ka?," Jiyū, Aug. 1965, p. 182.

Talmon, J. L. The Origins of Totalitarian Democracy. London, 1955.

———. Political Messianism: The Romantic Phase. London, 1960.

Tamura Norio. "Shihyō no Ronri Kōzō," Gendai no Me, June 1967, p. 174.

Tamura, Yoshirō. "Religion and Modern Life," Contemporary Religions in Japan, Sept. 1960, p. 40; Mar. 1962, p. 42.

Tanaka Jigohei. "Shinkyō no Jiyū to Sōkagakkai no Fukyō-hō," Shūkyō Kōron, Sept. 1962, p. 30.

Tanaka Kunio. Nihonjin no Shakaiteki Taido. Tokyo, 1964.

Tanaka Tadao. "Seiji to Shūkyō ni tsuite no Ikkōsatsu," Nihon oyobi Nihonjin, No. 1432 (Jan. 1966), p. 86.

Tanamachi Kennosuke. "Toshi-ron kara mita Danchi Shūkyō," Seiki, No. 194 (July 1966), p. 20.

Thomsen, Harry. The New Religions of Japan. Tokyo, 1963.

Thrupp, Sylvia. "Millennial Dreams in Action," Comparative Studies in Society and History, Supplement 2 (1962), p. 11.

Tilly, Charles. "How Protest Modernized in France," unpub. paper, Center for Adanced Study in the Behavioral Sciences, Stanford University, April 1969.

Tinder, Glen. The Crisis of Political Imagination. New York, 1964.

Toch, Hans. The Social Psychology of Social Movements. New York, 1965.

Toda, Jōsei. "Preface to 'Sōka Gakkai and the Nichiren Shō Sect,' " Contemporary Religions in Japan, June 1960, p. 48.

"To-Fuku-chiji Hiketsugeki no Butai-ura," Asahi Jānaru, May 28, 1967, p. 8.

Togawa Isamu. "Jidai no Gunzō: Hōjō Hiroshi," Chūō Kōron, Feb. 1967, p. 212.

———. Zenshin-suru Kōmeitō. Tokyo, 1966.

Tōkei Sūri Kenkyū-jo. Kokuminsei no Kenkyū: Dai Sanji Chōsa. Sūkyū Kenkyū No. 11. Tokyo, Sept. 1964.

Tokoro Shigemoto. "Kōmeitō ni okeru Kakushinsei no Jisshōteki Bunseki," Shakai Kyōiku Kenkyū, No. 6 (Oct. 1965), p. 101.

———. "Nichiren ni okeru Shūkyō to Seiji," Shūkyō Kōron, Sept. 1962, p. 7.

Tōkyō Daigaku Hokekyō Kenkyū-kai. Nichiren Shōshū Sōkagakkai. Tokyo, 1962.

Tōkyō Daigaku Shakaigakka and Tōkyō Joshi Daigaku Shakaigakka. Sōkagakkai. Tokyo, 1963.

Troeltsch, Ernst. The Social Teaching of the Christian Churches. Tr. Olive Wyon. 2 vols. New York, 1931.

Tsuji Kiyoaki. "Mūdo to Jitsueki to no Tatakai," Asahi Jānaru, Feb. 12, 1967, p. 12.

Tsuji Takehisa. "Kōmeitō no Kihon Seisaku," Ekonomisuto, Sept. 7, 1965, p. 52.

Tsunoda, Ryusaku, et al. Sources of Japanese Tradition. New York, 1958.

Tsurufuji Ikuta. "Yo wa Sōkagakkai wo Kaku Miru," *Shūkyō Kōron*, Sept. 1962, p. 57.
Tsurumi Shunsuke *et al.* Shakubuku. Tokyo, 1962.
Tuveson, Ernest Lee. Millennium and Utopia. New York, 1964.

Umehara Takeshi. "Sōkagakkai no Tetsugakuteki Shūkyōteki Hihan," *Shisō no Kagaku*, No. 33 (Dec. 1964), p. 83.
United States Congress. Senate Committee on the Judiciary. The Communist Party of the United States of America. Washington, D.C., 1955.

Verba, Sidney, *et al.* Unpub. survey of political attitudes of Japanese made in late 1966 as part of the Cross-National Project for Political and Social Change by associates of Sidney Verba, University of Chicago.
Vogel, Ezra. Japan's New Middle Class. Berkeley, Calif., 1963.
"Voting Characteristics Revealed in Pre-Election Opinion Poll—House of Councillors Elections, July 1965," United States Information Service, Tokyo, Oct. 6, 1965.

Wallace, Anthony F. C. "Revitalization Movements," *American Anthropologist*, LVIII (Apr. 1956), 264.
Ward, Robert. Japan's Political System. Englewood Cliffs, N.J., 1967.
——, and Dankwart Rustow, eds. Political Modernization in Japan and Turkey. Princeton, N.J., 1964.
Watanabe Baiyu. "Iwayuru Shinkō Shūkyō ni Jisshōteki ni Mirareru Bukkyō no Eikyō," *Seishin Kagaku*, No. 4 (Mar. 1965), p. 13.
——. "Modern Japanese Religions, Their Success Explained," *Monumenta Nipponica*, Apr. 7, 1957, p. 153.
Watanuki Jōji. " 'Chūdō Seiji' to 'Dai San Seiryoku'—sono Kotoba to Genjitsu," *Asahi Jānaru*, Feb. 19, 1967, p. 14.
——. " 'Kyū Chūkan-sō' no Seiji to Ishiki," *Chūō Kōron*, July 1962, p. 110.
——. "Patterns of Politics in Present-Day Japan," in Seymour Martin Lipset and Stein Rokkan, eds., *Party Systems and Voter Alignments* (New York, 1967).
——. "Political Attitudes of the Japanese People," *The Sociological Review Monograph, No. 10: Japanese Sociological Studies* (Keele, Eng.), Oct. 1966, p. 165.
——. "Social Change and Regional Differences in Japan." Unpub. paper, University of Tokyo, 1967.
——. "Tōkyō-to, Itabashi-ku ni okeru Seiji Ishiki Chōsa; Chūkan Hōkoku." Unpub. mimeo. Tokyo [1966?].
Weber, Max. The Sociology of Religion. Boston, 1963.
White, James W. California F-Scale administered to Sōkagakkai members in Tokyo, Oct. 1967.
——. "Mass Movement and Democracy: Sōkagakkai in Japanese Politics," *American Political Science Review*, XLI (1967), 744.
——. Mass Movement, Militant Religion, and Democracy: The Sōkagakkai in Japanese Politics. Unpub. Ph.D. thesis, Stanford University, 1969.
——. Militant Religion in Japan: The Sōka Gakkai. Unpub. A.B. thesis, Princeton University, 1964.

——. "The Sōkagakkai in Japanese Politics." Unpub. paper, Stanford University, 1966.
Wilson, Bryan A. "Millennialism in Comparative Perspective," *Comparative Studies in Society and History*, Oct. 1963, p. 93.
Wilson, Bryan R. "An Analysis of Sect Development," *American Sociological Review*, Feb. 1959, p. 3.
Woodard, William. "Study on Religious Juridical Persons Law," *Contemporary Japan*, Sept. 1958; Mar., Aug., Dec. 1959.
Wylie, Laurence. Village in the Vaucluse. New York, 1964.

Yamaguchi Akira. Issenman-nin no Kokoro wo Tsukanda Himitsu: Sōkagakkai no Shinri Senryaku. Tokyo, 1967.
Yanagida Kunio. "Ikeda Daisaku—soko de Kamigami wa Kawaku," *Gendai no Me*, Jan. 1966, p. 145.
Yanaihara Isaku. "Minshū Fuman no Sentōteki Nenshō," *Asahi Jānaru*, Aug. 5, 1962, p. 12.
Yano Jun'ya. " 'Kōmeitō no Jirenma' ni Hanron-suru," *Nippon*, Mar. 1965, p. 242.
Yokogoshi Eiichi. "Dai-toshi ni okeru Senkyo to Shimin," *Toshi Mondai*, Mar. 1955, p. 28.
Yomiuri Shimbun. Unpub. data from surveys made by Public Opinion Survey Department of *Yomiuri Shimbun* in Mar. 1966, Jan. 1967, Mar. 1967.
Yui Hiromichi. Datō Sōkagakkai. Fujisawa, 1967.

Index

Abe Ken'ichi, 117, 139, 169–70, 172, 287, 290
Adorno, T. W., 189–92 *passim*, 231
Akiya Einosuke, 87, 116f, 241, 332; mentioned, 51, 114, 238
Alienated, 190, 269; activists, 74; Gakkai appeal to, 47
Alienation, 80, 224–42, 248–49, 254–55, 271, 346; aspect of mass model, 222, 270; by Gakkai, 275, 283, 291; defined, 3, 6, 179–80; of "little people," 61; mentioned, 11, 266. *See also* Human alienation; Self alienation; Systemic alienation
Almond, Gabriel, 80, 195, 214; on secondary associations, 183, 247–49
Anomie, 5n, 25, 47, 239
Arendt, Hannah, 143
Authoritarianism, 192, 194, 259–60; causes, 275; of Gakkai leadership, 223, 230; mentioned, 200, 225, 250, 285
Authoritarian personality, 179, 189–90, 191, 216, 239; defined, 227–28
Authoritarian submission, 228–29
Azuma Ryūtarō, 169, 290, 296
Azumi, Koya, 75, 154, 198

Beliefs of Sōkagakkai, 30–38, 137. *See also* Buddhism
Bell, Daniel, 2–4 *passim*, 9
Block system, *see* Horizontal line
Board of Directors, 107–8, 114–20 *passim*
Boys' Division, 93f, 96
Braden, Charles, 77, 119
Buddha, 26, 114, 122, 280

Buddhism, 33f; authoritarianism, 194; *jihi*, 82; leadership, 43; political, 128–32; teachings, 232, 234; mentioned, 1, 17–21 *passim*, 83, 99, 293
Buddhist democracy, 128–32, 232

California Fascism Scale, 191–94 *passim*; activists' scores, 260
Charisma, 3, 40, 51–56 *passim*, 205; of Ikeda, 45, 52, 205, 207, 237, 264
Chiku, 89–90, 91, 94; chiefs, 117f
Christian Anti-Communist Crusade, 78, 182
Chūdō seiji, 126f
Citizens' Livelihood Discussion Centers, 108, 140, 159, 218, 258, 262, 285
Classes, social, 197f; differences, 187f; lower, 6ff, 61, 73, 77, 78–79, 196, 200, 210, 234, 284; middle, 78
Clean Government Party, *see* Kōmeitō
Cohn, Norman, 23, 39, 119
Communications of Gakkai, *see* Media, Gakkai
Communism, 227, 230, 256; compared with Gakkai, 77, 223, 228f, 239
Communists, 182, 191, 221; social class, 64, 80. *See also* Japan Communist Party
Constitution, 40; Article IX, 147, 149, 203; revision, 148–49, 160, 263; support for, 202–3, 246, 263, 264–65. *See also* Kōmeitō
Coughlin, Father, 78–79
Culture Bureau, 96, 108, 133; public relations, 113; and socialization, 98–99

Dahl, Robert, 238